NBA 75

THE DEFINITIVE HISTORY

A FIREFLY BOOK

Published by Firefly Books Ltd. 2020
Copyright © 2020 Firefly Books Ltd.
Text Copyright © 2020 Dave Zarum
Photography credits on page 255

First printing

Library of Congress Control Number: 2020936395

Library and Archives Canada Cataloguing in Publication
Title: NBA 75 : the definitive history / Dave Zarum.
Other titles: NBA seventy-five | National Basketball Association 75 | National Basketball
   Association seventy-five
Names: Zarum, Dave, 1986- author.
Description: Includes index.
Identifiers: Canadiana 20200225707 | ISBN 9780228102908 (hardcover)
Subjects: LCSH: National Basketball Association—History. | LCSH: Basketball—United States—
History.
Classification: LCC GV885.515.N38 Z37 2020 | DDC 796.3230973—dc23

Published in Canada by
Firefly Books Ltd.
50 Staples Avenue, Unit 1
Richmond Hill, Ontario
L4B 0A7

Published in the United States by
Firefly Books (U.S.) Inc.
P.O. Box 1338, Ellicott Station
Buffalo, New York
14205

Interior design by Noor Majeed
Cover design by Hartley Millson

Printed in China

 *We acknowledge the financial support of the Government of Canada.*

NBA 75

THE DEFINITIVE HISTORY

DAVE ZARUM

FIREFLY BOOKS

CONTENTS

INTRODUCTION
FRIDAYS WITH JERRY

It was a Friday afternoon like any other. I was quickly packing up my desk, looking forward to a weekend out of town. That's when my phone rang.

"Dave? This is Jerry West."

A couple of months earlier, I had reached out to West via the Golden State Warriors, for whom he was acting as a special advisor at the time. The Warriors had tabbed West to help turn them into champions (mission: accomplished). It was an obvious choice. West was a Hall of Fame player in the '60s and early '70s — the only player to win Finals MVP despite playing for the losing team — who transitioned to a front office role best remembered for architecting the Shaq-Kobe Los Angeles Lakers dynasty of the early 2000s. Oh, and his silhouette is the NBA's logo. No big deal.

As part of my job covering the NBA from Toronto, Canada, I have interviewed plenty of interesting figures. Dr. J really is one of the coolest people on Earth. Vince Carter's elaborate breakdown of the 2000 dunk contest blew me away. Wayne Embry's stories of playing with Wilt and Russell had me speechless.

But, I mean, *Jerry West*. Few figures have been a part of decade after decade of NBA history like he has. I put the receiver to my chest, took a deep breath, and tried my best not to geek out like I was hosting *The Chris Farley Show*.

I told Mr. West that I didn't plan to take up much of his time. He told me he was in rural California getting his car serviced at a mechanic and had all the time in the world.

Picturing Jerry West plopped down in the chair in a waiting room, waxing nostalgic, brought a huge grin to my face.

I had asked to interview West for a reason. But in the moment, caught off-guard like so many of his defenders, I couldn't remember what it was. Improvising, I asked him why he chose basketball as a lifelong pursuit. He paused. "Basketball chose me," he answered. He retraced his troubled childhood in West Virginia and the countless hours spent in refuge on a muddy, makeshift outdoor court. I asked him about teammate Elgin Baylor, and he lamented the "tragedy" of their Lakers finally winning a championship after six tries when Baylor was forced to retire. He talked about how few people realize how unstoppable Baylor was before injuries sidelined him. He talked about the landscape of the '60s and the hardships he watched his African American teammate — and many others — go through living in the spotlight during a time of overt racism. He talked about the way the game had changed and how gifted shooters like himself were tailor-made for today's NBA.

Here I was, a complete stranger, still early in my career, and navigating a truly unfocused interview. West was so candid and substantial in retelling the league's history through his own eyes.

For a fan like myself, who grew up devouring NBA history books and scouring the video bargain bins for old compilations and highlight-reels, this felt like every holiday wrapped up into one.

Hoops has a distinct advantage over other

major sports. The absence of facemasks or physical barriers between fans and players have helped make NBA stars the most accessible pro athletes around. We feel an uninterrupted connection as we admire the jaw-dropping physical feats on display every trip up the court.

And the dunks, crossovers, swats, swishes, and buzzer-beaters, they all have a story.

Of course, the NBA has always been more than basketball. The court is where social prejudices and societal ills play out in the spotlight. The NBA is where the fight against racism has been waged. It's where the AIDS crisis was better understood and where female athletes were provided a major stage to perform. It's where COVID-19 and the realities of the viral pandemic became a reality for millions.

Over 75 years, the greatest athletes from around the world have stepped onto NBA courts to compete. Like Jerry West, they each brought with them their hopes and dreams, but also their fears and struggles.

The history of the NBA is made up of these one-of-a-kind characters eager to tell their stories.

You just have to answer the call.

West races down the court in 1971 en route to the Lakers' 25th consecutive win.

1946
TIP-OFF

On June 6, 1946, a group of wealthy businessmen gathered at the Hotel Commodore in New York City. They were members of the Arena Association of America — owners of some of the largest venues in North America — and they had come to discuss a potential new venture: a professional basketball league.

These men had plenty going for them. Their arenas were located in the biggest cities in the eastern half of North America, including Chicago, New York, Boston, Toronto, Philadelphia and Detroit. They were skilled promoters, although only Ned Irish, who had staged marquee college basketball games at the Garden since 1934, had any experience in the sport.

The rest of the owners had cut their teeth in hockey, including Boston Celtics founder Walter Brown, who was responsible for establishing the Ice Capades traveling show in 1940. Brown had been looking for a steady draw to fill the Boston Garden on nights when the National Hockey League's Bruins weren't playing. The rising popularity of the collegiate game was impossible to ignore, and the fact a basketball court fit neatly within an ice rink made the proposition a no-brainer.

By the end of the meeting, the men had arrived at an ambitious plan: form an 11-team league called the Basketball Association of America. They hired Maurice Podoloff, president of the American Hockey League, to run the new venture. Tip-off was just five months away.

Basketball had come a long way since its very first game, played December 21, 1891,

The promotion advertised in the October 31, 1946, issue of the *Toronto Star*.

on the campus of Springfield College in Springfield, Massachusetts. Invented by Canadian-born educator James Naismith, the sport had seen a dramatic transformation over its 55 years. Gone were the peach baskets and the rugby-like violence of the first match.

"Well, I didn't have enough [rules] and that's where I made my big mistake," Naismith recalled during a 1939 radio interview. "The boys began tackling, kicking and punching in the clinches. They ended up in a free-for-all in the middle of the gym floor. Before I could pull them apart, one boy was knocked out, several of them had black eyes and one had a dislocated shoulder."

A new rule was added: no running with the ball. This led to a more skilled, faster-paced game built around coordination and ball movement. Naismith's students enjoyed the game and took it with them to college campuses

around the United States — as did Naismith, when he was hired by the University of Kansas in 1894. The sport was attracting sizable crowds in the college ranks, and by the 1920s and '30s several small regional pro leagues had been established, though few would last more than a few seasons.

One exception was the National Basketball League, which had been backed financially by General Electric, Firestone and Goodyear. The NBL operated teams in the Midwest between 1937 and 1949 and was where George Mikan, the 6-foot-10 giant, began his pro career, with the Chicago American Gears. For arena owners on the East Coast, the NBL wasn't seen as serious competition for their newly formed BAA.

With plans well underway for the inaugural season, fresh ideas were bandied about to help the league stand apart. A (thankfully) short-lived brainstorm was for one team to have possession of the ball for two minutes, after which the other team would take its turn, trying to score as many baskets as possible in that time — sort of like innings in baseball. Another idea was to allow fouls to accumulate and wait until the end of quarters to award the free throws. The only idea that stuck was that games would be 48 minutes long — eight minutes longer than the college game, and therefore offering more bang for the ticket buyer's buck.

The first game of the 1946–47 season took place at Maple Leaf Gardens in Toronto, Canada, between the Toronto Huskies and the visiting Knicks. Although it wouldn't be until 1949, when the NBL and BAA merged, that the National Basketball Association got its name, the league recognizes that Huskies–Knicks game as the first in its history.

Before the opening tip, the league's promoters had their work cut out for them when it came to selling a relatively new sport to a Canadian audience. Advertisements were placed in local papers signaling the arrival of "big-time basketball," proclaiming it as the "world's most popular sport!" Fans were promised "Thrills, Spills, Action, and Speed."

"Can you top this?" read another newspaper ad, with a photo of George Nostrand,

the Huskies' tallest player. "Anyone Taller Than NOSTRAND 6 ft. 10 Inches Will Be Admitted Free to OPENING GAME." For everybody else, tickets went for between 75 cents and $2.50.

The first basket in NBA history was scored by the Knicks' Ossie Schectman, a Jewish-American guard from Queens, New York. The Knicks roared to a 15-point lead early in the game, but Huskies player-coach "Big Ed" Sadowski helped Toronto narrow the lead to just 8 by halftime.

In the third, Sadowski fouled out and was replaced by Nostrand, who helped the Huskies gain a 48–44 lead heading into the final frame. Behind a team-high 14 points from forward Leo Gottlieb and 11 points from Schectman, the Knicks emerged with a 68-66 victory. Sadowski led all scorers with 18 points, followed by 16 from Nostrand.

The game played that night, and as it was played throughout the NBA's earliest years, hardly resembled the awe-inspiring action of today. Contests in those days more closely resembled a game of hot potato, with constant passing and cutting — and even more fighting. The league's formative years saw a product that featured plenty of brawls and fistfights.

These were even encouraged by the owners. After all, they had helped draw fans for hockey.

Basketball was played primarily on the ground, although there were exceptions. During the pregame warm-ups in Boston on November 5, 1946, 6-foot-7 Celtics forward Chuck Connors dunked a ball so hard, it shattered the new glass backboard. Brown, the team owner, was furious. Little did he know that, exactly three decades later, the slam dunk would help basketball's popularity soar higher than ever.

Still, in the NBA's formative years, two-handed set shots preceded the jumper, and hook shots were the go-to move for any center until Bill Russell appeared on the scene. It was Joe Fulks, a forward with the Philadelphia Warriors, who had the closest thing to a modern-day jump shot. Fulks was the league's biggest star in that inaugural '46–47 season and led the Warriors to the league's first championship.

The league saw major change after that first season. Four teams — the Detroit Falcons, Pittsburgh Ironmen, Cleveland Rebels and the Huskies — folded. The BAA was down to seven teams.

But the NBA was just getting started.

1ST GAME BOX SCORE

KNICKS

PLAYER	FG	PTS
Leo Gottlieb	6	14
Ossie Schectman	4	11
Stan Stutz	2	9
Ralph Kaplowitz	3	7
Jake Weber	1	6
Hank Rosenstein	2	5
Dick Murphy	2	5
Nat Militzok	2	5
Tommy Byrnes	1	4
Sonny Hertzberg	1	2
Bob Mullens	0	0
Team Totals	**24**	**68**

HUSKIES

PLAYER	FG	PTS
Ed Sadowski	8	18
George Nostrand	7	16
Charlie Hoefer	2	8
Mike McCarron	1	6
Ray Wertis	3	6
Dick Fitzgerald	3	6
Bob Fitzgerald	1	4
Harry Miller	0	1
Frank Fucarino	0	1
Hank Biasatti	0	0
Roy Hurley	0	0
Team Totals	**25**	**66**

1948
MR. BASKETBALL

The story of the NBA is told through its stars and the dynasties they helped create. In the league's earliest years, no star shone brighter than George Mikan — and no team won like his Minneapolis Lakers.

With five championships in six years between 1949 and '54, the Lakers were the NBA's first dynasty, and the 6-foot-10 Mikan was the game's first real star. As Mikan's teammate Vern Mikkelsen put it, "In our time, George was Michael Jordan, Magic Johnson and Larry Bird rolled into one."

Mikan was an anomaly, a giant in a sport dictated by the play of smaller, faster guards. The emphasis was on passing and movement, and the center's role was to rebound and protect the rim. That all changed when Mikan arrived on the scene, setting the stage for the big men who ruled the NBA for the rest of the 20th century.

Mikan was slow-footed and lumbering — hardly the makings of a star basketball player. But he was a quick study and had developed a reliable and surprisingly nimble hook shot that was virtually impossible for his smaller opponents to defend. Mikan created a training drill that allowed him to shoot his hook shots with either hand. It later became known as the Mikan Drill and is commonly used to teach low-post play to this day.

He spent his years at DePaul University honing his craft and developing the footwork and skill set that would take him to the Hall of Fame, all while dominating the collegiate scene. He was twice named the NCAA's Player of the Year and, en route to leading DePaul to a championship, once scored as many points as the entire opposing team in a 97–53 win over Rhode Island.

Mikan left college as a dominating post presence. Upon graduation in 1946, he joined the Chicago American Gears of the National Basketball League. He carried the Gears to a championship in his first season, but then team owner Maurice White left the NBL to form a new league in which he would own all 16 franchises. White's league barely lasted a month before it folded, leaving a 23-year-old Mikan without a team.

A young George Mikan during his early days as a Laker.

Meanwhile, the NBL had moved a team from Detroit to Minneapolis and dubbed it the Lakers, for the region's endless bodies of water. The team obtained Mikan's rights, and although collegiate games in Minnesota during its frigid winters had left him less than thrilled with the prospect of calling the Twin Cities home, he reported for duty.

New team, same results. In his first season in Minneapolis, Mikan won a championship, defeating the Rochester Royals, 3–1, in the best-of-five final series. The following season, the Lakers were crowned champs again, this time over the Washington Capitols and their young head coach, Red Auerbach.

Meanwhile, Mikan cemented his status as an unstoppable force. He led the NBA in scoring for three straight seasons between 1948–49 and '50–51, averaging 28 points per game in that span — in an era when whole teams averaged roughly 80 points.

So overpowering was Mikan that the NBA began to adjust its rules in an effort to level the playing field. In 1951 the league instituted what became known as the Mikan Rule, widening the lane underneath the basket from 6 feet to 12. As teams tried to deliberately keep the ball out of the Lakers' (and therefore Mikan's) hands, they employed all sorts of stall tactics, which led to the installation of the 24-second shot clock. The NBA even experimented with raising the baskets to 12 feet in order to make it harder for Mikan to score down low.

No rule change could tame those talents, though, and the same was true of Mikan. It wasn't until after Mikan retired that the NBA began awarding a Most Valuable Player

award, but it's safe to say he would have taken a run at Kareem Abdul-Jabbar's record six MVPs.

The Lakers were a formidable team beyond Mikan. Forwards Jim Pollard ("The Kangaroo Kid") and Vern Mikkelsen were All-Stars who filled the passing lanes, where point guard Slater Martin delivered them the ball — when he wasn't dumping it down low to a waiting Mikan, the team's go-to play.

For a league desperate to draw new fans, Mikan was a godsend. His immense size and distinctive appearance — bifocals and coiffed black hair that made him look like a supersized Clark Kent — made him instantly recognizable. Mikan became a popular pitchman, appearing in newspaper and magazine ads endorsing products such as Pabst Blue Ribbon beer, Mennen deodorant ("It's my favorite zone defense!") and underwear ("Mr. Basketball picks Munsingwear double-strength briefs").

He appeared on nationally televised talk shows and wore his title as NBA ambassador proudly. Mikan would regularly travel to road games ahead of his team to meet the local press and help promote games — and sell tickets (at a time when the league didn't want its games aired on TV for fear it would dissuade fans from purchasing tickets to watch in person). Mikan's star power helped the league make inroads in larger markets, a major step toward legitimizing the upstart venture.

When the NBL merged with the Basketball Association of America ahead of the 1949–50 season, officially creating the National Basketball Association, the new

DON'T HATE THE PLAYER...

Basketball would continue to change its rules when faced with all-time greats. In 1967 the NCAA passed the "Lew Alcindor Rule," banning slam dunks in response to the UCLA star. They kept the rule in place until 1976, after another dominant UCLA centre, Bill Walton, had left college for the NBA. On at least one occasion Wilt

Chamberlain, among the worst free-throw shooters in history, took a running start toward the free throw line and, as legend has it, opted to dunk the ball. This prompted the NBA rule that players must stand at the free-throw line until they've shot the ball.

league adopted franchises in such perilously small markets as Anderson, Indiana (the Packers), Moline, Illinois (the Tri-Cities Blackhawks), Waterloo, Iowa (the Hawks), and Sheboygan, Wisconsin (the Red Skins).

Franchises folded and materialized quicker than a Bob Cousy fast break, but by the 1951–52 season — Mikan's fourth with the Lakers — the NBA landscape featured 10 teams, all in respectably sized markets: New York City, Boston, Philadelphia, Syracuse, Baltimore, Rochester, Minneapolis, Fort Wayne, Indianapolis and Milwaukee.

On April 12, 1954, Minneapolis won its sixth title in seven years, following a hard-fought seven-game series against Dolph Schayes and the Syracuse Nationals. The Lakers' championship run drew to a close only once Mikan retired ahead of the 1954–55 season to pursue a career in law (he eventually set up a successful practice in Minneapolis).

Mikan sent an outlet pass through generations. His eight-season career, short by today's standards, established a formula for roster building. For decades, teams coveted a dominant big man to construct their team around

George Mikan polishes his own name on the Marquee at Madison Square Garden in 1949.

— Wilt Chamberlain, Kareem Abdul-Jabbar, Bill Russell, Shaquille O'Neal, Tim Duncan, Dirk Nowitzki. It's why Hakeem Olajuwon was drafted ahead of Michael Jordan, and why over 60 percent of first overall draft picks have been centers.

Among his countless accolades, Mikan was named the greatest basketball player of the first half of the 20th century by the Associated Press. There could be no other choice.

1948
GLOBETROTTERS 61, LAKERS 59

On February 19, 1948, a crowd of 17,823 packed Chicago Stadium for an exhibition match between the Minneapolis Lakers and the Harlem Globetrotters. It was the largest audience to attend a pro hoops game to date.

As the upstart NBA worked to grow its fan base, teams seemed to play more exhibition matches than league games. The league wanted to promote basketball as a spectator sport, and a clash between two iconic teams figured to do just that. Yet what started as just another barnstorming event would serve to challenge long-standing racial prejudices and become an important first step toward integrating the NBA.

Featuring an all-white roster built around bespectacled big man George Mikan, the Lakers had just won two consecutive championships. Serious and deliberate in their style of play, which revolved almost entirely around the 6-foot-10 Mikan, the Lakers were considered by fans and media to be the greatest team on Earth.

The Globetrotters, on the other hand, were undoubtedly the most popular. An all-black team known as much for its lighthearted comedic stylings as its athletic prowess, the Globies had risen to prominence thanks to

Wilt Chamberlain holds balls over Abe Saperstein during a luncheon in 1958.

their unique brand of showmanship and a tireless touring schedule.

True to their name, the Globetrotters traveled the world. They were also ambassadors for the United States, and their skill and celebrity were meant to imply that America wasn't a terrible place to live if you were black.

In reality, of course, race and prejudice had played an unavoidable role in the team's identity since it was first formed in the segregated America of 1926.

In those early days, the Globetrotters would arrive in new cities to headlines like "Colored Five Will Take on Shelby Stars." For decades, they played doubleheaders in front of separate white and black audiences. They weren't the

first all-black traveling team, and initially, they weren't the best (that distinction went to the Harlem Renaissance, from whom the Chicago-founded Globetrotters stole part of their name). But before long, the Globetrotters were certainly the biggest draw.

Their rise came soon after the team was purchased by Abe Saperstein, a London-born and Chicago-raised booking agent with a P.T. Barnum-esque nose for publicity. Saperstein recognized his players' superb skills and creative talents, and by the late 30s he'd transformed them from a traveling team into a traveling show — incorporating choreographed gags and tricks such as no-look passes or putting the ball behind a defender's head.

Saperstein was also an important ally of the early NBA, and the two did good business together, promoting doubleheaders in league arenas like Madison Square Garden, where the Trotters routinely drew more fans. By the mid-40s, white audiences were showing up in droves to watch Marques Haynes's dribbling wizardry or the comedic stylings of Goose Tatum, a former Negro League baseball player who seemingly held the ball on a string.

Yet when they traveled through America, the joy they spread seemed to matter less than the color of their skin. Globetrotters players were spat at on the street and refused service in stores and restaurants.

Despite consistently defeating all-white opponents, the Globetrotters, like African American basketballers in general, had to fight the perception that they weren't capable athletes. Globetrotters alum Mannie Jackson, who purchased the team in 1992, said, "I heard [sentiments] like 'Blacks can't play point guard because they can't think and they can't lead. Blacks are good for rebounding and hard work, but you can't really trust them on the floor because they can't think through the complex plays in the NBA.'"

The Globetrotters were easily dismissed as a trick show. But their 1948 exhibition match against the Lakers offered a prime opportunity to prove otherwise.

Adding fuel to the fire, the game was played in a climate of extreme racial tension. Just days earlier, a black teenager was beaten to death with a baseball bat by six white men. On the night of the game, U.S. president Harry S. Truman delivered a landmark speech to the nation against segregation and prejudice.

The Lakers and their plodding brand of ball jumped out to an early lead at Chicago Stadium. They dumped the ball to Mikan down low, where he methodically sank hook shots and fed teammates passes. By halftime the NBA champs held a comfortable 10-point margin.

The second half was a different story. The Globetrotters matched the Lakers' physicality on defense. They double-teamed Mikan in the post and held the future Hall of Famer to just 6 second-half points. On the other side of the ball, they used their speed and the fast break to put up points in bunches.

With the game tied as the clock ran down in the fourth, Marques Haynes dribbled the ball for what seemed like hours before delivering a pass to Elmer Robinson, who swished it as the buzzer sounded. In one of the most important basketball games ever played, the Globetrotters pulled off the upset, 61–59. They had beaten the best white team in America — without any tricks.

"That was like Joe Louis defeating Max Schmeling — this triumphant event," said Globetrotters historian Ben Green. "They were celebrating in the streets on Chicago's South Side. This black team that was viewed as a bunch of clowns beat the best basketball team in the world."

A rematch the following year set a new attendance record of more than 20,000, and the Globetrotters received national press after winning a second time. The victories made clear to team owners that the all-white NBA couldn't possibly claim to feature the best players in the country as long as African Americans were barred from its rosters.

The league might have been on its way toward integration already, but those Lakers losses fast-tracked the process. Within a year, the NBA's first African-American players were signed, including Nat "Sweetwater" Clifton, a key member of the Globetrotters teams that edged the Lakers.

But Saperstein and the Globetrotters had welcomed black athletes when other teams and leagues wouldn't.

Soon, the NBA found itself competing with the Globies for talent. Chuck Cooper, the first black player drafted, had been a target of the Globetrotters coming out of college, but he was offered more money by the Boston Celtics, with whom he ultimately signed.

The bidding wars went on throughout the 50s. Maurice Stokes, a talented forward out of St. Francis College, was coveted by both parties upon his graduation in 1955. Stokes, like more and more prospects, opted for the NBA, which was on its way to eclipsing the Globies in talent and becoming the destination of choice for black ballplayers.

One notable exception was Wilt Chamberlain. The Philadelphia-born center had already attained legendary status by the time he reached college at Kansas — stories of

unheard-of feats passed through schoolyards around North America.

Making easy work of the competition in college, in 1958 Chamberlain wanted to leave school early to pursue his pro career. The NBA's Philadelphia Warriors, who owned his pro rights (between 1950 and 1965, teams could forfeit their first round pick in order to select a player from within a 50-mile radius), had drafted Chamberlain when he was in high school, but league rules at the time stated that a player had to wait four years after high school before he could turn pro.

Warriors owner Eddie Gottlieb offered Chamberlain $25,000 to join the NBA ranks after his junior season; it would have made him the league's highest-paid player. The Globetrotters offered $50,000 plus bonuses, and so Wilt Chamberlain became a Harlem Globetrotter.

"I signed with them because they had great tradition," Chamberlain said. "In the 1940s and early 50s, it was the Globies who had the best black players. Playing for them was something that a young man of color often dreamed about."

After a year abroad with the team, Chamberlain returned to America and signed with the Warriors.

Ten years after the Globetrotters beat the Lakers and disproved the most bigoted theories about black basketball players, the NBA's roster of African American stars was rapidly growing. As the 50s gave way to the 60s, the league featured such generational talents as Chamberlain, Stokes, Elgin Baylor, Oscar Robertson and Bill Russell.

Now the NBA could claim it boasted the best players in the world, and mean it.

CAREER REBOUNDS

1.	Wilt Chamberlain	23,924
2.	Bill Russell	21,620
3.	Moses Malone	17,834
4.	Kareem Abdul-Jabbar	17,440
5.	Artis Gilmore	16,330

George Mikan grabs a rebound over Globetrotters Nat Clifton and Babe Pressley.

1949
THE NATIONAL BASKET-BALL ASSOCIATION

The New York Knicks' victory in Toronto over the Huskies in 1946 may be officially recognized as the first NBA game, but it wasn't until three years later that the National Basketball Association officially came to be.

The Knicks and Huskies had been part of the Basketball Association of America, but it wasn't until August 3, 1949, that the BAA and rival National Basketball League officially merged and renamed their league. For the NBL, the merger was necessary to survive.

The BAA was a clear threat to the NBL, which had been established nine years earlier. The arena owners who founded the BAA had deep pockets and represented the biggest markets in the Northeast. And they'd already persuaded four franchises, including the successful Minneapolis Lakers and Rochester Royals, to leave the NBL in 1947.

The NBL couldn't compete with the BAA's venues or its populous cities, but what it did have going for it was better all-around talent. In 1948 the NBL's Tri-Cities Blackhawks (who played out of Moline, Illinois) made waves when they signed New York University star Dolph Schayes, who had been heavily recruited by his home-town Knicks.

The next summer, just ahead of the merger, the NBL established a new franchise, the Indianapolis Olympians, whose roster featured the entire starting five from the reigning NCAA champion Kentucky Wildcats — four of whom had also led the United States to a gold medal at the 1948 Olympics in London.

Even though it was struggling to survive, moves like these made the NBL a valuable partner for the BAA. Newspapers across the country carried the news of the merger and the establishment of the new NBA.

The first game under the NBA banner took place on October 29, 1949, between the Tri-Cities Blackhawks and Denver Nuggets — the team farthest west in a league mostly on the Great Lakes and Eastern Seaboard.

With an odd number of teams (17) split into three divisions, along with greater distances to be covered by bus or train, scheduling became a logistical nightmare. Teams ended up playing as few as 62 games and as many as 68, with some clubs on the road more often than they were at home. Neutral-site games were a frequent occurrence, with the Nuggets playing a league-high 11.

Over the following years, the NBA would expand to cities to the north, south and west. Some franchises would fold, while others moved as often as an army brat. Throw in countless exhibition games in a host of small towns that dotted the map, and the early NBA was an ever-changing spectacle.

THE LEAGUE BACK THEN

Central Division	Eastern Division	Western Division
Minneapolis Lakers	Syracuse Nationals	Indianapolis Olympians
Rochester Royals	New York Knicks	Anderson Packers
Fort Wayne Pistons	Washington Capitols	Tri-Cities Blackhawks
Chicago Stags	Philadelphia Warriors	Sheboygan Red Skins
St. Louis Bombers	Baltimore Bullets	Waterloo Hawks
	Boston Celtics	Denver Nuggets

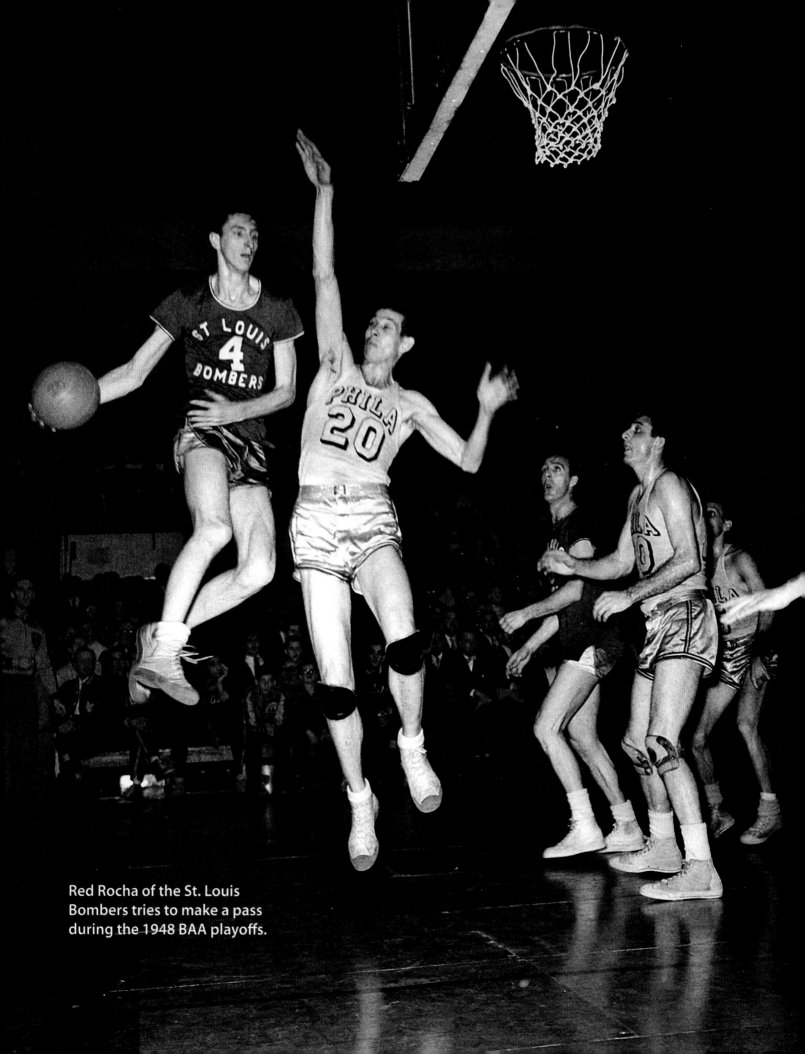

Red Rocha of the St. Louis Bombers tries to make a pass during the 1948 BAA playoffs.

Nate Clifton poses in his Knicks uniform in 1951.

1950
BREAKING THE COLOR BARRIER

There were no newspaper articles or radio broadcasts on October 31, 1950, announcing that Earl Lloyd had just become the first African American to play in an NBA game. The historic occasion came and went, but its impact on the game was immeasurable.

Apart from Wataru Misaka, a Japanese American point guard who played three games for the Knicks in 1947, the NBA had been operating as an all-white league. On April 25, 1950, Chuck Cooper became the first black player drafted, selected by the Boston Celtics in the second round. Lloyd, an eighth-rounder chosen by the Washington Capitols, soon followed. Before either could secure a deal with their new teams, Nat "Sweetwater" Clifton, a former member of the Harlem Globetrotters, became the first black player to sign with an NBA team, the New York Knicks.

The first black players in pro basketball, it should be noted, were Dolly King and Pop Gates, who joined the National Basketball League in 1946 before it merged to form the NBA. Earning the measly $500 the league could afford to offer, the two soon left to join the workforce instead.

At the turn of the 50s, racial tension was tightly wound across America, and the upstart league was no exception. When Cooper, a standout collegiate forward at Duquesne, was selected, some owners are said to have reached out to Celtics owner Walter Brown, raising concern over the color of Cooper's skin. "I don't care if he's plaid," Brown said. "All I know is that this kid can play."

Many owners were concerned about black players entering the league. For one, they thought fans might not pay to see them, something already disproven by the success of the Globetrotters. In order for NBA teams to sell more tickets, they often shared the bill with the Globies in doubleheaders during those early years. The Globetrotters would play first in order to ensure a packed crowd, and the stands would commonly empty by the time the NBA game tipped off later that night.

Second, the owners thought bringing African American players into the NBA would put it into direct competition with the Globetrotters, thus upsetting the team's

founder, Abe Saperstein, at that point the most powerful and influential man in basketball. That concern may have been more valid. Until that point, most black players played for Saperstein's Trotters, or for other, less-heralded traveling clubs like the Vagabonds.

In the case of Sweetwater Clifton, the Knicks were playing with fire by going after an established Globies draw, and the Globetrotters were actively trying to sign Cooper as well until he joined the Celtics.

Lloyd, Cooper and Clifton admired Jackie Robinson, who broke baseball's color barrier three years earlier under far more prejudicial circumstances. When Robinson entered the major leagues, opposing players would yell racial epithets at him. "We didn't have any trouble like that," Lloyd said. "Basketball players were college people. If they did harbor any racial prejudice, they were smart enough to keep it to themselves."

The fans were a different story.

Games in places like St. Louis, against the Hawks, were ugly for the NBA's first black players. Fans were known to hurl insults and spit on them. Trips to Fort Wayne, Indiana, to face the Pistons were always contentious.

The NBA's black players couldn't eat in the same restaurants as their teammates. When he heard that Lloyd had been refused service, coach Bones McKinney took his meal to Lloyd's room. The two ate together.

Lloyd, Cooper, and Clifton were together in making history, but by playing for different teams, they were mostly alone in their struggle. The trio made a point of hanging out when they could. "We were a support group for each other. We wanted the other guy to feel comfortable, and you can't feel comfortable sitting alone in a hotel room," said Lloyd. "A home-cooked meal with friends meant a lot."

Lloyd grew up in segregated Virginia, where he was raised under a canopy of prejudice that didn't allow him to go to the local whites-only swimming pool or share bathrooms with white kids. He had seen the ugliness. "These things had steeled me for anything I would face as an NBA player," he said. Sweetwater Clifton had also experienced the broad spectrum of racism during his time touring the world with the Globetrotters.

Chuck Cooper, on the other hand, was in for much more of a shock. Born and raised in Pittsburgh, he hadn't experienced segregation in the way Lloyd had become accustomed to. In an exhibition game in Charlotte in 1950, he was hurt at how differently he was treated than fellow rookie Bob Cousy, a white point guard from New York City.

"He couldn't stay at the same hotel, eat at the same places or even take a piss in the same place I did," Cousy recalled. "Chuck was upset by this — and he should have been."

Instead of looking for his own accommodations after the game, Cooper took a midnight train home. "I looked at this garbage," Cousy said, "and I was embarrassed to be white." Cousy joined Cooper on the train ride back to Boston.

At an exhibition game in Louisiana three years later, Cooper wasn't allowed to play.

The NBA's first black players were viewed as role players, not scorers, and therefore not stars. They set picks and rebounded. Coaches matched black opponents up against one another. "It was a 4-on-4 game with us as the odd men out," said Don Barksdale, who was one of many to have raised the issue with their coaches. "Was it intentional?" he asked years later. "They said it wasn't. No matter their intent, the result was degrading."

In the 1951–52 season, three more African Americans joined the NBA, including Barksdale, who in 1948 was the first black player on the U.S. Olympic Team and would become the NBA's first African American All-Star. In 1958 Elgin Baylor became the first African American drafted first overall.

As the years passed, it didn't get easier for the league's black players. During his rookie season, Baylor and his two black teammates, Boo Ellis and Ed Fleming, were refused service at the team hotel ahead of an exhibition game in Charleston, West Virginia. In a defiant act, Baylor, the game's biggest draw, refused to play that night.

While the NBA opened its doors to black players in 1950, it would be another 10 years before they had a decent representation across the league. By 1960, 26 percent of the league's players were black, still a vast minority. The 1958 St. Louis Hawks were the NBA's last all-white championship team.

Earl Lloyd fights for a rebound against Mel Hutchins in 1955.

"The phrase whispered was 'It's a white dollar,'" said former Laker Hot Rod Hundley. "Most owners were afraid that too many blacks would keep away the fans."

Black players suspected that a quota had been secretly put in place. There was believed to be an unwritten rule that teams should set a cap of two or three black players, and that those players had better be significantly better than their white counterparts in order to earn a spot on the roster. "It was racism, pure and simple," said Hundley.

There were also rumors of a related policy under which, if a black player joined a team, one of its existing black players had to be

dealt to balance the scale. When Al Attles joined the Philadelphia Warriors in 1960, for example, another black player was traded away. "There were too many examples of these kinds of player moves for it to have been a coincidence," said Attles.

There's no question that the league's African American stars helped the game reach another level. Baylor, Russell and Oscar Robertson all forged legendary careers. If anybody took issue with the NBA becoming blacker, Baylor had a message.

"They ask me where all the white players have gone. I've seen so many of them come into this league, and they've had great talent.

But they didn't last—they married some money or got a good outside job, things that don't happen to us. You give us a chance in other things, and you'll get your white ballplayers back right away."

But there was progress. In 1960 Earl Lloyd became the first black assistant coach. In 1961 the first all-black NBA lineup took the floor with the Chicago Packers.

"I think about how someone had to be first — how guys like Chuck Cooper, Sweetwater Clifton, Don Barksdale and myself paid the dues so those kids can have the chance they do today," said Lloyd. "They don't realize what we accomplished, but I do."

1954
TWENTY-FOUR SECONDS

It was Game 3 of the 1953 Eastern Division semifinals between the Boston Celtics and Syracuse Nationals. Late in the second half, Celtics point guard Bob Cousy uncorked his signature move — a dazzling dribbling display leading into a sweeping, running hook shot 15 feet from the basket. Boston took the lead, and the game ground to a halt.

It was hardly the exciting, fast-paced action ticket buyers had been promised.

Within a year, the NBA would institute a 24-second shot clock, putting a time limit on all possessions that drastically transformed the game for the better. But for now, as long as a team held a lead, its goal was to hold on to the ball for as long as possible until the final buzzer sounded. That was Celtics coach Red Auerbach's message to Cousy: Don't give up the ball until you're fouled. In a word, stall.

Cousy did. He took a beating and marched his way to the free-throw line as one overtime turned into the next. It took four extra periods before a winner was declared. What seemed on paper like an all-time classic was, in technical terms, a snoozefest.

Just a half dozen years into the NBA's existence, the sport was making progress. The league was regularly drawing fans to the arenas and beginning to secure television contracts. Pro basketball was on its way to becoming entrenched in North American sports culture. On the court, the game was evolving, with the two-handed set shot now

giving way to the more effective jump shot, while players like Cousy were creating exciting moves that mesmerized crowds.

But the foul-fest late in games had become problematic in recent years. With teams sitting on the ball — sometimes literally — basketball was becoming boring.

Never was this more evident than on November 22, 1950. The Fort Wayne Pistons were facing George Mikan and the Minneapolis Lakers, who were on their way to their second of five titles between 1949 and 1954. The Pistons devised a strategy to keep the ball out of the paint and away from the 6-foot-10 Mikan, resulting in the dullest game of hot potato you've ever seen. The final score, 19–18, was low even by the standards of the day.

"The fans hated it," recalled Lakers point guard Slater Martin. "They booed for a while. Then they gave up and started reading newspapers." By the end of the game, fans had tossed the papers onto the court and demanded refunds.

While not as dramatic, there were plenty of other examples. One particularly damaging game came on March, 20, 1954, between Boston and New York in front of a national television audience — a major promotional opportunity for the league. The game dragged on for over three hours as teams traded fouls. During a fourth quarter that took 45 minutes to play, viewers turned off

Bob Cousy demonstrates his famous dribbling skills.

their TV sets en masse. The network pulled the feed before the game even finished.

At first, the ball stopping and subsequent fouling had been encouraged. It added a physical element to the game that echoed that of hockey, the sport where most NBA owners held their roots. Referees were encouraged to ignore fouls late in games as the players wrestled each other for possession of the ball. It was physical, sure, but it was also ruining the game. Worse, it was keeping fans away.

Something had to give.

A number of rule changes about fouling were made during the first half of the 1950s, but none addressed the problem of a game that often appeared stuck in quicksand.

Syracuse Nationals owner Danny Biasone had been the most vocal in pushing for widespread changes. Having made his money running a bowling alley in his native Syracuse, Biasone was a football fan first, and he had come to own an NBA team without knowing much about the game. His fresh eyes would prove invaluable.

Biasone argued in favor of a time limit on possessions in the wake of the Pistons–Lakers 19–18 game. Football has four downs, he figured, and baseball has three outs, so why shouldn't basketball follow suit?

At the league's 1954 summer meetings, he proposed a 24-second shot clock. Why 24 seconds? "I looked at the box scores from the games I enjoyed," Biasone explained. "Games where they didn't screw around and stall. . . . I noticed each team took about 60 shots. That meant 120 shots per game. So I took 48 minutes [the length of a full game] and divided that by 120 shots. The result was 24 seconds per shot."

His math must have been sound. While the game has seen major overhauls as the decades have passed, the NBA has never strayed from the 24-second shot clock. As Syracuse star Dolph Schayes said, "Danny Biasone was the Wilbur Wright of basketball."

A demonstration game took place at Biasone's high school alma mater in Syracuse, with a mix of NBAers like Schayes and other local talent taking part. Initially, the players were forcing shots up early on each trip up the floor, after just seven or eight seconds.

But soon they settled into a rhythm that encouraged a faster pace, while still giving teams enough time to develop plays without bringing the action to a halt.

The impact of the shot clock was immediate, fundamentally changing the way the game was played. Suddenly, teams were incentivized to actually shoot the ball. In the 1953–54 season, the last season before the clock was installed, teams averaged 79 points per game. In 1954–55 the average leapt to 93 points. By the end of the decade, the average was 115 points, while Cousy's Celtics paced the league at 124 points per game.

The shot clock also made an even bigger star out of Cousy. Nicknamed the Houdini of the Hardwood, Cousy brought elements of showmanship to the game thanks to a magical ability to control the basketball.

Cousy, the son of French immigrants, was a local celebrity as a high school player in Queens, New York, earning a city league title and scholarship to Holy Cross in Massachusetts, just under an hour west of Boston. He became a national star in college, leading Holy Cross to 26 straight wins in his senior season, and became a local hero as a rookie in Boston when he led the Celtics to their first winning season in 1950–51.

A gifted scorer and passer, Cousy's ballhandling wizardry was his greatest attribute. He'd switch hands and bounce the ball between his legs, as if he'd wrapped it in twine. His behind-the-back dribbles defied logic. No player in the NBA could come close to matching his abilities with the ball — Harlem Globetrotters stars Marques Haynes and

Goose Tatum were perhaps his only rivals.

Cousy led the NBA in assists for eight straight seasons beginning in 1952–53, and as the game's pace increased in response to the shot clock, so did Cousy's flair. He was the precursor to Jerry West, Magic Johnson, Steve Nash and the great maestros that followed. The up-tempo style the new clock encouraged was a key part of Boston's success, and they supplanted the Lakers as the NBA's preeminent dynasty.

Cousy was the league's most magnetic talent and, with a salary of $20,000 per year, its highest-paid player. At 6 foot 1 he was an everyman compared to the towering Mikan, and his style put a premium on entertainment.

"Cousy, as pro basketball's greatest attraction, has almost single-handedly been carrying the league to a prosperity it could never otherwise enjoy," read a 1956 *Sports Illustrated* profile.

It didn't hurt that his teams won. By 1956, when Boston traded for a rookie center named Bill Russell, the Celtics had assembled a loaded roster that also featured Bill Sharman, Tommy Heinsohn, K.C. Jones and Frank Ramsey. With Cousy leading the fast break, the Celtics were the class of the NBA.

Cousy delighted sold-out Boston Garden crowds, firing no-look passes on the run, hitting big shots, setting up Russell in the paint and amazing his fans as the championships piled up.

With each passing year of his Hall of Fame career, Cousy continuously added to his legend — 24 seconds at a time.

COUSY'S RECORD NIGHT

In that quadruple overtime duel, Cousy did all he could to keep the ball from the Nationals. He dribbled behind his back, faked passes and ran around the court as the Nats chased him like a youth soccer team swarming the ball. But mostly Cousy held the ball and braced for contact. "Get a lead and put the ball in the icebox,"
he said. The Syracuse players fouled him — what choice did they have? — as Cousy made one clutch free throw after another. By the time the buzzer sounded, he attempted a record 32 free throws. He made 30 of them and wound up with 50 points — and a win.

Bob Cousy draws a foul against Dick McGuir during a 1954 game at the Boston Garden.

1955
SCHAYES AND THE CITY GAME

The 1954 NBA Finals featured a clash of styles. On one side were the Minneapolis Lakers. Like many teams from the Midwest, they played a controlled game, running set plays and finding success through repetition. On the other were the Syracuse Nationals. They played the "city game," a free-flowing style born on the concrete of New York.

The Nationals were one of the NBA's original franchises, and they boasted the league's most fervent fan base. They were led by Dolph Schayes — a top-10 scorer and rebounder for 12 seasons straight — and the Nats' hectic, give-and-go brand of ball was all he knew.

Schayes grew up in the Bronx. By the early 1920s, long before the game could be seen on the playgrounds of New York City, basketball was being played in the community centers in Jewish neighborhoods on the Lower East Side. It was the sport of choice among the children of European-born Jewish immigrants like Schayes's parents, who were born in Romania.

"You couldn't play football. They had no fields for baseball," explained Brooklyn-bred Red Auerbach. "Everything was basketball."

Soon, the top collegiate teams in the region, like New York University (Schayes's alma mater), featured predominantly Jewish rosters, including the 1950 NCAA champion Community College of New York. Those players went on to populate some of the earliest professional leagues, including the precursors to the NBA.

As had been the case with African American players, their inclusion in the sport was a lightning rod for anti-Semitism. In 1938 prominent sportswriter Paul Gallico alleged that Jews were drawn to basketball because "the game places a premium on an alert, scheming mind and flashy trickiness, artful dodging, and general smart alecness."

The NBA's Jewish roots are undeniable. Its first commissioner, Maurice Podoloff, was Jewish, as were such prominent early figures as Auerbach. The Philadelphia Warriors even began as the Philadelphia Sphas, which stood for South Philadelphia Hebrew Association, before changing their name to the Warriors (and, eventually, moving to California).

When the NBA tipped off its first game in November 1946 between the Toronto Huskies and New York Knickerbockers, four of the Knicks' starting five were Jews. "Playing in Pittsburgh, and we came out on the floor, I heard them singing: 'East Side, West Side, here comes the Jews from New York,'" recalled Nat Militzok, an original member of the Knicks.

By the time he left NYU, Schayes had been offered a contract by the Knicks, who saw a 6-foot-8 low-post player. The upstate Nationals, however, saw potential for Schayes to take on a far greater role and offered a $7,000 contract. He signed and joined the team for the 1948–49 season.

Even in his earliest days, Schayes was considered among the slowest players on his team. But he made up for lack of foot speed with a relentless motor. "He would overwhelm you with effort," said All-Star George Yardley. The quick-passing, frequent cuts to the hoop and constant motion were trademarks of the city game Schayes grew up playing. In the NBA, it exhausted defenders.

This was still the era of the low-efficiency set shot, and so Schayes's .380 career shooting rate, pedestrian by current-day standards, was considered elite. But his range extended beyond 25 feet. Later, those who shared the court with Schayes would draw comparisons to Larry Bird for his offensive arsenal. When he broke the wrist of his shooting hand during the 1954 playoffs, Schayes donned a cast and played left-handed.

Schayes became the first player to reach 15,000 career points and was the Nationals' leading scorer every season he played. The rest of the roster was potent as well. In 1954 Syracuse drafted center Johnny "Red" Kerr, giving them the post presence they lacked against Mikan and the Lakers. In the backcourt, George King was a ball hawk, while forward Earl Lloyd, the first African American to play in the NBA, was a load to handle. The players described their coach, Al Cervi, as "a street fighter," and the team took on his tough demeanor.

But the Nationals' biggest advantage was their home crowd.

Nats fans were ruthless, approaching games as if they were at the Colosseum, calling for the lions. When players fought — as they frequently did — fans would storm the court. Opposing players would often leave the floor drenched in drinks thrown from the stands. On at least one occasion, for their own safety, the visitors had to sit in the locker room during the game, the coach going back and forth from the court to make substitutions. It was a consistently intimidating environment.

In 1954 Syracuse dropped Game 7 of the Finals to Mikan and the Lakers. But the next year, following Mikan's retirement, the Nationals returned to the Finals, where they met Yardley and the Fort Wayne Pistons. For a league still looking to build a larger fan base, the matchup between Syracuse and Fort Wayne didn't exactly help push the NBA into the mainstream. But it produced a down-to-the-wire Finals.

Game 7 took place in Syracuse, where Schayes helped a Nationals fourth-quarter comeback. Pistons center Larry Foust — at 6-foot-10 and 250 pounds, the game's top big man now that Mikan was retired — had gotten the better of his matchup with the rookie Kerr, scoring 24 points.

With 10 seconds on the clock and the Nats up 92–91, all eyes were on Foust. But Pistons guard Andy Phillip dribbled the ball into the corner, and before he could get a pass off, Syracuse's King stole the ball before the buzzer sounded. The Nationals became the first post-Mikan champs.

For Schayes, it was the only title of his career. He retired in 1964 as the NBA's all-time leader in games played, its second all-time scorer, and its third all-time rebounder. He was named one of the NBA's 50 greatest players in 1996.

The Nationals' title marked the beginning of the end of the NBA's briefest era. Within two years, Bill Russell and the Boston Celtics would win the first championship of their dynasty. The league would never be the same.

Dolph Schayes attacks Bill Russell at the rim during a 1958 match-up.

OLD TIME GREATS

Paul Arizin: A ten-time All-Star who popularized the jump shot and led the NBA in scoring by just his second season.

Bob Pettit: "The Bombardier of Baton Rouge" was an 11-time All-Star and two-time MVP with the St. Louis Hawks.

Harry Gallatin: The New York Knicks forward was a punishing rebounder and stalwart on the Knicks frontline.

Bob Davies: Believed to be the man who brought the behind-the-back dribble to NBA courts, Davies was a dynamic guard for the Rochester Royals.

Joe Fulks: The league's most potent scorer, Fulks averaged over 23 points per game for Philadelphia during the first three seasons of the BAA.

1957
THE RUSSELL DYNASTY

Bill Russell is not a basketball player.
Bill Russell and Boston Celtics teammate John Havlicek were out about town one day when someone approached Russell, looked up and asked if he was a basketball player.

"No," Russell replied without breaking his stride.

"Why do you always say you're not a player?" Havlicek asked.

"John," Russell replied, "that's what I do. That's not what I am."

Bill Russell is the missing piece.

For their first 10 seasons in the NBA, the Boston Celtics were exciting. Point guard Bob Cousy delighted fans, and coach Red Auerbach's offensive schemes were ahead of their time. But the Celtics never won, advancing past the first playoff round just twice. In the summer of 1956, Auerbach needed a new centerpiece. He wanted a center who could protect the rim, rebound and ignite the fast break.

Russell, the incoming top collegiate player, fit the bill. Prior to the 1956 draft, Auerbach traded two future Hall of Famers — center Ed Macauley and forward Cliff Hagan — to the St. Louis Hawks in exchange for Russell's draft rights.

Auerbach told the 22-year-old center that points — or any other stats — were meaningless. The only thing he cared about was the result. Red was preaching to the choir; winning was all that mattered to Russell.

Russell was born February 12, 1934, in Monroe, Louisiana. Raised in the segregated South, he'd been subjected to racial prejudice all his life, including after his family moved to San Francisco during his childhood. When he was 12 years old, his mother passed away. She had taught him to be leery of his white neighbors and to fight for himself.

In college, Russell was one of the few African American players on the University of San Francisco squad. He was often a target of racism. In one game in Oklahoma City, fans threw coins at him during warm-ups. He picked the change up off the ground and proceeded to take his anger out on that night's opponent. His team won in a blowout and Russell felt vindicated.

"I decided early in my career that the only really important thing was to try to win every game," Russell explained, "Then, it's a historical fact, and nobody can take it away from me."

Russell led USF to a 60-game winning streak and two national championships and was named collegiate player of the year. He then went on to capture the gold medal for the United States at the 1956 Olympics in Melbourne, Australia, in November, which pushed his Celtics debut to December 22.

Having missed all of training camp prior to his rookie year, Russell came off the bench and played sparingly in his first game, which drew the largest crowd of the season at Boston Garden. Celtics fans were eager to finally see the 6-foot-9 rookie in person, although many had disapproved of the trade that put him in Celtic green. "I don't think they were ready for a black athlete," said teammate Tommy Heinsohn, "let alone a world-shaking black athlete who revolutionized a game they didn't know anything about."

The coach could care less what color Russell's skin was. Arnold "Red" Auer-

bach grew up in the Brooklyn, New York, neighborhood of Williamsburg and began his coaching career in Washington, D.C., where he was a standout collegiate player. A Jewish American whose father emigrated from Russia, Auerbach selected the first-ever African American, Chuck Cooper, in the 1950 draft, and in 1964 he played the NBA's first all-black lineup.

In Russell's first play as a Celtic, he leapt to block a shot. The referee called it goaltending, and Auerbach passionately argued the call, earning a technical foul in the process. Russell saw a coach willing to fight for him. So he was willing to fight for his coach.

As a rookie, Russell averaged a league-leading 19.4 rebounds per game. He quickly became the anchor for a fast-paced Celtics team that featured All-Stars Cousy and Bill Sharman in the backcourt, with Heinsohn, a fellow rookie, and forward Jim Losticuff running the wings.

After sweeping the Syracuse Nationals in the playoffs, Boston squared off in a seven-game series against league MVP Bob Pettit and the St. Louis Hawks. Game 7 went to double overtime. Heinsohn scored 37 points and Russell grabbed 32 rebounds, along with a game-saving block at the buzzer.

For the rest of his career, Russell's teams never lost a do-or-die game.

Bill Russell is a pioneer.

By his second season, Russell's reputation as the league's dominant defensive force was unquestioned. In a November game against Philadelphia, he set a record with 49 rebounds. But it was the shot blocking that really set him apart.

"Players just didn't block shots before Russell came into the league," Auerbach said. He was the most imposing player in the game and also its best athlete. He was the fastest down the court, jumped the highest, and could pivot on a dime. In old black-and-white footage, he's often reduced to a blur; film technology simply wasn't advanced enough to capture Russell in motion. It was as if LeBron were plopped onto an NBA court in the late 50s.

Cousy remained the most popular Celtic in Boston — fans didn't need encouragement to cheer on a flashy white player. But Russell confounded them. His dominance was less obvious to spectators who weren't used to measuring success on the defensive end. In order to bring recognition to his new star, Auerbach ranted and raved to the media about the myriad ways his center bolstered Boston's defense.

The Celtics came to rely on Russell's shot blocking. "Once, I blocked seven shots in a row," he recalled. "When we finally got the ball, I called time-out and said, 'This s★★t has got to stop.'"

It wasn't just that Russell swatted away shots. He was a cerebral defender who purposefully directed blocks in the direction of a teammate. The league didn't keep track of blocks in those days, but many estimate he averaged in the double digits. It had a profound psychological effect on opponents; the mere threat of Russell around the basket altered the types of shots teams took against Boston. There isn't a stat to measure that.

In 1958 the St. Louis Hawks got their revenge on an injury-riddled Boston squad, but the Celtics returned to the '59 Finals, where they faced Elgin Baylor and the Minneapolis Lakers. Boston swept the series. "He whipped us psychologically," Lakers coach John Kundla said of Russell after the series. "Every one of the five [Lakers] was thinking Russell is covering him on every play."

Behind Russell's defense, the Celtics were a powerhouse, bolstered by such new additions as Sam Jones, Tom "Satch" Sanders and Havlicek. From Russell's rookie season of 1956–57 until 1964–65, they finished in first place every year. Russell took home five MVP awards in that span, including three in a row from 1961 to 1963. His team won eight straight titles between 1959 and 1966.

After beating the Lakers in the '66 Finals, Auerbach retired as head coach and moved to the front office, naming Russell the Celtics' player-coach. He became the first African American coach in pro sports.

Bill Russell is guarded.

Russell was the heart and soul of the Celtics dynasty, but he always maintained an icy relationship with Boston fans and media.

Boston claimed to be a liberal Northeastern town — "the Athens of America" — but from his earliest days in the city, Russell was exposed to its toxic racist underbelly. He was a proud, intelligent and outspoken black man acutely aware of the power he wielded on the court. It gave him a self-confidence that was threatening to a prejudiced audience.

"Bill Russell did not ask permission to be a human being," Heinsohn observed, "and there were many whites in our society who were not exposed to a black person who thought that way."

The same fans who adored Cousy yelled slurs at Russell. Shortly after Russell bought a house in the white suburb of Reading, Massachusetts, and moved in with his family, locals broke into his home. They demolished his trophies, smeared excrement on the walls and defecated on his bed.

He never discussed what happened to him. "He doesn't want those bigots to know they hurt him," said Heinsohn. But from then on, Russell made it clear he played for the Celtics, not for Boston. He grew withdrawn and closed off to those outside the game. "Impersonal," in his own words. He refused to sign autographs and avoided media. When it came time to hoist his No. 6 jersey to the Boston Garden rafters, Russell would only allow it in a private ceremony with no fans present.

"I owe the public nothing," he said.

Bill Russell is an activist.

As the civil rights movement grew in America, Russell came to the forefront as one of the most outspoken and socially aware African American celebrities of his era.

When NAACP leader Medgar Evers was assassinated in Jackson, Mississippi, in 1963, Russell accepted an invitation to go to Jackson and hold an event to help calm racial tensions. In 1967 Russell was front and center when a group of the top black athletes in America convened in Cleveland, Ohio, to support Muhammad Ali's refusal to join the armed service in Vietnam. He was seated directly beside Ali during the iconic press conference.

In 1975 Russell became the first black player enshrined in the Hall of Fame. He refused to accept the gold ring, stating that there were other black players, like Chuck Cooper, who deserved to go ahead of him. It wasn't until 2019, when Cooper was finally inducted, that Russell accepted the ring in a private ceremony.

Bill Russell is a leader.

"There are two types of superstars," said Don Nelson, a former teammate of Russell's in Boston and the NBA's winningest coach of all time. "One makes himself look good at the expense of the other guys on the floor. But there's another type, who makes the players around him look better than they are."

That, by all accounts, was Russell.

He empowered his teammates to play to their strengths and promised to cover their weaknesses. It's one of the reasons why, in an age where Wilt Chamberlain racked up gaudy offensive stats, Russell never averaged more than 19 points per game in a season. His career averages of 15.1 points, 22.5 rebounds and 4.3 assists per game tell the story of the ultimate team-first player.

Russell led by example. He was the fiercest competitor in the game, even after countless miles on the court wreaked havoc on his knees. In 1966–67, his first season as player-coach, he played through a foot injury (later revealed to be a broken foot), but the Celtics fell short of winning the championship. The following season, Boston got back to its winning ways and captured two more titles, an aging Russell leading his team in minutes.

Bill Russell is a winner.

If winning is the ultimate measure of greatness, then Russell is simply the greatest ever to play the game.

In 1969, after the Celtics beat Chamberlain and the Los Angeles Lakers in a grueling seven-game series, Russell retired. He didn't tell the team, but instead announced the decision via a *Sports Illustrated* cover story titled "I'm Through with Basketball."

When Auerbach saw it, he phoned Russell and said, "Hey, you could sell them another story called 'Why I Changed My Mind.'"

All told, Russell won 11 championships in 13 seasons — the most of any player in professional sports. That's a historical fact; you can't take that away from him.

Bill Russell embraces Bob Cousy after the Celtics won their fifth consecutive NBA championship, beating the Lakers in Los Angeles, April 24, 1963.

1961
BAYLOR GOES FOR 71

Before there was LeBron James, there was Michael Jordan. Before Jordan came David Thompson and Julius Erving. And before all of them, there was Elgin Baylor.

The NBA's original high flyer and Los Angeles's first basketball star redefined how the game was played. He introduced flight to a game that had been beholden to gravity.

It's not that Baylor simply took off from the ground and glided until he reached the basket. He used his leaping ability smartly to create scoring opportunities where they hadn't existed before.

There isn't a lot of video footage from Baylor's prime, and so generations of NBA fans and followers grew up without an appreciation of the way he controlled the court and launched the game into the air during the 1960s. But if you can find old tape of Baylor, you'll see the way he would power his way to the hoop, leap in the air and wait for the defense to react. How he would then counteract, contorting his body, soaring from one side of the hoop to the other, putting all sorts of spin on the ball to help direct it off the backboard and through the net.

If it hadn't been for Russell, Baylor might have been the NBA's winningest player. He led the Lakers to the Finals in his rookie season, and, once he teamed with Jerry West, seven more times after that. But Baylor fell short each time, dropping seven consecutive title rounds to Russell's Celtics.

If it hadn't been for Wilt Chamberlain, Baylor would be remembered as the greatest scorer of his era. Between 1960–61 and 1962–63, he averaged over 35 points per game — including 38.3 in the '61–62 season — but never won a scoring title. His career average of 27.36 is third in NBA history, behind only Jordan (30.12) and Chamberlain (30.07).

In 1960, Baylor set the record for most points in a single game, scoring 71 against the New York Knicks, but the performance became a footnote in history two seasons later, when Chamberlain scored 100. Timing,

Elgin Baylor powers his way in for a shot against the Philadelphia 76ers, March 18, 1964 in Los Angeles.

it seems, is the only thing that could impede Elgin Baylor.

Baylor arrived at his first training camp with the Minneapolis Lakers in the fall of 1958 and dominated from day one, picking up where he left off in college. At Seattle University they called him Rabbit, and he led the Redhawks to the NCAA championship game. To nobody's surprise, Baylor was the first overall pick in the 1958 draft — making him the first African American to be selected with the top pick.

As a player, he had it all going for him: a stocky 6-foot-5 frame that rivaled that of most forwards of his day, brute strength that made him unstoppable with a head of steam, and, of course, hang time.

It was the latter that separated Baylor from his peers — and made him unpredictable.

"He was great using airspace . . . he was just ballet in basketball," said Julius Erving, who studied tapes of Baylor while growing up. "And that opened a lot of doors for young players, myself in particular, to try that stuff. Suddenly, it was like, 'Wow. This can actually work.'"

Baylor also had a twitch that only surfaced when he was on the court, causing his head to shake slightly. It threw defenders off guard. Was it a deliberate head fake? Or was Baylor even aware he was doing it? They had to ponder this question while trying to ground the hefty high flyer. Later in his career, Baylor consulted doctors, who chalked it up to a nervous spasm.

Baylor was named both MVP and Rookie of the Year for the 1958–59 season. He was the Lakers. So, in the summer of 1959 when Baylor was enlisted in basic training ahead of his second season, the Lakers moved their training camp to Baylor's army base in San Antonio, Texas.

While his teammates stayed in their own barracks — where they'd be woken from their late-night parties by marching soldiers — Baylor would go through military training from morning to night, and then join his team for practice once his fellow army men retired for the evening.

Baylor's military duty forced him to miss all the Lakers' preseason exhibition games, but in their first regular-season game that season,

he dropped a cool 52 points in a win over the Pistons. "I sat there in complete awe," said teammate Rudy LaRusso. "I kept thinking, 'He doesn't even practice and he gets 52.'"

The early-season matchup on November 15, 1960, at Madison Square Garden between the Lakers and Knicks felt like a typical Baylor performance to those on the court. He unleashed his usual arsenal of moves, jump shots from all around the court, sweeping drives through the middle of the lane, following up any missed shots to put back the rebound. "Each particular shot had nothing amazing about it," recalled Knicks forward Johnny Green. "It was just that Elgin was such an amazing player."

He had already established the NBA's single-game scoring record by dropping 64 points on the Boston Celtics a year earlier. But by the time the fourth quarter came to a close, he had established a new mark: 71 points. Almost as impressive? He also grabbed 25 rebounds.

Baylor routinely grabbed as many boards as the game's top centers and was as elite working the glass as he was putting the ball in the hoop. He combined basketball smarts with his physical gifts and turned the offensive rebound into a weapon, deliberately throwing the ball off the backboard from afar, running toward the basket and catching it while his defender was still guessing where the ball would go. "I don't know why guys don't use that play today," he said.

Just prior to the 1960–61 season, the Lakers moved from Minneapolis to Los Angeles. Newsreels announcing the move proclaimed Baylor as "the best basketeer in the world."

CAREER POINTS PER GAME

1.	Michael Jordan	30.12
2.	Wilt Chamberlain	30.07
3.	Elgin Baylor	27.36
4.	LeBron James	27.10
5.	Jerry West	27.03

Along with rookie sensation Jerry West, Baylor was tasked with drawing West Coast fans to the young league. The duo was paraded around LA, sitting on the back of a truck and holding a microphone, imploring locals to come catch the Lakers in action.

As Baylor captivated audiences and his team established itself as the class of the West — the perfect rival for Boston in the East — the Lakers went from the back page to the front page. In LA, Elgin paved the way for other one-name stars in the City of Light: Magic, Kareem, Shaq, Kobe, LeBron.

During the 1961–62 season, Baylor returned to army duty. Posted at a base in Seattle, he took weekend passes to join the Lakers in whatever city they were playing in before catching a red-eye back to Seattle to report for duty on Monday morning. He appeared in 48 games that season. In a little over half a season, Baylor averaged more than 38 points and 18 rebounds.

You can always tell retired ballplayers by their hampered gait — not a limp, per se, but close. The toll of spending countless hours bouncing up and down the hardwood catches up with everybody. For Baylor, who was always the rabbit ahead of the pack and

not the greyhound chasing it around the track, the physical strain caught up sooner than most.

Just five minutes into the first game of the 1965 playoffs, a 30-year-old Baylor suffered a terrible knee injury. He'd been in pain for at least a year before, but this was different: his teammates heard a pop. It was Baylor's left knee. The top of the patella had separated from the rest of the kneecap, sidelining him indefinitely. After several setbacks during the rehab process, Baylor was discouraged. "Finally, I just accepted the fact that I would never play again," he said.

But sure enough, by October of 1965, as the new season tipped off, he was back in the Lakers' starting lineup.

Eventually, the knee problems worsened. Too proud to carry on and too pained with each drive to the basket, Baylor retired abruptly, nine games into the 1971–72 season. He walked away at the age of 37, having never won a championship despite eight trips to the Finals.

It wasn't for lack of trying. In the '62 Finals, Baylor scored 61 points in the face of double- and triple-teams against the Boston Celtics. It was a playoff scoring record that

Dave DeBusschere winces as he and Elgin Baylor collide during a game at Madison Square Garden, April 24, 1970.

lasted until Michael Jordan scored 63 in 1986 — but Jordan needed two overtime periods to overtake him.

In a ruthless bit of irony, the Lakers were crowned champs in 1972. But Baylor's legacy had already been long established. In 2018, the Lakers unveiled a bronze statue of him in front of their arena, the Staples Center, in downtown Los Angeles. The gesture was long overdue. All the Laker greats came out to honor the original mayor of Lakerland.

West spoke eloquently of Baylor's graciousness as a leader and how he found him to be "regal" while on the court. Kobe Bryant talked about all of the lessons Baylor had imparted to him, and Shaquille O'Neal warned kids to do their homework and study up on the icons from a generation not always preserved on videotape.

"You did some things that Dr. J, Michael Jordan, Kobe and myself couldn't do," Magic Johnson told Baylor. "And I tried to do it — I just couldn't hang that long in the air."

Wilt Chamberlain shoots over Boston defenders in Philadelphia, in March 1960.

1962
LEGENDS OF WILT

*T*he story goes that Wilt was jumped by a mountain lion while in the Arizona wilderness. The NBA star grabbed the beast by the tail and threw it into the nearby brush. Later, a Knicks official recalled Wilt sporting huge scratches across his shoulders.

In a game of giants, no figure looms larger than Wilt Chamberlain. His exploits were mythic long before his playing days were over. He was a dominating figure — bigger than basketball. Wilt is an NBA tall tale. Sportswriters compared their first encounters with Wilt in person to one's first gaze at the New York City skyline.

Chamberlain spent his 14 NBA seasons writing and rewriting the record books. Over that time, he achieved what no player has before or since. For perspective, Michael Jordan reached the 50-point mark an impressive 31 times in his career. Wilt did it 45 times in one season.

Wilt was "one of the world's great athletes," said former head coach Alex Hannum, "and I'm talking about in the history of time." Yet, then as much as now, he was never celebrated in the same way as his peers. "I was too big for the game — my talent, that is," he once said. When you're as exceptionally sized and skilled as Chamberlain, the expectation is that you be exceptional. And when you are, people only expect more.

While at a party, Wilt challenged legendary NFL fullback Jim Brown to a race on the lawn. Wilt won. Brown demanded a rematch. Wilt won again.

Growing up in Philadelphia, Wilt carried the burden of expectations. He was colossal, an elite athlete in any sport he tried. But Philly was a basketball town, and it wasn't long before he dominated the local high school circuit. At 7-foot-1 and 1/16 and 275 pounds, he ran the 100-meter dash in 10.9 seconds and boasted a vertical leap of nearly 50 inches. Famously, he showed off his springiness by grabbing a quarter off the top of the basket.

Wilt quickly gained notoriety. Newspapers called the teenage prodigy Wilt the Stilt, a nickname he hated because it made him sound like a freak. He preferred Dipper or Dippy, names his friends gave him for the

Wilt Chamberlain holds a sign after he scored 100 points in a March 2, 1962 game. The Warriors defeated the New York Knickerbockers 169-147.

way he had to duck under doorways. Soon it became the Big Dipper, for his signature dunk. Standing sideways to the basket, Wilt would crouch and explode upward, windmilling his arm for the slam.

At 16 Chamberlain was paid to play in a Pennsylvania pro league and averaged over 40 points per game. At 17 he averaged 74 points in the playoffs for the Quakertown Fays. He played under the pseudonym George Marcus to avoid NCAA eligibility issues. Chamberlain later admitted to the ruse. "I've always been ashamed of having done that," he said. "Not of having played, but ashamed of having given in to the hypocrisy of the NCAA, rather than fighting it."

In his first game at the University of Kansas, he scored 52 points and grabbed 31 rebounds. He also starred in track and field, competing in the shot put, the high jump and the quarter-mile race. The Big Eight Conference high-jump champion three years in a row, he cleared 6 feet 6 inches. Growing up, he wanted to be a decathlete, but the pay was lousy. In the NBA, he became the first player to earn a $100,000 contract.

In the 1959–60 NBA season, Wilt was named the MVP. Chamberlain led the league in scoring and set records for points (37.6) and rebounds (27.0) per game. It was his rookie year. The following season, he broke both records. In his third season, he averaged 50 points per game — nobody else has ever averaged more than 37. But no game was bigger than the one on March 2, 1962, in Hershey, Pennsylvania, when the Dipper scored a record 100 points. (No video footage exists of the game.)

For basketball fans, 100 points was unthinkable. For Wilt, it was inevitable. He had already scored 78 and 73 points that season, and had topped 60 in his three previous outings.

Knicks rookie center Darrall Imhoff was powerless and quickly fouled out. Wilt played all 48 minutes, but when he scored his 100th point with 46 seconds remaining, the game was called.

Wilt outshot his teammates, 63–52. "I mean, 63 shots?" he said. "You take that many shots on the playground and no one ever wants you on their team again."

Two nights later, in a rematch at Madison Square Garden, Wilt tried for 100 again, but Imhoff and the Knicks limited him to just 58. Imhoff received a standing ovation.

Wilt would say he could bench press 600 pounds. During the filming of Conan the Destroyer, Wilt left costar Arnold Schwarzenegger in awe when he did 170-pound triceps curls. Schwarzenegger maxed out at 110.

Chamberlain earned a reputation as the strongest player in the game. He was superhuman. Chamberlain could palm a 16-pound bowling ball. He would effortlessly fling opponents around and pick a teammate up off the floor like a shopping bag. He was one of the first NBA players to embrace weight lifting. "I was stronger than everyone else because I made myself stronger," he said.

As his NBA career progressed, his once spindly frame filled out, reaching a hulking playing weight between 300 and 310 pounds of pure muscle.

Eager to prove that he was far more than a brute, Wilt constantly downplayed his size advantage. When the league outlawed offensive goaltending in light of his unfair ability to tap in his teammates' shots at the rim, Chamberlain was happy to show off his well-rounded game. He developed an deft turnaround shot in the post. Critics called it soft and implied that Wilt shied away from contact.

Tuned in to what the press said about him, Wilt took offense when he was called a selfish scorer. To prove otherwise, in 1967–68 Chamberlain led the NBA in assists — still the only center to do so.

It's said that Wilt once dunked so hard, the ball broke Johnny "Red" Kerr's toe. Kerr pretend to trip to hide the embarrassing injury.

The Dipper was the NBA's leading scorer for each of his first seven seasons. In 1965 he was traded from the Warriors (who had moved to San Francisco after his third season) to the Philadelphia 76ers. His return to Philly was front-page news for weeks.

Chamberlain joined the most talented team he'd played for. His coach, Alex Hannum, asked Wilt to adjust his game to accommodate such future Hall of Famers as Hal Greer, Chet Walker and Billy "The Kangaroo Kid" Cunningham. In response, Wilt scored less and passed more.

Philadelphia won the championship in 1967, the first of Wilt's career. After losing to Bill Russell and the Celtics in the playoffs year after year, Chamberlain's team beat Boston, 4–1, in the second round before a 4–2 Finals victory over his former team in San Francisco. Wilt averaged 17.7 points in the Finals, along with 28.5 rebounds and nearly 7 assists per game.

When a *Sports Illustrated* feature alleged that Wilt, who had just turned 30, couldn't score anymore, Chamberlain deposited 68, 47 and 53 points in his next three games. "As the years went on, my scoring went down only because I wanted it to," Wilt said. "I could always score 50–60 points if needed."

He went back to passing, and in a February 1968 game against the Detroit Pistons he had 21 assists, the most by a center in a single game. He also scored 23 points and grabbed 25 rebounds.

Although blocks weren't officially tracked until '73 Wilt is said to have recorded four quadruple-doubles in the playoffs en route to the championship. In a game in March 1968, he recorded 53 points, 32 rebounds, 14 assists, 24 blocks and 11 steals. In one game versus the Pistons, statisticians counted 26 blocks.

Wilt almost boxed against Muhammad Ali. The two were on television together, where Wilt's height and reach advantage were on full display. Rumor has it that Ali's manager backed out of the fight, fearing an upset.

After orchestrating a trade to the Los Angeles Lakers in 1968, Chamberlain — already the most famous and recognizable athlete of his generation — joined a star-studded cast featuring Jerry West, Elgin Baylor and Gail Goodrich. He remained the league's leading rebounder well into his 30s and returned to the Finals twice.

Chamberlain retired in 1973 as the NBA's all-time leading scorer. But the feat he was perhaps proudest of was the fact that, after 1,205 contests, he never fouled out of an NBA game. "To do that," he said, "you not only must be strong, but smart."

He still played hoops, and continued to dominate the best in the game well into his 40s, when he could be found in the summers owning Magic Johnson's pickup game on the campus of UCLA. All the top stars of the day played, and Wilt took delight in

WHAT WILT DID

- 100 points in one game
- 50.4 points per game in one season
- Most points in one season: 4,029 in '61-62
- Most 50-point games (118, Jordan is 2nd all-time with 31)
- Most 60-point games (32)
- Rookie scoring average (37.6 ppg)
- Career rebounding average (22.9 per game)
- Consecutive double-doubles (227, between 1964-67)
- Lead NBA in rebounds and assists in same season ('68)

Wilt Chamberlain extends a long left at world heavyweight champion Muhammad Ali at an ABC television studio in New York, March 10, 1967.

MOST POINTS IN A GAME

1.	Wilt Chamberlain	100 (1962)
2.	Kobe Bryant	81 (2006)
3.	Wilt Chamberlain	78 (1961)
4.	David Thompson	73 (1978)
	Wilt Chamberlain	73 (1962)
	Wilt Chamberlain	73 (1962)

blocking every shot in sight. When he was 50 years old, the New Jersey Nets and Cleveland Cavaliers wanted to sign him.

Wilt's 1973 autobiography, Wilt: Just Like Any Other 7-Foot Black Millionaire Who Lives Next Door, was a best seller. In his 1991 autobiography A View from Above, he wrote that he had slept with over 20,000 women.

As the years went on, Wilt would appear on TV to promote his latest book, and inevitably bemoan the death of the big man, asserting that the stars of the day, like Shaquille O'Neal, would've been nothing in his era. "I couldn't rely on my size," Wilt would say. "I had to do more than be big."

He spoke like someone carrying a grudge. Still waging war with the critics who told him he was scoring too much and, when he stopped, said he wasn't scoring enough.

"Wilt drove big cars, had a lot of girlfriends and was very opinionated," said Al Attles, Wilt's former teammate. "This bothered . . . the older people in the media."

Because he was expected to be perfect, Chamberlain's legacy remains complicated.

"He was so great that no matter what he did, people never accepted it as being enough," observed Bill Walton. It's why he finished second in MVP voting the year he averaged 50 points a game. It's why he was labeled a selfish coach killer, despite adapting his game for Hannum and the 76ers. It's why he walked away a two-time champ, but is remembered for falling short as a winner thanks to constant comparisons with Russell.

"All that loser crap," as Wilt puts it.

The Dipper always struggled with his identity, eager to write his own narrative. He was a giant who prided himself on his guarding skills. He was a young black man, yet he was a staunch Nixon supporter. He was a public figure who preferred to be alone.

Wilt helped design Ursa Major, his two-and-a-half-acre Bel Air mansion. To this day, it's a world-renowned architectural triumph. At the push of a button, his bedroom ceiling retracted so that he could stargaze through a state-of-the-art telescope. Most nights, the Big Dipper slept under the stars.

Chamberlain passed away at age 63 after

a long battle with heart problems. "He was so busy doing," said his sister, Barbara, "I'm not surprised he had a tired heart." His death came as a shock. "Dippy was so big," said friend and Harlem Globetrotter legend Meadowlark Lemon. "We thought he was going to live forever." How many times had Wilt been literally called "larger than life"?

Wilt had no children; he was America's most celebrated bachelor, who happily lived alone in that big house with his two cats, Zip and Zap. He left over 90 percent of his estate to charity.

Chamberlain also left behind a career that will never be replicated. Over 14 years, he tallied 7 scoring titles, 9 shooting titles, 11 rebounding titles and 4 MVPs. Every story and stat seems too good to be true, and each is more impressive than the last. When talking about his 100-point game, Chamberlain once said the following — a sentiment that could apply to his life:

"It has reached fabled proportion, almost like a Paul Bunyan story. And it's nice to be part of a fable."

Oscar Robertson scores from outside in a game with the Chicago Bulls in Kansas City, Mo., on Jan. 26, 1970.

1962
THE BIG O

There have been countless signature moves in NBA history, but there haven't been too many signature rebounds. Oscar Robertson had one. The point guard would leap and splay his tree-trunk legs, performing the splits in midair while grabbing the ball. It was a simple display of athleticism, and one hell of an effective way to create space.

Yet, save for the rebounding, showmanship was never a part of Robertson's game. He took smart shots, made sound passes and guided his team toward the most effective play. "The dunk, the behind-the-back garbage — those aren't great plays," he said.

There was nothing spectacular about the way Robertson played. Only the results.

"His greatness," said Jerry West, "was his simplicity."

But it's the rebounding that separated him from his peers: Robertson ranks 4th all-time in career assists per game. Among NBA players, he's 10th in points per game, and no guard has ever averaged more boards than the Big O.

For his first three seasons, Robertson averaged 11 rebounds per game and was a top-10 rebounder in the NBA. Standing 6-foot-5, he was dwarfed by the other players on that list. But compared to other point guards, he was a giant. Despite his size, he had all the maneuvers and lightning-quick moves of the most agile ball handlers. As Bill Sharman put it, "Robertson was a big man with the moves

of a really tremendous little man."

Put it all together and Robertson was the most complete player of his era.

At no time was that more evident than during the 1961–62 campaign. A 23-year-old Robertson became the first player to average in double digits in points (30.8), rebounds (12.5) and assists (11.4) in a single season. It took 55 years for someone else to accomplish the feat. There's a reason why they called Robertson "Mr. Triple-Double."

Robertson and his family grew up in the Lockefield Gardens housing project in Indianapolis, Indiana. He was a high school star, leading Crispus Attucks High School to back-to-back state titles in 1955 and '56. It was the first all–African American team to win the championship. And when the players returned to Indianapolis, the city redirected the parade route so that it would avoid white neighborhoods.

Robertson was the first black player at the University of Cincinnati, which he attended because its business program allowed him to work for local companies while earning his degree. In college, he became the first player to lead the country in scoring three years in a row — among all players in NCAA history, only Pete Maravich amassed more points over a three-year span.

Despite his successes, at Cincinnati he received threats from the grand wizard of the Ku Klux Klan. He felt isolated even among his teammates. Before a game in Houston, the team arrived to its hotel to find that the establishment didn't allow black guests. The team stayed there anyway, while Robertson got a dorm room at a nearby college.

He had reason to be ornery, and he developed a reputation for being short with teammates, coaches, referees — especially referees — and fans alike.

As he neared graduation, he was recruited by the Harlem Globetrotters, whose status as a beacon of sorts for prominent African American men was enticing. "There's a café and a movie house just a few steps off campus where I'm not welcome," he said. "Sure I'd like to play with [the Globetrotters]."

But when the Cincinnati Royals selected Robertson first overall in the 1960 draft and offered him a three-year, $100,000 contract, he opted for the NBA.

Robertson was a star from the beginning. In a sign of things to come, he finished his debut with 21 points, 12 rebounds and 10 assists. It would prove to be an off night. He was named Rookie of the Year in 1961, finishing third in the league with 30.5 points per game while also earning MVP honors at the NBA All-Star Game.

It didn't take long for Oscar to make history. In just his second season, Robertson averaged his triple-double.

He methodically carved up the league, and talked trash throughout the process. Robertson was relentless, eager to take his spot atop the NBA's hierarchy. He took particu-

lar delight in scoring on Wilt Chamberlain — "Too late, big fella." "You can't get that one, can you, big fella?" In his first meeting against Wilt and the Philadelphia Warriors that season, Robertson posted season highs in points (49) and rebounds (22).

He was at the forefront of a generation of new stars accelerating the pace and leading an all-around offensive boom. In a span of five years, scoring had risen by nearly 20 points per game. By Robertson's triple-double season in '61–62, teams averaged 118.8 points per game, the highest in NBA history. Robertson averaged 30.8 points that year, but finished tied with Jerry West for fourth in scoring, well behind Chamberlain's 50.4.

But Robertson's all-around game meant that he did damage without ever putting the ball in the hoop. His nightly dominance helped the Royals to their first season with a record above .500 since 1953–54. Whether through his own play or sheer intimidation, he made his teammates better in the process. His passes established Royals center Wayne Embry as an All-Star; Embry's scoring average rose more than 5 points to nearly 20 per game in 1961–62.

"He controls events on the court with aplomb and the authoritarian hand of a symphony conductor," is how New York Knicks forward Bill Bradley described Robertson's impact on his team.

But Robertson's individual brilliance alone couldn't help the Royals contend for a title. They lost in the first round in 1962, and only made it to the second round twice during his 10 seasons in Cincinnati. He took his frustrations out on those around him, wanting them to perform to his impossibly high standards.

"Oscar was so far ahead of us humans," said Wayne Embry, "that you could never come up to his level."

His brilliant play continued, and in 1964 Robertson was named NBA MVP, leading the league in assists, as he did seven times in his career.

By 1970 Robertson had grown tired of playing for a losing team. And the Royals had grown tired of their cantankerous star. The team's GM, Joe Axelson, traded him to the Baltimore Bullets, but Robertson vetoed the deal. A two-week standoff ensued.

On April 21, Robertson accepted a trade to the Milwaukee Bucks. For the first time in his career, the 32-year-old took a supporting role alongside Milwaukee's prodigious center, Kareem Abdul-Jabbar. His scoring average dropped to 19.4 — the first time it had ever been below 20 — but he still managed to fill the stat sheet, and in late January he posted his first of four triple-doubles that season.

More importantly, he and Abdul-Jabbar quickly established themselves as the NBA's top duo. The Bucks made it all the way to the Finals in 1971, where they swept the Bullets in four games.

"This is the first champagne I've ever had," Robertson said in the locker room after the game, "and it tastes mighty sweet."

In the years that followed, he maintained that his historic triple-double season had been "blown out of proportion."

"What matters is a guy who plays the total game," Robertson said. "He's not after stats."

But sometimes he couldn't help but wonder. "I wish I had played in a wide-open style like guys do now," Robertson said. "I would have liked to have seen the numbers I would have put up."

CAREER TRIPLE-DOUBLES

1.	Oscar Robertson	181
2.	Russell Westbrook	146
3.	Magic Johnson	138
4.	Jason Kidd	107
5.	LeBron James	94
6.	Wilt Chamberlain	78
7.	Larry Bird	59
8.	James Harden	46
9.	Fat Lever	43
10.	Nikola Jokic	40

Oscar Robertson brings the ball down against the New York Knicks at Madison Square Garden, Nov. 28, 1970.

ROUND 1
CELTICS VS. LAKERS

Rivalries are built through repeated confrontations, and the strongest ones take time to develop. Two of the fiercest rivals in the NBA, the Boston Celtics and Los Angeles Lakers, have been competing for basketball supremacy for over 60 years.

The best rivalries have the most at stake. These two teams have played for the NBA championship a record 12 times, and gone to a winner-take-all Game 7 five times.

The most captivating ones have a clear underdog. The Celtics have won nine of the matchups.

The ones that last boast adversaries of the highest caliber. The Lakers and Celtics have combined for 33 NBA titles. Boston's 17 are the most of any franchise in history — one more than the Lakers.

Like orange balls and hardwood courts, the Celtics–Lakers rivalry is a constant throughout NBA history.

The teams first met in the Finals in 1959, when the Lakers were still playing in Minneapolis. The Lakers hadn't been to the Finals in five years, but rookie forward Elgin Baylor emerged as one of the NBA's best, leading the team with 24.5 points per game. Still, they were no match for Bob Cousy, Bill Russell and the Celtics, who had won their first title in 1957, defeating the St. Louis Hawks in double overtime in Game 7. The '59 Lakers proved no match for the battle-tested Celts, who swept the series.

The rivalry as we know it began in earnest during the 1962 Finals. By now, the Celtics dynasty had gained steam, winning three straight championships. The Lakers, meanwhile, had relocated to Los Angeles, enabling the media to spin a narrative in which the gritty Northeasterners were pitted against the glamour of Hollywood.

The Lakers had also added Jerry West, who joined Baylor to form the NBA's most potent scoring duo. They, along with forward Rudy LaRusso and guard Frank Selvy, were named to the Western Division team in that year's All-Star Game. Boston countered with four All-Stars of their own: Russell, Cousy, Tom Heinsohn and Sam Jones.

"We knew we were facing the better team," said Baylor, "but we always felt like we could win."

The Lakers stars were a handful for Russell and the Celtics' vaunted defense. In Game 3, West stole the ball from Sam Jones and laid it in at the buzzer for a win. In Game 5, Baylor took his turn, scoring a Finals-record 61 points.

Los Angeles pushed the Celtics to a seventh game, at Boston Garden. It came down to the wire. The score was tied, with five seconds left, when Lakers point guard Hot Rod Hundley looked to get the ball to West, whose nickname, Mr. Clutch, was well earned. But West was smothered, so Hundley passed the ball to Frank Selvy for an open

18-foot jump shot. The ball clanged off the rim, and Russell smothered the rebound. The game went to overtime, where the Celtics won, 110–107. West finished with 35 points and Baylor with 41. Russell countered with 40 rebounds.

"Poor Frank," recalled Cousy. "I felt bad for those guys."

"I always thought that if Frank made that shot, the course of history would have changed a little bit," West said years later.

West and the Lakers would have hoped it

did. The Celtics and Lakers met in the Finals four times in the next six seasons, with Boston winning every time.

In '63, the series-deciding Game 6 served as Bob Cousy's send-off, enabling him to retire as a champ.

In '65, it took a difficult seven-game series against Wilt Chamberlain and the Philadelphia 76ers for Boston to reach the Finals. The Celtics were aided in that series by third-year star John Havlicek. With Boston up by two, Russell inbounded the ball from the baseline,

but it hit one of the wires holding up the backboard. Philly ball. With the game on the line, Havlicek picked off a pass as time expired, prompting the famous call: "Havlicek stole the ball!"

After the Philadelphia series, the Celtics were exhausted, but they still managed to take care of the Lakers in just five games.

Both teams added to their arsenals over the years, surrounding their stars with championship-caliber talent. In Boston, Havlicek joined the likes of K.C. Jones, Wayne Embry

Bill Russell drives to the basket during the 1969 NBA Finals.

and Bailey Howell to bolster a deep roster.

In 1965, the Celtics signed Don Nelson, who had been released after two forgettable seasons with the Lakers, partly because of his subpar rebounding. Russell pulled him aside after his first Celtics practice and told him he never had to worry about rebounding ever again. Always making his teammates better,

Russell promised to cover for Nelson's weaknesses. Nelson was a good shooter, Russell said, and that's all he wanted his new teammate to focus on.

In Los Angeles, Archie Clark and Gail Goodrich added fuel to the backcourt, while big man Mel Counts and forward Tom Hawkins saw action down low. But after another convincing loss to Boston in the '68 Finals, the Lakers brought in the ultimate reinforcement in the form of Wilt Chamberlain.

Not only did the Chamberlain trade give Los Angeles a "big three" that rivaled any that would follow, but it brought the NBA's greatest individual rivalry onto to its most important stage.

For both Russell and Chamberlain, their best years were behind them, but they remained game-changing talents. The 1968–69 season was to be Russell's last, and it was only fitting that it would come down to a matchup with Wilt.

In Game 1, West scored 53 points in a Lakers win. But once again, Russell's teammates came through when it mattered. In Game 4, Sam Jones hit a buzzer-beating jumper to tie the series at two. As it had already done three times in the decade, the series went to a winner-take-all Game 7.

For the first time, however, the deciding game was to be played in Los Angeles. Although they had been slow to come around to the team when it first arrived in LA, fans were now crazy about the Lakers — especially with a celebrity like Wilt wearing the purple and gold — and team owner Jack Kent Cooke wanted to make the most of what could be a once-in-a-lifetime opportunity.

He ordered the rafters to be filled to the brim with balloons and arranged for pamphlets to be placed on each seat in the Forum — a playbill announcing the order of that night's performance. Once the Lakers won the title, it read, the USC marching band would play "Happy Days Are Here Again." That would cue the balloons, followed by on-court interviews with, in order, Baylor, West and Chamberlain.

If the Celtics needed any more motivation to send Russell off as a champion the way they had done for Cousy, that was it. Boston erupted for an early lead that held for much

Jerry West plays keep away during the 1968 NBA Finals.

of the game. With Chamberlain on the bench due to injury, the Lakers mounted a comeback behind West's brilliance. Los Angeles outscored Boston, 30–17, in the fourth quarter, and West would finish with a game-high 42 points.

The Lakers narrowed Boston's lead to one point. Havlicek had the ball poked away, and it arrived in the hands of Don Nelson near the free-throw line. Without hesitating, he pulled up for a jump shot that hit the back of the rim and bounced straight up above the backboard, hanging for days before it fell through the hole. Boston held on to the lead and beat LA one more time. They were a perfect 6-0 against the Lakers.

All told, 12 Hall of Famers shared the court during those Celtics–Lakers championship battles. The teams were worthy adversaries, but the rivalry wasn't exactly heated. Was it too one-sided for bad blood to exist? That might depend on whom you ask.

"I never remember feeling a real hatred for the Lakers that might have existed for some of the other teams back east," said Cousy.

On the other hand, West said, "I hated green for a long time. I wouldn't wear anything green."

When Russell retired, the rivalry went dormant. Fans would have to wait 15 years for a rematch. It would be worth the wait.

EMERGENCY LANDING

The Lakers–Celtics rivalry almost never happened because the Lakers came perilously close to losing their entire team. On January 18, 1960, the then-Minneapolis Lakers were flying back home from a game in St. Louis on the team's small charter plane, which carried team staff and the entire roster, including Elgin Baylor. After getting lost in a whiteout snowstorm and running out of fuel, the plane was forced to make an emergency crash landing onto a cornfield in Carroll, Iowa. Miraculously, nobody was hurt.

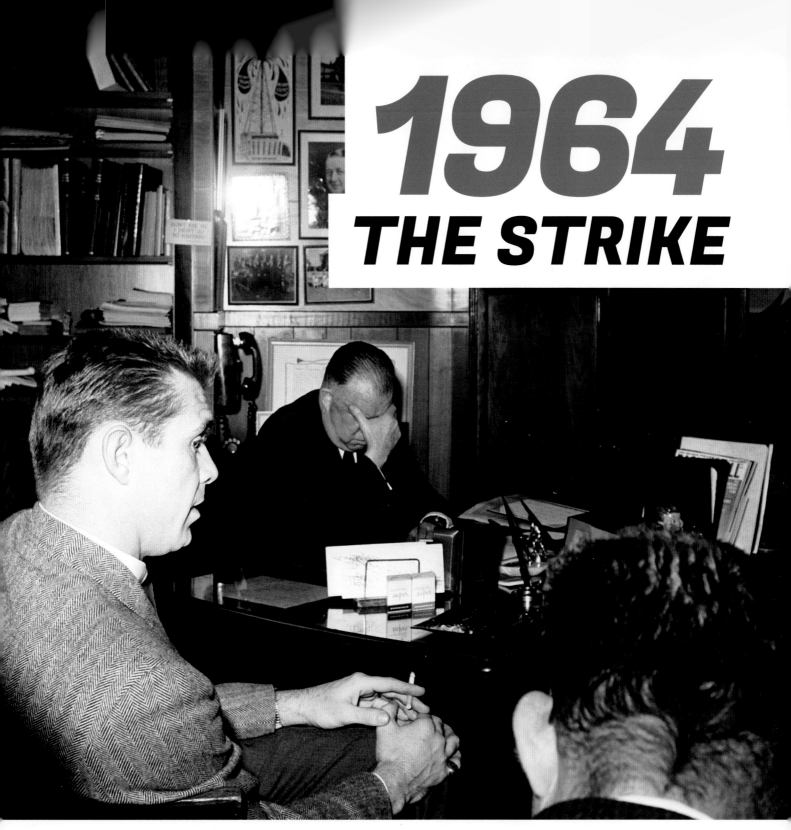

1964 THE STRIKE

Walter Brown, owner of the Boston Celtics, meeting with Tommy Heinsohn just before the 1964 All-Star Game.

"You tell Bob Short he can go f★★k himself!" Elgin Baylor yelled out from the locker room at the Boston Garden. It was a snowy January day and tensions couldn't have been higher ahead of the 1964 All-Star Game. With the league's top talent set to square off, owners from each team on hand, and the NBA's largest audience to date

waiting to tune in on live television, there was plenty on the line for everybody involved.

The Celtics locker room was filled with a who's who of future legends — 13 Hall of Famers in all, including Baylor, Bill Russell, Oscar Robertson, Jerry West, Wilt Chamberlain, Hal Greer and Tommy Heinsohn.

With lights and cameras in place to

broadcast the All-Star Game across America, the NBA was poised that night to usher in a new era. But an ongoing dispute between the

43

players union and the owners hung in the air like a storm cloud.

Now, just 15 minutes before tip-off, the players were refusing to play.

For the better part of a decade, tensions had mounted between the players and their employers — the team owners. In 1954, a players association was established after Boston Cetics star Bob Cousy reached out to the top players from each team. He intended to form a union to help give players a collective voice in negotiations with owners.

The players fought for basic employee rights. But the league and its owners barely gave the upstart union the time of day. Commissioner Walter Kennedy continually stalled any meaningful discussions.

Cousy wasn't long for the job; the clerical duties alone were a headache, and he soon passed the chores along to teammate Heinsohn, who was surprised to learn how little regard the NBA owners had for their players. He recalled meetings at Kennedy's offices when the commissioner would keep players waiting in the lobby while he invited their lawyers upstairs to talk.

Heinsohn was far more active in the role than Cousy had been, and he enlisted the help of Larry Fleisher, a Harvard law graduate, to assist in dealings with the league. Fleisher took control of the players association in 1962 and immediately recognized a huge disparity between the owners and players. The players earned $7,500 on average and almost all of them, big names included, worked summer jobs. They lacked job security and they lacked respect. "It was the stone ages of basketball," said Jerry West.

Owners bought into the stereotype of the dumb jock. They felt the players were lucky to have a gig playing games for a living. And that they were dispensable.

Fleisher took particular note of the owners' attitude toward black players. He heard players like Russell and Lenny Wilkens, so thoughtful and eloquent in their takes on the labor situation, and saw them as future senators. The owners saw running, jumping dollar signs. Nothing more.

But the times were a-changing. The burgeoning civil rights movement was giving prominent African Americans, as well as members of other ostracized groups, the courage to speak up. At the 1964 All-Star Game, they were given a platform.

The game was to be televised live on ABC to a national audience, with the unspoken agreement that if ratings were decent, the network could broadcast many more games the following season. As both the players and owners knew, it was the kind of exposure that could thrust the NBA onto a new stage and give it the legitimacy and popularity of leagues like the NFL, which already had a foothold on TV.

Decades later, broadcasting rights would prove to be the biggest driving force in transforming the NBA into a billion-dollar enterprise. But in 1964, merely getting the All-Star Game on TV was a major feat for the league. The NBA's nine teams were loaded with talent but still existed on the periphery of the American sports consciousness.

Russell was a few months away from capturing his sixth straight title with the Celtics, but collected his rings in relative anonymity. Baylor was redefining the game, but only in the eyes of the few thousands who attended the Lakers games in person.

TV was key. And everybody knew it.

The union had met with the league throughout the season. Following a series of failed negotiations, the players, most vocally led by Russell, hinted at boycotting the All-Star Game.

As the opening tip-off neared, no progress had been made between the two sides. If the players were to strike, now was the time — who knew how long it would be before they had this kind of leverage again? But the locker room was divided.

On one side, Russell, Wilkens and Heinsohn were adamant that none of the players should take the court until their demands were met. On the other, players like Wilt Chamberlain, easily the NBA's biggest celebrity, wanted to play for the cameras and hash things out later.

A narrow vote was held, reportedly ending 11–9 in favor of the strike. And so the players remained in the locker room. Fleisher darted between the locker room and the owners' suite, issuing player demands and relaying information back and forth.

In later years, player–owner disputes would hold billions of dollars in the balance, with months-long negotiations over the sharing of revenue resulting in roughly a 50–50 split. Players fought for free agency and other freedoms enjoyed by employees in virtually any other field.

But for now, the demands were simpler. The players wanted a pension — job security in an occupation in which a simple injury can cost a player his livelihood. They wanted full-time trainers in order to help maintain their health. And they wanted the NBA to limit the endless, exhausting parade of exhibition games and back-to-backs.

The scheduled tip-off time came and went. The court remained empty.

The owners were irate at being embarrassed in front of the viewing public. At one point, Lakers owner Bob Short tried to storm into the locker room but was stopped by security. From the doorway, he berated Baylor and West, two of the most respected men in the game. He threatened that unless they took the court, they would never play for him again. It only strengthened the conviction of those who wanted to strike.

"I was scared s**tless," recalled Milwaukee Bucks center Wayne Embry as he eyed the exchange and wondered what his own future had in store. But Fleisher was reassuring. He returned to the locker room and told the players they held all the cards.

Meanwhile, ABC executives were furious. They gave the league 20 minutes to start playing, or the network would soon be out of the NBA business altogether. It proved to be the incentive the owners needed.

Commissioner Kennedy approached the locker room and informed the players that they'd won. The union was officially recognized, and all of the players' demands were met. Most importantly, the players association earned a seat at the table for all future league negotiations.

Although none of the fans at the Boston Garden, or those tuning in on ABC, had any idea, the revolution had been televised.

Jerry Lucas lays up a shot as Wilt Chamberlain attempts the block during the NBA All-Star game at Boston Garden, Jan. 15, 1964.

1967
THE ABA: BASKETBALL'S WILD WEST

Imagine an NBA without slam dunks. Without 3-pointers. Without the stylish passes and jaw-dropping aerials that fill today's highlight reels. Without the freedom of expression that sets basketball apart from other sports.

Imagine a world in which the American Basketball Association never existed.

The league best remembered for its iconic red, white and blue basketball didn't just change how the game looked, it redefined how the game was played and how its stars were marketed. The life span of the ABA was just nine years in total, but the "gimmick" league changed the sport forever.

Of course, none of that was apparent when the league first launched in 1967.

The NBA was still in its relative infancy at the time, just 21 years old, and had already had to fend off such upstart competitors as the American Basketball League, which barely lasted one season.

Undeterred by the ABL's failure, entrepreneur Dennis Murphy sought to start a rival league with the eventual goal of merging with the NBA, in much the same way that football's American Football League had done with the NFL the year before.

A cattle call for prospective owners was put out, with franchises costing just $5,000

— a departure from the roughly $1.5 million that NBA franchises were fetching. Soon, 11 teams (one fewer than the NBA's 12) had been established across America, with an ownership group that ranged from a trucking executive to entertainer Pat Boone.

Murphy's biggest coup was bringing in George Mikan as commissioner. Mikan brought instant credibility — and a lot more — to a league that desperately needed it. The red, white and blue ball was an idea developed by the near-sighted Mikan, who had worn glasses on the court throughout his playing career and had struggled at times to see the NBA's brown leather ball. At a press conference at the Summit Hotel in New York City, he displayed the ABA's flashy ball and announced other unique features of the new league, most notably the 3-point line — or the "home run," as he called it.

"From the moment they first threw up that red, white and blue ball, we thought the ABA was a maverick league, a gimmick league," recalled NBA center Wayne Embry. "I thought it *was* a circus."

"We were a maverick league, but so what?" said Julius Erving, whose free-flowing Afro and high-flying acrobatics came to symbolize the style of the ABA. "What's wrong with a

little experimentation and encouraging an individual to excel in a team sport?"

But Embry wasn't entirely mistaken. The ABA was a circus. That was part of its appeal.

The league was home to an eccentric, free-wheeling cast of characters, including such stars as Fly Williams, Darnell "Dr. Dunk" Hillman (who earned the distinction of owning the ABA's largest Afro), Levern "Jelly" Tart and Marvin "Bad News" Barnes (who once refused to board a flight to a game in a different time zone — "I ain't getting on no time machine," he declared).

Rules were made on the fly and players often switched teams and markets without warning, almost always in the name of drawing new fans to the arenas.

Teams would try anything to sell tickets. While the NBA was content with simply putting the names of the two teams competing that night on the arena marquee, the ABA had to get more creative. And so it became the league where you could see a Willie Nelson concert before the game and a cow-milking contest at halftime. Where Victor the Wrestling Bear took on all challeng-

ers, and promotions like Denver's Halter Top Night regularly took place.

Lawlessness ruled. In a league featuring notorious bullies the NBA wouldn't dare allow on its courts — John Brisker, Warren Jabali and Wendell Ladner atop the class — coaches would often put bounties on opponents' heads. Knock out one of the ABA's bad boys and you could earn yourself some cash on the side. In one instance, Dallas Chaparrals forward Lenny Chappell didn't even wait until the game began; during the opening tip-off one night against Brisker's

The New York Nets and Denver Nuggets battle for a rebound at the Nassau Coliseum in Uniondale, N.Y..

Pittsburgh Condors, the players were watching the ball rise in the air as Chappell reared back and laid out an unsuspecting Brisker with a haymaker, earning a cool $500.

In Salt Lake City, they held John Brisker Intimidation Night, only adding to Brisker's mythical status as the ABA's premier tough guy. "Just in case the husky, sometimes ill-tempered Pittsburgh Condor forward gets out of line tonight, the Stars' management has taken steps to keep all in control. Surrounding the court tonight will be five of the top boxers the Intermountain Area has ever produced," read the program the game.

Compared to the NBA, it was the Wild West — little more than a sideshow. But it was hard to ignore how the game was evolving on ABA courts.

The 3-point line not only created a more exciting game — teams could rally from behind and make a comeback — but also opened up the middle of the court, providing more space for players like Erving to dazzle with displays of athleticism and improvisation. Players were encouraged to test the limits of their abilities and ply their trade with style.

Where the NBA showcased competition, the ABA sought to put on a show. Where the NBA executed textbook bounce passes, the ABA delivered no-look, behind-the-back dishes. It was a matchup of flair versus fundamentals. Hip versus square. Jazz versus classical. If the NBA was Lawrence Welk, the ABA was Little Richard.

During the late '60s, the NBA was the home of the big man: Russell. Chamberlain. Unseld. Thurmond. Reed. Every team worth its weight in sneakers featured a marquee center. The ABA, particularly in its early days, was guard-driven. The faster pace and emphasis on long-distance shooting gave the little man an opportunity to shine, creating stars out of the likes of 6-foot guard Louie Dampier, the ABA's all-time leading scorer.

Dampier, who let it fly from deep at a rate that would make Steph Curry blush, was a collegiate star at the University of Kentucky. Drafted in the fourth round of the 1967 NBA draft, he opted to join the ranks of the ABA's Kentucky Colonels for their inaugural season.

Others followed suit and gave the ABA a try — the more lucrative paychecks didn't hurt (although, like in the case of Jim McDaniels, the fine print would reveal that salaries were spread out over a 25-year period). But the majority of the ABA's players didn't have the luxury of choosing which league they'd join. They were NBA outcasts and basketball nomads.

There was Connie Hawkins, the Brooklyn high school prodigy who had been banned from the NBA for his alleged role in a collegiate point-shaving scandal during his freshman year. No matter, said the ABA, talent is talent. And the fledgling league needed as much as it could get. Hawkins was signed by the ABA's Pittsburgh Pipers, where he won a championship and became the league's first MVP.

"The young league will make do with what it has — the slightly too short and too old, the hoped-for sleepers and the discards," read a 1967 article in *Sports Illustrated*. But there were exceptions, like Rick Barry, a rising star with the NBA's San Francisco Warriors who scored 38 points in the 1966 All-Star Game before jumping ship the next year for the ABA's Oakland Oaks. Artis Gilmore, the ABA's 7-foot MVP, passed on the NBA in favor of an unprecedented $2.5 million contract with the Colonels, one of the league's few stable franchises.

Even Wilt Chamberlain, following his retirement in 1973, had a brief stint in the ABA as the butterfly-collared, sandal-clad coach of the San Diego Conquistadors.

And then there were those who began Hall of Fame careers in the ABA before becoming household names after the two leagues merged in 1976. Erving was the biggest star of a group that included George Gervin, Spencer Haywood, David Thompson, George McGinnis and Moses Malone, a future NBA Finals MVP. Malone became the first pro player signed straight out of high school when he joined the Utah Stars in 1973 — opening the door for the likes of Kevin Garnett, Kobe Bryant and LeBron James decades later.

By the mid-'70s, the league had developed a deep and growing talent pool that rivaled the NBA's; in exhibition games, ABA teams held a winning record over the NBA.

The league and its players reflected the style of the late '60s and early '70s. Afros, muttonchops, handlebar mustaches, mink coats and bell-bottoms were as much a part of the uniform as the flashy and inventive jerseys players donned. The play was loose and funky — basketball conducted by George Clinton.

The ABA resonated with its small but loyal following in a way the NBA couldn't. But

it remained firmly in the background. ABA players were confident they could outshine their NBA counterparts, but without the television coverage the rival league enjoyed, they could only play to the audiences that showed up on a given night — and crowds were sometimes so small, players recall being able to count them during the playing of the national anthem.

The ABA was "the invisible league." Even in later years, when crowds grew — mostly to catch Erving — the league didn't have enough exposure to make money or put a dent in the NBA's hold on America's living rooms. By 1976 a merger with the NBA was the only lifeline left. Four ABA teams — the San Antonio Spurs, Denver Nuggets, Indiana Pacers and New York Nets — joined the NBA.

Only after its demise would the ABA begin to earn recognition. In addition to giving us the 3-pointer, the ABA was the league where statistics like blocks, steals and turnovers were first tracked. It's where underclassmen were first signed and, famously, where the slam dunk contest was born. It's impossible to picture what the game of basketball would look like today had the ABA never came along.

Not bad for a gimmick league.

NOT A GIMMICK LEAGUE

A choice selection of some ABA promotions

- Victor the Wrestling Bear
- Halter Top Night in Denver
- John Brisker Intimidation Night
- Board Game giveaway
- Miami Floridians "Boo-Fest"
- Indy's Cow-Milking contest
- Ziggy the Dog
- Dancin' Harry vs. Robota, the Wicked Witch of the West
- Playboy Bunnies Night
- Glenn Campbell LIVE!

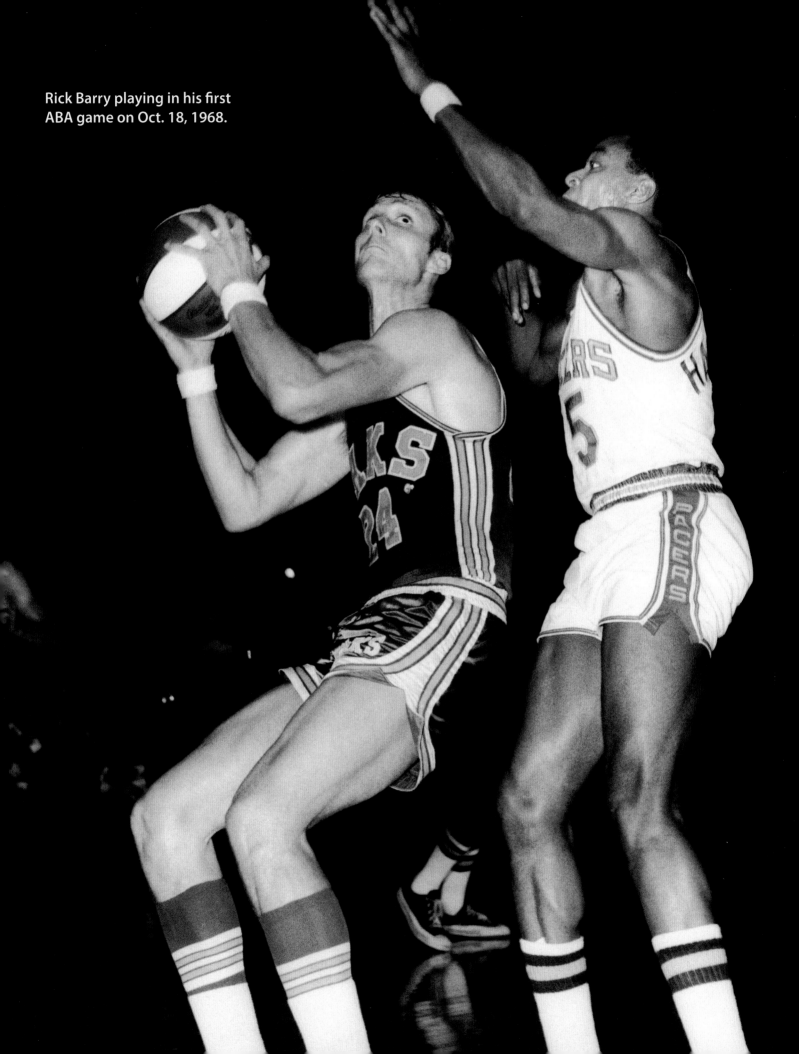

Rick Barry playing in his first ABA game on Oct. 18, 1968.

1969
"FELTON, THIS IS NORMAN"

William Felton Russell and Wilton Norman Chamberlain were two singular giants whose careers were unmatched — and always linked.

They combined to win nine MVP awards between 1958 and 1968. They remain the only two players with more than 20,000 career rebounds — nobody else is remotely close. In 1961–62, when Wilt averaged 50 points a game, he finished second in MVP voting to Russell.

The pair brought NBA basketball into the homes of Americans, who were captivated by the sight of two behemoths going toe to toe. Their rivalry was bigger than the game. "It took on biblical proportions," said Dolph Schayes. Team versus individual. Selfless versus selfish. Good versus evil.

Russell and Wilt were aligned from an early age. If Celtics coach Red Auerbach had had his way, they could have been teammates. Before the territorial draft system was eliminated in 1965, teams often had first dibs on local college stars. Red, who had coached Wilt in the summers at Kutsher's resort when he was a high schooler, wanted him to attend Harvard so that the Celtics could draft him. Wilt always maintained that Auerbach felt betrayed when he chose Kansas instead. That, Wilt said, was why Red spent so much time criticizing his game in the press while lauding Russell.

In 1959, when a 23-year-old Chamberlain entered the NBA, he stepped into a world where the 24-year-old Russell ruled. But the game had never seen a figure like Wilt, who presented Russell with his first real competition since coming into the league two seasons earlier. Wilt stood between five and six inches taller than Russell and was 70 pounds

Wilt Chamberlain tries to shoot over Bill Russell during the first period of the NBA Playoffs at the Forum in Los Angeles May 5, 1969.

heavier. He was a more skilled ballplayer and dunked the ball with more power than anybody. Russell was considered the only man on Earth capable of blocking it.

Russell's teammates recall that Chamberlain "destroyed" him in their first meeting on November 22, 1959. In truth, Russell "held" Wilt to a mere 30 points in a Celtics win. But there was no doubting that the Big Dipper was unlike any opponent Russell had ever faced. Wilt averaged 40 points and 30 rebounds in 12 games against Russell's Celtics during his rookie year.

Off the court, they were good friends —

Bill Russell outreaches Wilt Chamberlain for a rebound in 1967.

who else shared what they had in common? During Russell's first year with the Celtics, the sociable Wilt, then a sophomore at Kansas, reached out to meet with him. They remained close, and when the Celtics played in Philly, Chamberlain would invite Russell to his family home, where Wilt's mom, Olivia, cooked them dinner.

Publicly, of course, they were pitted against one another. Their differences — both real and perceived — were all anybody talked about. Chamberlain was the bad guy to Russell's hero. Wilt was more concerned about his own stats; Russell was the ultimate team player. Russell was a family man whose enduring image is of him surrounded by teammates; Wilt was a celebrated bachelor who, in his free time, would drive cross-country alone. Russell genuinely didn't care what people thought of him; Wilt desperately wanted to be liked. Russell worked hard for what he earned, whereas Wilt coasted on his talent.

As Bob Cousy imagined: "If [Wilt] had one-third of Russell's intensity, God . . ."

Chamberlain downplayed it all. "I played against teams and not individuals. Russell was just one of the players I played against," he said. But the comparisons never stopped.

Russell's Celtics eliminated Chamberlain's teams from the playoffs seven times — including twice in the Finals. But in the 1965 playoffs, Chamberlain averaged over 30 points and 30 rebounds and owned his matchup with Russell in the second round. In the closing moments of Game 7, Wilt dunked on Russell, who then turned the ball over on the inbounds pass, giving Wilt's 76ers a chance to win the game. Celtics guard John Havlicek famously stole the ball on the final possession to seal a narrow win.

That summer, Chamberlain became the first player to earn a $100,000 contract. When he heard the news, Russell demanded that the Celtics pay him $100,001. They did.

In 1967, Wilt flipped the script and eliminated Russell's Celtics en route to his first championship. The two would meet again on the Finals stage in 1969, with Chamberlain now a member of the Los Angeles Lakers. Wilt went down with a knee injury in Game 7. Although he wanted to return to action, his coach kept him on the bench during the second half. He could only watch as Russell and the Celts prevailed again.

After the game, a reporter suggested to Russell that he only won because Chamberlain didn't play. Incensed by the remark, Russell lashed out and said that, unlike Wilt, he would need to be on his death bed to miss a game of that magnitude. Chamberlain was hurt when he heard the remark, and the two didn't speak for years until Russell apologized.

The two matched up against one another 143 times. They knew each other's games better than anybody. Against Chamberlain, Russell would "let" Wilt score. The more baskets Chamberlain made, he noticed, the more his teammates stood around, watching in awe — like the paying audience. Wilt would try to get Russell in foul trouble, which would prompt Auerbach to switch Russell off of Wilt and have another Celtic guard him.

"I always wondered if Russell realized that, during his career, he was relegated to being a role player," Chamberlain said. But that was Russell's genius. He took on whatever task was needed to secure a win.

The difference between them, Russell said, was that Wilt's "teammates had to feed him, and I fed my teammates."

"When you played with Russell, you knew exactly what to expect from him each night," said Havlicek. "But Wilt, he was liable to decide, 'Tonight I'm going to score 60 . . . or tonight, I'm getting 40 rebounds . . . or 20 assists.' He was preoccupied with answering people who said he couldn't do things. . . . Russell never let himself get caught up in that."

Russell was aware of what was said about them. But after a decade of battles, he knew what kind of once-in-a-lifetime force Chamberlain was. "You know, Wilt," he'd tell him, "I'm the only person who really knows how good you are."

Wilt scored 40 points or more against Russell 26 times.

"Wilt and I were not rivals," said Russell. "We were competitors. You see, in a rivalry, there's a victor and a vanquished. He was never vanquished."

Their friendship was renewed post-retirement. Russell spoke at Chamberlain's funeral in 1999. He said he was "unspeakably injured" by the news of Wilt's passing.

They stayed in regular contact in their old age. Russell traded in his jersey for a collared shirt under a sweater only Grandpa would wear, his hair long since turned gray and covered by a ruffled baseball cap. Wilt was balding and sporting shades and a jet-black goatee, his still-impressive physique on display in a skin-tight T-shirt.

They used to call each other on the phone and talk for hours. Usually, Russell would leave a message on Wilt's answering machine: "Wilton Norman Chamberlain, this is William Felton Russell."

Wilt would call him back.

"Felton, this is Norman."

They'd reminisce, and Wilt would inevitably complain about the hype the current crop of stars received. "Do you believe this s★★t?" he asked after a *Sports Illustrated* cover debated whether Dennis Rodman was the best rebounder of all time. Russell would crackle his iconic laugh, more of a high-pitched howl. "Who cares about that crap?" Russell would say. Wilt would chuckle his baritone guffaw.

"Felton," Wilt would say, "you have 11 rings and just 10 fingers. How about you give one of those to me?" Russell would remind him that, once upon a time, Wilt had his chance.

NBA NEMESES

While it may be hard to top the stature of the Wilt–Russell rivalry, many individual standoffs have come close over the years:

- Bob Pettit vs. Dolph Schayes
- Walt Frazier vs. Jerry West
- Isiah Thomas vs. Michael Jordan
- Magic vs. Larry
- Shaq vs. Duncan
- LeBron vs. Kevin Durant

1969
THE TORMENTED
JERRY WEST

A wet and muddied ball bounces on a patch of dirt. A boy takes shot after shot on a makeshift net nailed to a shed in his neighbors' yard. His fingers are blistered and bloodied from the hours spent perfecting his craft. Don't call it practicing, he'll later say. "I was just afraid to go home."

Dusk turns into night and the boy refuses to go inside. It's here, surrounded by the mountain woodlands of rural West Virginia — alone — that he prefers. Three . . . two . . . one, he counts down in his mind. Swish.

When Jerry West plays out these games in his head, he always wins. But as he grows older, it's the losses that plague him.

"I never felt the fulfillment when we won," West said, long after his career had ended. "All I thought about was all the times we'd lost. It'll haunt me till I die."

Over the course of a 14-year career — all of it spent with the Los Angeles Lakers — West reached 9 NBA Finals, and lost all but one. His misfortune? Bad timing. When West entered the league in 1960, Bill Russell's Boston Celtics were in the midst of a title run that saw them win 11 championships in 13 years. In 6 Finals matchups with Boston, West's Lakers always had to settle for second place.

Never mind that West had led his team to a Finals stage most players could only dream of stepping onto. Or that he lays claim to some of the most iconic buzzer-beaters of all time. Or that he won more than 700 games as a player. Or that his jump shot was considered the purest on the planet. Or that his career average of 27.03 points per game ranks fifth in NBA history. Or that his 46.3 points per game remains a record for a single playoff series. Or that he was named to the All-Star Game *every year* he played. Or that he was such a big star that the NBA put his silhouette on its logo in 1969, and has never changed it.

West remembers his as a career wasted. It's why he's not only one of the NBA's best, but also its most tortured.

West grew up dirt poor in Chelyan, a West Virginia mining town (population in 2010: 778). He spent his childhood alone.

West's father was a coal mine worker who would return home from a long day's work and beat his children mercilessly. When West was 12, his older brother and hero, David, was killed in the Korean War. At home, the beatings got worse. "The wrong son died," West would begin to tell himself.

So shy that he could barely utter a word to strangers, West retreated to his neighbors' makeshift court. He wore mitts when it was cold, but never stopped dribbling. If he wasn't playing basketball, he was running furiously through the ravines at the foot of the nearby mountains. At one point, he needed to be injected with vitamin shots because he was so frail after many long hours outside.

After a childhood that left him scarred, isolated and deeply introspective, the basketball court was the closest thing West could find to sanctuary. In high school, West made the team, but, shorter than his peers, was relegated to benchwarmer status. The summer before his senior season, however, he shot up six inches and would go on to set a state scoring record while leading the school to a state title in 1956.

He stayed home to attend West Virginia University, where he became a legend, averaging 29.3 points per game as a senior — before the 3-point line existed — and carried West Virginia to the NCAA title game.

In 1960, when West graduated, the NBA was a big man's league. Larger-than-life centers like Russell and Wilt Chamberlain drew in fans and carried the league. That changed when West, the second overall pick, entered the picture alongside Oscar Robertson, the No. 1 pick. The two talented guards were already recognized across America, having just co-captained Team USA to Olympic gold in 1960.

West was an instant star in Los Angeles. He teamed up with Elgin Baylor to form a legendary duo — "Mr. Outside" to Baylor's "Mr. Inside" — that helped popularize pro basketball in California.

Basketball was more than a game. It was healing. And so, winning took on a deeper meaning. It made losing that much harder.

Los Angeles struggled to a 36-43 record in West's rookie year. It was the first losing season he had experienced. And he didn't like the way it felt. "I was afraid of making a mistake," he said of his first NBA campaign, "because I might hurt the team and make myself look bad."

Things began to click the following season. West's scoring average vaulted from 17.6 points per game as a rookie to 30.8. With Baylor averaging over 38 points that season, the Lakers made their first Finals appearance against the mighty Celtics in 1962.

In Game 3, with the series knotted 1-1, West scored four straight points in the last minute to tie the game. With three seconds remaining and Boston inbounding the ball, West intercepted a pass from Celtics guard Sam Jones and ran the length of the court for a game-winning layup at the buzzer — just the way he'd done it so many times in his mind growing up. The sequence earned West the moniker "Mr. Clutch," but the Celtics would go on to win the series in a decisive Game 7.

The Lakers reached — and lost — the Finals in four of the next six seasons.

West's obsession with losing was taking its toll. In the lead-up to games, he would sit alone in his locker-room stall, staring off into the distance, picturing the opponents he was set to take a lifetime's worth of angst out on. By the tip-off, he was mentally exhausted.

After home games, he would drive until the sun came up, going nowhere. On road trips, he lay awake all night in his hotel room, replaying key moments. West always blamed himself for losses, carrying a great burden that followed him off the court. He'd duct-tape his blinds shut to obstruct the light, but nothing could block out his thoughts.

West's agony would culminate in the 1969 Finals, Bill Russell's final year. That season, the Lakers traded for Wilt Chamberlain, the only player who could both dwarf Russell and match his athletic prowess. Having lost to Boston in the Finals in six of the last eight years, this was West's chance to flip the script.

He was brilliant during the seven-game series. In Game 1 he erupted for 53 points and the Lakers won by two. Boston would even the series, forcing a seventh game on the Lakers' home court.

Despite a hamstring injury that left one leg swollen and barely able to support his weight, West had one of the best performances in NBA history. He played all 48 minutes, scored 42 points, grabbed 13 rebounds and dished 12 assists. But, in a two-point nail-biter, once again, the Celtics won. He'd call it the most haunting moment of his career.

For the first and only time in league history, the Finals MVP award was given to a player on the losing team: Jerry West.

"Los Angeles has not won the championship," Russell said after the game, "but Jerry West is a champion."

The MVP distinction was meaningless to him. "A dubious honor," he called it. For winning the award, West was given a new car. He considered blowing it up with dynamite.

"I wanted to quit basketball in the worst way," West wrote in his autobiography, *West by West: My Charmed, Tortured Life.*

The following year, the Lakers returned to the Finals, where they faced the New York Knicks. In Game 3, West hit a stunning 60-foot buzzer-beater to send the game to overtime. The Lakers lost, and New York won the title — another would-be shining moment had been forever dulled in the mind of West.

In 1972, at the age of 34, West was finally crowned champion.

The Lakers won an NBA-record 69 games in the regular season that year, fueled by a 33-game winning streak. West thrived under new head coach Bill Sharman and led the league in assists for the first time. In the Finals, the Lakers made easy work of the Knicks.

Yet, even in victory, West couldn't enjoy the feeling.

Nine games into that season, Baylor, West's running mate since day one in Los Angeles and a cherished comrade through a decade of playoff disappointments, was forced to retire due to injury. West would call winning the '72 title without Baylor "one of the saddest things I've had to do." Nearly a week passed before West could feel happy about the victory. "Is it worth it to feel this bad all of the time?" he asked himself.

By his retirement in 1974, West had joined Wilt and Robertson as just the third player to score 25,000 points in league history.

His legendary career didn't end on the court. West transitioned to the front office, where he achieved the continued success he'd only dreamed of as a player. As a general manager, he was the architect of the "Showtime" Lakers dynasty of the 1980s. He traded for high-schooler Kobe Bryant on draft night in 1996 and recruited Shaquille O'Neal

from the Orlando Magic in free agency. As an advisor to the Golden State Warriors, he lobbied to draft Klay Thompson and brought in Steve Kerr as head coach.

All told, as an executive, he's responsible for 27 NBA finalists and 13 championships.

But the times he fell short will forever haunt him.

West never returned to the city of Boston once his playing career ended. Too many bad memories. "I'm still tormented by those losses."

"I was sure I was going to be labeled a loser forever," he wrote in his autobiography. "People will ask, 'When does the healing begin?' And I say, 'it never begins.'"

Jerry West poses for a team photo in 1969.

CAREER TRIPLE-DOUBLES

1.	Kobe Bryant	4
	Bob Pettit	4
3.	LeBron James	3
	Michael Jordan	3
	Shaquille O'Neal	3
	Oscar Robertson	3

1969
THE BATTLE FOR LEW ALCINDOR

The million-dollar check was in George Mikan's pocket. The meeting with Lew Alcindor was scheduled for the spring of 1969. Operation Kingfish was going according to plan.

Alcindor, the 22-year-old center who would later change his name to Kareem Abdul-Jabbar, had just wrapped up a legendary amateur career at UCLA. His soaring skyhook, the most recognizable — and unstoppable — signature shot in the history of the game, helped carry the Bruins to three straight championships between 1967 and 1969. The New York City native was named college basketball's Player of the Year in each of those seasons, with averages of more than 26 points and 15 rebounds per game.

So dominant was the 7-foot-2 Alcindor that, ahead of his sophomore season, the NCAA banned dunking to level the playing field. Ever since his high school days, when he rose to national prominence by leading Manhattan's Power Memorial Academy to state championships and a 72-game win streak, he had been considered the most promising NBA prospect the league had ever seen. Even segregated colleges in the southern US recruited him out of high school, promising to break the color barrier should he attend.

Kareem Abdul-Jabbar unleashes his hook shot against the Lakers in the 1972 NBA Finals.

He was a league-altering prospect. Of all the promising young stars that had entered pro ball in the late 1960s — Walt Frazier, Wes Unseld, Dave Bing — only Alcindor could be expected to single-handedly carry a league on his skinny shoulders.

So it's no surprise that when Alcindor left UCLA in 1969, at the height of the ABA and NBA's star wars, when the two leagues did whatever it took to snatch marquee talent away from one another, he was the most coveted of them all.

For the NBA, landing Alcindor meant bridging the gap between eras, from Chamberlain, whose prime years were in the rearview, to Lew. For the ABA, the stakes were far higher. If he were to choose the rival league, it would be established as "a permanent second league" to the NBA.

Operation Kingfish, as ABA executives dubbed it, had begun early in Alcindor's final UCLA season. The idea was simple enough. The league set out to do every possible bit of homework on Alcindor. They hired private investigators to follow him and his family and friends. Psychologists were put on the payroll to study the towering center and identify his motivations. They began compiling a list of those closest to him — any close confidant who could help sway his decision.

The results were comprehensive and painted a picture that would only ring truer as the years passed and the star center's fame grew: Alcindor was his own man. (In 1968, a *Sports Illustrated* feature was published with the headline "Lewie Is a Minority of One.")

He would meet with each league once and make his decision alone. Neither his parents nor his agent would be involved. Priding himself on his loyalty, once his decision was made, it would be final.

The ABA assigned Alcindor's "draft" rights to the New York Nets, in large part because they thought the notion of playing in his hometown would appeal to him. In the NBA, the Milwaukee Bucks held his rights. Advantage: ABA.

The ABA knew it needed to make a splash, and even held meetings with elusive billionaire Howard Hughes about putting up an enormous sum of money to sign Alcindor and establish a franchise for him to headline in Los Angeles.

When Hughes couldn't commit, the league was undeterred. It secured a meeting with Alcindor at a hotel in New York. It had also drafted a check for $1 million, a "signing bonus" that would make him instantly rich — something the research suggested would appeal to the big man. The brass also bought a mink coat for Alcindor's mother after learning that she had always wanted one.

Ahead of the meeting, ABA commissioner George Mikan said he wanted to represent the league — one great center to another — and would be joined only by Nets owner Arthur Brown. The plan was for Mikan and Brown to enter the room and simply place the check on the table. Actions speak louder than words.

Mikan tucked the check into his pocket and entered the hotel room with Alcindor. When they emerged a few hours later, the money was still in his pocket. "We decided it wasn't necessary to give him our best offer," Mikan told ABA executives, much to their horror. "We figure when he comes back to us, then we'll use the check for the second round of talks." Mikan had offered a salary of $1 million over four years.

The Bucks offered Alcindor $1.4 million over five years. He chose Milwaukee.

The ABA tried to find Alcindor later that night to present him with the check, but he had already boarded a flight back to LA. The ABA had missed the opportunity of a lifetime. That summer, Mikan was relieved of his duties as commissioner.

The ABA's worst fears were realized as soon as Alcindor played. In his first season, 1969–70, he was Rookie of the Year, averaging 28.8 points per game. Teaming up with Oscar Robertson, he lifted the Bucks from 27 wins the previous season to 56 wins.

He would go on to carve out one of the longest, most illustrious careers the NBA has ever seen.

The skyhook was just as unstoppable in the pros as it had been at UCLA and on the playgrounds of New York, where he honed his not-so-secret weapon. He had taken the hook shot — a staple of most every big man — and extended the range.

The move married practicality with grace, and it was the same every time: He'd post up his defender 10 or so feet from the hoop and spin away from the basket, his towering body lodged between the defender and the ball in his right hand. In one sweeping motion, a flick of the wrist sent the ball beyond the defender's hands and through the hoop.

"How do you block the skyhook?" he was asked in 2017. The answer: "You don't." The shot accounted for 75 percent of his points.

In 1971 a 24-year-old Alcindor led Milwaukee to its first-ever championship, sweeping the Baltimore Bullets, 4-0, in the Finals and dismantling the Lakers and Chamberlain — the player he'd been compared to since he first picked up a ball.

Within a month of winning the '71 championship, Alcindor officially changed his name to Kareem Abdul-Jabbar.

Abdul-Jabbar had always been political. In 1967, during the Vietnam War, he was at the table in Cleveland for a well-publicized meeting of top athletes who supported Muhammad Ali's refusal to report for military service. The lone collegiate athlete in the group, he was flanked by the likes of Ali, Bill Russell and football star Jim Brown — all outspoken public figures.

The meeting led to his decision to boycott the 1968 Olympics, a choice that didn't win fans over but reinforced the notion that public perception was a non-factor. As Abdul-Jabbar's legend grew on NBA courts, he doubled as one of its most unpopular. He treated interviews as if they were beneath him. The muttonchop sideburns and oversized goggles he wore (as a result of taking too many fingers to the eye from opponents trying whatever it took to stop the skyhook) covered his face. A chronic migraine problem only contributed to Abdul-Jabbar appearing closed off from fans. As he put it: "I'm the baddest of the bad guys."

Nor did he please fans when he asked to be traded from Milwaukee, where he felt isolated as a Muslim man in a mostly white, rural setting. In 1975 his wish was granted, and he was dealt to the Lakers, returning to the city he had owned as a collegiate icon.

In LA, Kareem was great as ever, although he never experienced the adoration such peers as Julius Erving and Pete Maravich

did. It wasn't until Magic Johnson arrived in 1979, sparking an '80s dynasty, that Abdul-Jabbar saw his popularity rise as the center-piece of the Showtime Lakers.

Still, it became apparent that Abdul-Jabbar would never satisfy his many critics — plenty of whom pointed fingers while simultane-ously debating whether he, Chamberlain or Russell was the best center of all time. Media and fans alike wanted Abdul-Jabbar

to take over games the way his predecessors had. Instead, his dominance tended to come within the flow of the action, while the smooth, calculated skyhook seemed almost casual. "Quietly," was how many described how he went about accumulating points.

After the Lakers captured the 1988 title, the writing was on the wall. His role in the offense was fading — he went from taking more than 21 shots per game during his first

year in LA to 11 that season — and while he had once been the Lakers' go-to player in crunch time, he only saw the ball once during the final minutes of Game 7 of the '88 Finals.

He still managed to make an impact, and remarkably was an All-Star every year but one, up until his retirement at age 41. "What Kareem still has is presence," one opposing coach said during his final season, 1988–89.

Rookie Lew Alcindor is measured by team trainer Arnie Garber as Bucks check in for medical examinations in 1969.

"He adds to the Lakers' aura."

After 20 seasons and 6 championships, 6 MVP awards, 11 All-Defensive Team honors and countless other accolades, Kareem was one constellation in the NBA universe that it seemed would never burn out.

By the time he retired, he had broken Chamberlain's record to become the league's all-time leading scorer with 38,387 points.

We'll never know what kind of tectonic shifts in the basketball landscape he would've sparked had he chosen the ABA over the Milwaukee Bucks, but his status among the greatest to ever play remains unquestioned.

STAR WARS

The NBA and ABA always battled over stars. For many players, the ABA offered an important leverage tool in contract negotiations with their NBA teams, who rightfully saw the ABA as a legitimate threat to poach talent. It wasn't uncommon to see NBA players nearing the end of their contract, like the Knicks' Earl "the Pearl" Monroe appear in the stands during ABA games — a message to owners that their talents were available to the highest bidder.

1970
IS WILLIS REED GOING TO PLAY?

That was the question hanging in the air at Madison Square Garden ahead of Game 7 of the 1970 NBA Finals.

Reed, the New York Knicks' captain, was the NBA's MVP that season. A skilled, burly 6-foot-9 center, seemingly as wide as he was tall, he was also the Knicks' leading scorer in 1969–70. He and point guard Walt "Clyde" Frazier — the only teammates named to the All-NBA First Team that season — helped a deep and talented squad to 60 wins and first place in the East.

The Knicks were the favorites entering the Finals against the Los Angeles Lakers, who starred living legends Jerry West, Wilt Chamberlain and Elgin Baylor. They entered Game 6 in Los Angeles with a 3-2 series lead and the chance to capture their first-ever title. But two nights earlier, Reed had torn a tendon in his right thigh and was forced to leave the game. With him on the sidelines for Game 6, there was nobody to slow down Chamberlain down low. The Big Dipper scored 45 points and snarled 27 rebounds in a blowout win.

With Reed's status for Game 7 up in the air, the Knicks' chances of ushering in a new era in front of a frenzied home crowd looked bleak.

The '69–70 season marked a changing of the guard in the NBA. It was the first campaign in 13 years without Bill Russell. After 11 championships with the Boston Celtics,

the league's winningest player retired before the season, leaving the door open for a new crop of contenders.

For the two teams squaring off in the first post-Russell Finals, his departure had given them renewed hope. The Knicks had been bounced from the playoffs by Russell's Celtics in two of the last three years. But that was nothing compared to their opponent — the Lakers lost to Boston in the Finals in seven of the last nine seasons.

As the minutes ticked away and tip-off time for Game 7 approached, a nervous Madison Square Garden crowd, joined by media members and even Reed's own teammates, had no clue whether he'd be able to suit up. As both teams took the floor for warm-ups, Reed was nowhere in sight.

When a player wearing a Knicks uniform emerged from the tunnel onto the court, the crowd erupted. Then, when they realized it was backup forward Cazzie Russell, and not Captain Reed, the cheers died in an instant.

Six minutes before tip-off, he appeared. As he limped out of the tunnel in full playing gear, the crowd went wild. It was as if Reed had come back from the dead. Longtime Knicks courtside photographer George Kalinsky called it "the most electric, passionate sound from a crowd I've ever heard."

Reed had arrived to save the day. What the fans didn't know was that, moments earlier,

Willis Reed races to the dressing room after capturing the NBA championship.

he had been administered 200 cubic centimeters of cortisone — enough painkillers to treat a racehorse — just to be able to stand on his injured leg. He could barely walk, but he wasn't about to let this moment pass by while watching from the sidelines.

When he emerged onto the court, the Lakers stopped their warm-ups. It was as if they'd seen a ghost.

"When I saw that," Walt Frazier later said, "something told me we might have these guys."

The 1969–70 Knicks were far greater than one player. They epitomized a team-first approach and tore through opponents with a balanced attack. Including head coach Red Holzman, the team featured six Hall of Famers and boasted talented shooters at each and every position, a precursor to the modern approach to sculpting an NBA offense.

When they got off to a record 23-1 start to the campaign, the basketball-mad fans in New York City knew their team had the potential to do something special.

In the backcourt, the Knicks' marquee player was Frazier, whose status as a superfly fashion icon of his era ran counter to his workmanlike approach to the game.

He was among the game's most potent defenders — they didn't count steals in those days, but he would surely have been a perennial league leader — and a versatile offensive threat who ran the Knicks' offense to perfection. Frazier was also one of the NBA's best shot-makers in the clutch and a player opponents did not want to see with the ball in his hands with the game on the line.

Throw in such supporting cast members as lefty shooting guard Dick Barnett and spry guard Phil Jackson, who went on to become one of the most accomplished coaches in NBA history, and it's no wonder the Knicks were a load to handle.

In the frontcourt, New York starred Bill Bradley, a Rhodes scholar (and future US senator, representing New Jersey) for whom the team waited patiently for two years after drafting him in 1965 while he studied at Oxford. In 1968 the Knicks acquired All-Star forward Dave DeBusschere from the Detroit Pistons in exchange for center Walt Bellamy. DeBusschere was a tenacious rebounder and natural power forward who allowed Reed to man the center position full time, helping to unleash his game further.

Reed, who grew up in the Jim Crow South, was the Knicks' heart and soul. He was the tone setter and peacemaker on a team made up of players from vastly different backgrounds. As a rookie, Bradley — the NBA's latest in a long line of Great White Hopes — was awarded a contract larger than any of his veteran black teammates. It was Reed who extinguished any potential trouble. When Cazzie Russell arrived to practice one day in Detroit (after being pulled over by a police officer who pointed a gun at his head in a case of racial profiling) and started throwing elbows at his white teammates in a rage, it was Reed who stepped in to defuse the situation.

He impacted his team without having to pick up a ball.

At Game 7 in Madison Square Garden, Reed's sheer presence as he went from the locker room to the hardwood instantly changed the atmosphere surrounding the deciding title game.

With the crowd still delirious that their hero had appeared to save the day, Reed stood at center court against the 7-foot-2 Chamberlain and won the tip-off. Two plays later, as he limped behind the action, Reed caught a pass from Frazier and pulled up for a jump shot. Swish. A few moments later, Reed faced up Chamberlain at the right elbow and hoisted a jumper over his outstretched arms. Swish.

"At that point," Bill Bradley said, "it's over."

Those were the only four points Reed scored that game. His inspired teammates picked up the baton from there. The Knicks' lead ballooned to as many as 29 points in the first half. Walt Frazier took control of the game with one of the most impressive Finals performances of all time, albeit one that was overshadowed by Reed's heroics. Frazier scored 39 points and dished 19 assists (then a Finals record) in a 113–99 victory.

Reed was named Finals MVP.

"They call it the Willis Reed game," Frazier joked years later, "and I call it bulls★★t."

The Lakers got their revenge against New York two years later, defeating the Knicks for the 1972 championship. But the following year, the Knicks retooled, adding forward Jerry Lucas, who was gifted with an incred-

ible memory — in addition to retaining opponents' plays and tendencies, he'd amaze his teammates by memorizing and reciting 50 pages of the New York City phone book on the spot.

The Knicks also added Earl "The Pearl" Monroe from the Washington Bullets. Monroe was a former streetball legend who had been dubbed Black Jesus. He and Frazier comprised the flashy Rolls Royce Backcourt.

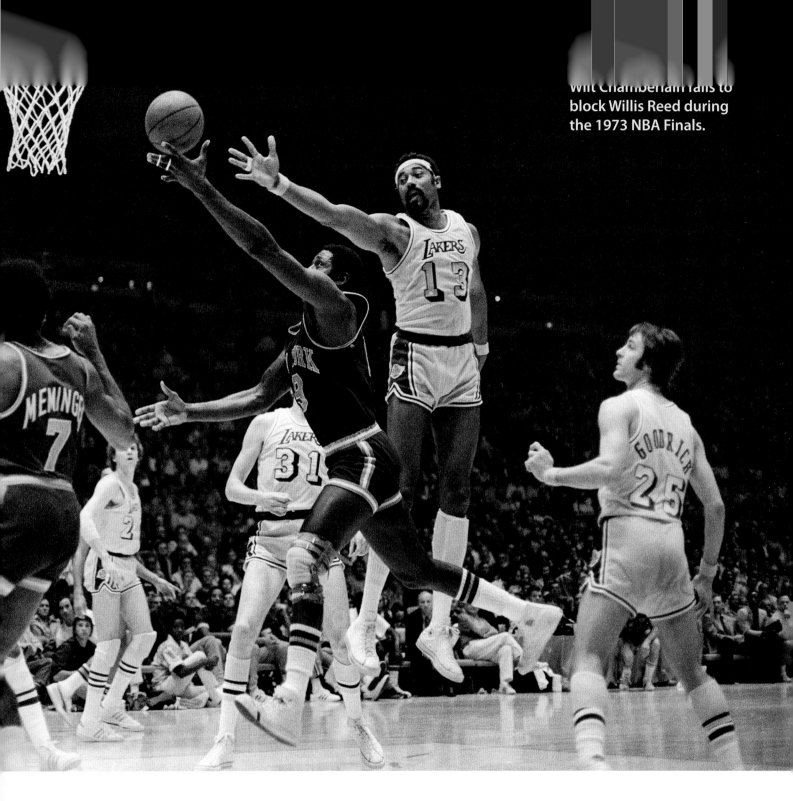

These new-look Knicks would reclaim the NBA title in 1973, in yet another matchup with the Lakers — this time winning easily, in five games. Reed was named Finals MVP for the second time.

From the street game to the marquee matchups on Madison Avenue, New York City has long served as basketball's unofficial home court. Madison Square Garden is the Mecca of the game, and

Knicks fans are traditionally among the most passionate anywhere.

But the Knicks have yet to recapture the glory of those early-'70s teams. They appeared in the Finals twice in the '90s, but never again hoisted the championship trophy. Along the way, their image has been marred by dysfunctional teams and misguided management. Their history traces back to the origins of the NBA — the Knicks and MSG

were the centerpiece of the league's earliest days — but only for that brief slice of time were the Knicks the greatest team around.

It's why the legacy of those early-'70s teams lives on so vividly in the minds of Knicks fans. Whether their team is winning or losing, the conversation always comes back to when the Garden was great.

1970
PISTOL

Neil Young famously sang, "It's better to burn out than to fade away." The Pistol did both.

Pistol Pete Maravich entered the NBA in 1970 as the highest scorer in the history of college basketball. He had the perfect nickname, which came from the way he shot the ball, stretching back to his right hip as if he was reaching for his holster. He also had an endless set of moves — passes, shots, handles — that had never been seen before . . . or since.

Maravich believed that basketball was a show, and he made sure ticket buyers got their money's worth each night. They called him "the first white Globetrotter."

He was a fan favorite, but he spent his career racking up points for perennially losing teams. It was only when he joined the Boston Celtics in 1980 that he played for a contender. But by then, Maravich had been ravaged by injuries. Worse, he was disillusioned by the game he'd dedicated his life to.

Pete Maravich was born to play ball. His father, Press, made sure of it. A former pro basketball player, including a stint for the Pittsburgh Ironmen during the inaugural NBA season, Press was preparing for his first college coaching job when his son, Pete, was born in Aliquippa, Pennsylvania, on June 22, 1947.

As soon he had the strength to lift it off the ground, Pete had a basketball in his hands. Beginning at the age of five, his father would run him through drills. Press was relentless, but Pete rarely tired.

As he got older, the exercises became more complex. Press invented dribbling drills with names like crab catch, punching bag,

seesaw, flapjack and pretzel. Dribbling alone, or under the watchful eye of his old man, on a slab of concrete in the family's basement, Pete perfected all of them.

In one drill, Press would have his son lie down in the back seat of a moving car with the door open, dribbling on the asphalt road. Maravich kept his dribble alive as his father changed speeds.

Press got more creative. At one point, he fashioned a pair of glasses with the bottoms blacked out so you couldn't look down while dribbling. At the bark of a whistle, he moved Pete around like a Tetris piece.

Press would show him off, bringing friends to the basement where Pete practiced and instructing him to perform the crab catch, marveling at his life's work.

He wasn't even a teenager yet, but Pete seemed to share his father's dedication to getting better. He was on a constant mission to find new ways to control the ball.

Maravich approached the game like a magician mastering new ways to manipulate and deceive the audience — or, in Pete's case, opponents. After team practices at school, Pete would routinely stay late and pass the ball off the wall to himself at every imaginable angle.

Maravich bounced around from school to school as the family followed Press's coaching career wherever it took them. Eventually, Press accepted the head coaching job at Louisiana State University in Baton Rouge. Pete became a top high school player, and although he wanted to attend West Virginia University, at his father's insistence, he enrolled at LSU to play for Press.

Pete had free rein at LSU. He wanted to perform, and Press gave him a stage to showcase his skills. In his first season, Maravich averaged 43.8 points per game. That's not a typo.

Maravich, who despite his rail-thin frame was sprouting to 6-foot-5, was quickly making a name for himself. He could deliver a two-handed bounce pass to one side — looking left, moving left — as the ball miraculously went in the opposite direction. Nobody had seen anything like it.

On one play, Maravich would sprint up the floor with the ball, leading a 3-on-1 fast break. Flanked by his teammates, he'd give the ball a hard bounce and trace his hand around it twice as it floated in midair. It put the defense into a trance, so mesmerized that they couldn't keep track once he finally slapped the ball with the back of his hand to an open teammate. When he tried the move in a game, he was called for traveling.

"How can you call it a travel when it's never been done?" he asked.

Maravich averaged 44 points in each of his three seasons at LSU. And he did it primarily as a long-distance shooter in an era before the 3-point line was introduced. He finished his college career with 3,667 points — one of his many NCAA records.

Herb White, who played against Maravich in college, said that guarding him was like "trying to catch a housefly in a really dark room full of refrigerators."

As word of his scoring exploits spread, photos of Maravich were plastered across

Pete Maravich is carried on the shoulders of his teammates after breaking the LSU scoring record.

newspapers and magazines across the country. His long, wind-swept hair fell just above a pair of sad eyes that brightened when they saw the back of the net. The floppy knee-high socks he wore became a fashion trend on the playgrounds. Most of his games went untelevised, and a mythos developed around Maravich.

As *Sports Illustrated*, which put Maravich on its cover before his junior season, described him, "Pistol Pete Maravich has the eyes of a lynx and the velvet grace of a panther."

By the time he was drafted, Maravich was a bona fide cult hero in the South. With the ABA's Carolina Cougars bidding for his services, the Atlanta Hawks ponied up $1.9 million in a five-year deal, rumored to be the largest contract in sports history at the time.

Maravich was Showtime long before Magic Johnson arrived on the scene, but both he and the fans were disappointed to learn that the Hawks wanted the Pistol to stay in its holster.

The Hawks had a roster loaded with established veterans. There was chatter that some teammates were jealous of his paycheck, which they deemed inflated by virtue of the fact that he was a white star trying to win over a mainly white fan base. Maravich grew suspicious that they were freezing him out.

He was still a potent scorer, but the ongoing battles between coach and teammates was taking a toll. In the summer of 1974, Atlanta traded Maravich to the expansion New Orleans Jazz ahead of their first season. Eager to attract a new fan base to its games in the massive Superdome, the Jazz brought Maravich back to Louisiana and gave up two players and four draft picks to get him.

Eight days before the start of the season, Pete's mother, Helen, committed suicide. A shaken Maravich reported for duty but averaged just 15 points during the first month of the season. New Orleans started the season 7-44. Once more, Maravich clashed with management, and he pleaded via the media for better teammates. He also complained about the way the media were portraying him: as the prolific scorer who couldn't win.

"I can't understand why everything is negative, negative, negative," he said in 1975. "I guess it says a lot about human nature that people would rather read about Pete Maravich the ball hog, not Pete Maravich the ball hawk."

Maravich had put so much into basketball but wasn't getting the love back. He was an icon at LSU who could do no wrong on the court, but in the NBA, they only seemed to notice his flaws.

He continued to score. In the 1976–77 season, Maravich put up 68 points against the New York Knicks — then a record for a guard — and led the league in scoring with 31.1 points per game. But the Jazz missed the playoffs, as they did in each of his six seasons in New Orleans.

"Pete Maravich knows he's bigger than the Jazz," said one NBA executive. "Pete thinks he's Smokey Robinson and the rest of the Jazz are the Miracles. The problem is that he's right."

But his former Hawks teammate, Lou Hudson, saw it differently. "He will be a loser, always, no matter what he does," he said. "That's his legacy. It never looked easy being Pete Maravich."

Things only worsened. By the 1979–80

Maravich unleashes a jumper in 1971.

Maravich blows past Walt Frazier in 1975.

season, he had been battling knee injuries for three years. The magic in his game was missing. His passion had pulled a disappearing act.

"There's a reason I never smile out there anymore," he said in 1978. "This is the coldest, flesh-peddlingest business around."

The Jazz placed Maravich on waivers partway through the season. He was picked up by the Boston Celtics. It was Larry Bird's rookie year, and Boston had the best record in the East.

"A championship would culminate my whole basketball life," he said after joining the team. "The other stuff — the trophies, plaques, scoring championships — you can throw it in the Mississippi River for all I care." But Maravich rarely left the bench as the Celtics lost in the second round.

Disappointed in his minimal role and the declining state of his knees, he retired following the 1979–80 season. He was fed up with having to please everybody but seemingly pleasing no one, least of all himself.

The next year, the Celtics won the title.

In retirement, Maravich became a recluse. It had been hard to ignore some troubling behavior at the tail end of his career, including drinking and unprovoked rants about everything from the meat industry to aliens.

As he retreated to his home in Metairie, Louisiana, he told his wife, Jackie, that he wanted to build a bomb shelter. He also said planned to draw a big circular landing pad on his roof with the message "Come take me."

When he walked away from the NBA, he distanced himself from the game of basketball entirely. He stopped playing — save for shooting around on a toy hoop with his infant sons — and removed all basketball-related memorabilia from his home.

Maravich became a born-again Christian to fill the void basketball once occupied.

In January of 1987, Maravich was inducted into the Hall of Fame. His father, Press, had taken ill with terminal cancer, but was there to learn the news. On April 15, 1987, Press passed away with Pete by his side. Before he died, Jackie overheard Pete whisper into his father's ear.

"I'll be with you soon," he said.

On January 5, 1988, Maravich flew from Louisiana to Pasadena, California, to appear on a national Christian radio program. He met with James Dobson, founder of a growing fundamentalist movement, who invited Maravich to play in his weekly pickup game at the church that morning.

For Dobson and his pals, who grew up rabid basketball fans, it would be the thrill of a lifetime to share the court with Pistol Pete. Maravich had avoided playing since his retirement eight years earlier. But he obliged.

After 20 minutes up and down the court, they took a break. "I feel great," Maravich announced. He headed to the water fountain and collapsed, dead. He was 40 years old.

An autopsy revealed that Maravich had suffered from heart failure as a result of a congenital heart defect. He had been born with only one coronary artery instead of two.

To mark its 50th anniversary in 1996, the NBA named its top 50 players of all time, and the honorees took the stage at halftime of the All-Star Game. Maravich was the only player no longer with us.

H-O-R-S-E

The NBA briefly experimented with an in-season H-O-R-S-E tournament. Pete Maravich was a finalist in 1978. Here are some of his moves:

- Tosses the ball from behind his back overtop his head, leaps and catches the ball in front of him mid-air and lays it in.
- Behind-the-back pass to himself from the right side of the hoop, catching the ball with his left hand and finishes the reverse layup.
- From the baseline, leaps inbound and lays it in off the glass with his back to the basket.
- Brings the ball behind-the-back, through-the-legs, and finishes a reverse layup.
- Palms the ball with his right hand and flicks his wrist upward for a funky-spin swish.

1971
DR. J

The ball bounces off the floor and disappears into Julius Erving's right hand. He takes one giant step toward the right side of the basket and readies for takeoff. It's the fourth quarter of Game 4 of the 1980 Finals between Erving's Philadelphia 76ers and the Los Angeles Lakers. Like countless others, Magic Johnson, the Lakers' star rookie, called Erving his favorite player growing up. Now he had a chance to watch the Doctor work his magic up close.

As Erving leaves the ground, he turns along the baseline for a layup. A swarm of Lakers defenders arrive, and one player tries to block the shot. Against anybody else, the timing would've been perfect. But this is Doc, the man gravity couldn't tame. He soars in the air across the baseline and doesn't stop until he's on the other side of the basket. He raises the ball up and around the outstretched arms of Lakers center Kareem Abdul-Jabbar, does the Sunday crossword and still has time to put enough funk on the ball that it spins against the glass and drops through the net.

"Should we ask him to do it again!?" Magic asks his teammates.

Dr. J's magic began with his hands — a pair of enormous paws that swallowed the rock like a pebble. Erving could palm the ball, leap into the air, show the ball on one side of the court and make it reappear on the other.

"I take my hands and I dip them in the paint and — bam — I begin to create," he once said. "But the hands are just an extension of my mind."

Those who followed Erving's exploits in the ABA were used to the Doctor's awe-inspiring flights. And it wasn't long before the rest of the world saw it too.

Doctor J was basketball's first real revolutionary figure. Rising to power in the late 1960s, he personified his era by challenging the norms. "Playing against Dr. J," Bill Walton said, "was Woodstock." His arrival is the dividing line between basketball's two major eras: Before Doctor and After Doctor.

Before he was the Doctor, Erving was Jewel — the nickname given to him early in his high school days on Long Island. Only his childhood friend, Archie, called him the Doctor, and it was in response to Erving jokingly calling his buddy the Professor for his encyclopedic knowledge of the basketball rule book. "If I'm a professor," Archie would ask, "then what are you? A doctor?"

In his college days, when he started showing up to play at New York City's Rucker Park, the streetball capital of the world, Erving was given more nicknames. They called him Little Hawk, a reference to '60s Rucker icon Connie "The Hawk" Hawkins. They called him Black Moses and the Claw, in reference to his oversized mitts. Erving didn't like any of them. "If you're going to call me anything," he said, "call me 'The Doctor.'"

Rucker Park was where the doctor operated. Dunks were still outlawed in college while Erving starred at the University of Massachusetts, and so it was at the hardtop that fans first saw him fly through the air, shape-shifting around defenders and dunking from impossible distances.

Still, he didn't realize his own powers. Erving knew he was good compared to those he grew up with, but it wasn't until he was invited to an Olympic camp along with the nation's top college stars that it dawned on him that he had a chance to be special. Erving led the team in scoring and rebounding. He was making an impression.

At 21 years of age, Erving was recruited by the ABA's Virginia Squires, who had heard rumblings of a bright, marketable kid with unheard-of talents. Erving had never heard of the team, but no matter. When they offered him a four-year, $125,000 contract, he left UMass early in 1971 to join the rebel league.

The ABA and Dr. J were a perfect fit. The league wanted its players to play without restraint, and Erving thrived when pushing the limits of what the body and mind are capable of on the court.

His high-flying moves captivated fans and opponents alike. He dunked the ball and scored in ways that had never been seen before. With his iconic look — the Afro, goatee, knee-high socks and swagger — Erving was the face of the ABA and was thrilled in the role. Among the league's cult following, the Doctor was a rock star.

It didn't hurt that he was also the league's best player. As a rookie, he averaged over 27 points per game, and led the ABA in scoring in three of the next four seasons. In 1973, he was traded to the New York Nets, which sent him home to Long Island. There, his star grew bigger than ever. Erving had signature sneakers, long before it was commonplace, and became the ABA's only crossover star, appearing on the cover of *Sports Illustrated*.

Julius Erving goes for the slam at the Great Western Forum in 1986.

It wasn't hard to see the appeal. He was gracious with the media, always gave time to his fans — particularly the kids, who looked up to him — and seemed intent on putting on a show. More important, he was cool. On the court, Dr. J was Superfly. He was Shaft. He was a bad motha-shut-your-mouth.

Aware and protective of his public image, it was a persona he left on the hardwood. "I didn't want to be Dr. J off the court." Away from basketball, Erving was a reserved man. His demeanor changed during his freshman year at college.

Erving's parents divorced when he was three, and his father passed away soon afterward. With his mother working full time to support her family, Erving was thrust into the role of father figure to his younger brother Marvin. In February 1969, Marvin visited the UMass campus to celebrate Julius's 19th birthday. While there, he complained about pain in his joints, and when he returned home, his health took a turn for the worse. Shortly after Erving's birthday, Marvin died. He was 16 years old. It was later discovered that he had been suffering from lupus.

Out of Marvin's death was born an intense focus for Erving. He had been endowed with rare physical gifts and was determined to put them to use. "I can't waste my life," he said in light of the fragility of those around him.

And he couldn't waste his talents. Erving was brilliant without knowing how. "One of my greatest challenges is to explain what I do," he said. "Did Beethoven have to explain how he wrote his Ninth Symphony?"

Nowhere was he more brilliant than during the 1976 ABA Finals. At 25 years old, Erving averaged 37.7 points against the Denver Nuggets and Bobby Jones, a future NBA teammate considered to be the best defender in either league.

Because of his growing celebrity and potential, the NBA saw Erving as a coveted tool to help grow the league and inspire a legion of new fans. When the league merged with the ABA in the summer of 1976, Erving's contract was sold to the Philadelphia 76ers, and he led the team all the way to the Finals in his first season, setting up a matchup with Bill Walton and the Portland Trail Blazers.

The Blazers won, and after two more years of playoff disappointment and a drop in his scoring totals, some began to question whether the Doctor had been of a specific time and place. In the NBA, Erving's game was tame compared to his ABA exploits of a few years earlier. Coaches employed zone defenses to block his access to the hoop, and by his own admission he was far too passive at times, conscious of not hogging the ball on a Sixers team chock-full of talented scorers. He even cut his famous Afro shorter. In March of '79, a *Sports Illustrated* story was published with the headline, "Hey, What's Up with the Doc?"

"Look. The ABA was a minor league," Celtics coach Red Auerbach said. "Over here, Erving is just another small forward."

Dr. J regained his form in time for the 1980–81 season. He was named the NBA's MVP, becoming the first non-center to win the award since Oscar Robertson in 1964. That same season, he became one of only two active players — joining Kareem Abdul-Jabbar — to be named to the NBA's 35th-anniversary team.

Still, six years had passed since the merger, and an NBA championship proved elusive. Erving and the 76ers returned to the Finals in 1982, but again lost to Johnson and the Lakers. A new opportunity came when another standout ABA alum, Moses Malone, joined Philadelphia that summer. The next season, Doc and the Sixers returned to the Finals for another rematch with the Lakers, and this time swept the series 4-0.

Erving was finally crowned an NBA champion, but a new day had dawned in the NBA. At 33 years old, he had become an elder statesman in a league being taken over by the likes of Magic, Larry, Michael, Barkley and Isiah Thomas — players who grew up idolizing the Doctor like so many of their generation.

He never returned to the Finals, and in the years leading up to his retirement he was determined to use his star power for good. He was an ambassador for the NBA, embracing the role that many stars who came before him had rejected. The Doctor appeared in commercials for every product under the sun, where his carefully worded vocabulary

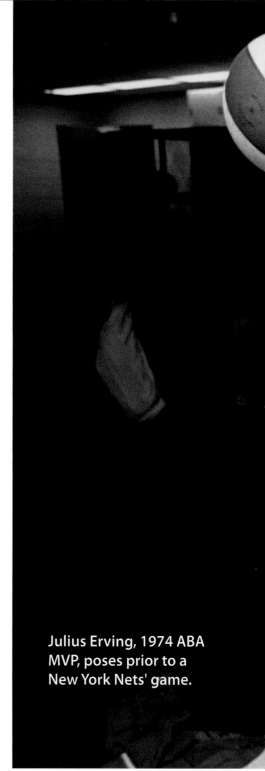

Julius Erving, 1974 ABA MVP, poses prior to a New York Nets' game.

and articulate manner were on full display. He was heavily involved with a large number of charitable foundations and spearheaded the NBA's support of the Special Olympics, where he coached the American team.

On the heels of an era in which the league, in the eyes of executives and advertisers, was deemed "too Black" for its mainly white audience, Erving almost single-handedly put an end to that stigma. As his career waned, he remained one of the NBA's most popular

figures and an undeniable role model. White parents wanted their kids to grow up to be like Doc — kind, intelligent, honorable.

"[Kids] come at me all the time, yelling, 'Hey, Doc! Hey, Dr. J!' That's cool," he said. "I want them to see I am a hardworking, successful Black man."

Ahead of the 1986–87 campaign, a 36-year-old Erving announced that it would be his last. He played 16 seasons of pro ball and was an all-star in every one of them.

His final season doubled as a farewell tour staged in the same arenas across America where he'd brought fans to their feet so many times. Against the Nets, the hometown team he once envisioned playing his entire career for, Erving was brought to tears as the crowd gave him a hero's send-off. In Los Angeles, they brought a rocking chair to center court at the Forum. Kareem gave Erving a touching eulogy. He talked about how Erving inspired a generation. How he changed the

game forever. How the class and creativity with which he approached his craft would never be forgotten.

Watching from the sidelines, Magic Johnson likely recalled Erving's unbelievable reverse layup in the 1980 Finals. If he'd had the microphone, Magic would have wanted to ask: How? How did you do it? *How???*

As the Doctor once said: "It's easy, once you learn how to fly."

1972
33 STR8

The familiar sounds of balls bouncing and sneakers squeaking against the hardwood rang through a Hawaii gymnasium during the Los Angeles Lakers training camp in the autumn of 1971.

Bill Sharman, 45 years old and embarking on his first season as head coach of the iconic franchise, surveyed the court and was pleased with what he saw — what coach wouldn't ?

Jerry West, a former NBA scoring leader and an All-Star in each of the previous 11 seasons, practiced free throws; Elgin Baylor,

the 10-time All-NBA First Team member and Los Angeles's first basketball star, weaved through imaginary defenders en route to the hoop; Gail Goodrich hoisted jump shots; Wilt Chamberlain, the dominant big man (who showed up in flip-flops) talked Xs and Os. "Muscle memory!" the new coach preached in a raspy voice weakened by ulcers.

As had been the case in his playing days, when he won four championships between 1957 and 1961 as part of the Boston Celtics, wherever Sharman the coach went,

success followed. The year before, he had led the ABA's Utah Stars to a title, and previously did the same with the Cleveland Pipers of the since-defunct American Basketball League.

But in Los Angeles he was inheriting an aging team seemingly on the decline, star-studded as it might be.

With 36 combined seasons under their belts, West, Chamberlain, and Baylor — 33, 35 and 37 years old, respectively — were all on the wrong side of their prime years. All

Wilt Chamberlain looks for Gail Goodrich during a 1972 playoff game.

three had recently suffered serious leg injuries, with West and Baylor requiring invasive surgery the year before, which contributed to the team missing the Finals for the first time in four years.

In total, the Lakers had been to the NBA Finals in seven of the last nine seasons, but they'd fallen short of a title each and every time. The physical effects of those grinding playoff runs, coupled with the emotional pain of losing, was taking a toll on the ultra-competitive West in particular.

The '72 Lakers were on their last legs — at least that's how Lakers owner Jack Kent Cooke felt when he decided to replace Joe Mullaney with Sharman after two seasons.

"Now, Bill, I don't expect you to win anything," Cooke told Sharman when he was hired. Sharman, he said, was brought in to rebuild the Lakers and usher in a new era of title hopes.

But on the morning of October 16, 1971 — as his team assembled a whopping eight and a half hours before tip-off, per the coaches' orders — Sharman had other plans. If he could get his veteran roster to embrace change and a new mandate to run, he knew his roster still had enough left in the tank to accomplish something special. But not even he could have anticipated what was to come.

The morning shootaround was one of the first changes Sharman introduced, forcing his players up and out of bed early on the days of road games and giving them an opportunity to loosen their muscles and get a feel for the arena's dimensions. It was unheard of for teams to assemble so early on game days, but Sharman himself had done it through his playing career (often to the dismay of his own teammates) and had made his teams in the ABA and ABL adopt the habit. So the Lakers would too.

Today the shootaround has become a part of each NBA team's game-day routine — just one of a number of habits, including such basics as healthy eating and regular training, that Sharman introduced.

Still, not everybody was on board with the new morning ritual, or so the story went.

Chamberlain, never shy to speak his mind and a notorious night owl to boot, supposedly drew a hard line and told Sharman he came to the arena once each day — and the coach could decide when.

"It's a great story," Sharman said, "but it never happened. I talked to Wilt right before camp and he said, 'You know, Bill, I usually don't get out of bed until noon. But if you think it will help, I'll go along — if we win.'"

There was already a degree of respect between the two, who had competed against one another early in Chamberlain's NBA career. They were even teammates during the summer pro-am games held in the Catskill Mountains of Upstate New York.

Chamberlain was familiar with Sharman's trademark intensity, which hid beneath a pleasant, upbeat demeanor; as a player, he'd been known as much for his shooting prowess as his willingness to throw a punch to get his point across.

A multisport athlete, Sharman also played baseball in the Brooklyn Dodgers farm system during the NBA off-season; he was in the dugout when Bobby Thomson hit his 1951 pennant-clinching home run, also known as "the shot heard 'round the world." But he couldn't crack the Dodger lineup, and in 1955 he turned full time to basketball.

Sharman's meticulousness bordered on obsessive; he was known to pack and unpack his socks and underwear in the same specific way when his teams were on the road. But this attention to detail worked. Sharman was considered the NBA's premier shooter and is the only player to win seven free-throw titles in a career. When the league announced its 25th-anniversary team in 1971, Sharman was among the 10 players selected.

As both player and coach, Sharman practiced what he preached: the importance of routine and the value of practice. And as the 1971–72 season began, that helped earn the ears of his Lakers players. A 4-0 start to the season certainly helped.

The Lakers were buying what their coach was selling. Chamberlain, who famously told former Lakers coach Butch van Breda Kolff that his team was "too old to run," was more engaged than he had been in years. He embraced his role initiating Sharman's fast-break offense.

Long gone were the days of averaging 50 points in a season — Wilt would fail to top 20 points per game for the first time in his career — but the 7-foot-1, 275-pound giant was still a game-changing force and led the league with over 19 rebounds per game in '71–72.

West, hampered by his persistent knee issues, remained a potent scorer and led the NBA in assists in his first season under Sharman's offense.

Perhaps no player flourished more than Gail Goodrich, who was given the green

light from his coach during training camp to shoot at will.

The Lakers star who wasn't thriving? Baylor, the elder statesman and team captain.

An Achilles tendon tear had cost the 37-year-old all but two games the season before, and it was clear the one-time high flyer had lost his bounce. He had earned his spot in the starting lineup on reputation — by then, he was the league's third all-time scorer — but after averaging 11.5 points in his final 11 games, it was clear that Baylor could hardly contribute like he used to.

A career spent bouncing like a pinball through the paint during the NBA's most physical era had caught up to the 13-year veteran. On November 4, 1971, nine games into the season, Baylor abruptly retired.

"I was depriving Jim McMillian of playing time," he said of the second-year forward Sharman inserted into the starting lineup in his place.

In their first game without Baylor, Goodrich scored 31 points, Chamberlain grabbed 25 rebounds and the Lakers beat the Baltimore Bullets, 110–106. The following night, West scored 28, while McMillian added 26 in another win. Soon enough, a month had passed and the team still hadn't lost. On December 12, the Lakers beat the Atlanta Hawks, breaking the league record of 20 straight wins. Another month passed before they lost a game.

In total, the win streak lasted 33 games, a staggering record that remains untouched.

In full command of Sharman's fast-paced offense, the Lakers scored 123 points per game and beat opponents by an average of 16 points during that stretch.

His team was flying high, but Sharman's vocal cord issues were worsening. His temporary solution — communicating via megaphone — wasn't helping. "The doctors told me that if I didn't rest my voice during the streak, I would cause permanent damage," he later said, "but how could I stop during such an incredible time?"

As Chamberlain said, "The man gave up his voice for us to win."

The team finished the season with a franchise-record 69 wins and steamrolled their way through the playoffs, losing just three games across three rounds. In a Finals rematch with the New York Knicks, who had beaten the Lakers in the 1970 championship series, Los Angeles made easy work of their cross-country rivals, 4-1.

It was the Lakers' first title since moving to LA from Minneapolis. After seven tries, West had finally won a title, although it would always feel bittersweet to have done so without Baylor, who had been by his side for each Finals defeat.

Chamberlain, who had been named captain following Baylor's retirement, was named MVP of the Finals, while Sharman was honored as the NBA's Coach of the Year.

The following season, each NBA team instituted its own morning shootarounds.

Sharman's coaching career ended early. By 1976 his voice issues had worsened, forcing a move off the bench and into the front office, where, as GM, he played a major hand in drafting James Worthy and Magic Johnson, setting the stage for the Lakers dynasty.

In 2004 — 28 years after his induction as a player — Sharman was elected to the Hall of Fame as a coach, becoming just the third Hall of Famer to enter as both, alongside John Wooden and Lenny Wilkens. He remains the only coach to win a title in three different professional leagues.

But it's the '72 championship that he will be remembered for most.

In the decades that followed, until his death in 2013, you'd spot Sharman driving around Redondo Beach in his silver Jaguar sedan. You couldn't miss it. The license plate read: 33 STR8.

WIN STREAKS

1.	Lakers	33
2.	Warriors	28
3.	Heat	27
4.	Rockets	22
5.	Bucks	20

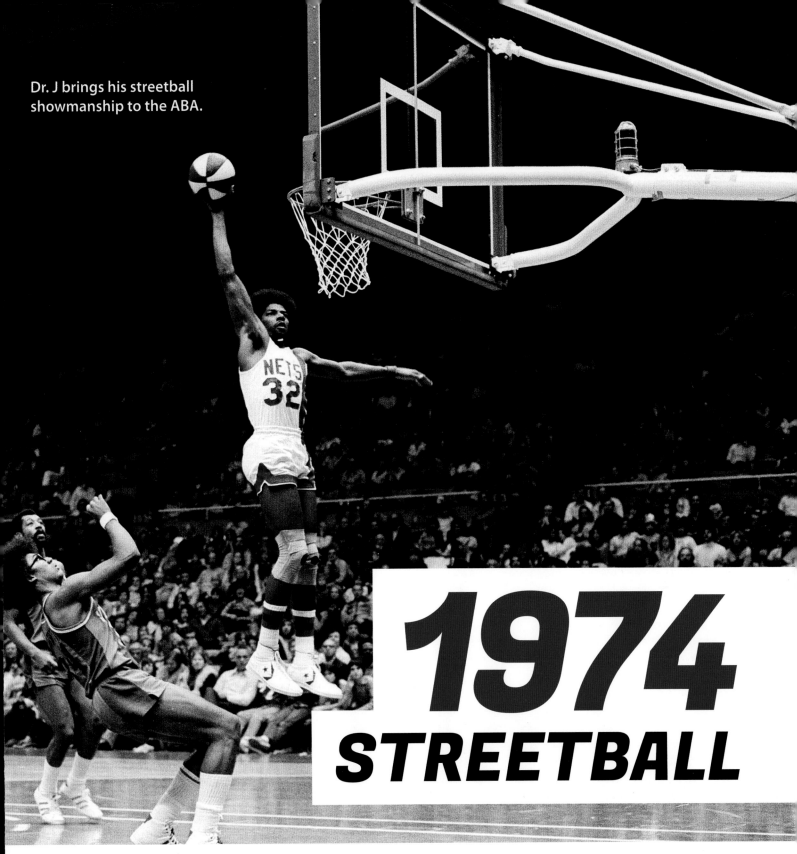

Dr. J brings his streetball showmanship to the ABA.

1974
STREETBALL

"Holcombe Rucker Basketball Courts," reads the sign at 155th Street and Frederick Douglass Boulevard in New York City's Harlem neighborhood. Inside a wrought-iron fence is a well-worn slab of concrete where a generation of NBA stars were born. It is where players like Dr. J were encouraged to create a new style that reshaped the pro game forever.

Nobody drew a crowd to the Rucker courts quite like Julius Erving. He brought the whole neighborhood out to watch him play. Fans in Harlem would climb onto the rooftop of the adjacent public school, gaze through the windows of the nearby Polo Grounds housing project, and hang off tree limbs in order to catch a glimpse of the Doctor in person.

It was under the summer sun where fans got the best version of the Dr. J experience. His Afro seemed even bigger, his strides longer and his hang time at an all-time high. It was also where the inventive moves that made him famous in the NBA were born.

"It had to do with the environment and the freedom," said Erving, "and the fact that it was showtime and the shackles were being taken off."

Free from the restriction of Xs and Os, players like Doc were granted the license to create. The bright blue asphalt courts were their canvas, the cradle dunks, free-throw-line leaps and gravity-defying up-and-unders their art.

Holcombe Rucker was a Harlem-based educator and recreation director for New York City. In 1950 he established a children's basketball tournament at the local courts.

"If you want to sound small, you say he was just a guy in charge of a playground," says Tom "Satch" Sanders, the Celtics Hall of Famer who first played at the Rucker tournament as a 16-year-old in 1953.

In 1954 Rucker established a pro-am division, and the event helped turn the courts into not only an incubator for talent, but an important community hub. For African Americans, it became a place of representation at a time when the NBA was still very much a white man's league.

In those days, every All-NBA honoree was white, and black players had to fit within an unofficial quota system. But on the asphalt courts they ruled the game. Players like the St. Louis Hawks' Cal Ramsey, one of just two African Americans on his team, and Harlem Globetrotter Carl Green were regulars.

Soon the playground became a popular stop for more stars, like Wilt "The Big Dipper" Chamberlain, who was already a streetball legend. As a 17-year-old, Chamberlain worked as a bellhop at a resort in the Catskill Mountains named Kutsher's. The resort's athletic director, Red Auerbach, organized summer games with some of the highest-profile players around.

On the famous Harlem court, Wilt continued to wow crowds with his feats of strength and athleticism. As one story goes, he dunked the ball so hard, it bounced off the concrete and over the fence onto 155th Street.

But a rising generation of New York–bred stars were beginning to make names for themselves on Rucker's courts. Erving, Kareem Abdul-Jabbar (then Lew Alcindor) and Nate "Tiny" Archibald were among the crowd favorites. While he was still in high school, Brooklyn's Connie "The Hawk" Hawkins became one of the most popular players in the city thanks to his summer performances. In one game, the teenager pinned Chamberlain's shot against the backboard. It was as if the crowd had just witnessed David toppling Goliath. On the next play, Wilt dunked on Hawkins's mug — you know, to reestablish the hierarchy.

Streetball's prominence wasn't exclusive to New York. In the 60s and 70s the city game was alive and well across the United States. In Washington, D.C., for example, Earl "The Pearl" Monroe made a name for himself, honing an endless stream of one-of-a-kind dribble moves and tricky layups — like Dr. J without the wings. Monroe and Baltimore Bullets teammate Archie Clark (nicknamed Shake and Bake) were the first players to bring the "crossover" move to the NBA.

In his hometown of Seattle, Elgin Baylor hosted annual pickup games that introduced local fans to a new side of their favorite NBA stars. Chamberlain would often show up, dazzling the crowd and leaving them in awe. But, as Baylor is quick to remind, Elgin's teams always won.

It wasn't long before you could recognize the influence of streetball on NBA courts. You could see it in the way players dribbled, improvised in midair, and generally tried to bring fans out of their seats.

In 1974 the City of New York officially renamed the Harlem public courts as Rucker Park. Its legacy as a gathering place for the top basketballers around continued into the 90s, when the likes of Allen Iverson, Kobe Bryant and Vince Carter all put on show-stopping performances (by now, they were all caught on videotape).

In 2011, the NBA lockout helped prompt a resurgence at places like Rucker. The league's top stars regularly took part in streetball games around the country, sporting matching shirts that read "Basketball Never Stops." In one of the most impressive showings in the history of the famous courts, Kevin Durant showed up for a game at Rucker Park and dropped 66 points. A jam-packed crowd, just like the ones that came out to see the Doctor operate forty years earlier, swarmed the court.

"It was a quick burst of joy that I hadn't felt on a basketball court before," Durant said. "It was amazing."

Streetball is alive and well in the NBA. You can see it today with every crossover; with every flashy dunk; every time a player hits a 3-pointer, turns to the crowd and waves three fingers in the air.

The playground game rewarded showmanship and creativity. Entertain the crowd, and you'll be an icon.

"It was the first time I experienced where two points was actually worth more than two points," Julius Erving said. "Two points might have been worth a dinner, a date . . . if somebody put on a pretty good show, they could walk off the court a winner."

AND-1

Streetball's influence returned to pro hoops in the early 2000s with the rise in popularity of the And-1 Mixtape series, a collection of videotapes that showcased some of the most inventive players on the hardtop. Once again, the killer crossovers and wild passes from the playground infiltrated NBA games. One notable And-1 legend, Rafer Alston aka Skip-To-My-Lou, carved out an NBA career after growing his legend on the streets.

1976
THE DUNK CONTEST

Dominique "The Human Highlight Film" Wilkins dunks during the 1985 dunk contest.

Julius Erving walked away from the basket, counting his steps as if measuring the distance.

"I had to get my stride just right," he would recall years later. "Everything had to be perfect for it to work."

It was halftime at the 1976 ABA All-Star Game in Denver, and Erving was the final contestant in pro basketball's first-ever slam-dunk contest.

The dunk contest was tailor-made for Erving, who became an instant superstar in just three seasons in the ABA thanks to his gravity-defying jams. But what Dr. J had in store on this occasion was something fans had never seen.

Erving had told a teammate what he was planning, and before the contest, the All-Stars placed bets on whether or not he could pull it off. Despite a tiring first half of action, none of them headed to the locker room. Who would miss this?

"It was like we all were back on the playground," recalled center Dan Issel, "watching this shoot-out to see who really was the master of the dunk."

As Erving paced away from the hoop, stopping just short of the top of the far key, the crowd was delirious. He turned around and, like any great showman, paused for effect. The crowd went silent.

Dr. J took off down the runway and planted his left foot on the free-throw line,

15 feet from the basket, then soared through the air, his Afro blowing in the wind.

By the time he landed, any notions of what we thought the human body was capable of had gone out the window. The contest was a success — nothing in sports could showcase the blend of creativity and pure athletic ability quite like it.

Unsurprisingly, the slam-dunk contest went on to become a staple of the NBA's annual All-Star festivities and served as a launch pad for the likes of Michael Jordan, Dominique Wilkins, Shawn Kemp, Kobe Bryant, Vince Carter, and Dwight Howard.

Of course, nobody in the ABA could have predicted any of that.

As Erving soared through the skies, the ABA was barely fending off extinction. Three teams had folded at the beginning of the 1975-76 season, leaving only seven.

But the All-Star Game was to be televised to a national audience. The league was desperate to drum up fan interest and potentially raise the stakes in merger negotiations with the rival NBA.

The idea for the dunk contest had been born out of the ABA's pregame layup lines, where players would take turns rocking the rim. In the empty arenas of the ABA, it wasn't hard to notice that the fans often seemed more amped by the warm-up dunks than the games themselves.

Five participants took part in the inaugural contest — Erving, David Thompson, Larry Kenon, George Gervin and Artis Gilmore. But everybody knew it would come down to Dr. J and Thompson, the man they called "Skywalker." Once Thompson amazed the crowd with the first recorded 360-degree slam dunk, it was Dr. J's turn.

For his first dunk, he dunked two balls at once. Next, came the free-throw line dunk. On his third, he grabbed the rim with his left arm and ferociously dunked the ball with his right. And for the finale, he uncorked the "Iron Cross" dunk, extending his arms out wide and dunking the ball behind him as he faced away from the hoop.

Sports Illustrated called that inaugural dunk contest "The best halftime entertainment

since the restroom." It was a feather in the cap for the ABA (its latest innovation), and it contributed to the Legend of Dr. J. After the merger, however, the NBA dropped the ball. In 1977 the league turned the dunk contest into an awkward, season-long tournament. By '78 it was done away with altogether.

The dunk contest made its return in 1984, with a 34-year-old Erving taking center stage once more. He recreated his iconic free-throw-line dunk but lost to Larry Nance, who spiked two balls through at once — a twist on another famous slam from Dr. J's 1976 repertoire.

The event may have reached its height in 1988 when Jordan, who paid tribute to Erving during his first contest appearance three years earlier, battled Atlanta Hawks forward Dominique Wilkins — the most gifted leaper in the game versus its most violent dunker.

The two traded perfect scores until Jordan took off for a free-throw dunk of his own, with more hang time than his predecessor. The image of Jordan flying through the air, his legs splaying out as he hauled the ball back, became the famous logo of the Jordan brand, recognized around the world.

The only duel that has come close to Jordan vs. Dominique came in 2016, when Aaron Gordon and Zach LaVine raised the bar. In a display of the basic principles of evolution, LaVine had a pair of free-throw dunks of his own: one where he passed the ball between his legs after takeoff, and another where he windmilled the ball.

In the 90s the contest faded again. It was thrown to the curb again in 1998 and '99, but returned in time for the greatest single contest performance of all time: Vince Carter in Oakland in 2000.

Carter had grown up analyzing tapes of past dunk contests like a lawyer studying for the bar.

"I used to think about Dee Brown pumping his shoes," Carter said. "I looked at the dunk contest like this: How can you get the fans in your pocket? Eating out of your hand?"

The answer, apparently, was by unleashing a series of dunks the world had never seen. His first was an impossible-seeming

reverse-360, followed by a 360 windmill. For one dunk, he jumped high enough to be able to jam the ball through the hoop — and his entire forearm with it. For his finale, of course, a free-throw-line dunk.

As he stepped off the court, the first person to greet him was Erving.

"If you know me, you know that Dr. J is one of my heroes," said Carter. "You win the contest, you're holding your trophy, you walk off and the first person you see is your hero? I mean, it doesn't get any better."

It didn't get much better for the dunk contest, either. There were other standout performers — Desmond Mason, Jason Richardson, Nate Robinson — but the league tinkered with the format (at one point, it even introduced a wheel players would spin as if they were on a game show, the "winner" having to recreate an iconic past dunk).

Eventually the game's top players stopped taking part. With so many ways to build your brand, who needed a dunk contest to become a star? Why risk injury — or worse, embarrassment? In response, the NBA rebranded the contest a "rising stars" event featuring young incoming talent.

But it's not hard to remember when the dunk contest meant something. If the ABA had thought of it sooner, maybe it would still be around today.

POST-VINCE TOP-5

1. Aaron Gordon one-handed 360 mascot-handoff ('16)
2. Zach LaVince through-the-legs from the free-throw line ('16)
3. Jason Richardson's through-the-legs one-handed reverse ('02)
4. Aaron Gordon beneath the legs ('16)
5. Andre Igoudala behind-the-basket reverse ('06)

Michael Jordan dunks the ball during the Slam-Dunk championship on Feb. 6, 1988.

1976
THE MERGER

The 1972 exhibition was billed as Supergame II — a rematch of a game between NBA and ABA All-Stars played the previous year. Held at the Nassau Coliseum on Long Island, the game pitted the NBA establishment against the up-and-coming talent from the rebel league.

It certainly lived up to the name.

All told, 12 future Hall of Famers shared the court. The NBA was represented by the likes of Wilt Chamberlain, John Havlicek, Oscar Robertson, Paul Silas and Nate Archibald. The ABA countered with Artis Gilmore, Dan Issel, Willie Wise, and a 22-year-old Julius Erving — after just one pro season, already on his way to becoming the most popular figure in the sport.

The leagues had played one another several times. NBA team owners welcomed the chance to have their fans pay tickets to watch the likes of Dr. J wow crowds with his aerial attack. And the ABA was eager for any chance to show that their players were every bit as talented as their more famous counterparts.

Supergame II came down to the wire. The ABA brought the game within two thanks to a Rick Barry jumper. Free throws from Robertson sealed a 106–104 victory.

The NBA may have won, but playing on their biggest stage yet, the ABA's stars shone.

The ABA found itself on life support as the 70s marched along, despite acquiring such talent as Erving, Moses Malone and George "The Iceman" Gervin. By 1975 the league had lost roughly $50 million since its inception in '67. Its franchises were folding faster than a poker player caught bluffing.

When the 1975–76 ABA season wrapped, the league was down to seven teams — six, once the Virginia Squires folded that summer.

ABA officials had long been pushing for a merger with the NBA — in fact, it was a goal from day one. But the NBA had little interest in obtaining the ABA's teams. It did, however, want its players. Badly. NBA commissioner Larry O'Brien and his lead counsel, David Stern, envisioned a future in which Erving donned a Lakers or Knicks jersey and sold out NBA arenas across America.

What's more, they had just seen such generational talents as David Thompson, drafted first overall by the Atlanta Hawks in 1975, spurn the NBA in favor of a higher payout with the ABA's Denver Nuggets. It was a trend O'Brien wanted to put to an end — now.

But the ABA owners put up a fight. They hired 35-year-old Dave DeBusschere as commissioner — the league's seventh in eight years. DeBusschere had been a key member of the 1970 and '73 champion New York Knicks and had even represented the NBA in the Supergame series a few years earlier. DeBusschere was an established "NBA guy," and the ABA team owners felt his presence in the room during negotiations would be an asset.

On August 5, 1976, a deal was made: the NBA would inherit four ABA franchises — the San Antonio Spurs, Denver Nuggets, Indiana Pacers, and New York Nets. Two ABA teams, the Kentucky Colonels and Spirits of St. Louis, were shuttered.

In San Antonio, fans celebrated in the streets — their beloved Spurs were in the NBA. But team ownership was more reserved. "This is no time to break out the champagne," owner Angelo Drossos warned, "because this isn't a good deal. We paid dearly to get in."

Each of the four ABA franchises paid $3.2 million to join the NBA. The Nets had to pay an additional $4.8 million (over a 10-year period) to the Knicks for infringing on their territory. In lieu of payment, the cash-strapped Nets offered the Knicks Julius Erving. They turned it down, and so the Nets sold their star to the Philadelphia 76ers for $3 million.

The surviving ABA clubs were allowed to retain their players, while the rest of the ABA's talent would be made available to NBA clubs in a dispersal draft — the Chicago Bulls selected center Artis Gilmore with the first pick. ABA teams weren't permitted to receive any television revenue for three years and were forced to sit out the 1976 draft.

One stipulation the NBA insisted on was that the arrangement wouldn't be referred to publicly as a merger — instead, it was to be considered an expansion. The merger — or expansion, or whatever you wish to call it — brought the NBA's total number of teams to 22. It also infused the league with the talent it had long coveted.

The impact was immediate. The Portland Trail Blazers traded for Atlanta's pick in the dispersal draft to select power forward Maurice Lucas, who teamed up with Bill Walton to create a killer frontcourt that carried the

Spencer Haywood drives around Craig Raymond in the ABA playoffs in 1970.

Blazers all the way to the Finals that year — where they met Erving and the new-look 76ers. Five of the 10 starters competing for the 1977 championship had been on ABA rosters the year before.

Ten ABA alumni were named to the 1977 All-Star Game, while four ABAers finished in the top 10 in scoring their first year in the NBA — with Pacers guard Billy Knight second only to Pistol Pete Maravich, and David Thompson fourth.

Meanwhile, the NBA adopted the ABA's 3-point line as well as elements of the gravity-defying, fan-friendly style of play.

As for the two ABA franchises that didn't make it to the NBA, it's hardly a tragedy. Kentucky owner John Y. Brown, who made his fortune by growing another franchise, Kentucky Fried Chicken, was paid $3 million by the four surviving ABA teams. He wound up purchasing the NBA's Buffalo Braves for $1.5 million later that year.

But nobody made it out better than the St. Louis owners, brothers Daniel and Ozzie Silna. Instead of accepting the same $3 million offer that Brown received, they negotiated a different — and ultimately, brilliant — settlement.

First of all, they would be paid for each of their players chosen in the dispersal draft,

which wound up netting them $2.2 million. But more important, the brothers would also receive a one-seventh share of media revenue from each of the four surviving ABA franchises "in perpetuity."

It's considered the savviest business deal in sports history. Over the decades that followed, the Silna brothers earned an estimated $300 million. In 2014, after trying for years, the NBA finally put an end to the deal, settling with the Silnas for a reported $500 million. Brown got $3 million for his team; Daniel and Ozzie pocketed $800 million.

In 1976, ABA owners felt they'd been fleeced in the merger. The $3.2 million fee to join the NBA was considered outrageous, and they only accepted the terms because they had such little leverage.

But as the years progressed and NBA basketball became big business, franchise values soared higher than Dr. J. In 2017 the Houston Rockets were purchased for $2.2 billion. In 2018 each of the 30 NBA teams was valued at over $1 billion.

In 2019, the Brooklyn Nets (the franchise that was forced to sell its best player because it couldn't afford the $480,000 annual fee it was ordered to pay the crosstown Knicks in 1976) were sold for a reported $2.35 billion.

Not bad for a gimmick league.

1977
THE CURSE OF BILL WALTON

The fast break was Portland's bread and butter, and the Trail Blazers executed it to perfection. They had all the ingredients — an innovative coach who preached ball movement, a selfless roster committed to his game plan, and the perfect center to facilitate his vision.

Bill Walton, 6-foot-11 and 250 pounds, entered the league as the No. 1 pick in 1974 and was anointed the face of the NBA.

By 1976–77 he would officially assume the mantle, carrying Portland to a Finals matchup against the league's newest superstar, Julius Erving, and the Philadelphia 76ers.

The 1977 championship series was a culture clash, in terms of personal and playing style. The Sixers were brash, ultra-athletic and overpowering. With Dr. J, George McGinnis and a 23-year-old specimen in Darryl Dawkins, Philly rarely passed up an opportu-

Bill Walton blocks this shot by Dan Issel during a game in Denver, April 20, 1977.

nity to dunk all over the competition.

On the Trail Blazers, however, you couldn't count on one hand the number of players who were capable of dunking a basketball. They relied on quick passes to get open layups and worshiped at the altar of team basketball.

But it wasn't always like that.

Walton's first two seasons in Portland were marred by injuries to his right foot — "The problem has not been exactly diagnosed," he said, "it's just that I have a lot of pain in my foot when I play" — and what he perceived as a slow, constrained style.

Walton knew he could unleash Portland's stagnant offense. A record-setting rebounder in college, his passing instincts set him apart from other big men in the game. He could corral a rebound on the defensive glass and, with pinpoint accuracy, rocket the ball up the court to ignite the fast break.

He was a student of the game and a proven winner. In college at UCLA, his teams went 30–0 in each of his first two seasons, capped by NCAA championships. In the 1973 title game against Memphis State, Walton scored a finals-record 44 points, shooting 21-of-22 from the field.

UCLA's win streak with Walton in the lineup was eventually snapped at 73 games, but stretching back to high school in his hometown of La Mesa, California, Walton's personal win streak totaled 126 games.

At UCLA he followed in the footsteps of another legendary center, Kareem Abdul-Jabbar (then Lew Alcindor). But in Portland, joining a franchise that had yet to reach the postseason in its four years of existence, he was blazing his own trail.

In his second season, Walton managed to play 51 games and averaged 13.4 rebounds, but Portland finished dead last in its division. In the summer of 1976, the team fired head coach Lenny Wilkens and replaced him with Jack Ramsay — or as he was better known, "Dr. Jack," for his Ph.D. in education.

It was Walton who drew the 51-year old Ramsay to the role. In the talented young center, Ramsay saw the perfect player for the style of basketball he wanted the Blazers to accept. In Ramsay, Walton saw a coach who shared his obsession for winning and perfecting one's craft. Each saw in the other an equal whose passion for the finer points of the game was as evident on the practice court as during real games.

That summer the ABA and NBA merged and the Blazers got another boost with the addition of Maurice Lucas, one of the ABA's most feared and most powerful forwards. Portland selected Lucas second overall in the dispersal draft, giving Walton a complementary player in the frontcourt whose physicality would more than make up for Walton's. The two were also devout vegetarians who sprouted a meaningful friendship.

The 1976–77 season wasn't without its growing pains, and it took a six-game winning streak at the close of the regular season to qualify for the playoffs.

The '77 Finals between Portland and Philadelphia was a promoter's dream: Dr. J vs. Dr. Jack. Walton vs. Erving. The high-octane Blazers vs. the high-flying Sixers. While it was easy for television networks to pit Walton against Erving — and therefore, white against black — both men represented the counterculture that had arisen in the 60s.

Walton, with his red locks often tied in a bandana, looked like he had just come to the arena straight from a Grateful Dead concert. In college he was arrested at an anti-Vietnam rally and would smoke pot after games to recover and to slow his mind from obsessively replaying each possession.

Erving, his iconic Afro swaying with each never-before-seen leaping move to the hoop, personified the modern game more than anybody. The verticality, the flair, the individuality. Dr. J was hip. He was cool. He embodied the evolution of basketball.

Heading into the series, Ramsay implored his players to try to stop Erving from dunking the ball. He can score points, the coach said. That's inevitable. But his electrifying dunks — celebrated by fans both at home and on the road — tended to change the entire tone of a game and turn the momentum in Philly's favor.

On the first play in Game 1, Erving took off for a soaring windmill slam. The 76ers led virtually the entire game and cruised to a win in front of a home crowd. They took a 2-0 series lead into Portland.

In Game 3, the Trail Blazers erupted for 42 points in the fourth quarter, sparked by a game-changing sequence early in the frame. Up by 4 points, Walton tipped in an alley-oop over top of Dawkins. The 76ers inbounded the ball, but it was intercepted by Blazers guard Dave Twardzik. Walton, wide

open underneath the hoop, signaled to him, jumping up and down and waving his arms in the air like a kid trying to get his parents' attention. Erving ran back toward the basket and thought about jumping, but it was too late. He looked up to see Walton jamming home another alley-oop with two hands.

An injured Bill Walton watches his team from the bench in 1976.

In Game 4, fueled in part by their rabid fan base, the Blazers got out to a 19–4 run to start the game and never looked back, tying the series at two games each. They would win the next game as well.

In Game 6, playing at home, the Trail Blazers had a chance to win it all. But in the first half, Dr. J set the tone, running the length of the court and taking off a step inside the free-throw line, on a collision course with Walton. Walton, who led the league with 3.2 blocks per game that season, jumped to meet Erving in midair, but was powerless as he ended up on another Dr. J poster.

But in the fourth quarter, Portland kicked it into high gear. The Trail Blazers worked the fast break and managed to funnel Erving toward Walton on the right side of the hoop, making the 76ers star work for his buckets. Undeterred, Erving finished the game with 40 points, but only one of his teammates finished with more than 10.

On the final possession, with the Sixers down 2 points, Walton swatted a missed jumper away from the rim and into the open court as the clock expired.

"All for One Sure Beats One for All," read a *Sports Illustrated* headline.

When the buzzer sounded, the Portland fans swarmed the court. Walton took off his shirt and flung it into the crowd. "If I had caught the shirt," Maurice Lucas said, "I would have eaten it. Bill's my hero."

Walton, who led all players not only in rebounds but also assists during the postseason, finished the game with 23 points, 20 rebounds, 8 blocks and 7 assists. He was named Finals MVP.

"Dr. J is incredibly tough," he said after Game 6, "but we are not into stardom here."

Portland had the makings of the NBA's next great dynasty, the successor to the great Celtics teams of the 60s, with Walton primed for the role of Bill Russell. The season after their championship, the Trail Blazers got off to a record 50–10 start to the season. That's when Walton went down again.

Continually hampered by his foot troubles, he was given an injection to numb the pain before a game on April 18, 1978. The bone in his foot split in half that night, and Walton would never be the same player again. "I spent the next eight years of my life chasing the dream," he said.

He was still named the NBA's Most Valuable Player in '78, but without Walton in the lineup, Portland was bounced from the first round of the playoffs. He was forced to sit out the entire next season as well.

The relationship between Walton and the Blazers — specifically the medical staff — soured. They disagreed over everything from diagnoses to recovery timelines. More than anything, Walton wanted to play. When the team acquiesced and allowed him, the center felt betrayed when he would inevitably injure himself again.

In 1979 Walton wanted out and joined the San Diego Clippers, his hometown team. He signed an unprecedented seven-year, $7

million contract, and the Clippers' first game that season against the Los Angeles Lakers — which also happened to mark the debut of Magic Johnson — was scheduled for national television. Walton didn't play.

He made it into just 14 games that season and was forced to sit out the next two seasons entirely. He only appeared in 169 games across six years with the Clippers, his once-gaudy stats declining with each injury-plagued campaign. Although he would briefly resuscitate his career as a backup center for the 1986 champion Boston Celtics, Walton was a shell of the dynamic force he once was.

The injuries continued to follow him after retirement: foot surgeries, ankle fusions and spinal problems. In 1990, following another foot procedure, he admitted he could no longer keep track of the number of times a scalpel had been taken to his cursed feet. At least 30, he guessed.

Bill Walton follows a game from the sidelines in 1974.

"I'd do anything to be able to play basketball again," he said in his retirement. "But you can't be bitter. I have too many good memories."

MOST GAMES PLAYED

1.	Robert Parish	1611
2.	Kareem Abdul-Jabbar	1560
3.	Vince Carter	1541
4.	Dirk Nowitzki	1522
5.	John Stockton	1504

David Thompson leaps
towards Pete Maravich
in 1979.

1978
SKYWALKER VS. ICEMAN

On April 19, 1978, the eyes of the NBA world were on Boston to witness John Havlicek's swan song with the Celtics after a storied 16-year career. But at Cobo Hall in downtown Detroit, where the Pistons were hosting a matinee game against the Denver Nuggets, all anybody cared about was the scoring title.

It was the final night of the 1977–78 regular season, and Nuggets guard David "Skywalker" Thompson was just 0.2 points per game behind the NBA's scoring leader, San Antonio's George "The Iceman" Gervin — 26.6 to 26.8.

Thompson and Gervin had been battling for the scoring crown all season long, and Gervin's Spurs were set to play later that night. It was the closest scoring race in league history — and it came down to the last game.

Thompson and Gervin were both imports from the ABA. So, too, were their franchises, which had joined the NBA in the previous season's merger, and their coaches, the Nuggets' Larry Brown and the Spurs' Doug Moe.

Brown and Moe were pals and day one members of the ABA. Brown had been a three-time All-Star in the ABA and was the league's all-time assists leader by the time he retired. He and Moe had been teammates and had risen through the ranks together. When Brown was hired for his first head coaching job, with the ABA's Carolina Cougars in 1972, he made sure to bring on Moe as an assistant.

Thompson, along with Gervin, had been one of the stars the NBA coveted, eventually forcing a merger. And it was obvious why. The game had never seen a leaper like Thompson. They called him "Skywalker" for a reason, and at 6-foot-4 with a penchant for dunking on — or over — anybody in his path, he also earned the nickname Giant Killer.

The first overall pick in both the NBA and ABA draft in 1974, Thompson took off with Denver, averaging 26 points per game as a rookie, and never looked back.

Thompson hadn't been following the scoring race between himself and Gervin all that closely in '78. His Nuggets were playoff bound and the final regular-season game

in Detroit — Gervin's hometown — was mostly perfunctory.

Knowing how close he was to the scoring lead, Brown asked Thompson if he wanted his teammates to funnel him the ball to help him surpass Gervin. "Nah," he told his coach, "let's just see what happens."

What happened was that Thompson nailed 20 of his first 21 shots. He scored 32 points in the first quarter alone, breaking Wilt Chamberlain's record for points in a single quarter, which had been set during his famous 100-point game. At halftime, Thompson had 53. He finished the game with 73, and the Nuggets needed all of them — they lost by 2 points, 139–137. But Thompson took the lead versus Gervin.

If Thompson hadn't been monitoring the scoring race too closely, the same likely couldn't be said of the Iceman.

Gervin was a gunner's gunner, an unabashed scorer who took pride in his ability to rack up points in a hurry. He'd become a superstar in the ABA — every bit as big as Julius Erving — and was the Spurs' first iconic player. "What Babe Ruth was to New York, George Gervin was to San Antonio," the team's owner once said.

He had a bottomless bag of tricks and could score from anywhere on the floor. But the finger roll, which required a perfect, delicate touch and spin on the ball, was his calling card.

In the ABA he'd routinely score 20 or 30 points in the first half before putting it in cruise control, and he was never shy about letting it fly. He embraced his role. "They didn't pay me to guard nobody," said Gervin. "They paid guys to guard *me*."

It's no wonder they called him "Ice." As in: cold as.

On the final night of the regular season, Gervin and the Spurs were in New Orleans to face the Jazz. He got a phone call to his hotel room from a reporter who told him that Thompson had just scored 73 points. If Gervin wanted the scoring title, he'd need to score 59 that night.

When he heard the news, Spurs coach Doug Moe was irate. He thought Brown had intentionally coached the Nuggets game so that Thompson could pad his scoring stats

and beat Gervin. As though it was some sort of prank.

Moe gathered his team in the hotel lobby and told them that Thompson had just "stolen" the scoring title from their Iceman. They needed to band together to get revenge — and take back what was rightfully Gervin's.

Gervin came out of the gates with guns a-blazin', but he was firing blanks. He missed his first six shots to start the game. But soon enough, he locked in and had 20 points in the first quarter. Shot after shot, his teammates set him up, and he was knocking them down.

In the second quarter, he scored 33 points, breaking Thompson's newly minted record. "It took me 16 years to break Wilt's mark," Thompson later wrote, "but it only took Gervin seven hours to break mine."

On the opposing bench, watching the scoring brilliance unfold, was injured New Orleans Jazz guard Pistol Pete Maravich, maybe the single most-gifted scorer the game has ever seen. Maravich began cheering Gervin on. "Get 'em, Ice!" he yelled from the sideline. "One artist to another," as Gervin put it.

By halftime Gervin had scored 53 points, and he finished the game with 63. The Spurs lost by 20. But the race was over, and the Iceman reigned supreme, taking the scoring title with 27.22 points per game to Thompson's 27.15.

Because this all took place during a time in which the league struggled for mainstream exposure, there is no footage of either performance.

The following season, Gervin won his second of four scoring titles, this time averaging 29.6 per game, just to be safe.

70S PPG

1.	Kareem Abdul-Jabbar and George Gervin	28.2
2.	Bob McAdoo	26.8
3.	David Thompson	25.1
4.	Jerry West	24.6
5.	Pete Maravich	24.2

1978
THE BULLETS WEAR RINGS

The Bullets were one of the most consistent winners during the 1970s. They began the decade in Baltimore before moving to Washington, D.C., in 1973, making the playoffs all 10 years and never finishing worse than fourth in the East.

But heading into the 1977–78 season, their window to compete was closing. The Bullets' star frontcourt of Wes Unseld and Elvin Hayes was on the wrong side of 30 and nearly a decade of NBA hoops was taking its toll on both.

Unseld, the team's 31-year-old captain and starting center, was entering his ninth season. He had been a lone constant on the Bullets throughout his career. In 1969 Unseld made history becoming the first player to win Rookie of the Year and MVP in the same season. He averaged 14 points and a career-high 18 rebounds that year.

At 6-foot-7 he was the shortest center in the game — even his Afro couldn't mask the height disparity between him and opposing bigs. But Unseld carried an imposing 250-pound wide frame and had Stretch Armstrong arms that allowed him to gain position against his larger opponents. What's more, he was the NBA's premier passer; he turned the outlet pass into both an art form and dangerous weapon.

Yet by '77 his numbers had steadily declined. He remained a lethal rebounder and matchup nightmare, but it had been five years since Unseld was a double-digit scorer.

Hayes entered the NBA the same season as Unseld. Following a standout career at the University of Houston, Hayes was the first pick in the 1968 draft and led the league in scoring his rookie year. He was traded to the Bullets ahead of the 1972–73 season and was an instrumental part of the team's run to the Finals in '75.

Like Unseld, Hayes was a high-volume rebounder, but unlike his teammate, "The Big E," as he was known, was a walking bucket. His fadeaway jumper was unstoppable and drove opponents mad. Hayes was consistently among the league's top scorers, but he had earned a reputation for disappearing down the stretch in close games.

If the Bullets were going to remain contenders, they'd need reinforcements. In the summer of '77 they signed forward Bobby Dandridge, a starter on the '71 Milwaukee Bucks team that beat Unseld and the Bullets in the championship series.

Washington's "big three" was in place, but the Bullets entered the season to middling expectations. After all, the campaign was shaping up to belong to Bill Walton and the Portland Trail Blazers, the defending champs who looked better than ever. Portland raced to a 50–10 start. That's when Walton broke his foot, sidelining him for the season and closing the door on the Blazers' would-be dynasty forever.

But there were still formidable teams led by a talented crop of ABA expats. In Phila-

delphia the 76ers were flying high thanks to Julius Erving, while in San Antonio George "The Iceman" Gervin was on the verge of one of the greatest scoring seasons of all time. The Sixers and Spurs finished atop the East, each winning over 50 games.

Washington finished the regular season in third with 44 wins, their worst result in six years. Injuries played a part. Guards Phil Chenier — a three-time All-Star between 1974 and '77 — and Charles Johnson missed significant time, which led head coach Dick Motta to throw his bench into the fire.

At one point in the season, the Bullets had just seven healthy players on their roster. But by the time the playoffs rolled around and the club was healthy across the board, the increased playing time for reserves like Tom Henderson, Kevin Grevey and Mitch Kupchak had helped develop a deep and versatile 12-man unit.

Unseld and the Bullets had been to two Finals in the past seven years. They were hardly also-rans. But they lacked the marquee talent of other contenders, and assumed the role of underdog in the minds of fans and media alike.

In the postseason, Washington ran the gauntlet against the NBA's best. After sweeping the Atlanta Hawks in the first round, the Bullets advanced past Gervin and the Spurs in six games, thanks in large part to superb defense on the Iceman from Dandridge.

Wes Unseld battles for a rebound with Ray Williams and Elvin Hayes in 1981.

In the Eastern Conference finals, they met Dr. J and the 76ers, who were looking to reach the Finals in back-to-back seasons. Six games later, the Bullets advanced.

"We had to go through the best," said Grevey, "and it made us the best."

The 1978 Finals were billed as David vs. David. Both the Bullets and their opponents, the Seattle SuperSonics, toppled the top two seeds in their conference en route to the championship round.

Nothing about the Bullets' 1978 playoff run was easy, and the Finals were no exception. In Seattle they went to battle in front of a record 39,000 fans at the Kingdome in Game 4, tying the series, 2–2, and breaking Seattle's 21-game home-court winning streak in the process. But the SuperSonics countered by winning Game 5. It seemed as if, every time Washington gained momentum, Seattle responded.

Coach Motta urged his team not to get comfortable on the heels of big wins. In the second round, the Bullets were leading the Spurs, 3–1, when a play-by-play announcer warned, "The opera isn't over until the fat lady sings." For the rest of the postseason, Motta repeated that refrain to his players. He even had T-shirts made bearing the team's new de facto slogan, and Bullets fans brought signs to game asking if the fat lady was ready to sing yet.

Facing elimination at home, the Bullets saved their season with a 117–82 win, setting up a Game 7 in hostile territory. The deciding game came down to the wire. Washington squandered an 11-point lead late in the fourth quarter, thanks to hot shooting from the Sonics' Downtown Freddie Brown, but a broken play with 1:30 remaining in the game resulted in a 3-point play from Kupchak.

When the final buzzer sounded, the scoreboard read 105–99, and the Bullets players and coaches gleefully sprinted toward the visitors' locker room to celebrate their first championship.

Elvin Hayes poses with the championship trophy in 1978.

It wasn't until 2016, when LeBron James and the Cleveland Cavaliers beat the Golden State Warriors, that another road team would win a Game 7 with the title on the line.

"What I feel," Unseld said after the game, "is relief." Although he averaged only 9 points per game, he was instrumental to his team's success and was named Finals MVP.

Despite winning it all, Hayes still couldn't shake his reputation for shrinking during big moments. He finished Game 7 with 12 points, having to watch the final moments from the bench because of foul trouble.

"They can say whatever they want," Hayes said. "But they gotta say one thing: E's a world champion. He wears a ring."

Eight thousand fans welcomed the Bullets at the airport that night to celebrate the city's first sports title in 36 years.

The next day, 100,000 spilled onto the streets for a victory parade that led to the White House. "Is the fat lady here?" President Jimmy Carter asked when the team arrived. In fact, she was — earlier in the day, an opera singer belted out "We Are the Champions" to the throng of cheering fans.

Washington's 44 wins during the regular season were the fewest of any champion in NBA history. Five members of the team made multiple All-Star appearances, and Hayes and Unseld are enshrined in the Hall of Fame. But the '78 Bullets are still remembered as the league's greatest underdogs.

Call them whatever you want. The Bullets wear rings.

UPSETS

1994: 8-seed Nuggets defeat 1-seed Sonics
2007: 8-seed Warriors defeat 1-seed Mavericks
1959: Minneapolis Lakers (33-39) defeat St. Louis Hawks (49-23) in round two
1981: Rockets (40-42, 6-seed) over Lakers (defending champs) in round one
1989: Warriors (7-seed) defeat Utah Jazz (2nd-seed) in round one

1979
THE NBA ON THE BRINK

Game 4 of the 1979 NBA Finals — a rematch of the '78 series between the defending champion Washington Bullets and the Seattle SuperSonics. With the seconds counting down in overtime and Seattle hanging on to a 114–112 lead, Washington brought the ball up the court in time for one last shot. Gus Williams, the 6-foot SuperSonics guard and leading scorer of the series, leaped to block a shot from the Bullets' Kevin Grevey — a clutch defensive play to seal the Seattle win.

If you were living on the East Coast, Williams's block would have appeared on your television screen at nearly 3 o'clock in the morning. Even if you were a fervent basketball fan, chances are you missed it altogether.

CBS owned the NBA's broadcast rights at the time. Concerned the series wouldn't draw significant audiences, the network opted to throw in the towel and air weeknight games at 11:30 p.m. in the Eastern and Pacific time zones, putting them up against ratings behemoth Johnny Carson. Many were aired on tape delay; Game 4 was shown live on the East Coast, but didn't tip off until the wee hours.

And so, fans were fast asleep when the Sonics took a commanding 3–1 lead in the best-of-seven series. The same was true when the Sonics captured their first championship two nights later.

The NBA was clearly in transition in the late 70s. Gone were such mythical figures as Wilt, Russell, Baylor and West and the epic rivalries that had captivated fans. The ABA merger of 1976 had ushered in a new generation of superstars like Julius "Dr. J" Erving, George "The Iceman" Gervin and David "Skywalker" Thompson, along with four new franchises, bringing the total to 22. But as the decade came to a close, they were tasked with resuscitating a fading league.

With more teams and stars spread out across the NBA, thanks in part to the introduction of free agency, the days of the dynasty seemed to be forever in the past. Eight different champions were crowned during the 70s, including those from smaller markets like Milwaukee, Seattle and Portland.

It wasn't enough to capture the casual fan, and by the turn of the 1980s, attendance and television ratings were plummeting. In 1983 a committee was formed to explore the notion of reducing the number of teams by five.

The league's problems went deeper than low viewership.

The numbers painted a bleak picture, stoking fears that the league had plateaued following the merger. By the close of the 1978–79 regular season, 12 of 22 teams had seen a dip in attendance.

There were exceptions, of course. Attendance was on the rise in San Antonio, where George Gervin's offensive brilliance was leading a competitive team. In Seattle the move to the Kingdome, which seated 27,000 for bas-

ketball, had sparked an eye-popping attendance rise of 45 percent, aided of course by back-to-back Finals appearances in 1978 and '79.

But in the league's largest markets, attendance was plummeting. New York, Los Angeles, Chicago and Philadelphia were all experiencing drops in the double digits. Even more troubling, national television ratings were down by a stunning 26 percent.

Meanwhile, players were making more than ever. In 1977 David Thompson signed a record five-year, $4 million contract. By the time 1980 rolled around, the average salary was over $160,000 — up from just $35,000 in 1970.

It was against this backdrop that a series of critical articles about the state of the NBA were written by an overwhelmingly

LEAST WATCHED NBA FINALS

Year	Rating/Share
2007	6.2/11
2003	6.5/12
1981	6.7/27
1979	7.2/24
1980	8.0/29

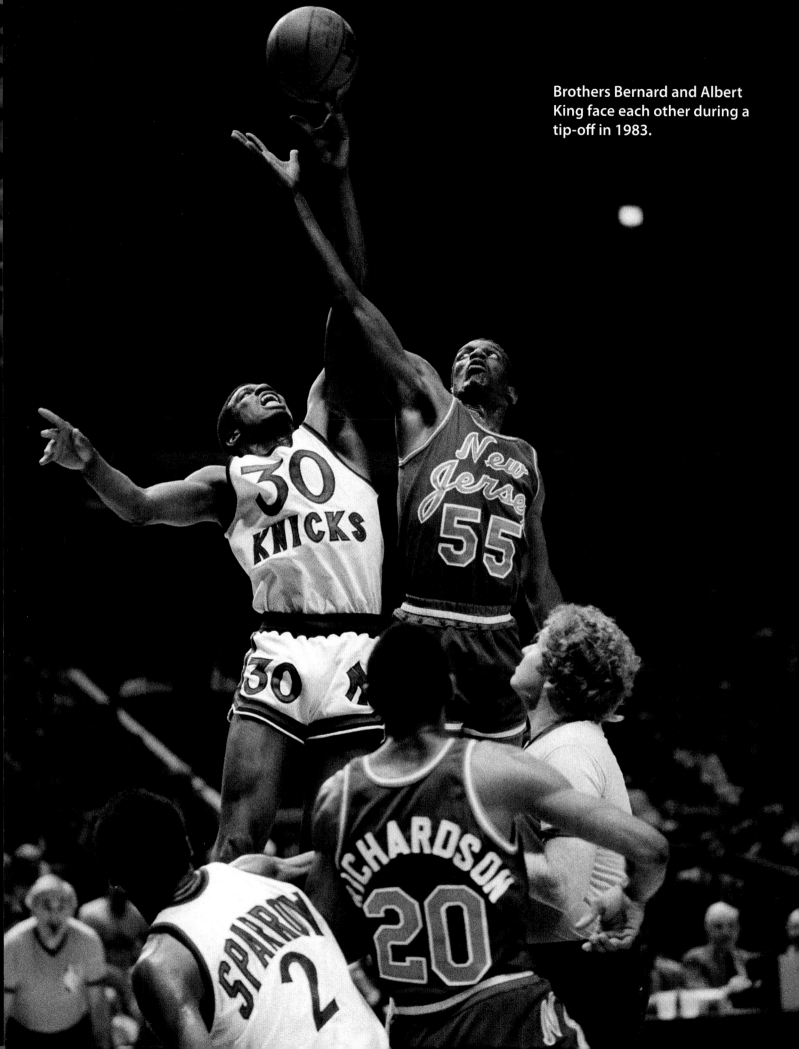

Brothers Bernard and Albert King face each other during a tip-off in 1983.

white group of reporters. Among them was a scathing piece published in *Sports Illustrated* in February 1979, titled "There's an Ill Wind Blowing for the NBA."

"Maybe the long-term contract, free agentry and big money have enabled the dollar-wise pro basketball player to contemplate retirement to an island villa at age 33," wrote John Papanek, "but they have also brought him a serious image problem."

It's true the larger contracts hadn't exactly endeared the blue-collar fan. In the 1980 season, the NBA dished out half a million dollars in marketing, quadrupling the previous season's budget — out of which came the popular ad campaign boasting "The NBA Is FANtastic."

The NBA was combatting an image problem that was supposedly about salaries, but was really rooted in racism.

Sonics guard Paul Silas, the (African American) president of the NBA Players Association, said, "It is a fact that white people in general look disfavorably upon blacks who are making astronomical amounts of money if it appears they are not working hard for that money."

"A lot of people use the word 'undisciplined' to describe the NBA," Hall of Famer Al Attles said in 1979. "I think that word is pointed at a group more than at a sport. What do they mean by it? On the court? Off the court? What kind of clothes a guy wears? How he talks? How he plays? I think that's a cop-out."

It can't be ignored that the "ill wind," as *Sports Illustrated* put it, blowing through the NBA also came at a time when the league's demographics were changing. In 1970, 60 percent of its players were African American. In 1980, 75 percent were black, while more than 75 percent of fans were white.

By the early 80s, a new issue had grown to alarming levels: drug use.

In that sense, the NBA and its players were no different than any other celebrity-driven industry in that time, when cocaine seemed to permeate all corners of the culture. In a transparent sport like basketball, where players can't hide behind helmets and face masks, the effects were plain for all to see.

"A lot of guys around the league were trying coke, and it was getting rave reviews," Lakers forward Spencer Haywood said in

1988. "The supply seemed unlimited. . . . If you were an NBA player, leeches lined up to stuff coke into your gym bag after the game."

During the 1980 Finals, Haywood passed out at practice because he had gotten too high the night before. He later told reporters he was merely tired from too much weight lifting and wind sprints. That summer, one general manager speculated that 75 percent of NBA players were using cocaine.

Players like David Thompson, a former first overall draft pick, went from dynamic superstars to lethargic and inconsistent, and were accused of going through the motions. Basketball's premier high flyer just a few years earlier, Thompson's career would take another downward turn in 1984 when he tore his knee after falling down a flight of stairs at Studio 54.

In 1986 Micheal Ray Richardson, an All-Star guard for the New Jersey Nets just a year prior, became the first player to be banned from the league for substance abuse after testing positive for cocaine for the third time since the league introduced a drug policy during the 1983–84 season.

The names of those who went public about their substance abuse issues doubles as a list of players who never reached their potential, or whose best years were too few: Haywood, Thompson, Richardson, Bernard King, John Lucas, Marvin Barnes, and so many others.

Drugs like cocaine had permeated society — as Haywood put it, "drug education was in the Dark Ages" — but it only contributed to the many criticisms surrounding the NBA during the first half of the decade. Pro basketball continued to reflect America's racial prejudice, much as it had throughout the league's history.

Whatever the reason, the NBA had been deemed "too black" for its largely white audience. "The teams are too black," one anonymous league executive told *Sports Illustrated*. "The question is are [the black players] promotable? How can you sell a black sport to a white public?"

You have to wonder what role that line of thinking had to play in the boardrooms at CBS, where the NBA took a back seat to such sports as football, baseball and even bowling.

The network reportedly had regrets about the 1977 broadcast deal before it was even signed, and the decision to air parts of the 1978 and '79 Finals on tape delay certainly sent a loud message that CBS didn't believe NBA basketball could be a ratings draw.

The tape-delay era did significant damage. The failure of the network and league to promote the game showed a lack of foresight. Even if a Washington–Seattle Finals didn't moved the needle as much as more popular recent championship squads like Bill Walton's Trail Blazers or Walt Frazier's Knicks, they needn't have waited long for reinforcements. The 1979–80 season saw the debuts of two rookies whose rivalry would help rescue the NBA: Magic Johnson and Larry Bird.

And yet it took years before the league would properly promote its two fastest-rising stars.

Take Game 6 of the 1980 Finals — Magic's coming-out party. Los Angeles held a 3–2 series lead over the Philadelphia 76ers but had just lost Kareem Abdul-Jabbar to injury. Johnson, the Lakers' rookie point guard, stood in at center for the opening tip-off and played all five positions that night. He finished the game with 42 points, 15 rebounds and 7 assists, and the Lakers captured the title.

The game was aired — you guessed it — on tape delay, with most fans fast asleep during one of the NBA's defining performances. The following year, Bird won his first championship with the Boston Celtics. Embarrassingly for the league, late air times meant Bird's breakout occurred during the lowest-rated Finals ever.

By 1986, networks finally took notice of the gold mine they'd been sitting on. The Lakers–Celtics rivalry, pitting Magic against Bird, pushed games onto live television and helped make megastars of the NBA's best and brightest. The '88 Finals between Magic's Lakers and the "Bad Boy" Detroit Pistons remain the highest-rated of all time.

By the close of the decade, Michael Jordan would propel the NBA toward becoming a major global enterprise, opening the doors for the $24 billion television contracts that came in the decades that followed.

The NBA: It's FANtastic.

1980
THE MAGIC AND LARRY SHOW

Larry Bird and Earvin Johnson won't forget the first time they saw each other play. It was an international exhibition tournament in April 1978, and the two were among a group of college All-Stars selected to represent the United States.

Johnson, the pride of Lansing, Michigan, had just wrapped up his freshman season at nearby Michigan State, in which he led the program to its first NCAA Tournament berth in 20 years and reached the quarterfinals. He turned down offers to sign with an NBA team in order to return to school for one more season.

Bird, a sophomore from French Lick, Indiana, was averaging over 31 points per game during his first two seasons. He had just been named a First Team All-American, although few had seen him in action playing at little-known Indiana State.

Within one year, Bird and Johnson would be competing for an NCAA championship in front of a record-setting audience for a basketball game, college or pro. Each would grace their own SI cover before graduation, and their celebrity would only grow as they took their talents to the NBA. There, the competition would continue to play out on center stage, as they combined to capture eight championships and six MVP awards in the span of just 10 years.

Magic and Larry lifted the league from the doldrums to unforeseen popularity and sparked a rivalry (and eventual friendship) that would equal any in basketball that came before or since.

But for now, nobody batted an eye when the two were placed on the same team during a routine scrimmage.

At 6-foot-9 — an exceptional height for a point guard — the game had never seen a playmaker like Johnson. Watching him manipulate the ball like a puppet on a string, Bird quickly realized why they called him "Magic."

Johnson's passing was as infectious as his smile, which stretched across his face wide as a Buick. The ball zipped around the court like a pinball. Bird would later return home proclaiming that he had just seen the best basketball player on Earth.

Of course, Bird was no slouch himself, firing no-look passes of his own, hawking the ball for steals and hitting shots from inconceivable angles — the result of untold hours and hours practicing alone with a hoop and a ball back home.

A gawky, shy young man with a big ol' flop of curly blond hair, Bird didn't exactly strike fear into opponents on first glance — he could barely even make eye contact with strangers. But once a game began, he carved up the competition like a master butcher. Johnson, like everybody else, was in awe. He called his pals back in Michigan, "This is the baddest white dude I've ever seen in my life."

The NBA was in trouble heading into the 1979–80 season, Bird and Magic's first in the pros. Ticket sales were trending in the wrong direction, and television viewership was plummeting. Weeknight games during the Finals weren't even aired live because the CBS network anticipated a ratings disaster.

The arrival of Magic and Bird couldn't have come at a better time. In their first meeting, in December, Bird and Johnson didn't shake hands before tip-off, and they even got into a fight when Bird delivered a hard foul on Johnson. Eager to promote the rivalry between the two as if they were heavyweight boxers, CBS broadcast the January rematch live from coast to coast.

Both were rookies, but Bird had actually been drafted a year earlier by Red Auerbach and the Boston Celtics, who took him sixth overall in 1978 even though they knew he was planning to return to school. Bird was so good that the Celts were willing to wait.

Johnson, fresh off a collegiate title after beating Bird and Indiana State — the opening salvo in a career-long game of one-upmanship — was selected first overall in 1979 by the Los Angeles Lakers. It was the NBA's good fortune that the two most anticipated prospects of all time had landed with its two most iconic franchises.

But the Celtics had fallen on hard times. When Bird joined the team, Boston had just missed the playoffs two seasons in a row. The Celtics' winning culture had eroded quickly after their 1976 title run, capped off by Curtis Rowe telling reporters in 1978, "The Ws and Ls don't show up in my paycheck."

Bird's arrival came with lofty expectations. To Celtics fans, he was put on Earth to rescue the franchise. Before his first game at the Boston Garden, a fan in the upper deck released a white dove. The crowd erupted.

The situation had been even worse in Lakerland. After winning their first and only title in LA in 1972, the team went into a tailspin two years later, when Jerry West retired. The lull was short-lived thanks to the arrival of Kareem Abdul-Jabbar, who was traded to the Lakers before the 1975–76 season. In his first two years in LA, Kareem was a back-to-back MVP, but the team made it past the second round just once in his first four seasons.

"People I talk to around Los Angeles all tell me that there isn't a great deal of interest in either the Lakers or the NBA," Jerry West said in 1978. That would change once Magic took the court.

His flashy game and desire to win were obvious from his first NBA game. Magic delighted the crowd with what would become signature moves: behind-the-back dribbles on the run, baby hook shots and, of course, the no-look passes — defenders watching his eyes widen as he gazed to the left, but dished to his right. When Kareem hit a patented skyhook to win the game at the buzzer, Magic leapt into the giant's arms and celebrated as if it were six months earlier, at the NCAA title game.

The Lakers finished 60–22 and returned to the Finals in a matchup with Julius Erving and the Philadelphia 76ers. Standing in for an injured Kareem at center, Johnson scored 42 points in Game 6 to win the series. Magic was named Finals MVP — to this day, he's the only rookie ever to earn the honor.

He may not have become an instant legend like Magic, but Larry Bird had also lived up to the hype in his rookie year. The Celtics' leading scorer and rebounder, he lifted the team from 29 wins the season before to a first-place finish overall. Both Bird and Magic were named All-Stars, but Bird took home the Rookie of the Year trophy after averaging over 21 points and 10 rebounds.

The next season, with Johnson sidelined

by a leg injury, Bird and the Celtics were crowned the champs over the Houston Rockets. The year after that? Magic and the Lakers won their second title in three years. And so on.

As the decade progressed, the two stars and their teams separated from the pack.

Magic's playmaking laid the foundation for Showtime basketball in Los Angeles, establishing a frenetic brand of ball appealing to the eye. Despite his reserved demeanor, Bird gained a reputation as the NBA's most ruthless trash talker. He took delight in winning and would toy with opponents. In one game, he decided to play the first three quarters shooting left-handed and wound up with 47 points. "I'm saving my right hand for the Lakers," he said afterward.

The Celtics and Lakers finished first in their conference seven times between 1979–80 and '87–88. Magic and Bird each won three MVP awards.

With the stakes rising, their rivalry only intensified. They didn't shake hands before games and maintained their distance. "When you compete, you're really not friends," Bird said during a 2012 appearance with Johnson on *The Late Show with David Letterman* to promote *Magic/Bird*, a Broadway musical based on their rivalry. "Earvin is an outgoing guy, he wants to love everybody and high-five. He's got that big smile — my goal was to take three of them teeth home with me."

Winning was all that mattered, no matter the game. When Bird was negotiating a deal with Converse sneakers — the same brand Johnson repped — he made sure he was paid exactly one dollar more than Magic. Throughout their careers, they both started each day by checking each other's box scores, keeping tabs on the latest exploits.

Magic read all about the 60 points Bird scored against the Atlanta Hawks in 1985, so amazing that by the end of the game, the opponents were openly cheering as each unbelievable shot fell. Bird saw that Johnson had set a playoff record with 24 assists in a single game in '84. Each set a standard of excellence the other worked tirelessly to match.

Writers and broadcasters were eager to fan the flames of the rivalry. They played up the obvious contrasts between the two: black vs. white; extrovert vs. introvert; the maestro of Showtime vs. "The Hick from French Lick."

It's true that, away from the game, the two lived distinctly separate lives. Magic lived in an extravagant Bel Air mansion and was a fixture on LA's disco circuit. Bird built a home in his hometown, moved his mother in and mowed his own lawn.

But the pair had far more in common than not. Both grew up in the industrial Midwest, Bird on the farm, Magic near the factories. Of course, the greatest commonality came on the court. Apart from being maniacal competitors, both had an otherworldly feel for the game of basketball. Neither were jump-out-of-the-gym freak athletes like other league-defining talents — Wilt, Julius, Kobe, LeBron. They were basketball players, pure and simple. They shared the same approach, finding the delicate balance between individual flair and team-first basketball in a way that few others ever have.

In the spring of '84, Bird's Celtics and Magic's Lakers met in the NBA Finals for the first time, a destiny that had been five years in the making. Boston outlasted LA in a thrilling seven-game series. After averaging over 27 points and 14 rebounds — plus shooting a perfect 8-of-8 from the free-throw line in the deciding Game 7 — Bird was named Finals MVP.

They renewed their rivalry the following season. This time the Lakers exacted revenge, winning the series 4–2. Magic, in the midst of a run of leading the league in assists four times in five seasons, delivered 14 in the deciding game.

The Magic–Bird rivalry was a marketable one on and off the court. Both were active pitchmen, as mainstream as any NBA stars had ever been. The league benefited as a result. After the '85 Finals wrapped, the NBA negotiated a new four-year, $173 million TV contract with CBS — $100 million more than the year before Magic and Bird arrived.

Their relationship changed that summer while filming a Converse commercial together. Johnson was hesitant to spend time with an established foe, while Bird only agreed to participate once producers agreed to shoot the ad at his mother's home in French Lick.

In the spot, a limousine with the license plate "LA 32" speeds through the Indiana backroads toward Bird, who grips a basketball as it arrives. The window rolls down and Magic flaunts his recent MVP award. "OK, Magic," Bird tells him, "show me what you got," as he tosses the ball at his enemy.

Between takes, Bird invited Johnson inside, where his mother, Georgia, fixed them meals. They had been linked since they were teens, and heated rivals. But for the first time ever, they found themselves in the same room, alone, and they talked. They traded war stories and laughed about how much they kept tabs on one another. They emerged from the experience as friends — no real surprise, given everything they had in common.

"It's hard to look at a white man and see black," said Magic, "but when I looked at Larry, that's what I saw. I saw myself."

The two would meet in the Finals again in '87. Magic hit a hook shot in the dying seconds of Game 4, giving the Lakers a 107–106 win and a convincing 3–1 series lead. At his postgame press conference, a dispirited Bird said, "Magic's just a great basketball player. He's . . . he's the best I've ever seen." His voice trailed off as he stared into the distance and pondered the reality that he'd met his match. "Unbelievable."

It was their last Finals appearance together. Bird had suffered a back injury in the summer of '85 while shoveling gravel in his driveway, and as the decade drew to a close he could no longer stave off the pain. He retired in 1992. Magic would continue to carry the Lakers until 1991, when he contracted HIV and was forced to walk away from the game. Among the first people he told, long before he went public, was Bird.

Magic and Bird met on the court 31 times in their NBA careers. As he'll remind Bird at every opportunity, Magic won 22 of those games — including two out of three Finals series. "I can still see him in my head, coming up court, faking right, faking left, then pulling it back and laying it in," Bird said following his retirement. "Still pisses me off."

Bird shoots over Magic during the 1984 NBA Finals.

1981
SHOWTIME LAKERS

"**M**agic's Bombshell: He Wants to be Traded," read the *Los Angeles Times* headline on November 19, 1981.

The news came as a shock to anybody outside the Lakers dressing room. After all, just a year and a half earlier, Magic Johnson had brought Showtime back to Hollywood, leading the most electrifying team in the game to the 1980 title as a rookie. In the off-season, he was awarded an unprecedented 25 year, $25 million contract, making him a Laker for life.

But now, just 11 games into the '81–82 season, Magic was clashing with his coach and wasn't happy playing the game he loved.

"I can't play here anymore," Johnson told reporters after a win in Utah. "I want to be traded. I can't deal with it no more. I've got to go in and ask [team owner Jerry Buss] to trade me."

Jerry Buss was a self-made man, a former chemist who built his fortune in real estate. In the summer of 1979, he purchased the Lakers and their iconic arena, the "Fabulous" Forum, for $67.5 million — to that date, the largest deal of its kind. Buss inherited Magic, who'd just been drafted first overall, along with moody veteran superstar Kareem Abdul-Jabbar.

In one of his first moves as owner, Buss hired the well-traveled Jack McKinney as head coach. McKinney had won a title in 1977 as an assistant with the run-and-gun Portland Trail Blazers, and he brought his fast-paced offense to Los Angeles. Soon enough it had a name — Showtime — and a leading man in Magic, who energized players and fans alike. Even Kareem was playing with joy during the '79–80 season, eventually capturing his sixth MVP award.

The Lakers were off to a 9–4 start when McKinney suffered a head injury that forced him off the bench for good. He was replaced by assistant coach Paul Westhead, who kept the Showtime offense in place as the Lakers went on to capture the title.

But the next season, Westhead scrapped Showtime for his own system, and the players weren't happy. Westhead's offense was conservative and tamed its star players. The

Magic Johnson runs into Pat Cummings in the 1984 NBA playoffs.

Kareem Abdul-Jabbar scores effortlessly during the 1984 playoffs.

smile quickly vanished from Kareem's face. Magic and the Lakers went from Technicolor to black and white. One year after winning it all, the Lakers were bounced from the first round of the playoffs.

The day after Magic's trade demand, Buss fired Westhead.

Assistant Pat Riley was promoted to head coach. Riley, who had won the 1972 title with the Lakers as a player, matched the flashy Hollywood persona his team acquired during its clashes with Boston in the '60s. He wore slick suits and even slicker hair, each strand held together by a healthy dose of gel. But beneath the designer duds, Riley was more substance than style.

In their first game under Riley, the Forum crowd booed Magic when he first touched the ball. The hardworking ticket buyer has no sympathy for a cantankerous millionaire. But it only took a handful of possessions to realize that Showtime was back.

Magic was pushing the pace, delivering dazzling passes with a flick of the wrist to Norm Nixon or Jamaal Wilkes on the wings. Kareem, reduced to a skyhooking statue under Westhead, was scoring in a number of ways. The Lakers' lead reached 30 by the second half. Johnson finished with 20 points, 16 assists, 10 rebounds and 3 steals.

The Lakers returned to the Finals that season, capturing their second title in three years in a six-game series against Julius Erving and the Philadelphia 76ers. For the second time in his young career, Magic was named Finals MVP. The Lakers appeared in the Finals for four years straight between 1982 and '85, finishing with the best record in the Western Conference each season. In 1985 they were crowned champs for the third time, this time in a star-studded matchup with Larry Bird and the Boston Celtics. A 37-year-old Abdul-Jabbar, the Lakers' leading scorer, was named Finals MVP — *14 years* after first winning the honor in 1971.

Behind the brilliance of Kareem and Magic and a loaded supporting cast that expanded to include defensive stopper Michael Cooper and former All-Star big man Bob McAdoo, the Lakers were Hollywood's top revue.

The Forum was the place to be in Los Angeles in the mid-80s. Celebrities flocked to games, where Buss ensured that they were seated courtside and in view of the television cameras. The arena even housed LA's most exclusive VIP nightclub, the Forum Club, which became a go-to spot for celebs and athletes alike.

Meanwhile, new stars were emerging. A trade during the 1979–80 season netted LA the Cleveland Cavaliers' first-round pick in 1982, which turned out to be first overall. The Lakers selected forward James Worthy, who'd just been named MVP of the NCAA tournament after winning a title with the University of North Carolina. At UNC, Worthy was the leading scorer on a team that featured Michael Jordan. When he joined the Lakers, however, he took a backup role to Jamaal Wilkes, who was averaging over 21 points per game.

By 1985–86, however, Worthy had established himself as a starter and an All-Star. Like in college, he had a knack for coming up big when it mattered, earning the nickname Big Game James. He could create his own shot but was particularly deadly on the fast break. The play must have happened a thousand times: Magic torpedoing the ball up the court to Worthy, who'd catch it in stride and take off, soaring to the hoop and slamming it down with one hand.

With Worthy in his prime, the Lakers were a machine, as well oiled as Riley's 'do. They blew opponents off the court. Like a basketball twister, you'd see it coming, but could only duck and cover. Before you knew it, you were down 18 points and there was a cow on your roof.

The Showtime Lakers were the NBA's elite. But they'd never won back-to-back championships, the hallmark — a prerequisite, even — of any great dynasty. After winning it all in '87, Pat Riley guaranteed his team would repeat as champs the following season. And he was in a position to make good on his promise.

"There's nothing really left [to accomplish]," Magic said ahead of the 1988 Finals. Their opponents were the Detroit Pistons,

who'd risen to the top the East thanks to their unique brand of bully ball, an ultra-physical style that seemed the polar opposite of LA's swift attack. Teams had often tried to slow the game down and pound the Lakers to get them out of their rhythm, and Magic & Co. had proven they could junk it up with the best of 'em. It took two physical seven-game series to reach the Finals. The Lakers were drained, but prepared for what the Pistons had in store.

Record audiences tuned in to watch the Pistons lay a beating on LA in Game 1 at the Forum, 105–93. But in Game 2, Worthy was a force inside and finished with a game-high 26 points as the Lakers evened the series.

After two convincing Pistons wins in Detroit's Pontiac Silverdome — the second before a crowd of over 41,000 — the Lakers were on the brink of elimination on their home court. Hobbled Pistons point guard Isiah Thomas put up 43 points, but Abdul-Jabbar sank a pair of free throws with 14 seconds remaining in the fourth to seal a 103–102 win, keeping the Lakers' back-to-back hopes alive and forcing a Game 7.

In front of a sold-out Forum crowd, the Lakers erased a first-half deficit and received timely performances from Magic and Cooper, who connected on a long-distance layup to give LA a 3-point lead with six seconds remaining. No player was more clutch than Worthy, who picked a hell of a time to notch his first career triple-double. In the biggest game of his life, Big Game James had 36 points, 16 rebounds and 10 assists. The Lakers won 108–105 and cemented an 80s dynasty cast in gold. It had been nearly two decades since a team won back-to-back championships, dating back to Bill Russell's final two seasons in Boston.

The Showtime Lakers joined an exclusive club and etched their place among the greatest dynasties in sports.

"We made a very strong defense," Riley told reporters after the win. "Now it's up to you, the prosecutors, to judge us, to give us our place in history."

Verdict: one of the best of all time.

Michael Cooper goes up and way over Isiah Thomas.

1984
THE GREATEST DRAFT

In April of 1984, Team USA held basketball trials on the campus of Indiana University in Bloomington. The Olympic Games in Los Angeles were four months away and the NBA draft was less than three months off.

Head coach Bobby Knight invited over 70 of the top collegiate players in the country (this was before professionals were allowed to compete in the Games). The trials were a chance for many to showcase their skills and compete for an Olympic roster spot. For others, it was an opportunity to cement their status as the top college players in the country. With the stands full of NBA scouts preparing for the draft, it was also a chance to open eyes and make it to the big leagues.

The gym was bursting with talent, including five future Hall of Famers: Michael Jordan, John Stockton, Charles Barkley, Patrick Ewing, and Chris Mullin. Ewing and Mullin would return to school the following year, but the others were NBA-bound.

Nearly a thousand miles away in Houston, Hakeem Olajuwon, the Nigerian-born center and top-ranked prospect in the class of '84, had just finished his second consecutive NCAA title game appearance and was preparing for his rookie NBA campaign.

Sam Bowie, the Kentucky big man who ran the floor like a gazelle, was also not on the Indiana campus for USA trials; he, too, was preparing for his NBA debut.

Those names would highlight the prospect pool for the 1984 draft, a league-altering collection of talent — and not just because it included Jordan, the man who would become the greatest player and most recog-

nizable star the game has ever seen.

When the 1983–84 season wrapped up, the NBA was in better shape than it had been in over a decade. It had been lifted to new heights of popularity, thanks in large part to the performances of a pair of young rivals by the name of Magic Johnson and Larry Bird. Just prior to the draft, the two met in the Finals for the first of three times, and a league whose public image was suffering at the turn of the decade was eager to market its new stars.

The consensus was that the '84 draft had promising talent at the top — Olajuwon one of the most coveted draft-eligible players ever — but few could have anticipated the impact the group would have on the NBA.

The first pick belonged to the Houston Rockets — they had "earned" it via a coin flip after finishing with the worst record in the West.

They'd held the number one pick the year before, too, selecting center Ralph Sampson, but this time around they landed the first overall pick under far shadier circumstances.

After a poor start to the 1983–84 season, and with Olajuwon waiting in the wings, the Rockets did everything they could to lose and take part in the coin flip. In the 81st game of the season, the Rockets played 38-year-old Elvin Hayes for 53 minutes in an overtime loss. Hayes was on his last legs and had averaged just 11 minutes per game that season. His extended run in that game was seen as a blatant attempt to tank.

In an effort to dissuade teams from intentionally losing, the NBA would institute the

draft lottery system in time for the '85 draft. But for now, the Rockets' plan worked. They selected Olajuwon. In an era where bigger was better, Houston had drafted the biggest frontcourt in the game.

Everybody knew Olajuwon would go first. Now, with Portland on the clock with the second pick, the real intrigue began.

The Trail Blazers' choice came down to two players: Bowie, the Kentucky kid, or Jordan. Today, that may seem like choosing between steak and pencil shavings for dinner. But it was a legitimate dilemma at the time.

Bowie had all the tools of a player built to dominate in the NBA. He was listed at 7-foot-1 and ran the floor like a track-and-field star. The Portland brass couldn't help but recall their 1977 title team, built around a versatile 7-footer in Bill Walton, and dream of recreating that success.

Bowie could be the natural heir to Walton, but there were red flags. Bowie had suffered a stress fracture in his right leg in college and was forced to sit out two full seasons at Kentucky. The injury woes were also reminiscent of Walton. Could Blazers fans suffer along with another injury-prone franchise player?

As for Jordan, there were no doubts about his talents. He was clearly the best player at the '84 Olympic trials and was a hero in North Carolina after hitting the game-winning shot in the national championship game in 1982.

Jordan had the makings of an unstoppable scorer, but his talents remained unknown. In college, he played under coach Dean Smith in a system in which everybody shared the

ball and there was no go-to player; it was said that the only person who could hold MJ to less than 20 points per game was Smith.

But Portland already had a shooting guard, having drafted Clyde Drexler the year before. They needed size. They needed Bowie.

That left Jordan to fall to Chicago with the third pick. Once Portland passed on Jordan, the Bulls received plenty of trade proposals for their pick. Philadelphia even offered Julius Erving, who had led the 76ers to an NBA title the year before. But Chicago had

a hunch that someone very special had just fallen into their lap. They took Jordan and never looked back.

Jordan's college teammate, forward Sam Perkins, went next, to Dallas, putting Philadelphia on the clock with the fifth pick.

The 76ers were just a year removed from winning a title, but a 1978 trade with the San Diego Clippers for guard World B. Free netted them a first-rounder in '84.

Of all the players at the USA Olympic trials, nobody made a bigger name for himself

NBA Commissioner David Stern shakes Charles Barkley's hand, June 19, 1984.

than the Alabama kid, Charles Barkley. A 6-foot-4½ forward from Auburn University, Barkley led his conference in rebounding three years running.

But he was perhaps best known for his heft. Barkley was asked to report to the camp at 215 pounds, but showed up tipping the scales at 284. He had earned a Rolodex of nicknames, including the Crisco Kid, the Goodtime Blimp and his personal favorite, the Round Mound of Rebound.

The stories of Barkley's eating exploits were legendary. Before one Auburn game, a fan dressed up as a Domino's pizza delivery-man came onto the court during the layup line to take his order. "At the training table, I just keep my hands away from Barkley's plate," said John Stockton.

You wouldn't know it to look at him, but Barkley was one of the more impressive physical forces in the game. He was a one-man fast break who abused the rim with his two-handed tomahawk dunks. But before the Olympic trials, few took him seriously as an NBA prospect. He was too short for his position and his belly didn't exactly inspire confidence.

So Barkley took the opportunity to prove the NBA scouts in attendance wrong. At the trials, he was on a mission, dunking every ball he got his hands on. "Every time I hear the rims rattling, I turn around and Barkley is walking away," another USA teammate said.

It was an incredible showcase, and by the time the tryouts were over, Barkley's had tipped the scales in his favor. Philadelphia was thrilled to land him with the fifth pick.

Notable players continued to come off the draft board. Alvin Robertson, a tenacious defender and one of the only players Jordan remotely struggled against, was drafted seventh by the San Antonio Spurs. Otis Thorpe, the ninth overall pick, was an All-Star and became an important member of the finalist Houston Rockets later in the decade. Eleventh pick Kevin Willis became the NBA's iron man, playing until the age of 44.

It didn't exactly move the needle when the Utah Jazz selected John Stockton with the 16th pick. Stockton, a point guard from Spokane, Washington, performed under mild anonymity during his four years at Gonzaga University. He was his conference's Player of the Year and led his team in scoring, assists

and steals, but it went mostly unnoticed because he played for a small program.

On draft night, thousands of Jazz fans gathered at the Salt Lake City arena to follow the action. When Stockton's name was called out, the crowd was silent.

They wouldn't stay quiet long. Stockton quickly established himself as one of the top point guards in the NBA. Once the Jazz drafted forward Karl Malone the following year, Stockton found a prime target for his passes, and he led the NBA in assists for nine straight seasons between 1987–88 and '95–96. He is currently the NBA's all-time career assist leader.

All of the top talent in the 1984 draft would go on to historic careers. They racked up championships and MVP awards and rewrote the record books. As the 90s got underway, their paths crossed on the NBA's biggest stage, establishing rivalries and a cast of characters that changed the game forever.

Hakeem Olajuwon holds up his new jersey after being selected by the Houston Rockets in the NBA draft.

CLASS OF '96

The '84 draft may never be matched, but the Class of '96 certainly comes close:

1. Allen Iverson (11X all-star, '01 MVP)
2. Marcus Camby ('07 Defensive Player of the Year)
3. Stephon Marbury (2X all-star)
4. Ray Allen (10X all-star, 2X champ)
5. Antoine Walker (3X all-star, champ)
6. Kobe Bryant (18X all-star, 5X champ, 2x Finals MVP, '08 MVP)
7. Peja Stojakovic (3x all-star, champ)
8. Steve Nash (8x all-star, '05 & '06 MVP)
9. Jermaine O'Neal (6x all-star)

Michael Jordan scores over Denver Nuggets' T.R. Dunn in 1985.

1985
AIR JORDAN TAKES OFF

History remembers the 1985–86 Boston Celtics as arguably the greatest single-season team. But in Game 2 of the first round of the '86 playoffs, the Celtics couldn't slow down a 23-year-old Michael Jordan.

Play after play, Jordan drove to the basket, hung in the air and stayed there, casually palming the ball while gravity took care of the defenders around him. Then, on his way back to Earth, he'd uncork a miraculous spinning shot.

Even when he wasn't defying the laws of physics, he was dismantling Boston. He pulled up for contested jumpers, ripped through triple-teams, and got to the free-throw line 21 times, his tongue sticking out while he worked, a habit he picked up from his father.

As the game neared its end, Jordan raised his play and took over.

With Chicago down 2 points and no time left on the clock, Jordan was at the free-throw line. In the biggest moment of his early career, he took in a deep breath and swished both shots to force overtime.

The Bulls ultimately lost. But Jordan's 63 points set a playoff record, breaking Elgin Baylor's 24-year-old mark of 61.

After the game, Larry Bird couldn't believe what he had witnessed. That wasn't an NBA player out there, he said. It was "God disguised as Michael Jordan."

Michael Jordan was born on February 17, 1963, in Brooklyn, New York. His mother, Deloris, was a bank teller, and his father, James, was a plant manager with General Electric. While Jordan was still an infant, the family moved to Wilmington, North Carolina, where Jordan spent his childhood playing baseball and basketball.

In the 70s he grew up watching David "Skywalker" Thompson, the game's most fearless dunker, who led North Carolina State to two undefeated seasons. On the playgrounds, Jordan would try to mimic the Skywalker, and before long he was routinely beating his older brother in games of one-on-one. "Once you feel like you can beat your brother, you can beat anybody," he said.

As a 5-foot-10 sophomore, Jordan famously didn't make the varsity team at Laney High School. Being left off the team was the first of a lifetime of "I'll show you"

moments that fueled his competitive fire. The next season, after sprouting closer to his eventual 6-foot-6, he joined the team and quickly became one of the most coveted college prospects in America.

He became a national icon at the University of North Carolina, sinking the game-winning shot in the 1982 NCAA championship game. In 1984, after declaring for the NBA draft, he led Team USA to a gold medal at the Olympics. By all accounts, Jordan had been constrained on both teams by playing within a system. It was obvious he was an outstanding athlete and great player, but the world had no idea how good Michael Jordan really was.

The NBA's elite did.

In the summer ahead of his rookie season, Team USA scheduled eight exhibition tune-up games against an NBA All-Star squad that featured the likes of Larry Bird, Bill Walton, Magic Johnson, Clyde Drexler, Alex English and Isiah Thomas.

Game after game, Jordan was relentless. He dunked on the centers, blazed past the forwards and stripped the ball from guards.

Jordan's USA squad won every game. The All-Stars resented this kid who was showing them up, in some cases in front of crowds as large as 67,000. They made sure to give Jordan a rude welcome. In one game, Jordan reached out to get the ball from Larry Bird following a time-out and Bird kicked the ball over his head. In another game, Jordan was knocked to the ground and Magic Johnson reached down to help him up. The All-Stars' coach, Oscar Robertson, yelled at Johnson from the sidelines to back off: "He's been over our backs all night!"

At 21, Jordan was already one of the best in the league, Johnson said afterward. And he hadn't even played a game yet.

That didn't stop Nike from giving him his own signature sneaker — the Air Jordan 1 — and putting millions of dollars behind a provocative ad campaign. "Who said man was not supposed to fly?" read the tagline of his first television commercial.

At the time, the NBA's uniform rules required all members of a team to wear the same shoes. Believe it or not, the Jordan 1s were banned.

In his rookie season, 1984–85, Jordan

was a scoring machine. In his third NBA game, he scored 37 points. Two weeks later, he dropped 45 on the San Antonio Spurs. He topped 30 points 31 times that year. In December, *Sports Illustrated* put him on the cover with the headline "A Star Is Born," and the *New York Times* anointed him the successor to the game's most popular aerial artist, Julius Erving.

After a sublime performance at Madison Square Garden, he was asked how he would defend himself. "I'd get out of my way," Jordan said.

In his first year, Jordan was named a starter at the All-Star Game, but the resentment on display during the Olympic warm-ups had only escalated.

During practice with the Eastern Conference All-Star team, Jordan wore his forbidden Nike apparel. It rubbed the veterans the wrong way. Thomas and Johnson, the East and West point guards, conspired to control the game — and Jordan's output. They would take it easy on each other on defense and work to keep the ball out of the hands of the cocky rookie. Jordan scored just 7 points.

"Natural jealousy is a part of professional sports," Jordan said when asked about it after the season. "I didn't work my way up to the top. I skipped a lot of steps."

Chicago's first game after the All-Star break was against Thomas and the Detroit Pistons. Jordan was out for blood. He went off for 49 points and 15 rebounds — including 12 of the Bulls' 16 points in overtime.

No slight — perceived or otherwise — went unnoticed to Jordan. He used everything as motivation. Just as much as his clutch shooting and ability to soar, that sense of vengeance became essential to Jordan's success. He always looked for an edge.

Seven years after the 1985 All-Star Game "freeze-out," when it came time to assemble the roster for Team USA's 1992 Dream Team, Jordan kept Thomas, one of the world's great playmakers, off the roster.

Nobody holds a grudge like Mike.

Jordan was named the 1985 Rookie of the Year. He led the Bulls in points, rebounds, assists and steals, and carried the team to its first playoff appearance in years. When he accepted his award, he referred to his first campaign as "experimental," a terrifying notion for the rest of the NBA.

In the playoffs the Bulls were bounced by the Milwaukee Bucks, but managed to win one game thanks to a last-second dagger from Jordan, who even as a rookie never backed down from the moment. "Twenty-six times, I've been trusted to take the game-winning shot and missed," he'd later say. "I've failed over and over and over again in my life. And that is why I succeed."

Jordan was grounded in his second season by a broken foot suffered after just three games. When his foot finally healed in March, the Bulls coaches and management wanted him to sit out the rest of the year to avoid reinjury. Jordan refused. The team tried to limit his minutes, but Jordan fought it publicly. He was giving the Chicago brass headaches, but the fans loved him for it.

That same season, Jordan made history against the Celtics in the playoffs. In Game 1 of their first-round series, he erupted for 49 points. Dennis Johnson, the Celtics' defensive wizard, couldn't stop him. "Michael's never going to have another game like that," Johnson said. The next game was Jordan's 63-point masterpiece. Nobody would question the limits of Michael Jordan again.

"I'd give all the points back if we could win," he said after the game.

Jordan was mastering the mental game, while his physical skills allowed him to do anything on the court, developing his style by learning from the legends before him.

"I believe greatness is an evolutionary process that changes and evolves era to era," he wrote in *For the Love of the Game*. "Without Julius Erving, David Thompson, Walter Davis and Elgin Baylor, there would never have been a Michael Jordan."

But evolution is a slow process. For Jordan, dominant from the very beginning, it was as though he emerged from the primordial soup slam-dunking. Like he said, he skipped a few steps.

Jordan's star continued to rise. His highlight-reel performances at the 1985 and '88 slam-dunk contests drew more and more

fans. In a matter of a few seasons, Jordan had reached rock star status. He was swarmed everywhere he went, and his celebrity pushed the NBA into the mainstream.

On the court, his dominance was unparalleled. In 1986–87 he led the league with 37.1 points per game, kicking off a streak that saw him win seven straight scoring titles. In 1988 he won his first of five MVP awards, and was also named the NBA's Defensive Player of the Year, He became the first player to record 200 steals and 100 blocks in a season.

Behind Jordan, the Bulls developed into a winner, making the playoffs each season, but getting to the Finals was proving difficult.

Year after year, one opponent got in their way: Isiah Thomas and the Bad Boy Pistons. Detroit employed an ultraphysical brand of

Jordan slams during the 1987 dunk contest.

Michael Jordan after signing a seven-year contract with the Chicago Bulls in 1984.

basketball and patrolled the court like a pro wrestling faction.

In '88 Detroit knocked out the Bulls in the second round. The following year, Jordan hit a buzzer-beater in round one to eliminate the Cleveland Cavaliers — "The Shot," as it has become known. The victory set up a rematch with Detroit in the Eastern Conference finals. The Pistons had devised a strategy for Jordan. They called it "the Jordan Rules," which essentially boiled down to double-teaming His Airness at all times — and knocking him to the ground every time he dared enter the paint.

The strategy worked, and at one point a frustrated Jordan retaliated, delivering an elbow to Thomas's face. With none of Jordan's teammates stepping up to provide scoring help, Detroit sent the Bulls packing once more.

Jordan needed help. In '87 Chicago drafted a relatively unknown forward from Arkansas named Scottie Pippen. But Pippen entered the NBA raw and would need years of seasoning before he was Jordan's costar.

And so Jordan continued to carry the Bulls. During the 1989–90 season, the NBA media paid close attention to Jordan's rising minute count and the unusually large burden he carried for the Bulls, by far more than any one player was being asked to do for any other team.

Publicly, Jordan dismissed the idea that his body needed a break. "Hey, I'm a young thoroughbred," he said, "and young thoroughbreds don't need rest."

Privately, he met with the Bulls' new general manager, Jerry Krause, and asked for help on the court. Krause told Jordan that his new eight-year, $25 million contract prevented the team from spending any more money on other players — as if it were Jordan's fault

that the Bulls couldn't surround him with better talent.

A furious Jordan took his anger toward Krause out on his opponents. In the last month of the season, he averaged over 36 points per game, including a career-high 69 points against Cleveland. But Chicago was once again destined to have their season ended by the Pistons — this time in a hard-fought seven-game Eastern Conference final series.

After six seasons in the NBA, Jordan had established himself as the best there is. But for all his brilliance, he'd fallen short of even a trip to the Finals.

But Air Jordan had barely left the runway.

MOST POINTS IN A PLAYOFF GAME

1. Michael Jordan	63	(1986)
2. Elgin Baylor	61	(1962)
3. Charles Barkley	56	(1994)
Michael Jordan	56	(1992)
Wilt Chamberlain	56	(1962)

1985
BOWIE OR BUST?

Sam Bowie will always be the player drafted one pick ahead of Michael Jordan. That's a complicated legacy.

In retrospect, the Bowie selection was an obvious misfire (how do you pass on Jordan?!), but he was universally considered one of the top prospects in the 1984 draft. He was a fluid athlete with a versatile skill-set who stood 7-foot-1. As a high schooler, he put little-known Lebanon, Pennsylvania, on the map when he was named the national player of the year in 1979, earning a scholarship to Kentucky. He was named an All-American in his sophomore season, and he helped his school reach the NCAA Final Four a few months before the draft took place.

If there was reason to pan the pick, it was Bowie's injury history. He'd missed two full college seasons after suffering a stress fracture to his left shin. Although he had returned and appeared healthy, the long-term risks were real.

The Portland Trail Blazers, who owned the second overall pick in the '84 draft, were keen on drafting a big man and had their sights set on Bowie. On paper he was the perfect center for coach Jack Ramsay's system: big, mobile and a good passer who could fill the lane and protect the basket.

Sam Bowie grabs a rebound as the Houston Rockets center Hakeem Olajuwon watches in 1985.

David Stern, center, Akeem Olajuwon, and Sam Bowie in 1984.

The Trail Blazers did their due diligence. They brought Bowie to Portland and put him through a seven-hour physical examination. "I don't know if that's referring back to the Bill Walton situation," Bowie wondered aloud on draft night after the team selected him. After Walton, the first pick of the 1974 draft, led the Trail Blazers to their first and only championship, his recurring foot injuries cut his career short, setting the franchise back in the process.

At best, the NBA draft is a crapshoot. Teams know they're rolling the dice, and no scouting report can accurately predict the course of a player's career. There are too many factors in play — what team they land on, the coach and the system, injuries, how they'll mesh with other pieces on the roster, how they'll adjust to the life of a pro athlete.

First-round draft picks in particular also carry the burden of expectations, which are always highest for those selected atop the draft — especially in the top three.

A top-three pick is supposed to signal a franchise savior of some kind — the caliber of player you can build a team around, or a missing piece to take a team to another level. When they don't fulfill that destiny, their shortcomings appear that much greater.

In his rookie year, Bowie looked the part of a potential future star, averaging nearly 9 boards and 3 blocks per game. He was named to the first All-Rookie team, along with Jordan, Hakeem Olajuwon, Sam Perkins and Charles Barkley.

In his second season, however, his left shin issues returned, and he was limited to just 38 games. In year three, Bowie was off to a flying start, averaging over 16 points per game. Five games into the season, he went up for a hook shot and felt what he described as an axe chopping through his leg. He crumpled to the ground, having suffered a broken tibia — this time it was his right leg.

"I remember seeing part of the bone sticking out of his leg, and how he was beating the floor over and over with his fist," recalled teammate Clyde Drexler.

The injury forced him to sit out his entire fourth season. He rebroke the bone during practice, and only returned to the court for the final 20 games of his fifth season in 1988–89. Jordan, meanwhile, was closing in on his third straight scoring title.

To that point in his NBA career, Bowie had played 139 out of a possible 410 games. He promised that if he suffered another major injury, he would walk away from the game entirely.

There has been a long list of top draft picks whose careers were cut short — or never even got off the ground — because of injuries.

Steve Stipanovich, the second overall pick of the 1983 draft, lasted only five years in the NBA until knee issues forced an early retirement. Pervis Ellison, the 1989 No. 1 pick, earned his nickname, Out of Service, because he struggled to stay on the court. The sixth overall pick in 1995, Bryant Reeves, had a promising start to his career but hung up his sneakers after just six seasons. Jonathan Bender, a fifth overall pick straight out of high school, played just one healthy season.

In Portland, center Greg Oden, the first overall pick in the 2007 draft, joined the list of heralded players who broke the hearts of Trail Blazers fans. Oden was drafted immediately ahead of two-time Finals MVP Kevin Durant, earning comparisons to Bowie.

But Oden only managed two injury-riddled seasons in Portland. A 2013 comeback attempt with the Miami Heat lasted just 23 games.

Sam Bowie was finally given a clean bill of health following the 1988–89 season. That summer, he was traded to the New Jersey Nets. "You'd have to call it a risk," said Nets GM Harry Weltman.

But the returns were promising. In his first season with the Nets, Bowie played in 68 games and averaged 15 points and 10 boards. For the next four years, he stayed healthy and helped the Nets reach the playoffs between 1992 and 1994. Sure, he wasn't the player Portland had envisioned on draft night, but he was a solid starter.

In the summer of '93, Bowie was dealt to the Los Angeles Lakers. He played two more seasons before calling it a career at age 33.

Bowie never became a star. But he played 511 NBA games, finishing in the top 20 in blocks in four separate seasons. He currently ranks 31st all-time in career blocks per game.

For many, Bowie's would be a dream career. But because of where he was drafted, he'll be remembered as a failure. *Sports Illustrated* put him at No. 1 on their list of the biggest NBA draft busts. ESPN named him the worst draft pick in the history of North American sports.

"I tell [Jordan] every time I see him: If he didn't turn into the player he was," Bowie said, "I wouldn't have to hear all this ridicule."

1986
THE DREAM COMES TO AMERICA

A keem "The Dream" Olajuwon uses his nimble feet and long limbs to dart out to the top of the key to help defend Magic Johnson.

Behind him, the ball is dumped to Kareem Abdul-Jabbar in the low post. Olajuwon doesn't look, but he sees. Abdul-Jabbar spins from the basket and hoists up his skyhook — only the most reliable go-to move the game has ever seen. Olajuwon turns toward the hoop, takes a stride and rises to meet Abdul-Jabbar at the apex, effortlessly swatting the ball away into the stands.

Later, the NBA's all-time blocks leader will take a page out of Bill Russell's book and perfect the art of blocking shots while directing the ball to an open teammate instead sending it out of bounds. But for now, Olajuwon is eager to make a statement.

At the other end of the floor, he's swarmed by as many as four defenders at once, while the 7-foot-2 Kareem hangs over his shoulders. Undeterred, Olajuwon leaps with his back to the basket, contorts his body in midair and dunks all over Abdul-Jabbar.

Hakeem Olajuwon outreaches the Dallas Mavericks during a 1988 playoff game.

It's Game 3 of the 1986 Western Conference finals between the Houston Rockets and Los Angeles Lakers. The NBA's defending champions, LA was eyeing its fifth straight Finals appearance.

But the second-year center from Lagos, Nigeria, is too much for the Lakers. Too big. Too quick. Too smart. In Game 2 he posted a double-double and added 4 steals and 6 blocks for good measure. On this night, he'll wind up with 40 points, and average 31 points, 11 rebounds and 4 blocks per game in the series.

It was a clinic in low-post play, the 23-year-old Olajuwon putting the 38-year-old Abdul-Jabbar through the wringer. For the first time in his 20-year career, Kareem looked old. The Rockets went on to beat the Lakers in five games, winning four straight after dropping Game 1. The Rockets would fall back to Earth in the Finals, losing to Larry Bird and the Celtics in six games, but Olajuwon had put the rest of the league on notice.

The Lakers had never come across a player like Akeem Olajuwon (he would add the H to his first name in 1991). Neither had the rest of the NBA.

Standing 6-foot-11, with the grace and agility of a guard, he was an effortless leaper and powerful presence down low. A multisport athlete growing up — everything but basketball, which he first played at the age of 15 — he merged elite athleticism with a sharp mind for the game and natural defensive instincts. As his career progressed, his offensive game did, too, as he developed a versatile post game and shooting touch that made him almost unguardable.

His road from Lagos to the NBA and status as the league's first international superstar only set him farther apart, while laying a path for generations of African basketball players to follow.

By the time he was dismantling Kareem and the Lakers, Olajuwon was no stranger to basketball fans. He was the first-overall pick in the 1984 draft after reaching three straight NCAA Finals with the University of Houston. In the NBA, he didn't skip a beat and would retire as one of the all-time greats, with all of the awards and accolades to back it up: MVP, two-time champion, Finals MVP and Defensive Player of the Year among them.

But when he first arrived in the United States, he was a 7-foot mystery.

Like all Nigerians, Olajuwon grew up playing soccer, and he also participated in track and field, excelling in the high jump. But handball was his sport.

As a teenager he was captain of the state handball team, which practiced in the same facility as the basketball team. Although he had never played, Olajuwon was mesmerized by the ballhandling. No-look crossovers, behind-the-back moves. It was cool.

The team's coach, Ganiyu Otenigbagbe, had long been begging the towering Olajuwon to give basketball a try. Now the kid was ready to give it a go. Ganiyu brought him to

Olajuwon shoots during the 1993 NBA Finals.

the court and walked him inside to the paint, which was coated with red. He pointed to the floor and told him it was red for blood. The low post was a ruthless place, he said, and to control it you have to be merciless. Block everything that comes near you. Slam the ball through the rim like you want to break it. You see, when you dunk on people they tend to stay out of your way.

Olajuwon was a quick study, and before long he caught the eye of an American-born scout who recognized his ability and arranged visits to five colleges across the United States. Olajuwon persuaded his mother to buy him a round-trip ticket that would take him from Lagos to New York City, then to Houston, Atlanta and Providence, before circling back to New York and, eventually, home.

He got off the plane in New York for a visit with St. John's University, in the heart of winter. He stepped off the plane, coatless, into the frigid air and headed straight to the ticket counter at the airport. "Can I go to Houston today?" he asked.

Four hours later he landed in the far more agreeable climate of southeastern Texas and took a taxi to the office of University of Houston head coach Guy Lewis. After the meeting, Olajuwon cancelled the rest of the visits.

Despite his obvious talent, it had still only been three years since Olajuwon first picked up a ball, and he played less than 20 minutes per game during his freshman season in 1981–82. That summer, however, Lewis introduced Olajuwon to NBA star and longtime Rockets center Moses Malone, who spent his off-seasons training at a local Houston gym.

A dominant center in his own right, the 27-year-old Malone had just been crowned the NBA MVP and would win the award again the following year, his third in total. He took the young Nigerian under his wing during heated scrimmages. Malone bodied the skinnier Olajuwon, who never backed down. By summer's end, Olajuwon was routinely dunking on his new mentor. The next season, he averaged over 5 blocks per game.

Heading into the 1984 draft, Olajuwon was unanimously considered the draft's top prospect — ahead of Michael Jordan. As

"luck" would have it, the Houston Rockets held the No. 1 pick. The choice was obvious.

Olajuwon continued to dominate the NBA just as he had done in the college ranks. Despite falling short of winning it all in 1985–86, the Rockets were anointed as the "team of the future" by *Sports Illustrated*. But the plague of cocaine use that had been poisoning the NBA throughout the 80s struck the Rockets hard, and all Olajuwon could do was watch as teammate after teammate was suspended or otherwise ravaged by the drug.

Between 1987 and '92 the Rockets couldn't even make it past the first round, while Olajuwon publicly admonished team ownership for not surrounding him with "championship-caliber" teammates.

While his teams were struggling, Olajuwon was expanding his game. Like a mad scientist, he worked endlessly on his footwork and developed an arsenal of low-post moves, including the patented "Dream Shake," a herky-jerky sequence where he fakes out his defender for a humiliating and picturesque 2 points.

Olajuwon reached the peak of his powers in 1993–94. With Michael Jordan sitting out the season to pursue a career in baseball, Olajuwon took over the title of the NBA's best. He was named the regular-season MVP for the first time in eight years and returned to the Finals for the first time since '86. The Rockets beat the New York Knicks in an intense seven-game series. Olajuwon was named Finals MVP, becoming the first player to ever be named MVP, Finals MVP and Defensive Player of the Year in the same season.

The Rockets repeated as champs in '95

against the Orlando Magic, as Olajuwon averaged 33 points per game while making easy work of rising star Shaquille O'Neal. By the next season, Jordan had returned to the Chicago Bulls and regained his form, ending the Rockets' title run — although we never got to see Jordan vs. Olajuwon in the Finals, a matchup of the 90s two most dominant players.

"If you ask Michael Jordan what one guy he ever feared," former Rockets forward Robert Horry said years later, "it was Hakeem Olajuwon."

When he hung up his sneakers in 2002 after 18 seasons — all but one in Houston — Olajuwon became the only player to have retired in the top 10 of all time in points, rebounds, steals and blocks. His total of 3,830 blocks leads all players in history. Nobody else comes within 500 of him.

In the years following his retirement, Olajuwon became a tutor to several of the game's brightest stars. Just as Moses Malone took the time with him, he has spent summers working with the likes of LeBron James, Kobe Bryant, Kevin Garnett and Dwight Howard.

He'd invite them to his ranch in Texas — after getting out of that taxicab in Houston, he virtually never left — and drill them on the physics and footwork of the low-post game. He'd share his secrets and demonstrate his moves, sweat dripping off of him as if he was back in the Finals.

Even into his 50s, there's an elegance and efficiency in the way he moves on the court. He brought a skillfulness to the center position that no player has, before or since. There is only one "Dream."

NBA AFRICA

Olajuwon opened the door to a continent of prospective talent. Today there have been more than 20 players from Nigeria alone, with the NBA making more inroads to Africa. In 2003 Toronto Raptors President Masai Ujiri, a native Nigerian, established "Giants of Africa," a program to help uncover talent in Africa that was founded on the simple question: "How do we find the next Hakeem Olajuwon?" Currently the league operates basketball camps across the continent, where all-stars like Joel Embiid and Pascal Siakam have been discovered. In 2019 the NBA partnered with FIBA to establish the first pro league in Africa.

ROUND 2
CELTICS VS. LAKERS

It was impossible to ignore the championship banners and retired jerseys hanging from the rafters at Boston Garden. They honored some of the game's most legendary figures and served as a reminder of the Celtics' heyday in the 60s, when Bill Russell's dynasty ruled the NBA kingdom.

The Los Angeles Lakers entered the Garden six times with a chance to win it all, and the Celtics walked away champs each and every time. If any of the Lakers forgot, all they had to do was look up.

In 1984 the Celtics and Lakers met in the Finals for the first time in 15 years. Game 1 took place at the Garden, and fans showed up draped in white sheets, dressed as the ghosts of Celtics' past.

But the Lakers were unfazed. Any mind grip Boston held over LA had been left back in the 60s. Los Angeles kicked off the 80s with a championship, thanks to the heroics of Magic Johnson, who in 1980 became the only rookie to win Finals MVP. They won it all again in '82.

The Lakers rolled out to an early lead in the opening game of the '84 series, ignoring the chants of "Beat LA!" that rained down from the Celtics faithful, who packed the Garden for its 168th straight sellout. Larry Bird, Dennis Johnson and Kevin McHale — three of the nine Hall of Fame players who took the court that night — all scored over 20 points. But Boston had no answer for Kareem Abdul-Jabbar's game-high 32. Los Angeles took Game 1, 115–109.

You could fill a whole wing of the Hall of Fame with the characters from the Celts–Lakers matchup, from the bench to the front office. The two head coaches — LA's Pat Riley and Boston's KC Jones — each won multiple titles as a player, and the architects of both clubs, Jerry West and Red Auerbach, helped lay the foundation for the NBA as we know it.

But all eyes were on the two young stars: Magic and Bird.

In Boston, Bird led the team to the title during his second year, 1980–81. That season featured the debut of McHale, who'd been drafted third overall. The pride of Hibbing, Minnesota, McHale's broad shoulders and sharp elbows were paired with a methodical low-post game that made the 6-foot-10 forward a nightmare to handle. By the '83–84 season, he'd earned the Sixth Man of the Year award twice.

He joined Bird, Johnson and center Robert Parish to give the Celtics a workmanlike reputation — blue-collar, like their fan base. In LA, Magic's smile could light up the Hollywood sign. When the Celtics players saw it flashed across newspapers, TV screens and billboards, they rolled their eyes. Ahead of the '84 Finals, they'd given Earvin Johnson a new nickname: Cheesy.

The teams left the Boston Garden tied at one game apiece. When the series resumed at the Forum in Los Angeles, Boston was run off the floor in a Game 3 blowout, thanks to a record 21 assists from Johnson. Boston "played like a bunch of sissies," Bird said after the game. He wasn't happy with the behind-the-back passes, uncontested layups and big smiles on the Lakers' faces as they dismantled the Celtics. "It seems like somebody would try to put a stop to it," he cryptically told reporters.

In Game 4, Boston was eager to send a message. During the third quarter, with the Celtics trailing by double digits, Lakers forward Kurt Rambis was en route to the rim for an open layup. The normally reserved McHale raced the length of the court and, before Rambis reached the basket, wrapped an arm around his neck from behind and violently pulled him to the ground.

Both benches erupted. The Lakers called it a cheap shot (which it was). Meanwhile, Bird later anointed Rambis's fall as the "birth of flopping." The hit knocked LA out of rhythm. Abdul-Jabbar and Bird got into a war of words, and Bird later shoved Lakers guard Michael Cooper into the stands. Boston erased the Lakers' lead and won in overtime, thanks in part to 29 points and 21 rebounds from Bird.

"That takedown of Rambis," Magic said one week later, "totally changed the complexion of the series."

It all came down to a deciding Game 7 back at the Garden. Boston maintained the lead during a close affair. Celtics reserve Gerald Henderson scored 9 points in the third quarter, and Boston held a 13-point lead heading into the fourth. But 19 fourth-quarter points from Kareem and James Worthy brought LA back.

Down 5 with less than a minute remaining, Magic danced to the hoop but was met by Parish, whose block sparked a Celtics fast break that iced the game.

Make it 7–0 Boston.

"I always thought [the Lakers] were soft," Finals MVP Bird said in victory, "and they were that all season."

Magic Johnson drives to the basket against the Celtics in 1984.

For the league, the Bird–Magic Finals matchup had been worth the wait. Game 7 was the most-viewed television game in NBA history.

The McHale knockdown greased the wheels for an intense rivalry. Unlike the 60s showdowns, there was real animosity between the teams this time around.

But when they met for a rematch a year later, it was the Lakers' turn to taste victory.

Los Angeles held Bird to 23 points per game in the series and staved off a breakout performance from McHale, who led the Celtics in scoring and rebounding. The Lakers got a boost from Worthy, the former first overall pick, and 14 assists per game from Magic. But the '85 Finals was Abdul-Jabbar's chance to shine.

His signature skyhook — the most reliable shot in the history of the game — proved unstoppable. At age 37, he became the oldest Finals MVP ever, a stunning 14 years after he first won the award with Milwaukee in 1971.

In 1985–86, the Lakers were upset in the playoffs by Houston. Meanwhile, the Celtics reclaimed their predominant position in the NBA, winning 67 games. McHale (now in the starting lineup) was blossoming, and Parish continued to own the paint. Boston got consistent contributions from such backcourt mainstays as Johnson and Danny Ainge, along with reserve guard Scott Wedman. And the team brought in another Hall of Famer, 33-year-old Bill Walton, who came off the bench in relief of Parish.

Throw in Bird at his best — he won his third straight MVP award — and the Celts were a juggernaut, cruising to the championship.

But Boston was aging fast and entered the next season worn down. They still managed to finish first in the East, but two grueling, physical seven-game series, against the Bucks and Detroit Pistons, left them ragged by the time they reached the '87 Finals.

The Lakers, on the other hand, seemed to be in peak condition. Their seven best players all played at least 78 games that season, and Magic Johnson was named league MVP.

The '87 Finals was the third and final installment of the Celtics–Lakers '80s trilogy. For the first time, the series began in Los Angeles,

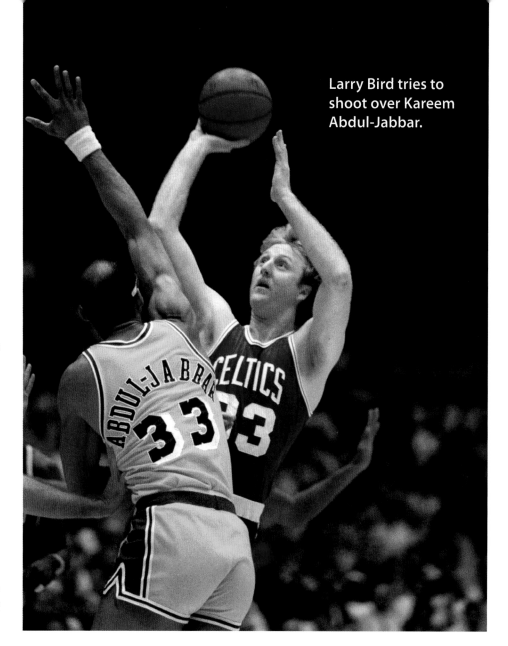

Larry Bird tries to shoot over Kareem Abdul-Jabbar.

where the Showtime offense was in full force. The Lakers shot nearly 60 percent from the field and averaged 133.5 points per game over the first two contests, both comfortable wins.

But the Celtics took Game 3 at home. "Now it's going to be easy," Bird said. And for the first three quarters of Game 4, at least, it was. The Celtics nursed a 16-point lead while Bird dropped 12 in the third quarter alone.

But as they'd done so many times before, the Lakers roared back. A clutch fadeaway from Worthy, followed by an alley-oop dunk by a 40-year old Abdul-Jabbar, gave the Lakers a 1-point lead with 29 seconds remaining. Celtics ball.

Bird eluded the defense and got open for a 3-pointer in the corner that swished through to give Boston a 106–104 lead. Lakers ball.

Kareem was fouled and split the free

throws to bring LA within one, but McHale fumbled the ball out of bounds to give the Lakers possession with seven seconds remaining. On a mismatch, Magic was guarded by the bigger and slower McHale. Johnson drove toward the hoop, hesitated and, with the defender off balance, uncorked a skyhook of his own — "the junior, junior, junior, sky-hook," he later called it. Lakers led, 107–106.

With two seconds left, Bird found himself open beyond the arc once more, but clanged the would-be game winner. The Lakers took a commanding 3–1 series lead.

The Celtics took Game 5 at the Garden, but back at the Forum for Game 6, the crowd helped propel the Lakers to an 18–2 run in a comeback win. For the second time in three tries, gold trumped green.

1986
LOSING LEN BIAS

"With the second pick in the 1986 NBA draft, the Boston Celtics select . . . Len Bias, of the University of Maryland." — NBA commissioner David Stern, on draft night, June 17, 1986.

"LEONARD K. BIAS, a 22-year-old Black male, died as a result of cocaine intoxication, which interrupted the normal electrical control of his heartbeat, resulting in the sudden onset of seizures and cardiac arrest." — Prince George's County toxicology report, June 19, 1986.

"Can't miss."

That's how they described Len Bias. As in you can't miss him. Six-foot-nine. Big smile. Soaring through the air with no regard for the rules of gravity. As in he can't miss a shot. As in: watch him on the court and the other nine players become a blur. As in, there is no chance Bias falls anywhere short of becoming a star.

That was in the summer of 1986.

It's hard to quantify just how good Bias was. The University of Maryland star dominated the college ranks like few others, a first-team All-American by his senior year and two-time Atlantic Coast Conference Player of the Year, the same award Michael Jordan had won two years prior before jumping to the NBA. In fact, opponents who played against both players referred to Bias as a "bigger and stronger" version of Jordan. Certainly, nobody attacked the rim quite like those two.

Len Bias at the 1986 NBA draft.

But the real excitement came over what he projected to be once he reached the pro level. If Jordan could transition so effectively to the big leagues, imagine the damage Bias could do. The perfect power forward for the time, Bias combined a tough, nasty inside game — he reveled in dunking on opponents and, like all of the greats, fed off hostile crowds — with sublime athletic gifts and a shooting touch that made him a threat from anywhere on the floor.

Only North Carolina center Brad Daugherty was a more touted prospect than Bias, and teams seeking to rest their fate on the skills of the 22-year-old would have to hope that the 1986 draft lottery broke their way. The Cleveland Cavaliers ended up with the first overall pick in the lottery, while the Boston Celtics scored the second choice.

Of all the teams in need of a serious talent boost, the Celts seemed to be at the bottom of the list. They were the defending champions, having just toppled the Houston Rockets in the Finals. Many were touting the '86 Celtics as one of the greatest single-season teams the NBA had ever seen, starring two-time MVP Larry Bird and an overqualified supporting cast that featured Kevin McHale, Robert Parish and Bill Walton.

Celtics president Red Auerbach made no secret of the fact that he intended to draft Len Bias that coming June, using a pick his team had acquired two years earlier in a controversial trade that sent championship guard Gerald Henderson to Seattle.

When the Cavs chose Daugherty, it was an unbelievable turn of events for Boston. Not only were the champs getting a top-flight player, they were being gifted with a lifeline that could keep their aging roster and dynasty status intact into the next decade.

That Bias was joining an esteemed fraternity like the Celtics was not lost on him. Boston represented the NBA's gold standard of success, from the unprecedented championship reign of the Bill Russell–led squads to the current Larry Bird era. Bias was eager to join their ranks.

Just before the draft, Auerbach invited Bias to watch the team in person during Game 1 of the NBA Finals against the Houston Rockets, seating him just one row behind the Celtics bench.

"It was a dream," Bias said. "I thought that could be me one day. It's a dream within a dream. My first dream was just to play in the NBA. To get drafted by the world champions is an extra one."

On draft night, June 17, in New York City, Bias couldn't stop smiling as his name was called out and he donned a Boston hat. Celtics green suited him quite nicely. After some celebrations that night, he and his agent traveled to Boston the following day, where he met with his new team and went over some contractual paperwork. In the evening, he signed an endorsement deal with Reebok, then made his way back home to Maryland.

Bias met up with friends at a party, and at two in the morning they made their way back to his dorm room on the University of Maryland campus. They stayed up chatting and snorting cocaine.

Bias had earned the nickname Horse for his sheer physicality and the manner in which he seemed to effortlessly gallop down the court in a breeze. As he sat on the edge of his bed, he proudly declared himself a horse, and then bent over a mirror to do what would be his final line of coke.

Paramedics rushed Bias to the local hospital, but it was too late. At 8:15 a.m., Bias was pronounced dead.

Forty hours earlier, Bias was the happiest kid in America; his dreams had come true. That morning, Larry Bird was called for a statement. "It's the cruelest thing I've ever heard," he said.

A medical examiner's report would reveal that Bias had suffered a heart attack as a result of the cocaine he snorted. Further test results suggested that he wasn't a regular user, which only heightened the fear that took hold across the country in the wake of his death.

"Few imagined a human as healthy and robust and muscular as Bias could actually die from a substance like cocaine," wrote Michael Weinreb in his ESPN feature article, "The Day Innocence Died."

"This was not John Belushi we were talking about."

The public at large knew little about cocaine. "There are still superb cardiologists who are surprised to find out that cocaine can cause a lethal cardiac event," said one renowned specialist.

Telephone hotlines were jammed with worried callers — parents and kids wondering aloud whether they were in danger for taking the drug. Bias's death was a rallying cry for the growing anti-drug movement and America's "War on Drugs." At a press conference the week after his death, Lefty Driesell, Bias's coach at Maryland, spread the message bluntly: "These are not recreational drugs," he said. "They're killers."

The NBA was no stranger to the drug, having gone through a crisis in the 70s when cocaine abuse gripped team rosters. But this was the mid-80s, and cocaine was as rampant as ever, a part of daily life for more than five million Americans representing a wide cross-section of the population. Cocaine was innocent, really, the thinking went. Not habit-forming. A drug with few consequences.

Until now.

Eleven thousand people attended a memorial for Bias. Friends and family mourned the loss of a 22-year-old, fans remained in shock, and a nation suddenly faced the danger of its most popular recreational drug.

Following Bias's death, his mother, Lonise, would describe her son as a martyr, a child whose death could teach others. His was a cautionary tale. Like that of Maurice Stokes, the powerful forward left permanently paralyzed after striking his head on the floor during a drive to the hoop, resulting in a debilitating brain disorder. Or Hank Gathers, the All-American who was stopped in his tracks, collapsed and died of a heart attack during a collegiate game. Or Ben "Benji" Wilson, the Chicago high school star destined for greatness until he was shot to death following a petty spat with another student.

When the league lost Bias, it lost a natural rival for Jordan, something that would prove elusive over the next decade. The Celtics lost their next great star, and players like Bird and McHale would run their bodies ragged trying to keep Boston's winning ways alive without the help of Bias.

Len Bias slams during a 1985
NCAA game.

1989
BAD BOYS

Long before they ever won a title, the Detroit Pistons had a reputation.

The Pistons were dubbed the Bad Boys and wore the moniker like a badge of honor. Detroit played a physical brand of basketball that habitually stepped over the line into sheer violence.

The Pistons were loathed around the NBA, and they earned that ire. The Bad Boys undercut opponents on their way to the rim. They took cheap shots — and not just after the whistle. They seemingly threw fists as often as jumpers.

They rubbed the basketball establishment the wrong way; in the eyes of Celtics architect Red Auerbach, the Bad Boys were nothing more than "classless bullies."

But they were also successful. The Pistons were the team that Michael Jordan couldn't beat. The team that got under the skin of Larry Bird and the Boston Celtics. The team that swept Magic Johnson and the Showtime Lakers in the Finals.

The Pistons franchise was one of the oldest in basketball, dating back to 1941, when they played out of Fort Wayne, Indiana. The team had its share of talent over the years — Bob Lanier, Dave Bing and Dave DeBusschere — but was never a winner. The organization set up shop in Detroit in 1957 and only made it to the second round of the playoffs (but never farther) three times in the two decades that followed.

By the end of the 70s, they were the worst team in basketball. But as the calendar flipped to the 80s, that was about to change — thanks to the addition of Hall of Fame point guard Isiah Thomas.

Thomas, fresh off an NCAA title with Indiana, was drafted by the Pistons second overall in the 1981 draft. He was, simply put, the perfect point guard and arguably the game's best one-on-one player until Jordan arrived on the scene.

Thomas had soft features and a gentle smile that masked his killer instinct. They called him the Baby-Faced Assassin. By his second season, he was an All-Star and would stay that way for 12 straight years.

With his cornerstone in place, Pistons GM Jack McCloskey got to work building a team around Thomas. During his rookie season, the Pistons traded for Vinnie "The Microwave" Johnson, who earned his nickname thanks to his ability to heat up in a hurry. The team also dealt a first-round pick to Cleveland for center Bill Laimbeer.

Laimbeer grew up rich, but his game was from the gutter. He set the tone for Detroit's aggressive play and was unapologetic about the way he liberally swung his elbows and threw players to the ground. When Laimbeer went to the bench, in came bruising big man Rick Mahorn, maybe the only player more eager to lay out the opposition.

In 1983 the team hired Chuck Daly as its head coach. Daly's coaching career began way back in 1955, when he coached high school ball in Punxsutawney, Pennsylvania. Daly was a players' coach, and his ability to manage egos and get the most out of his roster eventually earned him the Dream Team gig in 1992.

In 1985 the Pistons drafted shooting guard Joe Dumars 18th overall. He was the perfect complement to Thomas in the backcourt and quickly became the premier defensive guard in the game. The next year, they drafted Dennis Rodman, a rail-thin pogo stick of a power forward who went on to win two Defensive Player of the Year awards in Detroit.

The Pistons gained steam as the 80s rolled along. In 1984–85, Thomas had one of the best seasons ever for a guard, averaging over 21 points and an NBA-best 13.9 assists per game, but Detroit fell to the Boston Celtics in the second round.

The two teams met again in the '87 Eastern Conference finals. In Game 4, as Larry Bird went for a shot under the hoop, Laimbeer grabbed him from behind by the neck and slammed him to the court. As a pileup ensued, an irate Bird started swinging haymakers at Laimbeer.

"He was a dirty player," Bird said. "Bill tried to hurt you."

The Pistons' physicality was blatant. But it was the mental edge their hard-hitting reputation afforded them that served as Detroit's greatest advantage. Before tip-off, opponents were wary of driving the lane, lest they be on the receiving end of a vicious blow.

"We asked for no mercy, nor gave any mercy," said Laimbeer. "We were arrogant about how we did business."

Bird and the Celtics got their revenge. In Game 5, Bird stole an inbounds pass from Thomas before getting the ball to Dennis Johnson for a layup that won the game at the buzzer. Boston went on to win in seven.

The Bad Boys title was also an NBA marketing ploy introduced at the close of the

Joe Dumars defends
Xavier McDaniel during
the 1992 playoffs.

James Worthy goes up for a basket against Bill Laimbeer during the NBA championship game at The Forum in Inglewood, California, in 1988.

'87–88 season. The league's popularity was rising, and there were plenty of roles to fill. The Pistons were happy to take on the part of the villain. Yet, as the Bad Boys persona gained steam, Thomas issued a warning to his teammates: "We can use this reputation two ways," he explained. "We can use it to our advantage, or it's going to hinder us severely."

In 1988 Detroit ousted Boston in an Eastern finals rematch, setting up a matchup with the Los Angeles Lakers in the Finals. The series pitted the game's top point guards — Isiah and Magic — against one another. Close friends off the court, the two sent the viewing public into a frenzy when they'd meet for a kiss on the cheek at center court prior to the game.

But once the ball tipped off, that love was left at center court. The two teams engaged in a fierce series that went the distance. The Pistons entered Game 6 with a 3–2 lead. With Detroit trailing at halftime, Thomas came out on fire, scoring 14 points before rolling his ankle. But he remained in the game and, hobbling on one foot, ended up with 25 points in the third quarter alone — an NBA playoffs record for most points in a single quarter.

His heroic effort kept Detroit in the game, but the Lakers pulled out the win after a controversial foul call on Laimbeer that sent Kareem Abdul-Jabbar to the free-throw line to ice the game. An injured Thomas was unable to replicate his miraculous performance, and the Lakers won Game 7.

Halfway through the following season, Detroit made a controversial move at the trade deadline, sending their leading scorer, Adrian Dantley, to Dallas in exchange for Mark Aguirre. The Pistons went 30–4 after the trade and headed into the playoffs with a head of steam.

Apart from two losses to Jordan's Bulls in the Eastern Conference finals, the Pistons were undefeated in the playoffs, including a four-game sweep of their Finals rematch with an undermanned Los Angeles squad.

Lakers coach Pat Riley was succinct in his summary of events: "They kicked our ass."

The next season, the Pistons were crowned champions once more, this time with an equally convincing 4–1 Finals performance against the Portland Trail Blazers.

The Pistons were bullies, but they were also the best team around.

In 1991, however, their reign came to a swift end. After eliminating Jordan's Bulls in the playoffs for three years in a row — thanks to an especially aggressive tactic based around knocking MJ to the ground whenever he came near the hoop — Michael finally slew the beast. In the '91 Eastern finals, Detroit was swept 4–0.

"Good always overcomes evil," remarked Jordan, who averaged 30 points in the series. Game 4 was a 21-point blowout. Before the buzzer even sounded, Thomas led his team off the court, walking past the Chicago bench without making eye contact or shaking hands with their opponents.

Bad boys for life.

1991
MAGIC AND HIV

It's the most important press conference the NBA has ever held.

On November 7, 1991, Earvin "Magic" Johnson, the 32-year-old Los Angeles Lakers superstar, stepped behind a microphone in front of a group of family, friends, teammates and reporters.

"Because of the HIV virus that I have obtained," he announced, "I will have to retire from the Lakers today."

National newscasts led with the story of Magic's diagnosis. President George Bush addressed it, calling it "a tragedy."

Johnson was scared before he took the

Magic Johnson hugs Isiah Thomas before the 1992 All-Star Game.

podium. Not about making the announcement; he knew it had to be done. Not of facing the media; he'd done that his whole career. He was scared that once those around

Magic holds up the 1992 All-Star Game MVP award.

him knew he had the virus, he wouldn't see them again. They wouldn't call. They wouldn't reach out. They wouldn't come to his home to visit.

Despite an epidemic that was gripping parts of the globe and had made its way to the United States the previous decade, there was so much that was unknown about HIV and AIDS at the time. In 1981, when the first cases were reported in America, 337 people were afflicted. By 1989 the number of reported cases rose to over 100,000. In 1991, when Johnson went public, the World Health Organization estimated that over 10 million worldwide had contracted the virus.

The majority of citizens couldn't distinguish HIV — the immune system–attacking virus that Johnson had contracted — with AIDS, the condition that can develop as a result of HIV. In the early 80s the affliction had been obscenely dismissed as "gay cancer." It was seen as a disease reserved for homosexuals, or junkies sharing needles — a false perception Johnson himself had subscribed to.

"I didn't know the difference between the virus and the disease. While my ears heard HIV-positive, my mind heard AIDS," he wrote in a self-authored *Sports Illustrated* cover story published just 11 days after the announcement. "To me, AIDS was someone else's disease. It was a disease for gays and drug users. Not for someone like me."

To say the news came as a shock to Johnson as it did to everybody else is an understatement. His diagnosis came during the preseason, during which Magic had been playing at his usual All-Star level. In a series of exhibition games in Paris against his good friend Larry Bird and the Boston Celtics, Johnson was named MVP. Just one season removed from reaching the Finals, where the Lakers were upended by Michael Jordan and the Chicago Bulls, Magic and his team were preparing to contend for another title.

Magic felt healthy. But those around him kept telling him otherwise. Doctors told him they expected him to live for three more years, an optimistic guess based on his elite physical conditioning.

The night of the announcement, Pat Riley, Magic's former coach with the Lakers who was then coaching the New York Knicks, addressed the Madison Square Garden crowd and asked for a moment of silence.

Larry Bird, who failed to hold back his tears during a game that night, said it was the saddest he'd been since his father passed away.

"It's kind of like the death of a brother," said Charles Barkley when asked for his initial reaction to the news.

"My feeling was: dead man walking," said Karl Malone.

Before Johnson shared the news with the world, HIV was still living underground. Most people didn't know anybody with HIV, even though within a decade it was estimated that more than 900,000 Americans were infected with the virus, one-third of them not even aware because of a lack of testing. But *everybody* knew Magic. And so now everybody knew someone with the virus.

Johnson became a fervent spokesperson and activist. He established the Magic Johnson Foundation and joined the National Commission on AIDS. In 1999 he was the main speaker at the United Nations World AIDS Day Conference.

"This is a very courageous, heroic person and a heroic act," said commissioner David Stern. "What this means for the NBA is that one of our idols is human."

But nothing did more to dispel fear than the 1992 All-Star Game in Orlando.

Even though he wasn't playing that season, fans voted Johnson into the starting lineup of the Western Conference All-Star team. The league permitted Magic to play — Commissioner Stern had spent the season educating the NBA's players on the myths surrounding HIV, including dispelling notions that it could be transmitted through sweat.

Prior to the game, some players expressed concerns, but most were hesitant to speak up. "It's a sensitive issue," said Cleveland point guard Mark Price, "and Magic is a popular player."

Orlando point guard Scott Skiles admitted he was worried about Johnson getting a bloody nose. "I heard a doctor say the transfer risk was very, very, very, very low. But that's still too high," he said.

On February 9, Johnson made his return to the court. To prepare, he had been running four miles a day. He was also a regular at Lakers practices, where teammate Kareem Abdul-Jabbar would work out with him.

With the All-Star Game approaching, Johnson was nervous. He wasn't sure the other players would be comfortable playing against him; he worried they would no longer treat him as their peer on the court.

Before tip-off, the cameras — broadcasting to a worldwide audience — followed Johnson to half-court, where Eastern Conference opponent Isiah Thomas was waiting. Thomas planted a kiss on Magic's cheek, just as he had when the Lakers and Pistons met in the '88 Finals. During the pregame introductions, the sold-out crowd rained cheers on Johnson, and the East team came over to offer hugs and support. For the first time all night, the smile left Magic's face. The reality of the moment was sinking in.

On the first possession of the game, Johnson turned the ball over, but before long he found his stride. With his teammates encouraging him to shoot, Magic obliged. He uncorked a skyhook that swished through the net. He drove through the defense for an acrobatic layup. A 30 percent 3-point shooter during his career — his only real weakness — suddenly Johnson couldn't miss. He nailed two consecutive 3-pointers, howling with laughter as he watched the ball sink through the mesh.

Time away from the court hadn't dulled Magic's otherworldly abilities. He was dishing to teammates — no-looks, spinning zip passes, the whole arsenal that a generation of fans had grown up watching in awe and trying to replicate on driveways and hardtops around the world. Magic had 9 assists in the second half.

In the final minute, with Magic's Western Conference team up 148–115, the East stars began to challenge Johnson one on one — a show of respect for one of the game's greatest competitors.

First it was Thomas, who tried to dribble past Johnson before settling for an air ball. The next trip up the floor, it was Michael Jordan's turn. The eight other players cleared out, leaving half the court open for the two legends. Jordan planted a crossover on Johnson and pulled up for a jumper that clanged off the rim.

As Magic brought the ball up the court, the smile across his face was electric. A part of his life he thought was over had been rejuvenated, if only for one night.

With 18 seconds left in the game, Johnson backed Thomas down at the top of the 3-point line. He spun, stepped back, and hoisted a 3-pointer. *Swish.* The crowd lost it as players and coaches from both teams swarmed Magic in celebration. There were still 14 seconds on the clock, but the game was ended early. "It's the first game ever to be called on account of hugs," Johnson said afterward.

He would return to the court three years later, when he appeared for 39 games with the Lakers as a player-coach. But it's the 1992 All-Star Game that we'll remember.

Magic was awarded the MVP trophy that night, a fairy-tale ending befitting one of the most magical and memorable performances of all time.

"This was the perfect end to the story. I'd been trying to write this story all week, and that was like I was at my typewriter and I said, 'Here's my ending. Period.'"

MOST ALL-STAR GAMES

1.	Kareem Abdul-Jabbar	19
2.	Kobe Byrant	18
3.	LeBron James	16
4.	Tim Duncan	15
	Kevin Garnett	15
	Shaquille O'Neal	15

1991
THREE-PEAT

At age 23, Michael Jordan established himself as the NBA's best and transformed the Chicago Bulls into a rising power in the East. But after a demoralizing seven-game loss in the 1990 Eastern Conference finals to Detroit, there were questions surrounding MJ's ability to carry his team all the way. For the third straight year, the Pistons ended his season.

"I didn't have it to compete with them," Jordan said, for the last time.

If Jordan was going to beat Detroit, he couldn't do it by himself. That was the message first-year head coach Phil Jackson wanted to impart on his star.

The following year, after averaging over 34 points for the past four seasons, Jordan's scoring dropped to 31.5 (still tops in the NBA). The Bulls installed a new strategy called the Triangle Offense — the brainchild of Jackson's assistant, Tex Winter. The style created movement and flow in a half-court set. It helped turn Jordan's supporting cast — Scottie Pippen, Horace Grant, John Paxson and center Bill Cartwright — into legitimate threats.

Chicago won 61 games and earned home-court advantage throughout the playoffs. In their fourth straight meeting, the Pistons held Michael to under 30 points per game (29.6), but the Bulls swept Detroit.

When he was awarded the regular-season MVP trophy, Jordan made sure his teammates surrounded him on the court. But once the '91 Finals began, all attention was turned to the one-on-one matchup of Michael vs. Magic.

Chicago Stadium was a madhouse for Game 1, but the Lakers won after Jordan missed a jumper at the buzzer.

In Game 2, with Jordan in foul trouble, Horace Grant carried the scoring load in the first half while Pippen assumed the job of guarding Magic. Jordan led his team to a second-half blowout by scoring 13 straight baskets, none as mesmerizing as when he took off for a layup and switched hands in midair to elude multiple defenders. He finished with 33 points on 15-for-18 shooting in a 107–86 thumping.

After the game, some Lakers were upset Jordan had been taunting them during the Bulls' run. "Since he's Michael, I guess he feels he can get away with it," one said.

Chicago went on to win the series in six games. "I get to say I played against one of the greatest of all time," said Magic.

"I'm not sure people really know how good this guy is," said Lakers GM Jerry West. "If he didn't dunk a basketball, he would still be as great as anybody who ever played this game."

Jordan had been anointed. He cried and celebrated with his father. "It took a team to get to this point," he said.

The Bulls continued to steamroll through the league. In 1991–92 Pippen raised his game; the intense practice sessions against Jordan prepared him to take on anyone. He was already neck-and-neck with Jordan as the game's top defender, giving the Bulls an unrivaled one-two punch. That season, he upped his scoring to 21 points per game. Chicago won 67 games and returned to the Finals, against the Portland Trail Blazers.

The Blazers were one of the few teams with the athletes to match Jordan and Pippen. Their star, Clyde Drexler, was an MVP candidate and the West Coast's answer to Jordan. Who could forget that it was Drexler's presence on the roster that prompted Portland to pass on Jordan in the '84 draft? Eight years later the debate was reignited: Drexler or MJ?

Jordan took the comparisons as a personal affront. In Game 1 he scored 35 points in the first half alone, including six 3-pointers. After the sixth, he just turned to the crowd and shrugged, as if to say, "What did you expect?" The Bulls won by 33 points. Five games later, the Bulls were champs once more.

For the second year in a row, Jordan was named both the NBA's regular-season and Finals MVP. And didn't slow down. In 1993 he eliminated the Cleveland Cavaliers from the playoffs with a second-round buzzer-beater. After enduring a physical slog against the East, the Bulls made relatively easy work of Phoenix in their Finals matchup. "We felt liberated," said John Paxson, whose 3-pointer with 3.9 seconds remaining in Game 6 sealed the three-peat.

Jordan, who averaged 41 points in the series, earned his record third-straight Finals MVP award.

As the championships piled up and his game elevated, Jordan was driven not only to win but to dominate. For Jordan, Phil Jackson observed, "competition was an addiction."

The stories of his exploits began to circle. How he'd stay up until 5 o'clock playing cards, then play two rounds of golf before heading to the arena that night, where he'd drop 45 points in the Bulls' latest evisceration.

Basketball became too easy. Jordan began to manufacture additional motivation. "They're tricks I play against myself," he said; an effort to keep the games competitive. He took free throws with his eyes shut, and accepted challenges from fans sitting courtside. In one game in Utah, Jordan dunked on Jazz point guard John Stockton. "Pick on somebody your own size!" a fan yelled at him. A few plays later, he posterized 7-foot Mel Turpin. "He big enough for you?" he asked the fan on his way back down the court.

During an otherwise meaningless game in March 1993, LaBradford Smith of the Washington Bullets scored 37 points against Jordan. After the game, Jordan told his teammates that Smith approached him and said, "Nice game, Mike." That meant war.

The two teams played again the next night, and Jordan vowed to get 37 points — in the first half. When the game tipped off, Jordan made his first eight shots and outscored the entire Bullets team, 17–12. He was a man on a mission, and he finished with 47 points — 36 at the half — in a blowout win. Later, Jordan admitted that Smith had never said a word. He'd made the whole thing up. Fuel for the fire.

Jordan's never-ending quest to prove himself often put teammates in his crosshairs. He was a harsh leader with the highest expectations, quick to call out his teammates' mistakes. "If you let him ride you," said Horace Grant, "he'll ride you right out of the NBA, and out of your mind."

"You were scared to death of him," Bulls guard Steve Kerr said. "He was the most dominant force on the floor in every regard. It wasn't just the talent — it was the force of will. People, opponents were defeated by Michael before they even walked on the floor."

Pippen blocks Mark Price during the 1992 Eastern Conference finals.

1992
THE DREAM TEAM

The United States had dominated international hoops from the start. Going back to 1936, the year basketball was introduced as an Olympic sport, the American men had won the gold medal in all but two Olympic Games — a controversial finish in 1972 and the 1980 Games in Moscow that the U.S. boycotted.

But in 1988, Team USA lost fair and square to Arvydas Sabonis and a squad from the Soviet Union and settled for the bronze. It was a stunning disappointment.

The Americans had always sent amateurs — college stars — to represent them at the Olympics, but as the 1992 Barcelona Games approached, USA Basketball didn't want a repeat of the '88 embarrassment.

What resulted was the single greatest team to ever take the court: Michael Jordan, Magic Johnson, Larry Bird, Charles Barkley, Scottie Pippen, John Stockton, Karl Malone, David Robinson, Patrick Ewing, Christian Laettner, Chris Mullin and Clyde Drexler.

The team featured every NBA MVP between 1984 and 1999. In Magic, Bird and Jordan alone, it boasted the leaders of 10 of the last 13 NBA champions, with seven Finals MVP awards and nine regular-season MVPs among them.

The '92 Olympic basketball tournament had, in effect, become the NBA vs. the World. Their brilliant performance and perfect record en route to the gold medal was the greatest showcase the sport could get.

Charles Barkley goes for the basket against Croatia.

131

The team was selected nearly unanimously, but two decisions were made that history won't look back on so fondly. To honor USA Basketball's collegiate roots, the team agreed to include one college player and opted for Laettner, defending two-time champion at Duke, rather than Shaquille O'Neal.

Second, Isiah Thomas, one of the league's elite point guards and only two years removed from leading his Detroit Pistons to back-to-back championships, was left off the team entirely. The choice had come down to Thomas or Drexler. Michael Jordan let it be known that if Thomas, a longtime rival dating back to Jordan's rookie season in 1984–85, played, His Airness wouldn't.

The head coach of Team USA was Pistons bench boss Chuck Daly, who had proven his ability to manage strong personalities with the Bad Boy Pistons. When the team first assembled for practices in June in Portland, Oregon, Daly saw a talented roster but worried that the players' natural abilities would let them dominate in cruise control. He didn't want his team to approach the Olympics like another All-Star exhibition.

On June 24 he organized a scrimmage between his team and a select team made up of the best players in college basketball, including Chris Webber, Grant Hill and Penny Hardaway. Team USA, the greatest team of all time, played sloppy and loose. They lost their first game. It was Daly's plan all along.

"Chuck threw the game," assistant coach Mike Krzyzewski pieced together much later. "He knew what he was doing."

The Dream Team could be beaten — Daly just proved it. The two teams scrimmaged again the next day; this time Jordan played big minutes and his team wiped the floor with the kids. Order had been restored.

Team USA made its official debut on June 28 versus Cuba in a pre-Olympic qualifying event held in Portland. As the American players took the court, the Cuban team took a knee. The Americans won, 136–57.

What was most impressive was that, contrary to Daly's early concerns, his team played with an edge. They were playing angry. It didn't take much to tap into their competitive spirits.

"This is just a small step to going to Barcelona, winning the gold and bringing it back where it's supposed to be," Bird told a euphoric crowd after the game, emphasizing the word "supposed."

But before the Games began, the Dream Team first had to establish hierarchy.

Shortly after they arrived at training camp in Monte Carlo, Daly divided his teams for a scrimmage. One on side were Jordan, Pippen, Ewing, Mullin and Barkley. On the other were Magic, Bird, Robinson, Malone, Stockton, and Drexler.

It was no accident that Jordan and Magic were split. The two were just a year removed from meeting in the 1991 Finals. After a dominant run in the 80s, Magic and his Showtime Lakers lost to Jordan's Bulls. It was a passing of the torch in the NBA as Jordan collected his first of six titles.

HIV had taken Magic out of the league the prior November, but it hadn't taken any of his competitive fire away. And Daly knew it. He named Magic and Bird the team's co-captains.

As the scrimmage began, Magic was playing like he had everything to prove, and he set his sights on Jordan. He began calling him out, telling him that he was no bigger or better than the other players on the court. Jordan never needed much in the way of fuel to get him going. Magic was supplying enough to fill an ocean tanker.

The atmosphere changed entirely as Jordan took over the game the way he'd done countless times before. If there had been any confusion — especially on Magic Johnson's part — as to who the best player was on this team, Jordan put it to rest.

With the pecking order established, it was time for the Games to begin — but not without a bit of controversy courtesy of Charles Barkley.

Ahead of Team USA's first game, scheduled against Angola, Barkley, ever the diplomat, was asked what he knew about his opponent. "I don't know anything about Angola," he said. "But Angola's in trouble."

The international perception of Americans as brash and rude was confirmed during the game, when Barkley violently elbowed Angola's Herlander Coimbra, resulting in an

intentional foul and sending the wrong message to viewers around the world. "There just wasn't any place for it," Jordan said after the game. "There's already some negative feelings about us."

Barkley was unapologetic and, on the court, so was his team. The Dream Team led

Angola 64–16 after the first quarter. At one point they went on a 46–1 run, Angola's lone point coming from a technical free-throw by Coimbra as a result of Barkley's elbow.

As the tournament progressed, more and more teams were in awe of Team USA. Opponents would ask for autographs — and even the players' shoes — during games. In one instance, as Magic Johnson posted up an opponent, the defender yelled toward his bench, "Now! Now!" as a teammate snapped a photo.

On and off the court, the Americans were the biggest celebrities around. They had

John Stockton, Chris Mullin and Barkley celebrate their gold medals.

passed on staying in the traditional athletes' village in favor of $900-per-night rooms at a swank hotel. They were flanked by fans everywhere they went — it didn't matter what country you were from, there was something magnetic about the Dream Team, as if you were witnessing a moment in time that could never be captured again.

Basketball was already on its way to becoming a global sport by 1992. In the U.S. the rise of Air Jordan had helped make the NBA incredibly popular, and with worldwide Nike ad campaigns starring Jordan, the game was beginning to grow around the world.

The NBA had already proven it had an eye for the international market. It was the first North American pro league to play regular-season games outside the continent, with Utah and Phoenix competing in Tokyo, Japan, in 1990.

Since the '92 Olympics, the NBA has played on foreign soil over 150 times, with games broadcast in over 200 countries around the world. The Dream Team helped open many of those doors and show off the NBA brand to new audiences.

What they witnessed was a one-sided beating. Not that it had been in question, but the Olympics confirmed that the NBA was the best basketball league on Earth.

The Americans were dominating, but there were slight adjustments to be made. In the game against Croatia, Barkley was whistled for a technical foul after exchanging trash talk with a courtside fan. "If they gave Ts for that in America," he said, "I wouldn't make it past the first quarter."

While Jordan had established his alpha status in closed-door scrimmages, once the Olympics began, the Dream Team became the Charles Barkley Show. Barkley was the USA's most dominant force on the court and their leading scorer throughout the tourna-

ment, averaging 18 points per game.

Off the court, he was becoming a fan favorite in Barcelona, where he patrolled the streets near the hotel and partied with locals, leading *Sports Illustrated* to refer to him as "the Wild Bull of Las Ramblas." The following season Barkley, bolstered by his ascension on the Olympic squad, was named the NBA's MVP.

The Dream Team continued to crush opponents. On August 8, to nobody's surprise, it capped off a perfect record and took home the gold medal in a rematch with Croatia. This time Jordan and Pippen took it easy on a future teammate — they let Toni Kukoc score 16 points. Team USA won 117–85.

No matter your country of origin, chances

Magic Johnson rejoices after receiving his Olympic gold.

are you rooted for the Dream Team. You cheered for excellence. The Dream Team created basketball fans around the world.

For Jordan, the experience was another notch on his belt. He established himself as the greatest on a team of greats, and saw his star explode on a global scale. For Bird and Magic, the Olympic experience was a touching send-off. The two carried the league for years and could now walk into the sunset together, basking in gold.

In 2017 the Dream Team was inducted into the Hall of Fame.

Shaquille O'Neal dunks
over Michael Smith in 1994.

1992
SHAQ ATTACK

The NBA's draft lottery can change the course of a franchise. That was certainly the case in 1992, when Shaquille O'Neal was the top prize in the draft.

At the predraft combine, he was measured at 7-foot-1 (without shoes) and 305 pounds of pure muscle, with a 35-inch vertical leap to boot. His physical stature was without rival, dwarfing the NBA's preeminent bigs — who then included Patrick Ewing, David Robinson and Hakeem Olajuwon.

He spent his final season at Louisiana State University with opponents literally draped over his back as he destroyed rims. In the face of swarming defenses, aggressive fouling and triple-teams, Shaq averaged 24 points, 14 rebounds and 5 blocks per game before leaving school early for the draft. He had the makings of the NBA's next great center, the league's latest force of nature down low.

Three lottery teams in particular — the Charlotte Hornets, Minnesota Timberwolves and Orlando Magic — could desperately use a franchise player like O'Neal. Each had entered the league via expansion in the late 80s but had yet to make a mark in the NBA.

The Magic won the lottery and landed Shaq, who brought instant credibility to the hatchling franchise.

Orlando knew they had struck gold. In Shaq, they had a player who could own the paint the way Wilt and Kareem had done before him and who was poised to carry the baton from Michael Jordan as the NBA's most marketable superstar. Before he ever played a game, the Magic offered O'Neal a seven-year, $40 million contract — at the time, the richest contract in the history of professional sports.

Shaq wasted no time making his presence felt. His NBA debut on November 6, 1992, against the Miami Heat put opposing centers on notice. A 20-year-old O'Neal grabbed 18 rebounds and dominated the rim. He swatted shots, dunked on anybody who tried to get between him and the basket and, at one point, grabbed a rebound on the defensive end and dribbled the entire length of the floor before finishing with a powerful slam.

Orlando won, 110–100. After the game, Miami center Rony Seikaly was in awe. "He palms the ball like a grapefruit. He's as big as Mark Eaton and seven times as quick. And he's only 20," he said. "Give me a break."

As it turned out, Shaq didn't give Seikaly, or any opposing big, a break. He was named the 1992 Rookie of the Year in a landslide and became the only first-year player to average over 23 points, 13 rebounds and 3 blocks.

The Magic narrowly missed the playoffs during Shaq's first year in Orlando, but one memorable win came against Michael Jordan and the two-time defending champion Chicago Bulls, 128–124 in overtime. In one sequence, Jordan rose to dunk on Shaq — a baptism of fire for nearly all of the NBA's rim protectors in that era — but O'Neal knocked him to the ground, leaving Jordan in a heap on the floor. When the rookie made a move to help him up, Jordan waved him away. "Great foul," he said.

Shaq finished the game with 29 points, 24 rebounds and 5 blocks. Jordan answered with a cool 64 points, but O'Neal and the Magic would prove to be one of the few foils to Jordan's Bulls in the 90s.

Shaq's career was in its infancy, but his singular dominance was already drawing comparisons to the NBA's all-time great centers. During his rookie season, four of them assembled to film a Reebok commercial for O'Neal's signature sneaker. In the commercial, Shaq knocks on a virtual door. Bill Russell answers.

"You're early," the 11-time champion says.

"But I'm ready," Shaq responds.

"Then prove it."

O'Neal steps into a virtual world where Russell is joined by Wilt Chamberlain, Bill Walton and Kareem Abdul-Jabbar. With the four icons looking on — a living Mount Rushmore of NBA centers — O'Neal dunks so hard on a rim, the glass backboard shatters — something he'd done himself in real life.

Shaq's game was pure power. It was based on intimidation, brute strength and unrelenting force. A nasty, gnarling brand of basketball. Surprisingly, that set him apart from those who had come before him.

Many of the NBA's top centers and most powerful physical forces had long been hesitant to fully utilize their size and strength. They either didn't have the mentality to destroy or were out to prove that they were every bit as skilled as their smaller counterparts. Wilt's fadeaway jumper, Kareem's skyhook and Hakeem's shake-and-bake maneuvers were all go-to moves. Those weapons didn't exist in Shaq's arsenal — at least, not until later in his career. What he achieved was through sheer force.

A beast on the court, Shaq boasted a disarming smile and childlike joy away from it that appealed to fans of all ages. He seemed approachable and was extremely likable, a puppy dog disguised as a human wrecking ball. As his agent once put it, "He's a combination of the Terminator and Bambi."

That combo made him a valuable marketing tool, both for his personal brand and for a league searching for a new generation of stars to usher in the mid-90s. Before his rookie year, he'd already signed endorsement deals with toy manufacturers, apparel companies and countless other ventures. From day one he was one of the NBA's most active pitchmen and lapped up the newfound celebrity that came with it.

Shaq craved attention away from the court, too, which also set him apart from the legendary centers who came before him, many of whom were turned off by the crowds and constant flashbulbs. They were sick of questions like "How's the weather up there?" and had to resist the urge to spit and respond, "It's raining." They'd spent their whole lives being gawked at. And hated every moment of it.

Shaq always stood out. Raised by an army sergeant, he moved around a lot as a kid, and the oversized newcomer always drew attention. By age 13 he was 6-foot-9, meaning he couldn't exactly blend in to his everchanging surroundings. He was used to being in the spotlight. Maybe that's why he was so comfortable in the role.

Meanwhile, he was cashing in on his fame. Before his second season, Shaq released a rap album that went platinum, selling over a million copies. The single "(I Know I Got) Skillz" reached No. 35 on the Billboard Hot 100.

There were criticisms that O'Neal's extracurricular activities were a distraction. By the age of 22, he had an album, top-selling merchandise and a role in the film *Blue Chips*. During one game, with Lakers legend

Magic Johnson in the broadcast booth, the announcers discussed Shaq's many off-court interests. "Where were you at age 22?" Johnson was asked. "I was out on the court, trying to improve my game."

Once the ball tipped off, any concerns that his off-court activities would dull his performance were immediately put to rest. He started his sophomore season with 42 points and 12 boards against the Miami Heat. At one point he dunked the ball and hung on to the rim, bringing the entire backboard and stanchion crumbling to the ground — the second time he'd ruined an NBA net in as many years.

In his third season Shaq led the NBA in scoring and the Magic to a first-place finish in the East. He had teamed with bouncy guard Penny Hardaway to form the league's most dynamic duo.

In the second round of the '95 playoffs,

Orlando eliminated the Chicago Bulls in six games. Just prior to the postseason, Michael Jordan had returned from a two-year hiatus from basketball. Although Jordan wasn't in peak condition, it was still a significant win that signaled a potential changing of the guard in the NBA.

Led by a 23-year-old Shaq, Orlando made it all the way to the Finals. Facing the defending champion Houston Rockets, O'Neal was outplayed by the 32-year-old Hakeem Olajuwon, and the Magic were defeated in four straight games.

In 1995–96, the NBA celebrated its 50th anniversary. During the All-Star weekend, it announced the 50 greatest players of all time. At 24 years of age, and with just four years of service in the league, O'Neal made the list. He was the only player under the age of 30. What seemed premature at the time proved to be prescient. Shaq would go on to win

Shaq towers over his teammates during a huddle.

four championships and three Finals MVP awards, and he was named an All-Star 15 times in his career.

But his time would have to wait. In the '96 playoffs, Shaq's Magic met Jordan's Bulls once more. This time, Jordan got his revenge.

Orlando was swept in four games. After the final buzzer sounded to end Shaq's season, Jordan pulled him aside before he left the court. "Before you succeed," Jordan told him, "you must first learn to fail."

That summer, O'Neal left the Orlando Magic to sign a lucrative deal with the Los Angeles Lakers. Shaq had learned to fail before arriving amid the bright lights of Hollywood. Now it was his time to shine.

1993
JORDAN PLAYS BASEBALL

On October 5, 1993, Michael Jordan stepped onto the pitcher's mound at Comiskey Park to toss the ceremonial first pitch ahead of Game 1 of the American League Championship Series between the Chicago White Sox and Toronto Blue Jays. The baseball disappeared in the grip of his right palm. A huge smile crossed his face as he wound up and tossed a fastball wide and down in the dirt.

The following day, Jordan met the press to make the most shocking announcement of his career: Air Jordan was retiring.

At age 30, Jordan was a few months shy of capturing his third straight NBA championship. He would be named Finals MVP for the third time and had won his record seventh straight scoring title. A year earlier, he won an Olympic gold medal with the Dream Team, and his celebrity put a spotlight on the NBA. In every way, Jordan had conquered the game of basketball.

He'd long maintained that the moment the game became too easy, when his legendary drive began to fade even the slightest bit, it was time to walk away. So many greats before him hadn't, their legacies marred by hanging on too long. They hobbled up and down the court, bearing the scars from countless operations and the wear and tear of years spent landing on unforgiving hardwood. It wasn't a rite of passage Jordan wanted any part of.

"I have reached the pinnacle of my career," he told reporters, flanked by teammates, Bulls staff and NBA commissioner David Stern. "I don't have anything left in myself to prove."

But he did leave the door open for a return. "I think the word 'retire' means you can do whatever you want from this day on," Jordan said. "So, if I desire to come back and play again — maybe that's the challenge I need someday down the road."

It was an unprecedented decision — nobody had willingly walked away at the height of their powers. Plenty of theories were bandied about. The most prominent involved Jordan's well-known gambling issue. In May, during the Bulls' playoff series against the New York Knicks, Jordan was spotted in Atlantic City, New Jersey, the night before a game, gambling until the wee hours. That didn't stop him from dropping 36 points at Madison Square Garden in Game 2, but it wasn't a great look for the most recognizable figure in pro sports.

The previous year, the NBA had investigated Jordan's gambling habits to ensure he wasn't betting on basketball games. Rumors of a $1.2 million gambling debt surfaced, and Jordan told reporters it was closer to $300,000. As more stories of his betting exploits surfaced, the theory went, Stern and the NBA wanted to crack down on a potential PR disaster, and Jordan's surprise sabbatical was the result.

In truth, Jordan's reason for retiring was much simpler. And heartbreaking.

On July 23, one month after his son hoisted the NBA championship trophy, Jordan's father, James, was murdered during an attempted robbery at a North Carolina highway rest stop. James was driving the flashy red Lexus sports car Michael had bought him with the license plate UNC0023.

At first, James was presumed missing. His body wasn't found until August 12, and he wasn't identified until the following day.

James was a proud father and constant presence in Jordan's life. He'd originally dreamed of a career in baseball for his son. It was the first sport he introduced Michael to, and in the hours following the Bulls' third championship, the two talked about how amazing it would be if Jordan could switch sports in the middle of his career.

On February 7, 1994, the journey began. Jordan signed a deal with the White Sox. Two months later, to the day, he was stationed in right field for an exhibition game at a sold-out Wrigley Field against the neighboring Cubs. Legendary baseball broadcaster Harry Caray was behind the microphone when Jordan hit an RBI double to tie the game in the eighth inning.

"All of a sudden I felt like a kid again," Jordan said.

Jordan showed promise, but once the MLB season began, he was assigned to the Sox' minor-league affiliate in Alabama, the

Birmingham Barons. It was a far cry from life with the Bulls. He swapped the bright lights of Chicago Stadium and Madison Square Garden for baseball diamonds in places like Chattanooga, Tennessee. In Birmingham, he traded in private charter flights to games for a seat on the bus — granted, he arranged for the team to get a new state-of-the-art bus. He also autographed the outside door.

Making the majors was a long shot, but he was committed. His manager, future World Series winner Terry Francona, was among the Barons staffers impressed by his work ethic. Jordan routinely arrived at the crack of dawn to practice with legendary hitting coach Walt Hriniak, who was hired to fix Jordan's swing.

Hriniak had worked with such Hall of Famers as Carl Yastrzemski, Frank Thomas, Wade Boggs and Carlton Fisk. He was immediately drawn to what NBA coaches already knew was MJ's most valuable trait: "His mind," said Hriniak. "Disciplined. Focused. Determined. More so than anyone I ever saw."

Jordan was settling into his retirement nicely. Between morning practices and evening games, he'd play 36 holes of golf, excited to return to the diamond to test his new skills. "I really am having a good time trying," he said. "If I develop the skills to be [in the majors], great. But if I don't, at least I fulfilled a dream trying."

Fans and media alike weren't thrilled with Jordan's new venture. Some felt Jordan had used his stature to jump the line in baseball, taking a roster spot from someone more deserving.

"Bag It, Michael!" read the cover of *Sports Illustrated* in the summer of '94, adding "Jordan and the White Sox are embarrassing baseball."

Jordan never dreamed of being the best. And he wasn't. He hit .202 with 3 home runs in 497 plate appearances with the Barons. But he showed up each and every day, ready to put in the work. It's not as though he lacked motivation. Jordan later recalled how, during idle moments in games, he'd look out into the stands from his perch in right field and see a father and son taking in the action. He wanted so badly to be in their shoes, to be spending the time with his old

Michael Jordan in the Birmingham Barons' dugout in 1994.

man. In a way, by doing what he was doing, he still was.

"On my drive to practice in the dark every morning, he's with me," Jordan said, "and I remember why I'm doing this."

In Chicago, the Bulls were still potent without Jordan. His sidekick, Scottie Pippen, transitioned into a starring role, and the Bulls

Jordan scores a sixth-inning RBI double in 1994.

won 55 games in '93–94. However, they were bounced in the second round of the playoffs, losing to the Knicks in seven games.

In September 1994, Jordan played in a charity game organized by Scottie Pippen that doubled as the final basketball game held at Chicago Stadium. Jordan scored 56 points. But he was gearing up for his second full baseball season.

In March of '95, the effects of a strike in baseball threatened to keep Jordan away from the ballpark. He couldn't get better if he

couldn't play, Jordan figured. Meanwhile, in Chicago, the Bulls were struggling, reaching the All-Star break with a 23-25 record. Resurrecting the Bulls might just be the new challenge Jordan was looking for.

On March 18, Jordan's agent, David Falk, sent a fax to NBA teams and media. It contained two words: "I'm back."

JORDAN AT BAT

Year	Age	Team	G	PA	AB	R	H	HR	RBI
1994	31	Birmingham	127	497	436	46	88	3	51

1994
THE CHALLENGERS TO MJ

Michael Jordan scores past
Shawn Kemp in 1996.

Call it being in the wrong place at the wrong time.

In the 90s, Jordan claimed his spot atop the NBA with six championships in eight years. A by-product of Jordan's success was that nobody else enjoyed any. Superstars like Charles Barkley, John Stockton, Karl Malone, Gary Payton, Shawn Kemp, Clyde Drexler and Patrick Ewing all had their shot at Jordan's throne — they comprised an entire generation of legends that fell short.

Clyde Drexler

Drexler was the reason the Portland Trail Blazers passed on Michael Jordan in the 1984 draft. The Blazers had selected Drexler the year before and didn't need two players at the same position. Clyde spent his career in Jordan's shadow as much as anybody. Unlike most of Jordan's closest contemporaries, there weren't many consistently great shooting guards. Drexler was always runner-up to Jordan at the position.

He was an unbelievable leaper. Just not like Mike. He could score from all over the court. Just not like Mike. He was a two-way force. Just not like Mike.

Drexler even put up similar stats. Just not like Mike. Take the 1988–89 season, for example, when Drexler averaged a career-high 27.2 points, 7.9 rebounds, 5.8 assists and 2.7 steals per game. Jordan posted 32.5, 8.0, 8.0 and 2.9, respectively. Drexler made 10 All-Star teams. Jordan made 14.

Drexler led the Trail Blazers to the Finals in 1990, losing to the Detroit Pistons. In '92 they finished first in the West and made their return, bowing out to Jordan and the Bulls in five games. Clyde "The Glide" did win one championship — in '95, with the Houston Rockets, the season a "retired" Jordan largely missed.

Charles Barkley

Few stars of the 90s were closer to Jordan than Barkley. Part of the same draft class, they were cohorts off the court and relentless competitors on it.

Barkley was a one of a kind. He stood 6-foot-5 but scoured the court like the Tasmanian Devil. He tore rebounds off the glass and plowed through defenders like a wrecking ball. He was one of the NBA's most popular — and outspoken — stars. He played hard and partied hard. He once threw someone through a bar window. In an ad campaign for Nike, he put it plainly: "I am not a role model."

The Round Mound of Rebound got his start with the Philadelphia 76ers, where he began his career coming off the bench on a veteran-laden team led by Julius Erving and Moses Malone. But it wasn't long before the Sixers belonged to Barkley. He was the team's leading scorer for six straight seasons, and their top rebounder for seven, but Philly was never a contender.

In 1992 Barkley demanded a trade and was dealt to the Phoenix Suns. Surrounded by a high-octane roster that included All-Star guards Kevin Johnson and Dan Majerle, Barkley helped transform the Suns into a contender. In 1992–93, the Suns were the NBA's highest-scoring team and Barkley was named league MVP. They reached the Finals that year and pushed Chicago to six games.

John Stockton and Karl Malone

When the Utah Jazz drafted Stockton 16th overall in 1984, nobody could have imagined they'd just landed one of the greatest ever to play the position. "There's never been a point guard who made better decisions with the ball," said Barkley, who first shared the court with Stockton at the '84 Olympic trials.

Right out of the gate, Stockton had it all. He was a great passer with eagle-like court vision. Twice he led the league in steals, and he made the All-Defensive Team five times. He was consistent, piling up nine straight assists titles between 1987–88 and 1995–96.

On the receiving end of most of those passes was Malone. Big and bruising, with broad shoulders like a costumed superhero, Malone had a perfect touch near the hoop and kept defenses honest with a reliable midrange jumper.

When the Jazz drafted Malone the year after Stockton, they created an unstoppable pick-and-roll combo. Stockton to Malone was the most reliable source of 2 points in basketball. The Jazz were a perennial threat, and Malone was named MVP in both 1997 and '99.

In 1995 Stockton passed Magic Johnson and became the NBA's all-time leader in assists — a title he still holds. Two years later, he added "clutch shooter" to his résumé, drilling a 3-pointer in the 1997 Western Conference finals against the Houston Rockets to send Utah to the Finals. The Jazz and Bulls played for the title in back-to-back years, each series going six games.

Gary Payton and Shawn Kemp

If Stockton and Malone were the league's premier one-two punch, Payton and Kemp were the most fun. The duo produced a highlight reel that few have ever matched.

Seattle took a flier on Kemp. He was the top scorer in the 1988 McDonald's High School All-American showcase game and a prized recruit at the University of Kentucky. But he failed his SATs and was ruled ineligible. He transferred as a freshman to Trinity Valley Community College in Athens, Texas, but never played a game. Seattle drafted him 17th overall in 1989. Within four years he was a perennial All-Star.

The second overall pick in 1990, Payton was the reigning NCAA Player of the Year and a promising rookie. But it wasn't until his third season, when the SuperSonics hired George Karl, an offensively minded head coach, that his game really took off.

Under Karl, Payton was encouraged to push the ball, and Kemp was his favorite target. The passes came from anywhere on the court and arrived somewhere high above the rim, where the ball was miraculously caught and slammed home with force. The Payton–Kemp alley-oop was one of the NBA's most thrilling plays.

They were the reason Seattle was everybody's second-favorite team. They had the nicknames: Payton, an elite pickpocket, was the Glove, while Kemp was the Reign Man. They had the credentials, finishing with at least 55 wins every season between 1992–93 and '97–98 and teaming up in six straight All-Star Games. And they had swagger, like pro wrestlers in NBA jerseys.

Payton was an ultra-confident, swashbuckling trash talker who always backed it up. "Some people can't play the game and do all that talking," said Payton. "It was a gift that I had." Kemp was the fiercest dunker around and would gleefully point at opponents after knocking them to the ground with the force of his slams.

In 1996 the SuperSonics reached the Finals for their shot at the throne. Payton was up for the task, openly jawing with Jordan throughout the series, but once again, the Bulls won in six games.

Patrick Ewing

No player or team fell short against Jordan more often than Ewing and the New York Knicks. Ewing was an NCAA champion and Final Four MVP at Georgetown and the first overall pick in 1985. Hailing from Kingston, Jamaica, Ewing was one of the most physical centers of his era, anchoring the grit-and-grind Knicks under coach Jeff Van Gundy.

The Knicks were the spiritual successors to the Bad Boys from Detroit, but they always hit a roadblock when Jordan was on the court. The 1992–93 season would prove especially heartbreaking, given Ewing and New York finished first in the East and took a 2-0 lead on Chicago during their conference finals matchup, only to lose the series in six games. The Bulls knocked Ewing's Knicks out of the playoffs four times in six years, and five times in total, during Jordan's reign.

Karl Malone fouls Charles Barkley in the 1994 Western Conference finals.

1995
GRANT HILL

It's clear Grant Hill's ankle has a story to tell. A tale of how it once carried the weight of a generational athlete. How it deteriorated because of stress and injury. How skin grafts and countless surgeries left it discolored and permanently swollen. And how team doctors let it get worse and worse and worse.

If it weren't for his ankle, Hill would be rated among the greatest to ever play the game. Instead, he's a Hall of Famer plagued by a lingering question: What if?

Following one of the most successful collegiate careers of all time — two national championships and a Defensive Player of the Year award at Duke — Hill was as close to a sure thing as there was.

He was an out-of-this-world athlete, a natural on the level of Michael Jordan. "He doesn't even run," observed Duke coach Mike Krzyzewski, "he floats." Shaquille O'Neal called him "the perfect player." And for six years, at least, he was.

A 6-foot-9 forward, Hill handled the ball like a point guard, wielded a deadly mid-range game, defended all five positions and exploded through the air like few players ever had. They called him a "point forward."

When Hill was selected by the Detroit Pistons with the third overall pick in the 1994 NBA draft, the NBA was getting not only a thrilling basketball player, but a worthy ambassador for the league. He was clean-cut, good-looking and well-spoken, with an impressive lineage. His mother, Janet, was a senior partner at a law firm in Washington, D.C., and his father, Calvin, was an ex-NFL

standout and a former vice-president of baseball's Baltimore Orioles.

The NBA was ecstatic to make him the face of a new generation, expectations that were laid before he ever took the court.

Once he did, however, the "nice guy" persona stayed on the sidelines. In his earliest days, Hill was ruthless. One night, he'd be crossing up Jordan, making the game's premier perimeter defender look like a high schooler. The next, he'd drive to the basket and put elite rim protectors like Dikembe Mutombo on a poster. So bouncy was Hill that his body would often spin in midair as he reached the net, as if he was trying to slow himself down from flying past the basket.

In his rookie season, Hill became the first and only rookie to lead all players in fan voting for the All-Star Game. And he got better with each season, leading the NBA in triple-doubles as a second- and third-year player, carrying the Pistons to the playoffs. Those who were quick to compare Hill to Jordan might have been on to something.

As the 90s drew to a close, the league and its fanbase were desperate to anoint the "Next One." It wasn't long before Hill assumed the mantle. In fact, even during Jordan's first full season back from his brief hiatus between 1993 and '95, Hill remained the leading All-Star vote-getter — the only player to surpass Jordan in eight years. The fans had spoken: Hill would be the face of the post-MJ era.

By the 1998–99 campaign, Hill was the league's third-leading scorer and finished third in MVP balloting. Through the first

six seasons of his career, Hill averaged 21.6 points, 7.9 rebounds, 6.3 assists and 1.6 steals per game. The only players ever to match that productivity six years into their careers were Oscar Robertson and Larry Bird (and, later, LeBron James).

But just as Hill was reaching another stratosphere, his story took a turn. In April of 2000 he was diagnosed with an ankle sprain on his left foot. In truth, he had been playing on a hurt ankle for months before the Pistons team doctors intervened.

The timing of the injury complicated matters. Hill's contract was set to expire that summer, and after years as Detroit's lone star, it was widely believed that he would look to sign elsewhere, making him one of the most coveted free agents in history.

As the 1999–2000 season drew to a close and Hill's ankle ailments continued, he was forced to sit out the final two games of the regular season. Amid criticism that he was taking it easy in his final games in Detroit — already eyeing his next destination — Hill wanted to prove otherwise and played through the pain.

When the playoffs began versus the Miami Heat, Hill played 38 minutes in Game 1 before removing himself from an eventual 10-point loss. Still, critics felt Hill should have stayed in the game — after all, these were the Pistons, the same team with which Isiah Thomas earned hero status after playing through an ankle injury of his own in the 1989 Finals.

In the second quarter of Game 2, Hill felt a pop in his ankle. He tried to play in the

Grant Hill rebounds over Charles Outlaw in 1998.

third quarter, but could barely put weight on the left foot and exited the game after just 21 minutes of action. Later that night, he received the news: he had broken his left ankle. MRI results revealed that what was previously deemed a sprain had in fact been a stress fracture the whole time.

"I was told everything was fine. I even found out that certain team doctors were questioning whether I was really hurt," Hill said. "When I found out I had broken my ankle, as crazy as this sounds, I was relieved. I finally had some confirmation, I finally had proof that I'm really not making it up."

On April 28, 2000, he went under the knife.

His injury status didn't dissuade teams from trying to sign the All-NBA forward. In Chicago, Oprah Winfrey tried to recruit him for the Bulls. In New York, Jerry Seinfeld pleaded for him to sign with the Knicks.

Ultimately he chose the Orlando Magic, signing a seven-year, $92 million deal. That summer, Orlando also acquired up-and-coming shooting guard Tracy McGrady. The Magic were building a surefire contender in the East; the two stars were poised to form a one-two punch that would rival Jordan and Pippen's status as the most lethal wing tandem in the NBA.

Although Hill wasn't aware, his surgeon had informed the Magic's medical staff that he couldn't resume basketball activity until December. Yet that summer, just three months after the surgery, the Magic put Hill on the court for informal pickup games, doing untold further damage and setting back the recovery process. His ankle pain worsened.

"I just kept thinking, 'I can't believe how mismanaged this has been,'" he said.

Hill was never the same player. Not even close. In the 2000–01 season, his first in Orlando, he appeared in just four games, although that didn't stop fans from voting him in as an All-Star starter once more.

Hill celebrates a career high 46-point game in 1999.

By 2003 a now 30-year-old Hill had played in just 47 games for the Magic over three seasons. He continued to go under the knife — three surgeries in three years — in order to repair his ankle. Following an operation in the summer of 2003, he suffered a staph infection and was hospitalized, forcing him to sit out the entire upcoming season. In a cruel twist of fate, his former team, the Pistons, were crowned NBA champions that year.

Hill successfully returned to action for the 2004–05 season. He averaged over 19 points per game and was named an All-Star for the seventh and final time. With his world-class hops grounded because of the injuries, he managed to successfully reinvent his game and remained a relevant player for the next seven seasons.

He joined the Phoenix Suns and carved out a reputation as a valued role player and esteemed locker-room presence. He retired in 2013 after a brief stint with the Los Angeles Clippers.

His would have been a great career for most, but Hill was never part of the majority. "It does bother me that I was hurt, that I was on this trajectory early on in Detroit and things were coming together and then it's incomplete," he said. "I didn't get a chance to see it through, to see what could have been."

In 2018 Hill was enshrined in the Hall of Fame, an acknowledgement of his longevity and recognition for what he represented when he was at the height of his powers.

Hill himself was always too entangled in the everlasting rehab process — as he put it, too "focused on the struggle" — to be able to look back and enjoy his success.

It wasn't until the twilight of his career, when his daughter would pull up old highlights from his Detroit days on YouTube and marvel at her father's abilities, that he began to acknowledge his career with pride.

"I was elite, for a period of time, you know," he'd say. "It wasn't all bad."

1995

THE NBA COMES TO CANADA

On July 17, 2019, the streets of Toronto were painted red. Not the red of the maple leaf, but Raptors red. An estimated two million fans filled the streets of Canada's largest city for nearly five miles, jamming the freeways.

The Toronto Raptors had won the championship, the first NBA title outside U.S. soil.

The Raptors' playoff run captivated the entire country, and basketball was suddenly more popular than ever. The championship parade felt more like a long-overdue coronation of the sport in Canada.

In truth, basketball is as Canadian as poutine. Its inventor, James Naismith, was a Canadian, and in 1936 Canada won the silver medal the first time basketball was played as an Olympic sport.

Ten years later, the Toronto Huskies were one of the NBA's inaugural franchises, and the league's very first game was hosted at Maple Leaf Gardens. But the Huskies folded after just one season, and with the exception of visits from the Harlem Globetrotters and the occasional Buffalo Braves game in Toronto during the 70s, basketball took a back seat for the next 50 years.

On September 30, 1993, the NBA awarded an expansion franchise to Toronto — the league's 28th team — with a tip-off date set for the 1995–96 season. The ownership group was headed by John Bitove Jr., president of a financial services firm, beating out a rival bid from a group that included Magic Johnson. To make matters worse for Magic, Bitove's group brought on Hall of Fame point guard and 1990 Finals rival Isiah Thomas as the team's vice-president. Thomas also held an ownership stake.

On the other side of the country in Vancouver, Arthur Griffiths, owner of the NHL's Vancouver Canucks, had put in a bid of his own for a franchise on the West Coast. Like Toronto, Vancouver was a large metropolis with the resources to support a team — and, unlike Toronto, it already had a new arena ready to house NBA hoops.

The NBA agreed that establishing a nationwide presence all at once made sense. "I think timing is important," said Jerry Colangelo, owner of the Phoenix Suns and chair of the league's expansion committee, "to have both east and west representation."

The NBA had been expanding rapidly by the time the 90s rolled around. When the NBA and ABA merged the summer of 1976, the league comprised 22 teams. The rise of Michael Jordan and the popularity of Magic and Larry Bird in the mid-80s established NBA basketball as a valuable, coveted property. Sports ownership had become a billionaire's playground, and more and more deep-pocketed investors were looking to get into the basketball business.

In 1988 the NBA opened shop in Charlotte (the Hornets) and Miami (the wildly inventive Heat), and in 1989 two more franchises were added, in Orlando (the Magic) and Minnesota (the Timberwolves).

Just as it had been since the league's inception, the NBA was always looking to infiltrate new, untapped markets. It had nearly covered the continental United States. Now it was time to go north of the border.

By the time Toronto and Vancouver were added to the mix, the number of teams was 29. The franchise fee was set at $125 million — a far cry from the mere $32.5 million it cost the NBA's previous four teams to join.

Before the Canadian clubs played, they needed names.

In '94, Toronto held a fan contest to vote for their team's nickname. Among the finalists were the Towers, Grizzlies, Hogs, Terriers and Bobcats. The winning name — the Raptors — was a result of the popularity of Steven Spielberg's blockbuster film *Jurassic Park*, which ruled the box office the previous year. To promote the new team, Isiah Thomas appeared on *The Late Show with David Letterman* sporting a letterman jacket with the Raptors' purple dinosaur logo on the front.

Vancouver, sensibly, adopted the Grizzlies moniker.

On November 3, 1995, the Raptors played their first game in front of over 33,000 fans at SkyDome, a cavernous 54,000-seat stadium designed for baseball. That same night in Portland, the Grizzlies made their NBA debut. Both teams won, although it wasn't a feeling fans in either city were about to get used to.

But they showed up nonetheless. The Raptors ranked third in attendance during their first season, while the Grizzlies were a respectable 14th. In Vancouver, the team's first-ever draft pick, Bryant "Big Country" Reeves, a 7-foot, 275-pound mountain of a man from rural Oklahoma, became a popular figure in his rookie year.

Toronto's first draft selection, Damon "Mighty Mouse" Stoudamire, who couldn't have been further from Reeves in stature, was an early fan favorite. Thomas saw shades of himself in the diminutive point guard and described him as "a daredevil."

One of the lone bright spots during the first season came on March 24, 1996, when over 36,000 were on hand when Michael Jordan and the Chicago Bulls came to town.

The Raptors had the second-worst record in their division, and the Bulls were in the midst of a record-setting 72-win campaign. But Stoudamire, proving Thomas right, was fearless down the stretch, matching Jordan shot for shot. He finished the game with 30 points and 11 assists.

The Raptors held a one-point lead heading into the final seconds. It all came down to Jordan, who — of course — nailed an impossible turnaround bank shot as the buzzer sounded. But the referees ruled he got the shot off a

fraction of a second too late. Raptors win!

"The best thing about us back then," recalled Thomas, "was that we were naive. We didn't know we weren't supposed to win."

The Raptors won only three more games the rest of the season.

Things were worse in Vancouver. The Grizzlies were dead last in the NBA and remained in the basement for years, finishing no higher than 11th in the West during their first six seasons.

It was a bad omen for the franchise when, at the 1999 draft, their second overall pick, Steve Francis, cried after he was selected. Francis wanted no part of the Grizzlies and demanded a trade. "I was not about to go up to freezing-ass Canada," he said years later. The Grizzlies missed out on a three-time All-Star, and Francis missed the opportunity to learn that Vancouver is warmer than half the cities in the league, including his hometown in Maryland. (Years later, Raptors forward Antonio Davis would request a trade because he didn't want his kids growing up learning the metric system, as is taught in Canadian schools.)

The Grizzlies were hemorrhaging money, and the team was sold in 2000 for $160 million. A year later, after just six seasons, they were moved to Memphis.

As the Grizzlies experiment came to a close, in Toronto a new basketball hero had emerged in high flyer Vince Carter. Thanks in part to a jaw-dropping performance at the 2000 slam-dunk contest, Carter had quickly become one of the NBA's most popular figures and was helping to popularize the sport across the country. By 2015 more kids were playing basketball in Canada than hockey. In 2019 there were more NBA players born in Canada than any other country save for the U.S.

The millions of hoops fans who showed up to celebrate the Raptors championship were proof of the sport's growth and success. But the legacy of the NBA's first major foray into Canada will always be bittersweet.

"I consider [Toronto] to be a great success," former commissioner David Stern said in 2019 amid the Raptors' hoopla, "just as I consider Vancouver to be one of our greatest failures."

Vince Carter sticks his arm through the basket after dunking the ball in the 2000 slam-dunk contest.

1995
THE BIG TICKET CASHES IN

On an early summer day ahead of the 1995 draft, NBA scouts and executives descended on a Chicago gymnasium to watch an invitation-only workout of Kevin Garnett, a 19-year-old prospect fresh off his senior year of high school.

They'd heard stories of a spindly teenager from South Carolina as tall as Shaquille O'Neal with handles like Mookie Blaylock, defensive instincts like Alonzo Mourning and ups like Dominique Wilkins. They knew that he had been named National High School Player of the Year by *USA Today*. Also he once notched a triple-double in a quarter.

They also knew that he had declared his intention to skip college to enter the upcoming NBA draft — a rare move that hadn't been done in nearly two decades, prompting skepticism among the scouts.

Any doubt was quickly dispelled. The kid was unbelievable. His skill set was endless. Dribbling drills. Hook shots. Left-handed. Right-handed. On the run. Jumpers from the elbow. Jumpers behind the 3-point line. Anything they asked, he did.

"Man, what do you want?" Garnett remembered thinking, the sweat pooling and turning the paint into a watercolor. "Let's see him chili sauce. Let's see him break dance.

Let's see him do the salsa. That's how it was."

For the finale, Garnett lifted off with the ball in both hands, tapped it off the backboard and threw down a powerful dunk while letting out a primal scream that would soon be known worldwide.

Then, without saying a word, he packed up his things and left the gym. Thank you for coming.

There was no doubting Garnett's talent. But if the NBA had its way, he would have gone right to college just like most every other American prospect. There was concern that the teen would be a bust and that his potential failure would hurt a league forever concerned about its public image.

"If it were up to us, we'd prefer not to see someone come into the league at that tender age," Russ Granik, the NBA's deputy commissioner, said at the time, "but the courts say otherwise."

Indeed, there had been legal precedent. In 1969, following his sophomore season, University of Detroit forward Spencer Haywood left school to join the American Basketball Association. Unlike the NBA, the ABA had no rules regarding drafting underclassmen. In his first season, Haywood averaged 30 points and 19.5 rebounds per game and was named both Rookie of the Year and MVP.

Contract disputes led Haywood to sign with the NBA's Seattle SuperSonics the following season. But league rules required a player to be four years removed from the graduating date of his high school class, and Haywood was only three years past it. The battle resulted in the 1972 landmark case of *Haywood v. National Basketball Association*. The Supreme Court of the United States ruled 7–2 in favor of Haywood — that the league could not prevent a player from earning a living.

Kevin Garnett soars during
a game against the LA
Lakers in 2007.

As a result, the NBA adopted a new "hardship rule" to make exceptions for underclassmen who might be in financial need.

The first player to make the jump from high school to the pros under the hardship rule was Moses Malone. A towering center from Petersburg, Virginia, Malone won 50 straight games and two state championships in high school. He was the most sought-after college recruit in the nation.

But Malone grew up in extreme poverty and watched his single mother, Mary, battle ulcers while working long hours and earning $100 a week at a local meatpacking plant. In 1974, after his senior year of high school, Malone signed with the ABA's Utah Stars for $565,000 over four years. As stipulated in the contract, Mary was given $10,000 on the spot.

When the ABA merged with the NBA in '76, a 21-year-old Malone became one of the game's greatest centers. He was named MVP three times and was the Finals MVP when his Philadelphia 76ers swept Kareem Abdul-Jabbar's LA Lakers in the '83 championship.

In 1975, following Malone's success, two NBA teams drafted high schoolers — Darryl Dawkins and Bill Willoughby.

There wasn't another high schooler to enter the league until Garnett.

By his senior season he had risen to the ranks of top teenage player in the world. But with concerns over college eligibility due to poor grades, and with a family in need of financial aid, the Big Ticket, as he'd later be known, decided to cash his in.

Garnett's 1995 workout confirmed that he was NBA-ready, and the Minnesota Timberwolves promptly selected him fifth overall. Although it wouldn't result in wins until later in his career, his arrival took the NBA by storm. He led the charge of the new age do-it-all big man and quickly became one of the league's defining characters as a maniacal, trash-talking competitor.

When Garnett was drafted, Minnesota hadn't won a playoff series in its entire six-year existence. After missing the playoffs his first season, he carried the team to eight straight postseason appearances. Garnett was an All-Star by his second season — at 20 years old, the youngest since Magic Johnson in 1980 — and league MVP by his ninth. In his 13th season, after being traded to the Boston Celtics, he was a champion.

In October 1997, when he was just 21 years old, the Timberwolves signed Garnett to the richest contract in NBA history — $126 million over six years.

The prospect of instant fame was enormous. An entry-level deal in 1999 paid a guaranteed salary of at least $1 million if you were picked 13th or higher. Unsurprisingly, more and more high schoolers were looking to make the jump from prep to pro.

In 1996 Kobe Bryant and Jermaine O'Neal were first-round picks, and Tracy McGrady was a top-10 selection the following year.

With those players flourishing (Garnett, Bryant, O'Neal and McGrady were All-Stars between 2002 and 2005), GMs around the league looked to find the next Big Ticket. Suddenly potential was being coveted more than production. In 2001 three of the first four picks were high school players, including Kwame Brown, the first overall pick.

As the trend blossomed, the success rate plummeted. The list of flameouts reads as long as a Tolstoy novel.

Even as teenagers, players like Garnett and Bryant viewed being drafted as simply the first of many steps toward greatness. But the league's GMs underestimated how rare that mentality is. They also didn't put

enough weight on the fact that someone like McGrady happened to be a generational talent — by definition, exceptional.

In 2005 a record nine high schoolers were drafted — but only one ever made it to an All-Star Game (10th pick Andrew Bynum, who was out of the league by age 26). Worse, others, like Korleone Young, a second-round pick, didn't make it at all. Young was a star who slid in the draft and only appeared in three games for the Detroit Pistons during the lockout-shortened 1999 season, and never graced an NBA court again.

Robert Swift was a 7-footer and 12th overall pick who never made an impact in the 97 games he appeared in between 2004 and 2009. His career ended at age 23, when he spiraled into substance-abuse issues.

It was becoming difficult to evaluate talent. The draft became a roulette wheel, and NBA teams kept putting their chips on the wrong numbers. Everybody suffered. To stop the bleeding, the league pushed for a new rule that NBA officials would ultimately attribute to Garnett.

Beginning in 2006, players must be at least 19 years of age and one year removed from

A rookie Garnett smiles during media day.

the graduation date of their high school class — the "one and done" rule. The impact on the college basketball landscape was chaotic, with the majority of top talent attending college for just one year and then jumping to the pros.

Some players, like Brandon Jennings and R.J. Hampton, circumvented the rule by graduating from high school and spending a season playing professionally in Europe or Australia before entering the draft.

After establishing the NBA Development League (later the NBA G League), a minor league where young players can develop while still earning a paycheck, the NBA plans to open the draft to high schoolers once more in 2022.

As for Garnett, he reopened a door that granted amateur athletes the autonomy to earn a living. In 2016, after 21 seasons, Garnett walked away from the game having earned $326 million, the most of any player ever.

It's no wonder so many tried to traverse the same path from prep to pros.

1996
REPEAT THREE-PEAT

As the Chicago Bulls entered the 1995–96 season, Michael Jordan and Scottie Pippen were the only remaining members of the original '91 title team.

Over a two-year span marked by back-to-back second-round playoff exits (against New York in '94 and Orlando in '95), a new-look roster was assembled alongside the two veterans. Defense-first guard Ron Harper, center Bill Wellington and 3-point specialist Steve Kerr settled into their roles. Third-year Croatian forward Toni Kukoc gave the team a dynamic third scoring option. Kukoc was a 1991 draft pick who made his NBA debut two years later, during Jordan's baseball hiatus.

But no Bulls newcomer made a bigger impact than their biggest free-agent signing: Dennis "The Worm" Rodman, brought in to replace the departing Horace Grant. Rodman had been a key factor in the Pistons teams that repeatedly beat up on Jordan and the Bulls en route to NBA titles in 1989 and '90.

Despite averaging more than 10 points just once in his 14-year career, Rodman could change the dynamic of a game as profoundly as any scorer. *Sports Illustrated* declared that Rodman "deserves a place next to Wilt Chamberlain and Bill Russell as one of the greatest rebounders of all time."

By the time he arrived in Chicago, he was in the midst of a seven-year run as the NBA's top rebounder, using his strong, wiry

Dennis Rodman feeds off the crowd during the 1996 NBA Finals.

6-foot-7 frame to hurtle toward loose balls. He described himself as a computer for his ability to calculate where the ball would land. The press called him Demolition Man.

"Let's just say I have the bite marks and scratches from going up against him in practice," said one teammate.

Rodman was the wildest card in the Bulls deck. He'd clashed with the front office on his previous team, the San Antonio Spurs, and missed more than half the 1994–95 season because of a motorcycle accident. He dyed his hair all the colors of the rainbow and reached fame after a highly publicized affair with pop star Madonna.

His celebrity status made him a good fit for the Bulls. Jordanmania had lifted the team to Beatlesque levels, except Jordan was John, Paul and George all in one. Bulls apparel was a perennial best seller, and the team was greeted by enormous crowds every time it arrived at a hotel. The Bulls came into town, signed some autographs, beat the crap out of the opposition and left. They were a traveling road show in the guise of a professional sports team.

If the hoopla was growing out of control, the '95–96 Bulls were as polished as ever on the court. They ran the Triangle Offense to perfection and resumed their dominance as if Jordan had never left. Rodman averaged 15 rebounds (and 5.5 points), Kukoc and Pippen combined for over 32 points, while Jordan led the league with 30.4 points per game — capturing his 8th of 10 scoring titles.

With more scoring options around him, Jordan could focus more energy on the defensive end of his game. He averaged over 2 steals per game and was named to the All-Defensive First Team for the sixth time.

The Bulls finished with a then-record 72 wins and capped off a dream season with a 4–2 victory over the Seattle SuperSonics in the NBA Finals. After walking away from the game to play baseball and fulfill his deceased father's dream, Jordan had returned as a champion. The title-clinching game was played on June 16 — Father's Day. After he won, Jordan collapsed in a heap of tears while latching onto the championship trophy.

The next season saw the Bulls match up in the Finals with the Utah Jazz, whose combination of John Stockton and Karl Malone were a handful. With the series tied, 2-2, an exhausted Jordan fought through a flu in Game 5 to finish with 38 points and the win.

In Game 6, the Bulls had a chance to win the series. With the score tied in the fourth quarter and 28 seconds remaining, Chicago called a time-out. Two games earlier, Stockton had stolen the ball from Jordan late in the game after a double-team. Jordan expected the same swarming defense this time, and he warned Steve Kerr that if he was open, Michael was passing it to him. "After my heart stopped beating for a few seconds," Kerr recalled, "I said, 'I'll be ready.'"

With the clock down to five seconds, Jordan, as if on cue, passed out of the double-team to an open Kerr, who sank a 17-foot jumper. "I thought to myself, 'Well, I guess I've gotta bail Michael out again,'" Kerr joked at the championship parade a few days later.

Phil Jackson was already calling the 1997–98 season "the last dance" before it began. "And it was a wonderful waltz," he'd say eight months later to a crowd of 300,000 at the Bulls' sixth championship parade.

But the final haul was the toughest. Chicago started the season 8-7 and were without Pippen until January because of a back injury he suffered during the '97 Finals. Pippen, like Jackson and Jordan, was in the final year of his contract. He'd finished in the top seven in MVP voting in each of the last three years, yet was the 122nd-highest-paid player in the league. But Chicago GM Jerry Krause had already made it clear that although he was willing to break the bank for Jordan, the same wasn't true of his cohorts.

For the second year in a row, the Bulls toppled the Jazz in six games — this time thanks to Jordan's most iconic shot of them all, a pull-up jump shot just ahead of the buzzer. Trailing by 3 points with 41 seconds remaining, Jordan tore through the Jazz defense for a layup, stole the ball out of Malone's hands on defense, and then strutted past half-court for the game winner.

Jordan took home his sixth Finals MVP award — twice as many as any other player. "To be the best at anything," Jordan said,

"you have to have a love for it."

After Bill Russell and the Boston Celtics dynasty captured 11 titles in 13 years, nobody thought another team would ever come close. With Michael Jordan, the Bulls came

close. Chicago's second three-peat enshrined them among the best. Jordan wouldn't have had it any other way.

The summer after the three-peat, Pippen, as expected, left the team and signed with the Houston Rockets. Jackson prepared for a year off. Jordan's future plans remained up in the air, where he belonged.

Rodman, Michael Jordan and Scottie Pippen take the court in 1997.

1996
SPACE JAM

It's hard to fathom just how popular Michael Jordan was by the summer of 1996.

The most recognizable sports figure on the planet, no athlete had ever reached the zenith of both on-court performance and off-court marketability quite like Mike.

"Air Jordan" was a one-man industry. His likeness appeared on every bit of merchandise imaginable; he starred in industry-defining commercials; he endorsed a wide range of products around the globe. Wherever Jordan went, swarms of admirers followed like moths to a flame.

Jordan had ushered in the era of the athlete mega-celeb, creating a platform that helped make stars out of those who shared the court with His Airness. Shaquille O'Neal, Penny Hardaway and Charles Barkley, for example, were becoming household names.

Basketball was big business — and the film industry was paying attention.

So massive was Jordan's celebrity that he had been offered countless starring movie roles. His agent, David Falk, had been turning down offers from Hollywood for years. When Jordan asked why, Falk explained that there was only one role befitting a player of his magnitude and cultural status.

"What's that?" Jordan asked. "The first black James Bond?"

No, the agent responded. The role of Michael Jordan.

The two set out to find the right vehicle. The result was *Space Jam*.

Space Jam merged Jordan with another massive brand, Warner Brothers and Bugs Bunny's *Looney Tunes* universe. Between his record-setting contract with the Bulls, his lucrative endorsement deals and the swaths of money he generated through ticket sales and television revenue, Jordan was a $10 billion business. Warner Brothers, meanwhile, committed over $170 million to the film's budget, making it one of its most expensive projects to date.

The plot, for the uninitiated, was as follows: Michael Jordan, playing himself circa 1994, at the height of his fame and success, is transported from a golf outing with Larry Bird and Bill Murray to *Looney Tunes* Land, where he is asked to help save its cartoon citizens by winning a basketball game. Needless to say, he is the ultimate ringer and helps Bugs Bunny & Co. defeat the Monstars, a team of giant aliens who have stolen the basketball powers of some of the NBA's biggest stars — Charles Barkley, Patrick Ewing, Larry Johnson, Muggsy Bogues and Shawn Bradley.

Barkley was only a couple of years removed from a Finals appearance against Jordan's Bulls; Patrick Ewing was established as one of the most popular Knicks of all time; Johnson seemed like the next big thing in Charlotte, while Hornets teammate Bogues, the 5-foot-6 point guard, was nearly a decade into his career and one of the league's most recognizable figures. And then there was Bradley, the second overall pick in the '93 draft and a player the NBA was desperate to market, whose 7-foot-6 frame translated well to the Monstar motif.

Filming took place during the 1995 off-season, following one of the most disappointing endings to a campaign Jordan had experienced.

After sitting out the entire '93-94 season to pursue a career in professional baseball, Jordan returned to the court in March of '95 — just in time to play the last 17 games of the regular season. While his scoring numbers suggested that he hadn't missed a beat, the Bulls struggled in the playoffs, losing in the second round to Shaq, Penny and the Orlando Magic. It was the first playoff series Jordan had lost in five years.

As one of the conditions for Jordan agreeing to take the part and dedicate much of his summer to filming, Warner Brothers built him a massive air-conditioned dome housing an NBA-sized basketball court. The opportunity to grow his brand through cinema was enormous, but nothing could overshadow his first full season back from retirement. He needed to stay in game shape.

Jordan flew out NBA stars like Reggie Miller, Alonzo Mourning and Grant Hill to take part in heated scrimmages between filming. Some of the extras, who donned green suits to play the Monstars in basketball scenes (later to be replaced by cartoon versions through state-of-the-art technology at the time), took part as well. Even they weren't spared from Jordan's incessant trash talk.

On November 15, 1996, two weeks into the NBA season, *Space Jam* hit theaters worldwide. That night, Jordan dropped 38 points in a blowout win, one of 12 straight to begin the season (which would end with yet another Bulls title).

Space Jam wasn't the first NBA-based

movie released in 1996. That honor goes to the Judd Apatow–penned *Celtic Pride*, in which Dan Aykroyd and Daniel Stern play Celtics superfans who kidnap fictional Utah Jazz star Lewis Scott (played by Damon Wayans) ahead of the NBA Finals.

Other '96 hoops movies included *Eddie*, which starred Whoopi Goldberg as a fan who wins a contest to become the New York Knicks' head coach and which featured a cattle call of NBAers, including Mark Jackson and John Salley in supporting roles, as well as *Kazaam*, a movie about a magical genie starring Shaquille O'Neal — probably the second-most recognizable NBA star behind Jordan — in the title role.

That so many basketball films were being produced during Jordan's brief hiatus was no coincidence. The NBA movie boom was, in part, an effort by a league eager to retain its growing fan base in a Jordan-less world — and it coincided with the league's 50th anniversary.

But none held a candle to the scale (and success) of *Space Jam*. The film's existence as a marketing tool — the latest frontier in capitalizing on NBA celebrity — was impossible to ignore. It helped establish a blueprint for a generation of upcoming star athletes.

The movie studio shelled out an unheard of $70 million on marketing tie-ins, including a limitless line of products, from *Space Jam* Happy Meals to *Jam*-branded Jell-O to literal *Space* jam. For its 20th anniversary in 2009, the Jordan Brand even released a *Space Jam*–themed Air Jordan sneaker based on the pair Jordan wore in the film.

Responses to Jordan's performance were positive, citing the fact that by playing himself, he hardly had to test the boundaries of his comfort zone. One *New York Times* review read, "As a sports star so celebrated that even the backs of his ears are famous, Mr. Jordan need do little more here than show off his

sportsmanship and play ball."

Reviewers were less kind to O'Neal, whose second marquee role, playing the title character in the '98 superhero film *Steel*, was an enormous flop. "Mr. O'Neal should have slam-dunked the script into the nearest wastebasket," read one review.

By starring in his own major motion picture, Michael Jordan had broken the mold. But in playing the role of a basketball player — a glorified cameo — he was following a road well traveled by NBA stars before him.

In 1979, Julius Erving played a streetball legend in the low-budget comedy *The Fish that Saved Pittsburgh*.

One year later, in 1980, Kareem Abdul-Jabbar, the NBA's most recognizable star, made a far more memorable appearance in the smash hit slapstick comedy *Airplane!* Abdul-Jabbar plays copilot Roger Murdock, but in one scene, he memorably breaks character.

Abdul-Jabbar had appeared in the movies once before — a kung fu–fighting cameo in the 1972 Bruce Lee film *Game of Death* — but by the close of the decade he was combating a negative reputation off the court. Fans perceived Abdul-Jabbar as surly, unfriendly and joyless. *Airplane!*

proved to be a successful PR gambit for a superstar whose image was in need of saving.

"I'd already been typecast [by fans] as the brooding black guy," Abdul-Jabbar said. "I just seemed to be like Mr. Grump. Being able to poke fun of my image . . . changed people's minds."

Despite coming out in the same year as major blockbusters like *Independence Day*, *Twister* and the first installment of the *Mission: Impossible* franchise, *Space Jam* still managed to finish in the top 10 at the box office, grossing over $250 million worldwide.

On the heels of that success, it's no wonder Hollywood opened its doors wide for NBA stars. Because of Jordan, the line between athlete and celebrity had been forever blurred.

By 2018 powerhouse agency William Morris had over a dozen NBAers on its client roster. Several players, like Elton Brand and Kobe Bryant, would start successful production companies — Kobe even won an Oscar for Best Animated Short Film as the executive producer of 2017's *Dear Basketball*.

In the summer of 2019, LeBron James began filming the *Space Jam* sequel, proving that, more than 20 years later, everybody still wants to be like Mike.

NBA GOES HOLLYWOOD

In the years following Kareem's 1980 cameo in *Airplane!*, several NBAers made their big screen debuts. In 1984 Wilt Chamberlain played a villain opposite Arnold Schwarzenegger in *Conan the Destroyer*. Before they were teammates in real life, Shaq and Penny played college basketball stars in the 1994 cult classic *Blue Chips*. In 1998 Ray Allen starred opposite Denzel Washington in the Spike Lee joint *He Got Game*. James flexed his comedic muscles alongside Bill Hader and Amy Schumer in the Apatow film *Trainwreck* in 2015. Kyrie Irving starred in 2018's *Uncle Drew*, a movie based off a successful ad campaign for Pepsi.

1997
NBA INC.

The timing was perfect. A few months before the 1984 Finals tipped off, David Stern, the New York–born lawyer who had worked with the league since 1966, replaced Larry O'Brien as NBA commissioner.

Stern inherited a league with financial problems and a souring reputation among North American sports fans. But he surveyed his new empire, saw the emergence of Finals-bound stars Magic Johnson and Larry Bird and crafted a vision not only to rescue the league but to grow it to unimaginable heights. He would rebuild the NBA's image off of the mainstream appeal of its brightest talents.

However, Stern's first shot was an air ball — one that unintentionally sparked the NBA's move into a multibillion-dollar enterprise and made moguls out of its stars.

Around the same time Stern was getting his feet wet as commissioner, Michael Jordan, the third overall pick of the '84 draft, was negotiating with Nike on his first signature sneaker, to be called the Air Jordan 1. MJ was the perfect pitchman for the struggling company. He was handsome, well-spoken and the most breathtaking athlete in sports.

It was incredibly rare for a player to have his own branded shoe — let alone a rookie. The first was Chuck Taylor, a semi-pro basketball player in the early 20th century who went on to work for Converse and design the iconic shoes that bore his name. They

The Jumpman logo outside the Niketown store in Portland, Oregon.

became the go-to footwear for ballers for over 50 years.

In 1973 New York Knicks point guard Walt "Clyde" Frazier joined forces with Puma to release the Puma Clyde. When Jordan and Nike teamed up, Magic and Bird's Lakers- and Celtics-colored Converse kicks were still two years away.

Jordan's agent, David Falk, made sure the shoe contract included a clause that forced Nike to spend at least $1 million promoting the product ahead of Jordan's rookie year. The apparel company went to work marketing Air Jordan to a mass audience with billboards and television ads.

When Jordan wore the black-and-red sneakers in his first preseason game, however, they were deemed to have violated the NBA's "uniformity of uniform" rule because they weren't the Bulls' official team colors. Stern and the league banned the most-hyped signature sneaker.

The people at Nike knew a PR opportunity when they saw one, and they released a print ad across the country that read, "On Oct. 15, Nike created a revolutionary new basketball shoe. On Oct. 18, the N.B.A. threw them out of the game. Fortunately, the N.B.A. can't keep you from wearing them."

Jordan occasionally wore the shoes anyway, opting to pay the fines that were handed down. The sneakers flew off the shelves. The "banned" Air Jordans generated over $100 million in sales in the first year alone, helping to launch Jordan into a stratosphere of celebrity. Over time, Nike cornered 90 percent of the sneaker market.

Unwittingly, Stern helped the Jordan Brand skyrocket from day one. Nike's success in marketing Jordan was impossible to ignore, and the commissioner quickly learned to embrace — and not fight — individual player branding.

Stern looked to replicate the Walt Disney model. As Disney had done with Mickey Mouse, Pluto and Donald Duck, the league would sell its stars more than its teams. That's where Stern's timing was impeccable. His first full season as commissioner saw a crop of rookies enter the NBA that included Hakeem Olajuwon, Charles Barkley and, of course, Jordan. Within a decade, the talent pool was replenished again with the likes of Shaquille O'Neal, Grant Hill and Penny Hardaway.

To further promote the NBA's marquee talent, the league was aggressive in securing licensing deals with some of the biggest companies in the world — more than 150 in all by the mid-90s. McDonald's and Coca-Cola were among the most notable to partner up. At McDonald's, kids got toys dressed in their favorite player's NBA jersey as part of their Happy Meals. In '94 Sprite became "The Official Soft Drink of the NBA." These kinds of deals not only generated a massive amount of revenue, they grew the celebrity of NBA players worldwide.

Factors beyond Stern's control helped. In 1989 FIBA, basketball's international governing body, changed its rules to allow pros to play on national teams. The NBA capitalized on the opportunity by working with USA Basketball to form the Dream Team, whose members served as global ambassadors during the 1992 Olympics in Barcelona.

And the NCAA college basketball tournament saw a spike in popularity in the early 90s. With dozens of games televised nationally (between 1990 and '95, the title game averaged 31 million viewers in the U.S.), college hoops helped make stars of future NBAers before they arrived in the league.

As a result, more and more players were receiving big-money sneaker deals accompanied by inventive ad campaigns, before they had ever played an NBA game. Shaq, Hill and Allen Iverson were among the many beneficiaries.

Of course, when it came to branding, nobody could touch Jordan. Thanks to the success of the Air Jordan shoes, by 1996 Nike accounted for 44 percent of the athletic shoe market, with sales in excess of $3.6 billion.

In September 1997 Nike awarded Jordan his own off-shoot brand, Team Jordan — the first of its kind. Jordan took a hands-on approach, hand-selecting the players who could wear his Jumpman Pros. He tabbed second-year star Ray Allen as the first player to endorse the brand. Allen withdrew from a prospective deal with Fila to join Jordan.

In the years since, basketball sneaker culture has become an industry of its own. Air Jordans are collected and traded like fine art. A rare pair can go for as much as $30,000 at auction. The whole scale of the industry has transformed. When Jordan first signed with Nike in 1984, his deal earned $2.5 million over five years — plus royalties. In 2019 alone, Kevin Durant's Nike deal paid him over $30 million.

When he was promoted to commissioner, David Stern was tasked with taking a floundering league and making it a multibillion-dollar corporate jewel. Within 10 years he succeeded. He worked to build the NBA's brand and went about it blatantly, plastering the league and its stars on every product under the sun. He was aggressive in getting NBA basketball on television around the world, securing broadcasting deals in over 180 countries.

And it worked. In 1986 ticket sales and TV rights garnered $255 million in revenue. By 1996 the number was $1.2 billion. Throw in the corporate partnerships, and the NBA earned over $4 billion in league revenue that year alone, along with massive riches and opportunities for star players.

The NBA was big business thanks in part to Stern, but it's hard to imagine the league transforming as it did had it not been for the meteoric rise and Madison Avenue appeal of Michael Jordan.

After all, there's no Disneyland without Mickey Mouse.

SPEND IT WISELY

Few players have cashed in on their NBA earnings quite like Junior Bridgeman. A 12-year veteran who played between 1975 and '87, mainly with the Milwaukee Bucks, Bridgeman spent his summers learning the ins and outs of the fast-food industry. He invested in the Wendy's franchise and, after his playing days, owned over 100 Wendy's and Chili's restaurants. In 1988 he became President and CEO of Manna Inc., adding more food franchises to his portfolio. Bridgeman is currently the second-largest Wendy's franchise owner on the planet. His company has reportedly earned profits in excess of $700 million.

1997
WE GOT NEXT

Cheryl Miller leads the USA to Olympic gold in 1984.

During the 1995–96 season, the NBA was looking to capitalize on Jordan-mania. There was talk of launching two leagues under the NBA banner: a minor-pro development league and an all-women's league to be called the WNBA.

The women's game was growing rapidly thanks to the popularity of Texas Tech's Sheryl Swoopes, Lisa Leslie of the University of Southern California and University of Connecticut's Rebecca Lobo — the three most recent winners of the NCAA women's Player of the Year award.

The NBA was still riding high from the global reach of the 1992 Dream Team, and with the Atlanta Games kicking off in the summer of 1996, the league saw another opportunity to use the Olympics as a springboard.

In the leadup to the Games, the NBA agreed to handle the bulk of the marketing duties and costs to promote USA Basketball's 1996 women's team. In exchange, the league would be able to gauge any potential interest in the women's game.

The league organized an exhibition tour for the team and secured a deal for ESPN to broadcast 10 games. The response was encouraging. There was an audience for women's hoops — and a major gap in the market.

Women's leagues had come and gone over the years. There was even a rival league, the American Basketball League, set to launch in '96. The ABL, like so many before it, lasted a year. But for years, prospective American pro players could only secure semi-reliable work in European leagues.

The women's pro game could never find a foothold in the United States. And it wasn't for a lack of talent; there were plenty of standout female players in the decades leading up to the WNBA's inception. Cheryl Miller was a national star at USC — a two-time NCAA champion and gold medalist at the 1984 Olympics — but she didn't play professionally.

Nancy Lieberman earned the nickname Lady Magic after setting assists records in college while at Old Dominion, and she played in the first American women's pro league, the Women's Professional Basketball League. The WPBL folded in 1981 after three years. With limited options, in 1986 Lieberman became the first woman to play in a men's pro league when she signed to play in the United States Basketball League.

But a lot had changed over the ensuing decade. On April 24, 1996, the NBA's board of governors gave the okay, and the launch of the WNBA was announced. Tip-off would take place the following summer.

In July 1996 the women's Dream Team appeared on the cover of *Sports Illustrated*. "Seeing that magazine cover was an incredible moment," recalled Val Ackerman, the WNBA's inaugural president.

The issue hit newsstands the same morning that Ackerman and NBA commissioner David Stern were set to meet with prospective WNBA sponsors. Stern grabbed a copy on his way to the meeting and as it began, without saying a word, he placed it on the table. The message had been sent.

"If the NBA was willing to put its own name in the league, it gave people confidence that this wasn't just a 'We'll try it and see.' It was a long-term commitment," said league executive Rick Welts.

As Stern saw it, the WNBA was a win-win for the league. There was an opportunity to sell tickets and fill arenas during the NBA's off-season, and the women's league had the potential to inspire an entire generation of young girls. In Stern's eyes, they would also grow up consumers. "Because if you play, there's more chance you'll be a lifelong basketball fan," he explained.

But the bounty was far more than a financial one. "We were all united by this sense of purpose," said Ackerman. "We were moving the ball forward."

Like the American Basketball Association before it, the WNBA wanted to stand out, and that started with the look of the ball. Thanks to its NBA affiliation, the WNBA's games would be broadcast nationally in its first season and it wanted to catch the eye of a new audience. In 1967 the ABA went with red, white and blue. The WNBA opted for a shade it called oatmeal—or off-white—and orange.

Teams were established in eight cities — all existing NBA markets — and the league tried to link clubs to NBA counterparts. The Los Angeles Sparks, for example, wore purple and gold like their brothers, the Lakers.

The first WNBA game was played on June 21, 1997, between the Sparks and the New York Liberty — it was not a coincidence that the league's first national showcase featured its two largest media markets.

Before the game, billboards went up across LA featuring larger-than-life versions of Sparks star Lisa Leslie and the Liberty's Rebecca Lobo. In print next to their faces was the perfect slogan: "We Got Next."

For Liberty veteran Teresa Weatherspoon, who'd spent the past eight years playing in Russia and Italy, the opportunity was immense. "We were scared to death," she said. "Not afraid to play the game, but we wanted to do well because it was televised."

The game was broadcast on a Saturday afternoon on NBC. A generation of future WNBA stars tuned in to witness history.

Tamika Catchings, who was celebrating her 18th birthday, remembers watching the Sparks' Penny Toler score the first basket in league history. "I wanted to be there," Catchings said. "I wanted to be a part of the movement." Catchings went on to spend 15 seasons with the Indiana Fever.

The Liberty beat the Sparks that afternoon and went on to the WNBA Finals, falling to the league's first No. 1 draft pick, Tina Thompson, and the Houston Comets.

In the years that followed, the WNBA gained a foothold in the sports market. More moments, like Cynthia Cooper's full-court heave to win Game 2 of the 2000 Finals. Two years later, Tina Charles, the 2010 first overall pick, watched in amazement when Lisa Leslie slammed home the first dunk in WNBA history.

Sustaining the success of those early years has proven difficult. Average league attendance peaked at over 11,000 per game in 1998, but had dropped to 6,800 by 2019.

"I never could understand the disconnect and the absence of media coverage," said David Stern. "So that became a source of intense focus for us."

But the WNBA's impact on a generation of young girls borders on immeasurable. In 2017, as she was being enshrined in the

Naismith Hall of Fame alongside George McGinnis, Tracy McGrady and others, Rebecca Lobo took the podium and told a story about her daughter.

Like her friends, she grew up exposed to the women's game, following her favorite league, the WNBA, and her favorite player, her mom. One night while at home with her father, who was watching an NBA game, Lobo's daughter was stunned to see men playing the sport.

"Are boys playing *basketball*?" she asked. "I didn't know boys played basketball, too."

Lisa Leslie knocks the ball from Camille Little during Game 1 of the playoffs in 2009.

MOST WNBA TITLES

1.	Minnesota Lynx	4
	Houston Comets	4
3.	Los Angeles Sparks	3
	Detroit Shock	3
	Phoenix Mercury	3
	Seattle Storm	3

1999
LOCKOUT

There have been plenty of impressive streaks throughout NBA history. The Los Angeles Lakers' 33-game win streak in 1972. Wilt Chamberlain scoring at least 30 points in 65 consecutive games in 1965. Tim Duncan making a field goal in 1,310 games in a row. And the San Antonio Spurs' 22-year run without missing the postseason.

But in 1998 the longest streak of them all came to a startling halt. Dating back to the NBA's inception, the league had enjoyed 52 straight seasons of NBA basketball. That changed during the 1998–99 campaign, when a long-simmering dispute between the players' union and owners resulted in a lockout that lasted 207 days, cost the NBA half a season and stunted the NBA's growing popularity.

The '97–98 season ended spectacularly. A record television audience of nearly 36 million tuned in to watch Michael Jordan hit the title-winning shot against the Utah Jazz.

On the wings of Air Jordan, the NBA had risen to unfathomed heights. The league and its players were reaping the financial benefits. Players were earning more, teams were generating more revenue than ever and the league enjoyed a global reach.

The NBA appeared to be riding high, but behind the scenes, owners and players were preparing for the first work stoppage in league history long before Jordan's iconic shot.

The lockout of '98–99 was the third in four years. In 1994, the existing collective bargaining agreement (CBA) expired, and negotiations toward a new deal went on throughout the 1994–95 season. The players were seeking to lift salary restrictions and eliminate teams' right-of-first-refusal to re-sign players, all in an effort to put more control in the players' hands. They also wanted to abolish the college entry draft in favor of letting all rookies hit the open market — something players had spent decades arguing for.

During the off-season, the National Basketball Players Association (NBPA) sued the league, claiming those restrictions were illegal. A U.S. District Court judge disagreed, and scolded both sides for "using the court as a bargaining chip in the collective bargaining process."

Immediately after the 1995 Finals, team owners imposed a lockout. The NBA shut down for three months over the summer, but patchwork solutions were put in place to ensure that no games were sacrificed during the upcoming '95-96 season. Meanwhile, a group of players led by Michael Jordan and Patrick Ewing pushed to decertify the players union altogether. With no union in place, a lockout would be illegal. In September 1995 a vote was held, and the movement failed, 226–134.

Another lockout was imposed following the '96 Finals, but this time it only lasted two hours as the sides completed a new CBA. The agreement contained an opt-out clause that could be exercised in 1998 if player salaries exceeded 51.8 percent of the league's basketball-related revenue.

By the 1997–98 season, the players' share was at 57 percent. And on March 23, 1998, 82 days before Jordan's famous shot, team owners voted to exercise the opt-out and reopen the CBA.

The previous agreement had been meant to prevent player salaries from ballooning. But player agents found creative ways to circumvent the cap rules — in particular, a loophole that allowed for big-money contract extensions to second-year players. The result? Twenty-one-year-old Kevin Garnett's record-breaking six-year, $126 million deal in 1997, which enabled him to join Shaquille O'Neal, Juwan Howard, Alonzo Mourning and Shawn Kemp among the NBA's growing $100 million club.

The NBA had become a billion-dollar industry and the players were cashing in. But there were concerns on both sides, and years of distrust had taken hold. After all, the league was never in a hurry to protect its players.

The NBPA, organized by Boston Celtics star Bob Cousy in 1954, was the first of its kind among team sports. The merger of the NBL and BAA six years earlier had given birth to the NBA, but it meant players could no longer play the leagues against one another to give them leverage in negotiations. Owners held more power than ever. The players union was necessary. Still, it took another 10 years — thanks to a players' strike moments before tip-off at the '64 All-Star Game — for the union to be recognized by the league.

The emergence of the ABA in 1967 added a new wrinkle to the management–labor dynamic. Players again had negotiating leverage, and they made a pickup game

David Stern announces the cancellation of NBA games due to the 2011 lockout.

out of playing the two leagues against one another. In 1970, when talks of a merger first began, Oscar Robertson led a lawsuit against the league in an effort to block it. *Robertson v. National Basketball Association* wasn't successful in stopping the NBA from swallowing up the ABA years later, but in 1977 a judge ruled that the league could not bind a player to one team. The landmark case led to the implementation of restricted free agency, granting teams the right of first refusal but allowing players to explore their value on the open market.

The threat of a player strike ahead of the 1987–88 season resulted in more concessions for players, including the establishment of unrestricted free agency for all non-rookie deals. But the relationship between the players and the league soured in 1991, when the NBPA learned the NBA had not fully disclosed its revenues. A court ruled in favor of the players, who moved forward with a healthy dose of skepticism in any future negotiations.

By 1998 the players' voice was stronger than ever. The NBA that Jordan built during the 90s created a different world. The players were more vocal in their discontent. Owners, doling out record-level contracts, were even less sympathetic to their needs.

When the owners voted to reopen the CBA, both sides braced for a lockout and lengthy negotiations.

The union hired Billy Hunter to represent them. A former NFL player turned federal prosecutor, Hunter had taken the Hells Angels and Black Panthers to court. A group of 29 billionaires presented a new challenge, and Hunter found a worthy adversary in NBA commissioner David Stern, a shrewd and ruthless negotiator who belied his self-appointed nickname, Easy Dave.

The players again pushed to limit salary restrictions, and the owners fought for salary caps. Both sides eyed the growing revenues and wanted a larger slice of the pie.

On August 6, 1998, during one of the earliest formal meetings between players and

owners, the tone of the negotiations was set. Fifteen minutes after a break for lunch, the owners left their seats in unison and stormed out of the room.

The talks remained heated. In December, Jordan, who had officially retired in January 1999, made an appearance and silenced Washington Wizards owner Abe Pollin by telling him that if he was worried about losing money, he should give up and sell his team. Another 12-hour day ended in a standstill.

By October the NBA had cancelled the preseason and first 20 games. Then came All-Star weekend. Two days before Christmas, Stern announced he'd recommend that the season be axed entirely if a resolution wasn't reached by January 7.

On January 6, the two sides finally reached an agreement, and the season was set to start

on February 5.

Fans followed the ongoing dispute between millionaires and billionaires and didn't hold much sympathy for either side. Just when the NBA had built it up, it was turning off its fan base. A charity game in December between All-Star teams captained by Patrick Ewing and Alonzo Mourning barely managed to sell 1,200 tickets.

Merchandise sales plummeted by an estimated 50 percent during the lockout, and, once the games tipped off, there was a leaguewide attendance drop. Ticket sales wouldn't reach pre-lockout numbers again until 2003–04, when LeBron James led a new generation of stars into the league. The '99 Finals, which saw the San Antonio Spurs sweep the New York Knicks and begin their modern dynasty, experienced a 40 percent drop in viewership from the year before.

As a result of the lockout, teams were forced to cram a 50-game schedule into 90 days, featuring multiple back-to-back-to-backs and resulting in even more nagging injuries than usual around the league.

The players got a health benefits package. The owners got a limit on individual player salaries. Neither side walked away happy.

It took 52 years for the first lockout to cost the NBA any games. It was barely a decade before it happened again.

Ahead of the 2011 All-Star Game, a war of words broke out between Hunter and Stern, who found themselves back at the negotiating table. With the CBA set to expire after the season, the two addressed the players before tip-off. Hunter spoke highly of the '64 All-Star Game, when players threatened not to play until their demands were met. Stern responded by telling Hunter and the players that he knew where the bodies were buried — he had dug the graves himself.

This time the main dispute was over revenue sharing. The players wanted 53 percent

Karl Malone and Alonzo Mourning speak out during the NBA labor talks in New York in 1998.

of the pie. Owners didn't want to concede more than 47 percent. The players were locked out once more. This time, the dispute went on for 161 days, delaying the start of the 2011–12 season until December 25.

Few found themselves in a more precarious position than Michael Jordan, who, 13 years after the longest lockout in history, was now on the other side of the table. Now the owner of the Charlotte Bobcats, Jordan led a group of owners who refused anything more than a 50/50 revenue split.

The NBA's current collective bargaining agreement is due to expire after the 2022–23 season. There is talk of another lockout.

2000
THE KOBE-SHAQ LAKERS

The Los Angeles Lakers are on a 22–4 run in the fourth quarter of Game 7 of the 2000 Western Conference finals against the Portland Trail Blazers. Ten minutes ago they trailed by 15. The Trail Blazers have no answer for the Lakers' superstar duo. Kobe Bryant, the 21-year-old two-time All-Star, has been brilliant down the stretch. His

Shaquille O'Neal puts his arms around Kobe Bryant and Co. during a 1999 game against the Houston Rockets.

Richard Hamilton guards Bryant during the 2004 NBA Finals.

teammate, Shaquille O'Neal, the league MVP, has been unstoppable, as per usual.

With 50 seconds left and the Lakers up four, Bryant brings the ball up the court. He crosses over and blasts into the lane. As the double-team arrives, he sees Shaq point up to the rafters and floats a pass toward the hoop. O'Neal slams home the alley-oop to seal the win. The Lakers go on to win the championship, their first of three in a row to begin the new millennium.

Behind Shaq and Kobe, Los Angeles ruled the league — winning 12 of 15 games in the Finals between 2000 and 2002. The duo gave the Lakers the NBA's best one-two punch — on paper, one of the best of all time. But they grew to loathe each other. Their relationship was tailor-made for Hollywood and served as the NBA's biggest soap opera — one that cut the Laker dynasty short.

In the summer of 1996, O'Neal was in search of new surroundings after four years in Orlando, where he'd beaten Michael Jordan in the playoffs and led the Magic to the Finals. He was the biggest game changer in the NBA — and Lakers GM Jerry West knew it. Los Angeles opened the vault for Shaq, inking him to a $120 million deal that made him the NBA's highest-paid player.

When Shaq and West met in person to finalize the deal, the Lakers legend and executive said, "I just traded for a kid, and you two are going to win three or four championships."

Kobe Bean Bryant was born in Philadelphia and raised in Italy, where his father, former 76er Joe "Jellybean" Bryant, played after his NBA days. Kobe often felt isolated as he tried to learn the language and fit in with the kids around him. The experience left him guarded. But he felt like he was wearing impenetrable armor whenever he stepped onto the basketball court.

He was a natural, and equally unnaturally self-assured in his own abilities. By the age of 11 he was regularly challenging his dad's teammates to games of H-O-R-S-E and one-on-one — and winning. When he met Michael Jordan, the player he patterned his every move on the court after, he told the game's greatest that he'd "kick his ass" once he got to the NBA. He was a dominant high

schooler when his family moved back to the United States. He made the jump straight from Philly's Lower Merion High to the NBA — the first guard ever to make the leap from high school to the pros.

At 18 years and 72 days, he became the youngest player to appear in an NBA game when he came off the bench for his debut on November 3, 1996. His rookie season was mostly uneventful (he did win the slam-dunk contest), but he had a career-shaping performance in an elimination game in the playoffs versus the Utah Jazz.

With the Lakers trailing the series, 3-1, and Shaq fouling out near the end of Game 5, Bryant was thrust into the spotlight. He responded by shooting three air balls down the stretch, including two in the final minute of overtime. The Lakers lost, but Kobe left a favorable impression in Lakerland. "[Kobe] was the only guy who had the guts at the time to take shots like that," said Shaq, who put his arm around the rookie on their way off the court.

The next season a 19-year-old Bryant became the youngest All-Star in NBA history. He joined Shaq on the West All-Star team and led the squad in scoring. Bryant was an instant superstar, marketed as the league's Heir Jordan, and happy to take over long stretches of games just as his idol did.

Although he'd said that Kobe played too selfishly at times, Shaq was content to let a burgeoning Bryant dominate in the regular season. But by the time the playoffs came around, the big man wanted the ball. The Lakers' new coach, Phil Jackson, agreed.

After all, O'Neal was in the midst of one of the most dominant stretches in decades. In the 1999–2000 season he averaged 29.7 points, 13.6 rebounds and 3 blocks per game, earning his first MVP award in the process. In the playoffs, his numbers rose, and plays like his Game 7 alley-oop jam against Portland put the rest of the NBA on notice. Shaq was named Finals MVP that year, and he'd earn the honor the next two years as well.

Shaq and Kobe's exploits were being written into the history books. They were the latest in a world-class lineage of star duos in Los Angeles — West and Baylor, Magic and Kareem. Now it was their turn.

After winning their first championship, Shaq arrived at training camp out of shape and nursing injuries. Bryant, who spent the summer in the gym and took another leap forward that season, resented O'Neal and clamored for a bigger role on the team. Jackson obliged. Shaq wasn't happy.

"When it was clear that everything went through me," O'Neal told reporters in January, referencing the prior campaign, "the outcome of it was 67-15, playing with enthusiasm, the city jumping up and down and a parade. And now we're 23-11. You figure it out."

Asked about the comments, Bryant responded by criticizing Shaq's defensive effort. It went back and forth like that for the next two years, a spat played out in public.

On the court, however, the Lakers remained a force. Shaq and Kobe were surrounded by a group of veteran role players including Robert Horry, Derek Fisher and Rick Fox, as well as Horace Grant and Ron Harper, who'd been members of Jackson's title-winning Chicago Bulls teams in the 90s. In 2001 the Lakers swept the New Jersey Nets in the Finals. In 2002 they beat the Philadelphia 76ers in five games.

O'Neal had been hampered by toe issues during the 2001–02 season. Instead of undergoing surgery in the off-season, he waited until the start of training camp. "I got hurt on company time, so I'll rehab on company time," he said. Kobe, who patterned his tireless approach to winning after Jordan, was disgusted. But without Shaq, the Lakers started the season 11–19. They lost in the second round of the playoffs to the San Antonio Spurs.

In the summer of 2003, a 19-year-old hotel employee at a spa in Eagle, Colorado, alleged that Bryant had raped her. On July 4, Kobe was charged with felony sexual assault. He admitted to the encounter and infidelity with his wife, but denied the allegations of rape. The case went to trial and Bryant spent the 2003–04 season flying back and forth to the courthouse in Aspen, Colorado. Ultimately the case was dropped after the accuser refused to testify in court.

That same summer, the Lakers made a splash by adding two future Hall of Famers in

Gary Payton and Karl Malone, easily giving LA its most star-studded roster of the Kobe–Shaq era. With Bryant at trial during training camp, O'Neal let it be known he wasn't missed. "The full team is here," he said.

It was a dysfunctional season. Bryant was apart from his team often, and when he was around, he alienated teammates and mouthed off against Jackson, who wanted Bryant traded. For one game against Denver, Bryant went straight from one court to another, arriving during the second quarter. He proceeded to hit the game-winning jumper at the buzzer. "How he manages to compartmentalize is beyond me," said Jackson.

The simmering Shaq–Kobe feud boiled over into Bryant's court case. In a police report, Bryant alleged that Shaq had been in Kobe's shoes before, but had simply paid women millions of dollars to keep his indiscretions quiet.

Behind the scenes, the two had to be physically separated after Shaq threatened to kill Bryant. In front of reporters, Shaq suggested that Kobe should opt out of his contract at the end of the season and find a new team. The Lakers were Shaq's team, and he had three Finals MVP awards to prove it.

In a nationally televised interview, Bryant agreed that the Lakers were Shaq's team — and that's what frustrated Kobe: "It's time for him to act like it. That means no more coming into camp fat and out of shape."

During their championship run, Jackson had often played the two against one another. He was a puppet master who believed that it was a means to get the most out of his star players. But by the 2003–04 season, even he knew things had gone too far. Jackson went as far as to hire a psychologist who dealt with narcissists to work with his dysfunctional team.

But lines had already been drawn in the Lakers locker room. Bryant's otherworldly abilities and work ethic made him the team's best player, but he struggled as a leader. Kobe would often yell at teammates after they made mistakes during games. Jackson would tell Kobe that Michael Jordan waited until he was in private before calling out his fellow Bulls.

Shaq, on the other hand, was a good teammate. "He's telling you he's got your back," recalled Luke Walton, son of Bill and a rookie that season. "If somebody is fouling you, he'd tell you to 'run them into me.'"

The writing was on the wall. Divorce was near. Bryant wanted out of Shaq's shadow and was rumored to have had a backdoor meeting with the LA Clippers. "Get me over here," he told their staff during a game.

In the meantime, Shaq was unhappy with Lakers management and had been vocal in wanting a hefty pay raise at season's end.

Despite the ongoing drama, the Lakers raced to an 18-3 start to the season and returned to the Finals in 2004 — thanks in part to Derek Fisher's miracle buzzer-beater with 0.4 seconds on the clock against the Spurs in the Western finals.

In the Finals, the Lakers were upset by the Detroit Pistons, who played Shaq and Kobe's egos against one another. Early in games, they would single-team Shaq, knowing the Lakers would work to get him the ball down low. "What's going to happen," explained Finals MVP Chauncey Billups, "is Mr. Bryant is going to get a little discouraged with getting no touches. . . . Now he's pressing."

After the Lakers lost, Kobe, a pending free agent, began looking for a new team. He and his family scouted homes and schools in the Chicago area, and Bryant was dead set on signing with the Bulls.

"I wasn't going to play with Shaq anymore," he said. "I put that individual s★★t aside to win championships, and now I'm getting criticized for it. Now I'm going to show you f★★ks what I can do on my own."

The 2004 off-season decided the Lakers' future. Jackson maintained privately that he didn't want to return to the team if Kobe was still on the roster. But the Lakers brass were hesitant to break the bank for a 32-year-old Shaq who was past his prime. Sensing that the organization was backing Bryant, Shaq demanded a trade. On July 14 O'Neal was dealt to the Miami Heat. The next day, Kobe signed a seven-year, $136 million contract extension with the Lakers.

The next season, the Lakers missed the playoffs as Bryant was left with a subpar roster, learning that the grass isn't always greener.

In 2006 Shaq won a championship alongside the NBA's next great shooting guard, Dwyane Wade.

Shaq and Kobe made up publicly, but their beef never really died. During a 2019 inter-

view, Bryant said he would have 12 championship rings if Shaq had stayed in shape. O'Neal said that Kobe would have his 12 rings if he had passed the ball more against the Pistons.

Shaq runs down the court after a monster dunk against the Dallas Mavericks.

2001
MJ GOES TO WASHINGTON

A game winner with the championship on the line — the perfect end to Michael Jordan's career.

In January of the following year, Jordan announced his retirement for the second time. And this time, at 37 years old, it seemed like the greatest player of all time was done for good.

He had lost the competitive drive that fueled him to be the best, he said, adding that he was "99.9 percent certain" we would not see His Airness on an NBA court again. Which meant, there was a chance . . .

The game had lost its icon, and in Jordan's absence the next generation of NBA stars struggled mightily to fill the void. In the lockout-shortened 1998–99 season, the first since MJ's retirement, the likes of Keith Van Horn and Shareef Abdur-Rahim finished in the top five in scoring, where only two players, Allen Iverson and Shaquille O'Neal, managed to average more than 24 points per game — well below the 31.5 Jordan had averaged in his career with the Bulls, the highest scoring mark of any player in league history.

Fans wouldn't have to wait long for Jordan's (sort-of) return. On January 19, 2000, he became a part owner of the Washington Wizards and the team's president of basketball operations.

Washington had long been the NBA's model of futility. The championship team of 1978 was forgotten, lost to history when the team changed its name from the Bullets to the Wizards amid the mass of gun violence that plagued the D.C. area in the 90s.

No matter the name, the team was wholly inconsequential: since 1989 it had reached the playoffs just once, getting swept in the first round in '97 by Jordan's Bulls (ever the mind-f★★★er, Jordan strutted into Washington's locker room before Game 1 of the series, lit cigar in hand, asking, "Who's going to check me tonight?").

Since Jordan joined the NBA ranks in 1984, he had appeared in 179 playoff games. The Wizards in that span? Fifteen.

So, Jordan brought instant credibility — and attention — to a team severely lacking in both. But his résumé as an executive was nonexistent. Even so, he was given the final say on all basketball decisions and sought to put his mark on his new team.

He hired Doug Collins, who had coached him for three seasons in Chicago, as head coach. At the 2001 draft, Jordan used the first overall pick to draft high schooler Kwame Brown, the 7-footer who would eventually be remembered as one of the biggest draft busts of all time.

With the team mired in more losing and the ultracompetitive Jordan watching from the executive suites, it was only a matter of time before Jordan took matters into his own hands. Speculation about a potential comeback was rampant, and ESPN even ran a "Jordan's Return-o-Meter" on its website throughout the 2000–01 season.

The seeds for a return to action had been sown before Jordan ever joined the Wizards.

November 11, 1999, was an otherwise meaningless day on the NBA calendar. Except that, for the first time since his retirement, Jordan returned to Chicago's practice facility in an effort to "help the morale a bit," as he put it. The Bulls were 0-4 to start the young season, facing the harsh realities of a post-Jordan world.

Jordan played a game of one-on-one against 21-year-old Bulls sophomore Corey Benjamin, which Jordan won, of course. "The good thing about it is he's more worn out then I am," Jordan, noted trash talker, said afterward.

"I think he cheated a couple of times," Benjamin later told reporters. "There were a lot of flagrant fouls."

Jordan was quick to dismiss the possibility of another return, saying that basketball was no longer a challenge to him, unlike one of his most fervent hobbies, golf.

"I decided to stop by, don't take it further than that," he said. When asked if he was eyeing a return to the Bulls, Jordan said no, adding, "I've never pictured myself in another jersey."

However, by the close of his first season running the Wizards, things had changed. The Wizards won just 19 games. It killed Jordan to watch the team he had assembled

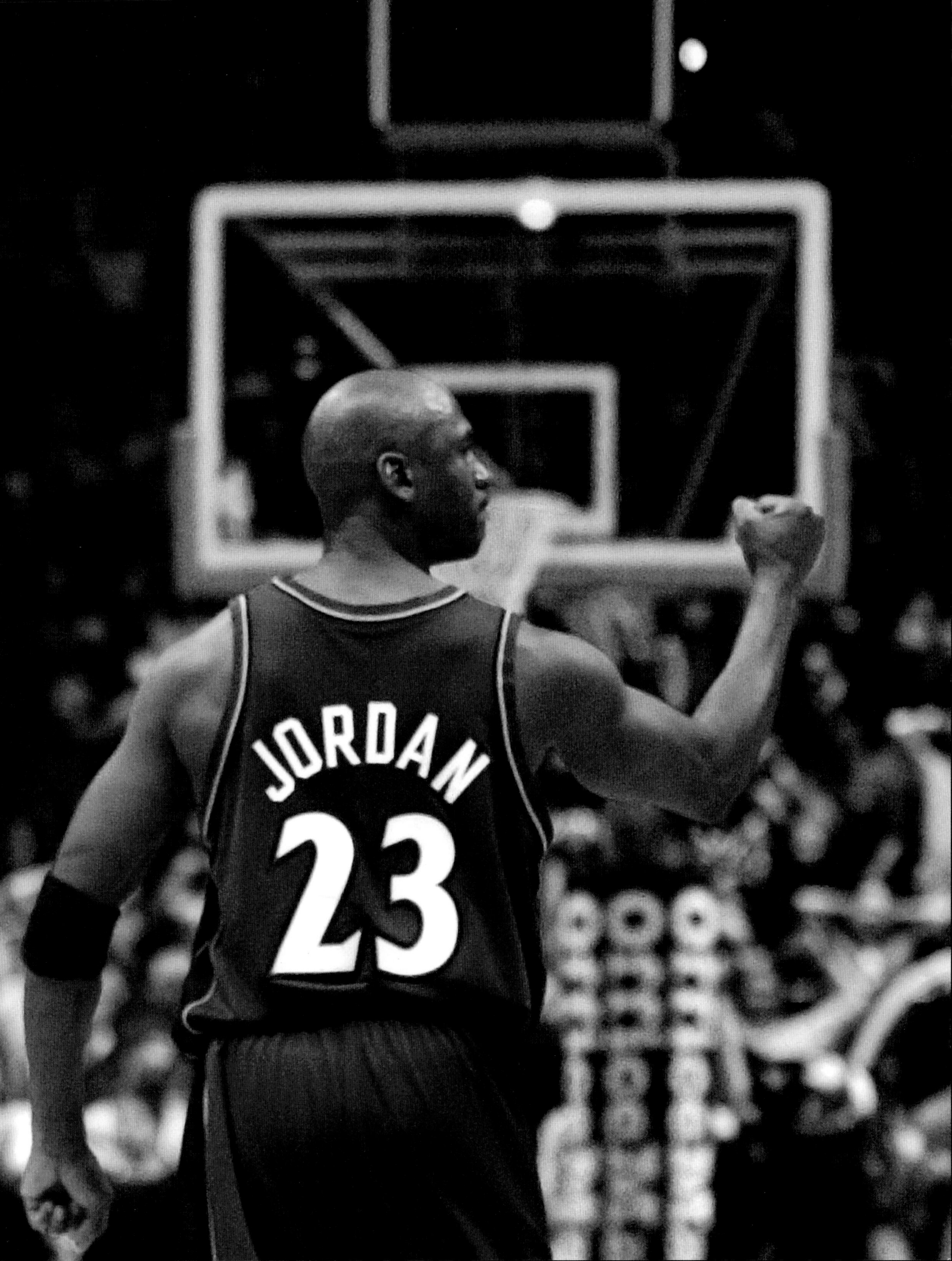
JORDAN
23

lose. Especially when he knew full well that he could still whoop some ass.

He likely replayed the conversation he'd had two years earlier, while meeting a 19-year-old Kobe Bryant — the supposed heir to his throne — over and over in his head. The Lakers' rising star told Jordan he would "kick his ass" in a game of one-on-one. That's the fuel MJ runs on.

Jordan also kept a close eye on another sports icon of his generation, NHL star Mario Lemieux, who had successfully returned to the ice after his own retirement. Jordan would call Lemieux often, asking in detail how he prepared for his comeback.

Late in the summer of 2001, Jordan could be found in the Wizards weight room. Collins would catch the gleam in his eye. "He's going to play," the coach told anybody who would listen.

The pathologically competitive Jordan — remember, this is the same man who would ask arena officials before home games which mascot would win the predetermined halftime race, and then con teammates into betting against him — didn't need much in the way of convincing.

On September 25, 2001, Jordan announced that he would return to the court and suit up for the Wizards that season. He stepped down from the front office, sold back his 10 percent stake in the team and donated his $1 million salary to relief efforts stemming from the recent September 11 attack on New York's World Trade Center.

Needless to say, it was jarring to see Jordan plying his trade in the NBA in anything but a Chicago Bulls jersey. Sure, there have been plenty more legends who ended their careers in strange uniforms — Hakeem Olajuwon in the Toronto Raptors' purple dino jersey, Karl Malone in Lakers' gold and Patrick Ewing with the Orlando Magic come to mind.

But Jordan was synonymous with the Bulls logo. He took a sorry franchise and made it the most recognizable team brand on Earth. (Jordan's brand was even bigger, and the Wizards would become the NBA's leader in home and road attendance during the 2001–02 season.)

Jordan was 38 years old, and three years removed from the game. Expectations were tempered.

"We're going to start calling him Floor Jordan," one ESPN analyst said ahead of his return.

It was true that the high-flying acrobatics were gone, but Jordan the Wizard remained an extremely effective player. In his first season back, he averaged 23 points per game and finished 10th in the league in scoring — although his campaign was cut short after 60 games, the years of impact on his knees catching up to him.

He had his moments. On December 29, 2001, Jordan became the oldest player to score 50 points when he dropped 51 on the Charlotte Hornets — it was of no consequence that, in his previous game, he scored just 6, the lowest output of his career.

Jordan's proudest moments came in match-ups with the NBA's rising stars, where he was eager to remind the kids that he was more than just a great scorer. Facing Paul Pierce, he limited the Celtics star to just 2 points in the fourth quarter of a tightly contested win. Against the Raptors, he held Vince Carter scoreless down the stretch. Rumor has it that Carter asked Jordan for his phone number while on the court.

The respect among his peers was evident. At the 2003 NBA All-Star Game, in the middle of Jordan's final season, fellow All-Stars Tracy McGrady, Allen Iverson and Carter, the leading vote-getter, offered their spots in the starting lineup to the 40-year-old Jordan.

That game, MJ's 14th all-star appearance, offered one last shining moment: with the game tied in overtime and 10 seconds on the clock, Jordan received the ball on the right elbow. Like he had so many times before, Jordan posted up his defender, took two dribbles toward the baseline and soared for a fadeaway jump shot with the game on the line. *Swish.*

On March 16, 2003, before the final game of the season, legends were on hand to bid farewell to MJ. Julius Erving and Moses Malone gave Jordan a personalized golf cart. It was a blowout loss for the Wizards, and Jordan spent much of it on the bench. "We want Mike!" the fans chanted.

Jordan's presence was never enough to lift an otherwise uninspiring team. The Wizards missed the playoffs during both of his seasons in Washington.

As in Chicago, Jordan's breakup with the Wizards would turn ugly. Following the 2003 season, he clashed with an ownership group that told him his services were no longer needed. Not since his high school varsity team had he been cut. Jordan maintains he was promised that he could regain his ownership stake upon his latest retirement, though that never happened.

He returned to the front office in March 2010, becoming the majority owner of the Charlotte Bobcats (renamed the Hornets in 2014). His track record hasn't improved much; Jordan the executive seems to have an effect on his teams that is the polar opposite of Jordan the player.

These days, you can find his latest highlights on grainy cell phone videos, like the one showing a 43-year-old Jordan crushing top-ranked high schoolers at his summer training camps. Every now and then, following a Hornets practice, he'll challenge a player to a heated game of one-on-one, even if it means he'll be icing his knees for days.

MJ's Wizards days are often dismissed as an asterisk on an otherwise unmatchable career. But they are also a fitting end for a competitor who couldn't stay away from the game.

As Jordan said during his Hall of Fame speech in 2009: "Never say never. Because limits, like fears, are often just an illusion."

MOST NBA TEAMS PLAYED FOR

1. Chucky Brown	12	(1990-2002)
Jim Jackson	12	(1993-2006)
Tony Massenburg	12	(1991-2005)
Joe Smith	12	(1996-2011)
5. Mike James	11	(2002-2014)
Kevin Ollie	11	(1998-2010)
Ish Smith	11	(2011-2020)

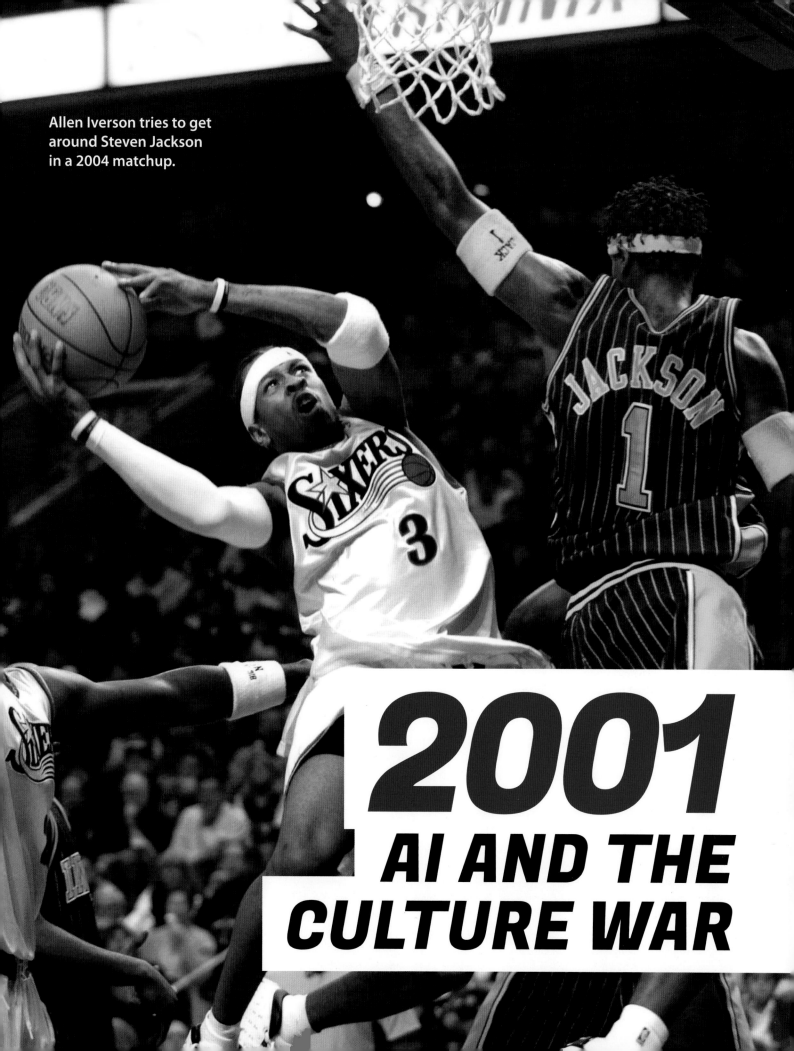

Allen Iverson tries to get around Steven Jackson in a 2004 matchup.

2001
AI AND THE CULTURE WAR

On March 12, 1997, the defending champion Chicago Bulls were in Philadelphia to face the 76ers. The Sixers were in the midst of a lousy 22-win season, but the arena was packed for the matchup between Michael Jordan and reigning first overall pick, Allen Iverson.

Like a generation of stars, Iverson grew up idolizing Jordan. He used to tell anybody who would listen that one day he would unleash his rapid-fire crossover on the perennial champ.

Iverson collected a handoff at the top of the key. "Michael!" Phil Jackson yelled from the sideline, as Michael Jordan switched onto the 76ers rookie. Jordan towered over Iverson, who was barely 6 feet tall and was generously listed at 165 pounds.

The other eight players cleared the way for the one-on-one battle fans had been waiting for. Iverson planted a quick crossover that brought the Philly crowd to its feet. Jordan didn't bite. As soon as MJ's feet were set, Iverson crossed him again and left the former Defensive Player of the Year in the dust. He took off to his right and pulled up for a jumper. By the time Jordan recovered, it was too late. The ball swished through the mesh, to the delight of the roaring crowd.

If a single moment in an otherwise meaningless regular-season game can shape the future of a league, this was it.

After a standout career at Georgetown, Iverson was selected first overall in a loaded 1996 draft that included such guards as Kobe Bryant, Steve Nash and Ray Allen. Iverson had separated himself from the pack with his flashy, streetball-influenced game built on deceptive handles and daring drives.

He connected with young fans. Despite being a prodigious athlete — a two-sport star and champion in football and basketball — Iverson was relatable. His small stature made him an everyman bushwhacking his way through the trees on his way to the hoop. He soon came to embody the hip-hop movement that was rising in popular culture. "Tupac with a jump shot," as critic Michael Eric Dyson once put it.

After the draft, he signed a $50 million deal with Reebok, which was eager to promote him as an "anti-corporate guy." In other words: the anti-Jordan.

Jordan wore a suit and tie to work every day. He adored golf and chomped on cigars; he was the image of corporate America. Iverson, needless to say, was not. He opted for do-rags and baggy clothes adorned with gold chains — the uniform of his generation.

Reebok hoped that Iverson could change the look and feel of the NBA in the same way Dr. J had in the 70s, ushering in a new style and attitude to a game that felt stale to its growing young audience. The league had different ideas.

Iverson was named Rookie of the Year in 1997 after averaging over 23 points per game. He showed up to accept the award at a press conference wearing a white Reebok-branded skullcap. "It looks like something people wear in prison," said deputy commissioner Russ Granik.

The next season, Iverson arrived sporting a new hairstyle — braided cornrows — and established himself as a new age trendsetter.

Meanwhile, as Iverson's star grew — by his third season, he was leading the league in scoring — the NBA continued to tangle with his hip-hop image. When he appeared on the cover of the NBA-published *Hoop* magazine in January 2000, the tattoos that adorned his upper body had been airbrushed out.

"They could have used somebody else if they didn't want me as a whole," Iverson said. His tattoos included the names of his mother and grandmother and kids. "Airbrushing them, that's a slap in my face."

The league may have been trying to curb its hip-hop image, concerned it would make the NBA harder to sell to its corporate partners. But the fans weren't having it. With Iverson — "The Answer," as he was called — as the poster boy of a generation, his Reebok apparel outsold that of every other player. Like hip-hop itself, he was the counterculture gone mainstream.

On the court, Iverson was blossoming. In the summer of 2000 the 76ers bolstered their lineup, adding center Dikembe Mutombo and hiring Larry Brown, who tailored Philadelphia's attack around their superstar guard. In 2000–01 the Sixers finished first in the East, and Iverson averaged 31.1 points per game to take home his second of four scoring titles. He was named 2001 MVP.

He led the Sixers to their first Finals that season in a David vs. Goliath matchup with Shaq, Kobe and the Los Angeles Lakers. In Game 1, Iverson scored 48 points in an overtime win — the Lakers' only loss that postseason. Los Angeles would eventually take the series, 4-1.

Iverson continued to rack up points (between 1998 and 2006, no player scored more), but he never reached the Finals again.

In the years since Michael Jordan's retirement in 2003, Iverson took over the mantle of the league's most popular player. But television viewership was dropping each season. Effective November 1, 2005, the NBA instituted a clothing ban. Ostensibly it was a reaction to the Malice at the Palace brawl the season before, an incident that had done nothing to diminish the thuggish image of the league and its new stable of stars. But in essence, it was a response to Iverson.

The ban outlawed T-shirts, chains and other hip-hop paraphernalia. Commissioner David Stern called the ban "liberal and easygoing."

"They're targeting my generation — the hip-hop generation," Iverson retorted.

Several prominent players spoke out against the ban. Jason Richardson called it "kind of racist," and said that the rule blatantly targeted black players.

Stern maintained that the dress code was for good, and that conversations about race are inevitable in a league that has almost always featured a predominantly black membership. "At every collective bargaining negotiation, I was accused of having a plantation mentality," he said.

It wasn't the first time Iverson had been in the center of a racial tensions.

As a high schooler he'd been involved in a brawl between a group of black and white teenagers in his hometown Newport News, Virginia. Iverson was a boisterous star in high school, brash and unashamed of his ability to dominate on the field or court.

He was a minor when the incident took place, but prosecutors prolonged the case so that Iverson could be tried as an adult.

Iverson tries to fake out Hakeem Olajuwon during a game in 1997.

Iverson watches a loose ball from the floor in 2006.

With a prominent figure from the African American community on trial, courts were eager to make an example of Iverson. He was convicted of "maiming by mob," a charge originally added to Virginia statute law to combat lynching after the Civil War and that hadn't been used in years. He was sentenced to 15 years in prison. After four months of his sentence, L. Douglas Wilder, Virginia's first black governor, pardoned him, and the conviction was eventually overturned.

Iverson's career never reached the apex that those of other greats did. After the 2001 Finals, he never made it past the second round. But his legacy as an all-time great is without question. He was revered by his peers for being unstoppable despite often being the smallest player on the court. His MVP award was validation of his stature among the best in the game. And his role as the new face of African American superstars

paved the way for LeBron James and the proudly outspoken generation that followed.

In 2016 Iverson was inducted into the Hall of Fame. "What makes me proudest," he told the crowd during his enshrinement speech, "is that I did this my way. I never changed who I was."

NBA RECORDS

Allen Iverson didn't just represent hip-hop; he was a rapper. But Iverson's 2005 single, *40 Bars,* was hardly the only time an NBA star took a trip into the world of music:

- *Shaq Fu: Da Return* — Shaquille O'Neal
- *The Album That Never Was* — Lou Williams
- *Shaq Diesel* — Shaqulle O'Neal
- *The Letter O* — Damian Lillard
- *40 Bars* — Allen Iverson

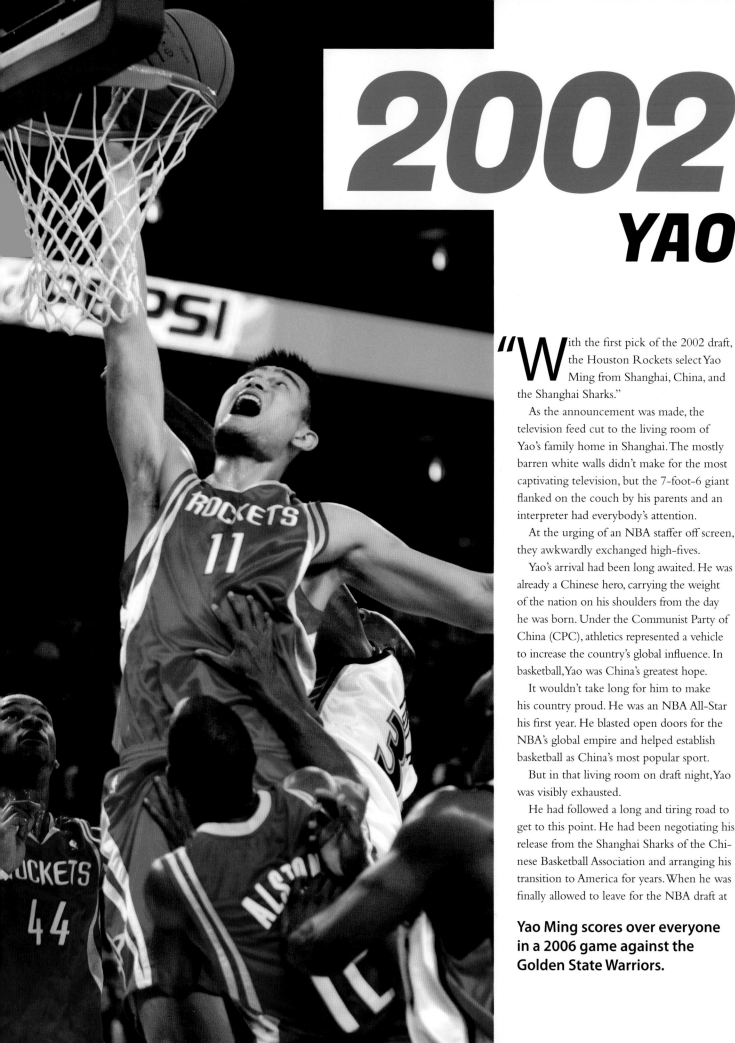

2002
YAO

"With the first pick of the 2002 draft, the Houston Rockets select Yao Ming from Shanghai, China, and the Shanghai Sharks."

As the announcement was made, the television feed cut to the living room of Yao's family home in Shanghai. The mostly barren white walls didn't make for the most captivating television, but the 7-foot-6 giant flanked on the couch by his parents and an interpreter had everybody's attention.

At the urging of an NBA staffer off screen, they awkwardly exchanged high-fives.

Yao's arrival had been long awaited. He was already a Chinese hero, carrying the weight of the nation on his shoulders from the day he was born. Under the Communist Party of China (CPC), athletics represented a vehicle to increase the country's global influence. In basketball, Yao was China's greatest hope.

It wouldn't take long for him to make his country proud. He was an NBA All-Star his first year. He blasted open doors for the NBA's global empire and helped establish basketball as China's most popular sport.

But in that living room on draft night, Yao was visibly exhausted.

He had followed a long and tiring road to get to this point. He had been negotiating his release from the Shanghai Sharks of the Chinese Basketball Association and arranging his transition to America for years. When he was finally allowed to leave for the NBA draft at

Yao Ming scores over everyone in a 2006 game against the Golden State Warriors.

the age of 21, reports surfaced that the Chinese government planned to take half of his earnings. "I've already had many frustrations," Yao reportedly told local newspapers in April, "a few more won't break me."

Even just hours before the draft, Yao's mother, Fang Fendi, threatened that her son would quit the game altogether if they weren't given a fair release.

His mother had always played a pivotal role in his development. Standing 6-foot-2, Fang had played professional basketball in China, as well as for the national team. Yao's father, Yao Zhiyuan, was a 6-foot-10 center from Shanghai.

The local basketball club played matchmaker, and their relationship had been encouraged by the CPC. When Chairman Mao Zedong rose to power in the middle of the 20th century, he urged athletic citizens to breed a pool of genetically gifted future stars for his future sports empire.

When they married in 1979, a year before their son's birth, Yao's parents were China's tallest couple.

Yao was born weighing 11 pounds and stood 23 inches — double the nation's average. Upon his birth, word spread to the Shanghai Sports Commission, and the shot clock on Yao's future in basketball began to tick.

"We had been looking forward to the arrival of Yao Ming for three generations," said a local youth coach and former teammate of Yao's father.

By the age of eight, Yao was as tall as the average Chinese man. Before his 10th birthday, he was selected to attend a junior "sports school" in Shanghai, where he would live and train basketball. The sport felt like a job, and the monotony of the routine — the same drills day in and day out — had swatted away any joy Yao might have had toward the sport. He would come home dejected, wanting to never pick up a ball again.

It was around this time that the Harlem Globetrotters passed through Shanghai on a tour of Asia. On a Sunday afternoon, Fang bought tickets for her and her son. It was a life-changing experience for Yao. The Globies appeared to be having a laugh riot playing the game, and he was particularly drawn to their showmanship. Basketball could be fun.

With a renewed appreciation for the game, Yao continued to sprout — in both size and skill. At 13 he was 6-foot-7 and playing for the Shanghai Sharks junior squad, and he made the senior team in his teens.

In 1996 Yao (by then a 16-year-old standing 7-foot-2) was spotted by Nike reps as they visited Shanghai, seeking to make inroads into a lucrative Chinese market. The Chinese government allowed Yao to take part in a Nike basketball camp in Paris in '97 and a U.S. tour in '98, where he would meet Michael Jordan — he was so nervous that he failed a basic shooting drill in front of the icon. It was a rare gesture by an authoritarian regime, but the CPC saw an opportunity for their biggest sports commodity to work on his game and spread the strength of China.

By 2002 a 21-year-old Yao (standing 7-foot-5) had become an unstoppable force. He carried the Chinese National Team to a gold medal at the 2001 Asian basketball championship. He also dominated the Chinese Basketball Association, averaging 39 points and 20 rebounds per game while leading the Sharks to a championship. It was time to take over the world.

When the Houston Rockets selected Yao first overall, there were plenty of skeptics. To some, Yao was merely a sideshow whose on-court success had come against inferior competition in China. The NBA would eat him alive.

Due to obligations with the Chinese National Team, he missed training camp and the preseason during his rookie year. An estimated Chinese audience of 300 million tuned in for his NBA debut. Yao went scoreless in just 11 minutes of action.

The NBA had first made contact with Chinese officials in 1989, when David Stern met with officials from CCTV, the state-run television network, to persuade them to broadcast NBA games. Within five years the NBA Finals were regularly aired across China. But the league had never witnessed viewership numbers like it had for Yao's rookie season.

As he got more comfortable in the NBA, Yao's skill became obvious. He paired his remarkable height and tree-trunk legs with a deft shooting touch, remarkable footwork

and passing instincts, and an ability to finish with either hand.

Unlike past giants in the NBA, such as 7-foot-7 Gheorghe Muresan or Manute Bol, Yao had been playing the game as far back as he could remember. And it was beginning to show. In December of his rookie year, he averaged 17 points, 10 rebounds and nearly 3 blocks per game.

Even in a league of giants, Yao stood out like a 7-foot-6 guy in Shanghai. As his star began to rise in the NBA, there were some cringe-worthy moments, like the fortune-cookie giveaway night in Miami when Yao's Rockets faced the Heat.

And just before their first matchup, video surfaced of an interview in which Shaquille O'Neal appeared to mock Yao while speaking in gibberish that loosely mimicked Chinese. The league did little to intervene.

Shaq apologized, sort of. It was a bad joke that didn't land, he said. Yao gracefully diffused the situation. "I believe Shaquille O'Neal was joking with what he said," he told reporters, "but I think a lot of Asian people don't understand this kind of joke."

The initial meeting of the two giants came on January 17, 2003, when the Los Angeles Lakers visited the Rockets. It was appointment television. Shaq, the only NBAer who weighed more than Yao, was the exact type of player the Chinese rookie was said to be unable to handle. In Yao's defense, nobody, save for Hakeem

MOST POINTS BY AN INTERNATIONAL PLAYER

1.	Dirk Nowitzki	31,560
2.	Hakeem Olajuwon	26,946
3.	Pau Gasol	20,894
4.	Tony Parker	19,473
5.	Steve Nash	17,387

Yao Ming and Shaquille O'Neal battle for a rebound during the 2004 playoffs.

Olajuwon, could slow Shaq down.

On the first possession of the game, Shaq posted Yao up and called for the ball. He didn't want to simply overpower Yao. That would be too easy. Instead, he tried a crossover dribble and rose to the hoop for a layup. Yao blocked it. It looked effortless. The crowd lost it.

On the next play Yao posted up Shaq below the basket and spun for a smooth hook shot. *Swish*. It was Shaq's turn again, and the three-time Finals MVP bodied Yao below the rim for his patented drop step. Yao blocked it again. The Rockets rookie raced up the court and his teammates found him for another basket. Yao 2, Shaq 0.

A few plays later Yao backed O'Neal down and turned for a fadeaway jumper that effortlessly fell through the net. Now O'Neal was furious. He backed Yao down and used his brute force to dunk on him. For the third time in a row, Yao blocked Shaq. The Rockets went on to win by 4 points.

Back home in China, there were celebrations at viewing parties across the nation. NBA games were drawing 10 million viewers on average, and Yao was a marketing angel for the league, starring in countless commercials, both at home and abroad.

The performance against Shaq and the Lakers opened eyes, and Yao was voted into the starting lineup of the All-Star Game. As

he got more comfortable in his new surroundings — and in his ability to hold his own against NBA talent — Yao's personality began to show. He was funny, self-deprecating and sharp.

In 2004 Tracy McGrady, the league's leading scorer, was traded to Houston. The Rockets won 51 games and, with the help of his fans in China, Yao was named an All-Star starter for the third year in a row, earning a record 2,558,278 votes.

McGrady and Yao had the makings of an elite duo, but following his third season Yao began to suffer foot injuries that would derail his career. Until then, he had been a model of good health, missing just two games out of

Yao poses in for a team photo in front of a portrait of Mao Zedong in 2004.

246. But there is a long history of foot problems in the NBA — as the careers of Bill Walton, Greg Oden and Kevin Durant illustrate. Even Jordan broke his foot his sophomore year.

Yao wasn't immune to the curse.

The foot problems persisted. He was forced to sit out the entire 2009–10 season. He returned the following year, but after just five games he was sidelined again. He never appeared on an NBA court again.

Yao retired after just eight seasons of action — an All-Star every year and five-time All-NBA honoree. For the first time in his life, basketball took a back seat. Yao never dreamed of being in the NBA. As a kid, he wanted to be an architect, or a politician. He continued to be a global ambassador for the game, but now had time to explore other interests. He dove into charity work and became an active spokesperson promoting wildlife preservation.

In 2017, the same year the Rockets retired his No. 11 jersey, Yao was appointed chair of the government-backed national basketball program. The Chinese Basketball Association grew and became a popular destination for aging NBA stars like Stephon Marbury, Steve Francis and Kenyon Martin.

Today the NBA is the most popular league in the country. The growth of basketball in China was unprecedented and remains Yao's lasting legacy.

Despite a relatively brief career, Yao was inducted into the basketball Hall of Fame in 2016 in a class alongside O'Neal. He was introduced by Bill Russell, Bill Walton and Dikembe Mutombo.

During his speech, Yao thanked his mother first, as well as teammates and coaches from throughout his basketball life.

"The game has inspired billions of people around the world," he said in closing. "As one of them, I will do my part to continue to grow the great game of basketball."

BIG IN CHINA

Thanks to Yao, basketball exploded in popularity in his homeland. In 2004 the NBA became the first North American sports league to play exhibition games in China. In 2008 the league founded NBA China, which has since been valued at over $4 billion. In 2015 the league agreed to their largest international partnership, a $500 million deal with Tencent, a Chinese tech company. During the 2017 Finals, the NBA logged 2.9 billion video views in China via Weibo, a social media app, and in July 2019, the NBA extended their partnership with Tencent for another five years for $1.5 billion.

2004
MALICE AT THE PALACE

November 14, 2004. Ron Artest's Indiana Pacers jersey is torn and soaked with beer as he's escorted off the court at Detroit's Palace of Auburn Hills. The neckline hangs below his chest. There's a crazed look across his face.

Moments earlier, with 45 seconds left in the game, a brouhaha had broken out between the Pacers and Pistons. Amidst the melee, a blue cup sailed from the stands and landed on Artest. He charged into the crowd, looking for the culprit, laying out a fan — the wrong one — with a blow to the face. It started the biggest and ugliest brawl in the history of North American pro sports.

Artest's teammates, led by newcomer Stephen Jackson, followed him into the stands. The players exchanged punches with fans, many of whom had rushed the court as unprecedented chaos unfolded.

Later, in the visiting locker room, Artest turned to Jackson and said, "Jack, you think we're going to be in trouble?"

Fighting had been part of the NBA since its earliest years, when players threw punches and cheap shots almost as often as jump shots; in the 40s and 50s there would be boxes in each locker room to house false teeth. But the NBA hadn't seen anything like this.

It all started with an elbow during the

Ron Artest returns to the court after climbing into the stands.

2004 playoffs. With a deep roster starring big man Jermaine O'Neal and a 38-year-old Reggie Miller, the Pacers had finished with a league-best 61 wins and were favorites to return to the Finals for the second time in three seasons. The Detroit Pistons had other plans. On the brink of eliminating their division rivals in the Eastern Conference finals, the notoriously rough Artest laid out Pistons star Rip Hamilton with a blow to the face (with no regard for the protective mask Hamilton wore as a result of a broken nose).

It was a cheap shot, and certainly not out of character for Artest. Born and raised in the Queensbridge housing development in New York City, by the time he landed on the Pacers at the age of 22 he had already developed a reputation as one of the NBA's best defenders and a certified hothead. By 2004 he already had eight suspensions to his name through six seasons. (He raised that number to 14 by the end of his 15-year career.)

Artest was also arguably Indiana's most important player, a two-way All-Star who helped set the tone for one of the league's contenders.

On paper, the 2004–05 Pacers were even better than the season before. Although Miller would start the season sidelined with a broken hand, the team had picked up Jackson in the off-season, adding a dynamic third scorer behind O'Neal and Artest.

The November 14, 2004, rematch between the Pistons and Pacers had been circled on the calendar and was broadcast to a national audience on ESPN. This was the Pacers' chance to send a message to the Pistons and the rest of the league: we won't be stopped.

Indiana was in control throughout the game, easing their way toward a blowout. Despite being up 15 points near the close of the fourth quarter, Pacers coach Rick Carlisle kept his starters on the floor, eager to deliver the message by running up the score. That's when things turned ugly.

With 1:11 remaining in the game, Pistons center Ben Wallace delivered a hard foul that sent Artest tumbling into the stanchion — clear retaliation from the season prior. On the next trip down the floor, Artest responded, pushing Detroit's big man from behind. Wallace turned to see who shoved him, saw Artest and rammed his arms into Artest's neck. You could practically hear the ringside bell sound.

Wallace continued after Artest, who retreated toward the sidelines. While players from both sides continued to jostle in front of him, Artest lay down on the scorer's table that doubled as a pseudo-dividing wall between players and fans. It was an attempt to show his maturity, that he wasn't going to get involved in the fight and would wait until the situation calmed. It would be a long wait.

As he lay there, the blue cup flew down onto him, hitting him in the face and spilling its contents onto him. He followed his first impulse and took off into the stands.

Before anybody could react, Artest was 10 rows up, making a beeline for the innocent fan he thought had thrown the beer. He shoved him to the ground as Pistons fans began to swarm Artest. John Green, the man who actually threw the cup, grabbed Artest from behind, punching him in the back of the head as more beer was tossed onto the raging Pacers star. Jackson, eager to defend his teammate, was hot on Artest's heels and threw a wild, swinging punch at another fan.

More Pacers and Pistons players and coaches filled the stands, looking less to calm things down than to get the players the hell out of Dodge — the fans outnumbered the players, 10 to 2, and many fueled by alcohol had grown brave enough to try to duel with basketball players twice their size.

Teammates helped steer Artest back to the court, where he was challenged by two fans, one of whom was decked by O'Neal. With what seemed like a bona fide riot breaking out, the Pacers were fighting as if their lives were on the line. They were slowly escorted off the court, pummeled by flying bottles and liquids as they made their way through the tunnel toward the locker rooms.

In the aftermath of the brawl, the NBA handed out some of its strongest punishments to date. Jackson was suspended 30 games for his role. "I don't regret defending my teammates," he said years later. "I regret going into the stands and punching fans."

O'Neal would get a 25-game sentence, reduced to 15 games upon appeal, while Wallace was suspended for 6 games for his part in initially escalating the situation.

Meanwhile, several charges were laid. Green, the fan who threw the cup at Artest, was already on probation stemming from his third drunk-driving conviction and was banned for life from all Pistons games, his season tickets revoked. He would eventually serve 30 days in jail. In total, five players and five fans were charged with assault. The players pleaded no contest. Artest, Jackson and O'Neal were sentenced to a year's probation and ordered to attend anger management counseling.

The hammer fell on Artest the hardest of all. He was suspended for the remainder of the season and the playoffs, missing an unprecedented 86 games in all. It remains the longest suspension resulting from an on-court incident in NBA history.

"It took me a while [to recover]," he said years later. "When I had the brawl, I went into a real depression. I had been in really good shape. I was an All-Star the year prior, and I probably had more All-Star years ahead of me in the East. I was 245–250 pounds and feeling good. After the brawl I got up to 275 pounds — quickly. I was ready to retire."

In search of a fresh start, Artest requested a trade midway through the following season, landing with the Sacramento Kings, whom he helped to make the playoffs. Eventually he wound up in Los Angeles, where he was a key member of the 2010 champion Lakers. In the deciding Game 7 versus the Boston Celtics, Artest scored 20 points, nabbed 5 steals and played a game-high 46 minutes. As the confetti rained down on the court during a postgame interview, the first person Artest thanked was his psychiatrist.

In April 2011 he won the NBA's J. Walter Kennedy Citizenship Award. That summer, he legally changed his name from Ron Artest to Metta World Peace.

Rasheed Wallace blocks a Ron Artest shot in Game 3 of the 2004 Eastern Conference finals.

NBA FIGHT NIGHT

The NBA has been marred by infamous incidents between players:

Kermit Washington's running punch broke Rudy Tomjanavich's face in 1977 and effectively ended both careers; superstars Larry Bird and Julius Erving famously traded blows during a heated game in '84. On more rare occasions, non-players have been involved. Vernon "Mad Max" Maxwell punched a heckler in 1995, earning a 10-game suspension; Dennis Rodman kicked a courtside photographer in the groin in 1997 for the crime of occupying the same spot on the floor where Rodman fell; Latrell Sprewell choked his coach later that same year.

2005
THE SPURS WAY

In the summer of 1999 thousands of fans lined San Antonio's River Walk to watch the floating barges, draped in silver and black, slowly make their way down the river.

San Antonio Spurs head coach and GM Gregg Popovich, a normally reserved air force vet, whooped and hollered to the crowd. The year before, he had drafted Tim Duncan first overall — the easiest decision he made in his career. As the crowd cheered them on, 34-year-old center David Robinson, the team's anchor and a former league MVP, smiled and waved like a politician on the campaign trail.

The Spurs were celebrating the franchise's first title since the ABA–NBA merger. Behind Duncan and Robinson, the team went 15-2 in the '99 playoffs. Duncan, at just 23 years old, was named Finals MVP — the youngest since Magic Johnson — after averaging 27 points, 14 rebounds and 2 blocks against the hapless New York Knicks.

The Spurs rose up during the lockout-shortened 1998–99 season and surprised many en route to the title. Few would have guessed that these championship celebrations would become a tradition in southeast Texas. With five championships in 15 years, the Spurs set a standard of excellence — and longevity — in the NBA that few teams have ever matched.

The Spurs win. They won in the ABA behind the scoring brilliance of George Gervin. When the team drafted Robinson,

nicknamed the Admiral for his service in the navy before joining the NBA, the winning ways continued.

After the 1976 merger, San Antonio had just five losing seasons over the next 20 years — but none worse than '96–97. With Robinson sidelined for all but six games by injury, the Spurs went 20-62, the second-worst record in the West. As their reward, they won the draft lottery, and the right to draft Duncan, the NCAA Player of the Year.

Duncan was born and raised on the island of St. Croix in the U.S. Virgin Islands. But he was never going to be a basketball player. Growing up, he practically lived in the water. With his broad torso and long limbs, he was a natural swimmer and on track to become an Olympian in the sport. But after he was discovered by Wake Forest head coach Dave Odom, Duncan decided to try basketball.

He was a fast learner.

Duncan was named Rookie of the Year in his first NBA season and Finals MVP in his second. He won back-to-back regular-season MVP awards in 2002 and '03, when he also earned his second Finals MVP award after leading the Spurs to a championship over the New Jersey Nets.

Duncan's game became symbolic of the Spurs Way. He quietly went about his business, supported his teammates and stepped up when it mattered most. Duncan embraced the little things that bred winning basketball

and could care less about the glitz and glamour that typically followed NBA stardom. The fact that his go-to was an unspectacular midrange bank shot says it all.

For the first eight years of his career, Duncan averaged over 22 points and 12 rebounds

a game — numbers that always went up in the playoffs. He played until the age of 40 and was so consistent that opponents began referring to him as "Groundhog Day."

They may as well have been referring to the Spurs. After that first title in '99, San Antonio won 50 games or more in each of the next *18* seasons. In six of those seasons, the Spurs topped 60 wins.

Duncan and Popovich were the Spurs' constants. They set the tone for every player that wore the silver and black.

Popovich served five years on active duty in the air force, during which he also represented his country on the court, with the U.S. Armed Forces Basketball Team. He earned a degree in Soviet studies and considered becoming a CIA agent before he

decided to give coaching a go.

After a four-year stint as an assistant with the Spurs, he returned in 1996 as the team's general manager. Eighteen games into the Spurs' abysmal '96–97 season, Popovich fired coach Bob Hill, hired himself as the replacement and never looked back.

With a steely demeanor cut with a witty, deadpan sense of humor (when he sat out Duncan during meaningless regular-season games later in his career, he listed the star forward as "DNP-Old"), Popovich's approach connected with his teams.

Pop didn't ask for the best from his players; he demanded it. No matter the size of your paycheck or the number of rings you got, everybody was held to the same standard. He made a particular point of calling out his star players in front of the team. It's the kind of act that tends to get coaches fired — it's a players' league, after all — but Popovich knew Duncan could take it. For the rest of the team it was eye-opening, and the coach knew that too.

"If your superstar can take a hit every now and then," Popovich explained, "everybody else could shut the hell up and fall in line. [Duncan] allowed me to coach."

Duncan was the centerpiece, but the Spurs

had an uncanny ability to discover talent. They filled their roster with second-round draft picks, minor-league journeymen and countless treasures from the scrap heap.

Bruce Bowen was undrafted and bounced around three teams in four years before the Spurs picked him up in 2001. He went on to make eight All-Defensive teams. Danny Green was toiling in the NBA's Developmental League before the Spurs signed him, and he became a starter. In 2013 he set a record for most 3-pointers made in a Finals. Kawhi Leonard fell to the 15th pick when San Antonio traded for him on draft night. In his third season, 2013–14, he was named Finals MVP, defending and outplaying LeBron James.

The list goes on.

"They do the due diligence to find out what kind of person you are," said Jaren Jackson, an undrafted guard who played for 12 teams in three leagues before the Spurs signed him in 1997. During their '99 title run, Jackson led the team in 3-point shooting.

"We get guys who want to do their job and go home," Popovich said. "One of the keys is to bring in guys who have gotten over themselves. They fill their role and have a pecking order."

But when the game is on the line, the

The Spurs' big 3 take the court to play the Oklahoma City Thunder in 2008.

Spurs don't care who gets the last shot. In the 2005 Finals against the Detroit Pistons, it was journeyman role player — and noted clutch shooter — Robert Horry who took the game-winning 3-pointer in overtime to seal the win. Still, there was no mistaking who the Spurs' biggest workhorse was. When they won in Game 7, Duncan took home his third Finals MVP award.

When it comes to uncovering diamonds in the rough, the Spurs' crowning achievements were Tony Parker and Manu Ginobili.

Parker, raised in France, was the 28th pick in the 2001 draft. As a 19-year-old rookie he was thrust into the role of starting point guard. He was lightning-quick, and his ability to get past the first line of defense, pull up in the paint and uncork a teardrop floater maddened opponents. Popovich saw the makings of a bona fide floor general and was especially hard on him during his early years in San Antonio. It paid off. In 2007 the Spurs swept the Cleveland Cavaliers in the Finals — their third championship in six

years — and Parker was named series MVP.

Ginobili was already an accomplished player in his native Argentina when Popovich drafted him 57th overall in 1999. He made his NBA debut in 2002 and established himself as one of the more unique players in the league. He seemed to play the game on fast-forward and owned a series of herky-jerky moves and wild, circus-like takes to the hoop.

During Ginobili's first season, Popovich repeatedly told him to slow down and temper his manic game. "This is what I do," he told Popovich, and the coach had the sense to let go of the reins. Ginobili became a critical piece of the Spurs' puzzle. He was a tenacious defender and disruptive force on the offensive end. Like Duncan, he played until he was 40 and was effective until the end.

One of the most remarkable things about Popovich's Spurs was how they were able to reinvent themselves over the years. They evolved with the game, which changed in front of their eyes. Over the course of their extended dynasty, they went from a slow, plodding, defensive juggernaut to a swift-moving offensive machine.

Perhaps the most rewarding of all was the 2014 title. The previous season had ended in a Finals loss to LeBron and the Miami Heat, a crushing defeat thanks in part to Ray Allen's Game 6 heroics. With an aging nucleus — Duncan in his 16th season, Parker in his 12th, Ginobili in his 10th, all with added miles of perennial playoff runs — the Spurs went into the series as underdogs. But thanks to a breakout performance from Kawhi Leonard and 15 points and 10 rebounds per game from Duncan, they won convincingly in five games.

Leonard was the consummate Spur. He did whatever was asked of him and worked tirelessly to improve. He emerged as Duncan's likely successor, equally quiet in his approach and just as domineering on the court. Leonard was eight years old when the Duncan-led Spurs won their first title. Fifteen years later, he helped bookend a remarkable run of winning basketball.

Five championships for Tim and Pop.

Although they never won back-to-back, by every measure, the Spurs were one of the NBA's great dynasties.

What you can't measure is the Spurs' chemistry. Aided by the continuity of their star trio and the selflessness of their leader, Duncan, the Spurs were a team in every sense.

Duncan celebrates after winning the 2014 NBA Finals.

On the road, Popovich organizes grand meals for his team, and if you look around the table you'll spot plenty of ex-Spurs among the group — retired players who happen to be in town, assistant coaches who have since switched teams, and even opponents. Once a Spur, always a Spur.

Hard work, commitment, fun, family and, above all, winning — that was the Spurs way.

ALL-TIME PLAYOFF WIN PERCENTAGE

1.	Los Angeles Lakers	.597
2.	Boston Celtics	.568
3.	Baltimore Bullets	.563
4.	Miami Heat	.554
5.	San Antonio Spurs	.551

2005
THE SSOL SUNS

It was a simple concept: a possession should be less than seven seconds.

Grab a defensive rebound, and it's off to the races. Don't waste time dribbling. Catch-and-shoot is the name of the game. Maximize possessions and play at a frenetic pace the rest of the NBA can't keep up with.

"We wanted to wear teams down," said point guard Steve Nash. "We reveled in watching our opponents just wither away at the end of games."

Heading into the 2004–05 campaign, the Phoenix Suns were in need of an identity. The team was coming off a 29-win season and willing to try anything.

Midway through the previous season, Phoenix fired its head coach and promoted assistant Mike D'Antoni in the role. A former point guard who had a cup of coffee in the freewheeling American Basketball Association and spent most of the 90s coaching in Europe, D'Antoni was given the reins of a team looking for a fresh start and that was expected to finish in the middle of the pack at best.

Free from the burden of expectations and with an offensive-minded roster, D'Antoni was encouraged to experiment. The result? The Seven Seconds or Less offense that propelled Phoenix, made a superstar out of their conductor and turned the Suns into not only the NBA's winningest team but — by far — its most exciting.

D'Antoni employed a frenzied offense while coaching in Italy, but he never thought the style could translate to the NBA. "Everyone told me, 'You'll kill your players. You'll get fired.'" If it was going to work, the Suns needed the perfect point guard to accelerate their offense to warp speed. Enter Steve Nash.

Born in South Africa and raised in Vancouver, Canada, Nash grew up playing soccer (as a baby, his first word was "goal"). A group of basketball-loving friends introduced him to the sport, and had it not been for the NBA's global spike in popularity in the late 80s, chances are he would've become a soccer pro.

"The NBA was really, really big, with Magic, Michael and Larry," he recalled. "I totally fed into the game and totally fed into the hype machine."

Nash translated the field vision he'd developed on the pitch onto the hardwood. He was a natural playmaker who saw passing lanes others couldn't and thrived on setting up his teammates.

Early in his career, he was hesitant to score and needed to be coaxed into shooting. He quickly developed into one of the league's most consistent shooters, and realized that his jumper meant defenses couldn't strictly play the pass, which opened up the court.

Canada was hardly a hotbed of NBA talent, and only one school, California's Santa Clara, offered Nash a scholarship. He defied the odds and was drafted in the first round of the 1996 draft by the Suns. After two seasons as their third-string point guard behind Jason Kidd and Kevin Johnson, Nash was traded to Dallas, where he blossomed into an All-Star playing alongside Dirk Nowitzki.

Despite never being the fastest or most athletic player, Nash's endless arsenal of creative passes seemed to defy logic. "He's driving into trees, getting trapped in midair and somehow throwing the ball through his legs to a shooter in the corner," Nowitzki said in awe of his former teammate.

With long, floppy hair he habitually tucked behind his ears and a thin, 175-pound build, Nash looked more like the bass player for an alt-rock band than an elite NBA player. But when he returned to Phoenix in the summer of 2004, signing a lucrative six-year deal, D'Antoni saw his perfect point guard.

The Suns didn't call plays — that wasted too much time. Instead, Nash was given full control to run the offense and instantly blossomed into the game's premier table setter.

"Steve was the perfect basketball player for what we were trying to do," said D'Antoni. "He took it to heights I couldn't even imagine."

With their new-look offense in place, Phoenix raced to a 31-4 record to start the '04–05 season. Nash reached double-digits in assists in 26 of those games.

But for Phoenix's offensive experiment to truly thrive, Nash needed the perfect running mates, players who could race down the court, corral a pass on the run and explode to the rim in a flash — or better yet, catch lobs and alley-oops for even greater efficiency.

Enter Amar'e Stoudemire and Shawn Marion. Marion was a great leaper and versatile defender. What he lacked in height, he made up for with fast-twitch muscles and great instincts.

Stoudemire was a physical freak seemingly born to run the pick-and-roll with Nash. Drafted out of high school in 2002, he was Nash's favorite target and one of the

Steve Nash streaks to the hoop during the 2010 playoffs.

league's most ferocious and ready dunkers. Stoudemire gave himself the nickname STAT, which stood for "Standing Tall and Talented."

"I was caught off guard by how easy the game [became]," he said once he started playing with Nash.

For the final pieces of the Suns' puzzle, Phoenix needed shooters parked behind the 3-point line, ready to let it fly at a moment's notice. Enter Joe Johnson and Quentin Richardson. As the years passed, more wing players would assume the role as the Suns became the NBA's gold standard for 3-point shooting. Instead of crashing toward the hoop on a fast break, the Suns would peel to the corners — a novel idea that has since become de rigueur across the league.

Phoenix led the league with 796 3-pointers in 2004–05 and broke its own record the following season.

With everything in place, the Suns were the closest thing to the Harlem Globetrotters in the NBA. The team finished with 62 wins, the most in the NBA. They averaged 110 points per game — 7 more than any other team — during a season in which the league average was 97.

For his part as maestro of the league's most potent offense, Nash was named NBA MVP.

He averaged 11.5 assists per game, along with 15.5 points (with a shooting percentage over 50 percent), the lowest scoring rate of any MVP since Wes Unseld in 1969. Nash registered nearly 200 more assists than any other player, and he kept up that pace throughout his Suns tenure — between 2004 and 2011, Nash registered an NBA-best 5,933 assists, which was over a thousand more than second-place Jason Kidd.

"[Nash] showed what can happen when a great point guard has an open court and the freedom to make choices," D'Antoni said. "The game explodes."

With the Seven Seconds or Less offense in full bloom, Phoenix repeated as Pacific Division champions in 2005–06. And again Nash was awarded the MVP trophy. He joined Wilt Chamberlain, Kareem Abdul-Jabbar, Moses Malone, Larry Bird, Magic Johnson, Michael Jordan and Tim Duncan on the exclusive list of back-to-back MVPs.

Nash's Suns teams were all or nothing. All offense, no defense. They outscored opponents but also gave up more points than any other team. The style didn't translate to the playoffs — the adage that defense wins championships was proving true.

The Suns were bounced from the Western Conference finals in 2005 and '06. But in 2006–07 a balanced and potent Phoenix club seemed poised to reach the Finals for the first time in 14 years.

But a controversial ruling during Game 4 of their second-round series against the San Antonio Spurs proved too much to overcome. The Suns entered the game trailing the Spurs, 2-1, but thanks to 15 assists from Nash and 29 points from Stoudemire they won the game and tied the series.

However, during the final minute, a hockey-inspired hip check from the Spurs' Robert Horry sent Nash flying into the scorer's table. Stoudemire and fellow Suns starter Boris Diaw leapt off the bench to come to his defense. Although no real brawl or skirmish ensued, the two had violated league rules by leaving the bench and walking onto the court. Each was suspended for the next game — an 88–85 Spurs win.

In 2008 the Suns fell to the Spurs in the playoffs for the fourth time in six years, this time a swift 4-1 first-round exit. That summer, D'Antoni left the team to coach the New York Knicks. With veterans Grant Hill and Shaquille O'Neal joining Nash in the upcoming season, the days of the run-and-gun Suns were all but over.

Nash remained an elite playmaker. In 2010–11, at the age of 36, Nash became the oldest player to lead the NBA in assists in a

Nash bleeds during the 2010 Western Conference final against the Lakers.

single season. But Phoenix failed to make the playoffs and Nash moved on to a new challenge shortly thereafter. In the summer of 2012, he signed a deal with the Los Angeles Lakers. After just one game, he broke his left leg. It was the beginning of the end.

In their day, Nash's Suns were outliers. But within a decade, their run-and-gun style proved to be the template for modern basketball. Push the pace, maximize possessions, shoot early and often, and launch 3-pointers like layups. The Suns played small ball, moving Marion to power forward and Stoudemire to center — experimental at the time, but basic common sense in today's NBA.

RUN TMC

Before the SSOL Suns redefined what it meant to run a high-octane offense in the NBA, the Golden State Warriors created a blueprint for "run-and-gun" basketball under head coach Don Nelson. Between '89 and '95 Golden State led the league in scoring multiple times during Nelson's first of two stints with the club. He played small lineups starring Tim Hardaway, Mitch Ritchmond and Chris Mullin with three guards and two forwards, pushed the pace and reached the playoffs four times in that span, proving that you can win while prioritizing scoring over defense. He retired from coaching in 2010 as the NBA's all-time wins leader.

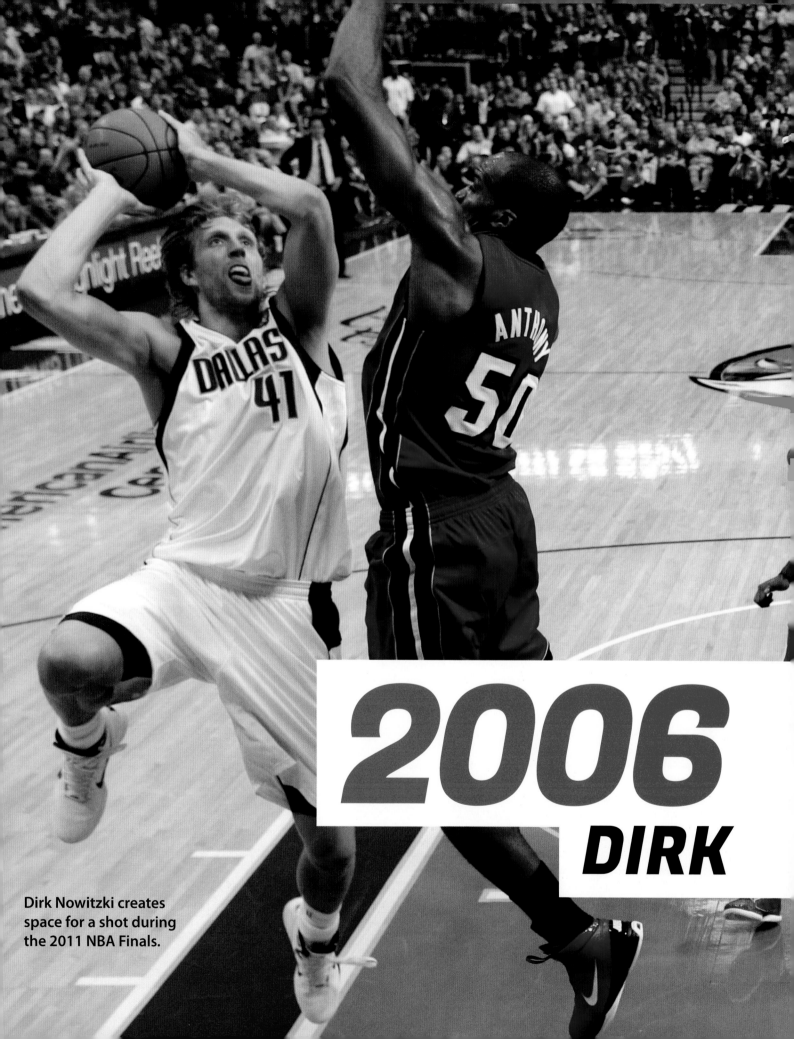

2006
DIRK

Dirk Nowitzki creates space for a shot during the 2011 NBA Finals.

It's Game 7 of the second round of the 2006 playoffs. The Dallas Mavericks are down three points against the defending champion San Antonio Spurs. Dirk Nowitzki and Tim Duncan, the NBA's premier power forwards, have been dueling since the opening tip.

With just 26 seconds left on the clock and the Mavericks' season on the line, Nowitzki knows the ball is coming to him.

From a tiny gym in a suburb in Germany to the NBA's greatest stage, it has taken decades and untold thousands of hours of shooting drills to get to this moment. Nowitzki is ready.

He posts up Bruce Bowen just inside the 3-point line. Bowen, an eight-time All-Defensive Team member, holds his own, but can't contain the 7-footer leaning all of his weight against him. Nowitzki backs Bowen down, spins right and barrels toward the hoop. He lifts off the ground, barely — gravity has always been an obstacle — and lays the ball in the hoop while getting fouled. He sinks the basket and heads to the free-throw line for a chance to tie the game.

To help calm himself down, Nowitzki, a 90 percent free-throw shooter this season, has been in the habit of humming tunes to himself while at the line. Lately, he's been singing David Hasselhoff's, "Looking for Freedom," a chart-topping hit from his childhood. Nowitzki swishes the free throw. At the other end of the floor, he blocks a Duncan layup and helps lead Dallas to an overtime — and series — win.

As far as basketball hotbeds go, Wuerzburg, Germany, is pretty far down the list. But it produced the NBA's sixth all-time leading scorer, a champion and league MVP.

"He made everybody change," Spurs coach Gregg Popovich said later, "and the league had to respond because guarding him was different than guarding anybody else his size."

Dirk Nowitzki was one of a kind from the beginning. He came from an athletic background — his mother was a pro basketball player and his father was a member of Germany's national handball team — with a sprouting frame that would eventually reach 7 feet.

Holger Geschwindner saw nothing but potential.

Geschwindner, who played for West Germany's Olympic Team in 1972, was playing in a senior's league outside Wuerzburg and was waiting for a local youth game to wrap up. When the game went into overtime, he went to the court to watch the action. His eyes fixated on a tall, skinny kid with an impressive feel for the sport.

After the game, the kid ran toward the locker room and Holger stopped him. "Who is teaching you the basics, the tools?" he asked the 15 year-old.

"Nobody," Dirk answered.

With the support of Nowitzki's parents, the two began to train at a local gymnasium.

Holger's methods were unorthodox, to say the least. He brought in a saxophonist to play jazz while his students practiced, urging them to dribble and pass the ball to the rhythms of the music. He didn't believe in weight lifting for young athletes; he used rowing to gain upper-body strength and fingertip push-ups to improve shooting. He didn't measure the court in feet, but in steps, and used geometry to inform many of his on-court principles. Today he calls his basketball clinic the Institute of Applied Nonsense.

While working with Dirk, Holger discovered that the perfect shot is released at a 60-degree angle. He then used precise measurements to determine the optimal shooting arc and release point for Nowitzki's frame.

After years of experimenting, they landed one of the most memorable jump shots the NBA will ever see: Dirk would plant his feet, rise up, fade back, kick out his right leg for balance and release the ball high into the air. Like Kareem's skyhook and Gervin's finger roll, the fadeaway jumper became Dirk's signature move — equal parts deadly weapon and iconic visual.

In that tiny barn in Wuerzburg, Holger and Nowitzki were producing a masterpiece for the entire world to see.

The 1998 Nike Hoop Summit in San Antonio — a predraft showcase event that pitted the world's best against a team of American star prospects — was Nowitzki's coming out party. He scored 33 points and grabbed 14 rebounds as Team World stunned the USA with a win. Nowitzki was the best player on the floor, and the notion of a 7-footer with an unstoppable jumper and

high basketball IQ placed him firmly in the crosshairs of NBA scouts.

Dallas Mavericks GM Donnie Nelson was in attendance that night and traded up to select the 20-year-old German ninth overall in the 1998 draft.

When Nowitzki and 24-year-old point guard Steve Nash, whom the Mavs acquired via trade that summer, were introduced at a press conference, both sporting long blond locks and matching awkward smiles, it didn't exactly inspire confidence in Dallas's new foundation.

"I thought a couple members of the Beach Boys got lost," Nelson said.

Nowitzki's arrival in the NBA was quite possibly unlike that of any player the league had seen before — there had been 7-footers who could shoot, though none who counted it as their greatest attribute — but it would take a long time before anybody mistook him for an NBA star.

He struggled during his rookie season. Unsure how to utilize Nowitzki, the Mavs played him at multiple positions — or, if he was struggling, not at all. He averaged eight points per game his first season, and he was losing confidence by the day.

Before the off-season, Geschwindner met with head coach Don Nelson. Then he and Dirk went back into the lab in Wuerzburg. A strong summer league showing gave Dirk a boost, and he formed a potent combo with Nash that helped unlock his game.

By his third season, Nowitzki's scoring average had shot to over 20 points per game, putting him eighth in the league — he would remain in the top 10 in scoring the rest of the decade.

Built around the trio of Nash, Dirk and Michael Finley, the Mavericks qualified for the playoffs in 2001, the first time in 11 years, and Nowitzki made his first of 14 All-Star teams.

When Nash left for the Phoenix Suns in 2004, it forced Nowitzki into an even bigger role. No longer was he the nervous, uncertain teen; now he was Dirk, the confident scorer who wanted the ball with the game on the line.

When Nowitzki hit that clutch driving layup against the Spurs in the 2006 playoffs, it was only the beginning. In the next round,

against Nash and the Suns, he scored 50 points in a Game 5 blowout and carried the Mavs all the way to the Finals against the Miami Heat.

The NBA had seen plenty of European talents over the years. Toni Kukoc. Vlade Divac. Drazen Petrovic. Detlef Schrempf. Stars in their homeland, the best reached their NBA apex as valuable role players. But Nowitzki was redefining what European players were capable of, setting an example for the likes of Kristaps Porzingis and Luka Doncic — whose rookie season in Dallas was Nowitzki's last.

In the 2006 Finals, the Mavs got out to a 2-0 lead, though Nowitzki struggled. By the time he got back on track, it was too late. Miami's Dwyane Wade, a 26-year-old tour de force, put on one of the greatest Finals performances of all time. Wade averaged 39.3 points and a whopping (or, if you're a Mavs fan, suspicious) 18 free-throw attempts per game in the series.

In 2007 Nowitzki was named the NBA's MVP. The Mavericks finished a league-best 67-15, making them favorites and the No. 1 seed heading into the playoffs. In the first round they were stunned 4-2 by the Golden State Warriors, the biggest postseason upset the NBA has ever seen.

Exhausted and dejected, Nowitzki

retreated to Australia, where he spent the summer. He didn't touch a basketball for two months, the longest stretch of his adult life.

"When I look back on the season, I don't think about the MVP," Nowitzki said that summer. "I think I take losses harder probably than anyone else in this league."

As the years passed, he and Holger went back to the lab in Wuerzburg each summer, refining and improving Nowitzki's ever-advancing game. In Dallas they would practice shooting drills all through the night. Occasionally, teammates would join in before tapping out.

No matter the effort, his reputation remained as of one of the best players to never win a title. But in 2011 Nowitzki got another chance at a championship — a rematch with Wade and the Heat.

This time Miami looked different. A lot different. Wade was now flanked by All-Stars LeBron James and Chris Bosh in the first year of their newly formed superteam.

Just before Game 4, with his team trailing 2-1 in the series, Nowitzki came down with a 102-degree fever, but played that night. During time-outs he sank into his seat on the bench, draped a towel over his head

Nowitzki celebrates during the 2011 Western Conference finals against the Thunder.

and chugged Gatorade. His own version of Michael Jordan's "flu game," Nowitzki finished with 21 points, including the game-sealing layup to even the series. Two games later, the Mavs were crowned champions.

As his team celebrated on the court in Miami, Nowitzki went back to the locker room and cried. Back out in the arena, sitting in the stands, was Holger Geschwindner, wiping away tears of his own.

For 20 years they had done the same drills, the same workouts. "Tomorrow," Geschwindner said through his smile, "he gets a day off."

Nowitzki played until the age of 40. Although he wasn't the same volume scorer in his final years, when he hoisted up into the air and kicked that leg out for his trademark shot, it seemed certain it would fall.

At his retirement ceremony, some of the greats of the game were on hand to pay the respects: Larry Bird, Charles Barkley, Scottie Pippen, Shawn Kemp and Detlef Schrempf. Everyone was in agreement: There'll never be another Dirk.

2006
KOBE'S 81

In the summer of 2004, following a shocking Finals loss to the Detroit Pistons, Kobe Bryant got his wish when the Los Angeles Lakers traded away Shaquille O'Neal.

Freed from the oversized shadow of his now-former costar, Kobe could claim, for the first time since he entered the NBA in 1996, that the Lakers were his team.

And they stank.

Gone were Bryant's three Hall of Fame–bound teammates — Shaq, Karl Malone and Gary Payton. Gone was Phil Jackson, the mastermind head coach who manipulated the egos of Shaq and Kobe. In their place was a roster of unproven talent, and Kobe.

Life after Shaq wasn't the utopia Bryant had envisioned. Sure, there were more shots, and the daily drama had subsided (as much as it can in the soap opera that is Lakerland). But for the first time in eight years, the Lakers were losing.

In the first post-Shaq season, Bryant finished second in the league in scoring, but missed over a month with an ankle injury. He was back in the lineup by the time his team went 2-19 to close the season. For the first time since 1994, the Lakers missed the playoffs.

For a player who maniacally patterned his game after Michael Jordan — even mimicking his on-court mannerisms — it was a tough pill to swallow. Jordan never missed the postseason.

The next season called for drastic measures. By the fall of 2005 the Lakers roster had been further gutted with the departure of Caron Butler, one of the primary pieces LA had received in the O'Neal deal. Save for

Kobe, the collection of players was among the league's worst. But, looking to avoid another playoff absence, Bryant was determined to do whatever it took. So he shot. A lot.

What ensued was a scoring tear the league hadn't seen in 40 years.

In December Bryant scored a career-high 62 points in three quarters in a blowout win over the Dallas Mavericks. He dropped 50 twice in the following weeks, taking a stranglehold on the NBA's scoring race. Through nine games in January, he was averaging over 41 points, on the cusp of joining Wilt Chamberlain as the only player to sustain that level of scoring for an entire month.

But it didn't look like fun, and Bryant's reputation as an arrogant ball hog only grew in this new phase of his career. Now that the Lakers were no longer title contenders, it was less endearing than ever.

One particular target of Bryant's ire was Smush Parker, a former streetballer who made the team following a training camp tryout and was thrust into the starting lineup from day one. "He shouldn't have been in the NBA," Bryant later said, "but we were too cheap to pay for a point guard. So we let him walk on."

In his estimation, Bryant needed to dominate the ball in order to give the lowly Lakers a shot at winning each night. And he was right. That's what many forget about the night Kobe Bryant made history.

You'd be remiss if you didn't have January 22, 2006, at the Staples Centre circled on your calendar. The Toronto Raptors were in LA for the Sunday evening matchup and, at 14-27, were barely hanging on in a post–

Vince Carter world. Even Jack Nicholson decided to skip this one — a decision he'd soon regret.

The Lakers fell into an early hole as the Raptors took a comfortable lead into half-time. Bryant scored 26 through two quarters, but Toronto led 63–49. Kobe came out of the locker room looking for blood. He carved up the Raptors in every way. He twisted his body around defenders at the rim, threw down angry dunks and let it fly from deep.

In the third quarter, Bryant scored 27 points, and the Lakers took a 6-point lead, 91–85. As LA's lead ballooned in the fourth quarter, Kobe refused to take his foot off the gas. The home crowd chanted, "MVP! MVP!" as Bryant sank his final shots — a pair of free-throws — with 43.4 seconds remaining. He finished the night with 81 points. *Eighty-one.* He took 46 shots and single-handedly out-scored Toronto, 55–41, in the second half.

It was the highest-scoring game for a non-center in NBA history, and second all-time only to Wilt Chamberlain's 100-point night in 1962.

"I couldn't even dream of this as a kid," said Bryant. "No way possible." Most importantly, he said after the game, "the points I put in the basket were instrumental" to the Lakers' comeback win.

"That was something to behold," said Jackson. "It was another level." But, he added, "it's not exactly the way you want to have a team win a game."

That was a sentiment shared by players and coaches around the NBA. It was as if scoring 81 points was no big deal. "We've got a lot

Kobe Bryant saves the ball
during a 2005 game.

of guys in this league, if they took 70 shots, they'd score a lot of points," Miami Heat coach Pat Riley said the following day.

Years later, when discussing the historic game, Bryant was reminded that the Lakers' second-leading scorer that night was Smush Parker. "Now you know why I had to score 81," he said.

That season, Bryant took more shots than any player since Jordan in 1986–87. His 2,173 shot attempts that season were the seventh most of all time, and the only season among the top 35 that took place after 1990.

Bryant finished the season averaging 35 points per game and captured his first scoring title. He successfully carried the Lakers into the playoffs. The Lakers got off to a 3-1 lead against the Phoenix Suns in the first round, but lost the series in seven.

Within two seasons, support arrived in the form of All-Star big man Pau Gasol, and Kobe's legacy was bolstered with a Finals return and two more championships. His image as an all-time great — and not simply an all-time gunner — was resuscitated. But an Achilles tear in 2013 effectively ended his career.

He played two more injury-shortened seasons, his final days spent once again jacking up shots on an inferior team. In 2014, a 36-year-old Kobe was back to his old habits. In December he stormed out of a practice, yelling at Lakers GM Mitch Kupchak on his way out. "We're supposed to practice to get better, Mitch. How am I supposed to get better with these motherf★★★★★s?"

The last game of Bryant's career came on the final night of the 2015–16 regular season. In front of a Staples Center crowd, he took 50 shots, fittingly breaking Jordan's record for most field goal attempts in a single game. He wound up with 60 points, the crowd fawning over his every move as the Lakers won by 5 points — just their 17th win that season. When the final buzzer sounded, he was engulfed by his teammates.

"It was a weird year," Bryant reflected after the game. "You go from being the villain to some kind of hero, from everybody telling you to pass the ball to them telling you to shoot it."

His final NBA play: a pass.

Bryant beats the buzzer in the 2006 playoffs.

JANUARY 26, 2020

Kobe Bryant's preferred mode of transportation was helicopter. To skip the notorious L.A. traffic, he took a chopper from his home to the Lakers' practice facility or the arena throughout his career. On the morning of January 26, 2020, a 41-year old Bryant was in a private helicopter on his way to a basketball tournament with his 14-year-old daughter, Gianna, a rising star in the mold of her father. They never made it. The helicopter crashed over Callabasas, California, killing Kobe, Gianna and all nine people on board. The tragedy left the NBA world at a standstill. The Lakers and Clippers canceled a scheduled game the next day, while the Lakers held a touching memorial service for fans at Staples Center. Mourners paid tribute around the world. The Empire State Building, Los Angeles Airport, Madison Square Garden and Dubai's Burj Khalifa — the tallest tower on Earth — were all lit up in purple and gold in Kobe's honor. At the 2020 All-Star Game two weeks later, players from one team all wore Kobe's jersey number 24, while the other team wore Gianna's number 2 in memoriam.

2007
KING JAMES

May 31, 2007. Game 5 of the Eastern Conference finals in Detroit. The series was tied 2-2, and the score was tied at 107 with 11.4 seconds remaining in second overtime. LeBron James held the ball and surveyed his kingdom.

James is just five months past his 22nd birthday, but in this grueling series he looks like he's aged five years. It's a rematch of last year's second-round series between James's Cleveland Cavaliers and the veteran-laden Detroit Pistons. A series win will send Detroit to the Finals for the third time in four years. The Cavs are eyeing their first-ever Finals appearance in franchise history — a chance to fulfill James's destiny as Cleveland's savior.

At the top of the key, LeBron cradles the ball like a running back. He gives a tug on his shorts, flashes right and explodes to his left toward the basket. He weaves through the Pistons defense like an ambulance through traffic. The Pistons swarm him. LeBron has scored 23 points in a row.

LeBron had been crowned king long before he ever played an NBA game. In high school, local papers referred to the Ohio phenom as King James, and the nickname stuck.

James grew up in Akron, Ohio, an only child raised by a single mother, Gloria. Apart from two years in foster care, LeBron lived with Gloria in Akron, moving from apartment to apartment in the city's public housing units.

James's talent was clear from the beginning. He was the first sophomore to be named Ohio's Mr. Basketball. By the time James entered his junior season of high school, he was already pegged as a future NBA star.

LeBron James's pregame routine in 2008.

The media seemingly covered the high schooler more than any active player in the NBA. In 2003, when his mother took out a loan and bought him a Hummer H2 SUV for his 18th birthday, it made national news and launched investigations into boosterism. But James was above the controversy. He was NBA-bound — a lock as the first overall draft pick.

There was a rocky track record for high schoolers entering the NBA. But no high schooler who entered the draft ever compared to LeBron James.

"[Other players] can put the ball in the hoop," LeBron said as a teenager, "but I see things before they even happen."

Scouts saw LeBron as an evolution of Magic Johnson, a 6-foot-8 floor general — except he also had hops like Kobe and was a consistent winner à la Jordan.

In any era, James would be lauded as a top pick. But his ascent during the cusp of the Internet age propelled him. LeBron's high school battles were televised nationally on ESPN, and St. Vincent-St. Mary games were such a hot ticket that they were moved to the higher-capacity gym at the University of Akron. James graced magazine covers, including a February 2002 issue of *Sports Illustrated* in which the 17-year old was dubbed the Chosen One. James liked the moniker so much, he got it tattooed across his upper back.

With a Madison Avenue smile like Jordan's and otherworldly ability on the court, James was anointed a crossover star before he ever played an NBA game. Before his rookie season began, he was already earning the same endorsement dollars as Jordan received in his prime, reported to be north of $100 million.

With LeBron as the draft's top prize, for the first time the NBA turned the draft lottery into a 30-minute live television broadcast. The Denver Nuggets and Cleveland Cavaliers held equal odds at landing the top pick — a franchise-altering, league-defining occasion. The Ping-Pong balls fell Cleveland's way, setting up a scenario where the hometown kid would be coming in to save a moribund franchise.

The Cavaliers had been on the wrong end of history throughout most of their 33-year existence. They were twice bounced from the postseason thanks to Michael Jordan game

winners. Now, for once, the basketball gods had given Cleveland a break.

LeBron's NBA debut came against the Sacramento Kings on October 29, 2003. The largest audience to watch a regular-season game since Yao Ming and Shaquille O'Neal's first meeting tuned in. What they saw was a teenager taking charge. LeBron scored 25 points — by far the most by a high schooler in his debut (for comparison, Kobe Bryant and Tracy McGrady went scoreless in their first games). Within two seasons, he was an All-Star. By age 21, he was already one of the NBA's most dominant forces, averaging 31.4 points, 6.6 assists and 7 rebounds per game.

Away from basketball, his star was burning bright. Cohosting parties with Jay-Z. Appearing in countless ads on TV. Hosting *Saturday Night Live*. All the typical benchmarks of a mainstream star.

On the court, he'd established himself as an elite talent and unselfish star who made those around him better. But in the postseason, where legends are made, he had yet to make his mark. It wasn't for lack of trying.

In 2006, during his first playoff series, James scored 45 points against the Washington Wizards, but the Cavaliers were bounced in seven games in the second round by Detroit. The Pistons were a tough defensive team reminiscent of the franchise's Bad Boy era. In the deciding game, the Pistons held Cleveland to just 61 points — the lowest total in Game 7 history.

The Pistons were unexpected title contenders. In 2004 a roster of afterthoughts and basketball nomads led by Chauncey Billups and Ben Wallace shocked a star-studded Los Angeles Lakers team featuring Shaq, Kobe, Karl Malone and Gary Payton to win the title. They returned to the Finals the following year, falling to the San Antonio Spurs.

Detroit had proven a formidable foe for James and the Cavs. In Game 1 of the 2007 Eastern Conference finals, LeBron was limited to just 10 points, but he still managed 10 boards and 9 assists. That didn't matter. In the aftermath, all anybody cared about was that, with the game on the line, LeBron drove to the hoop and dished the ball to teammate Donyell Marshall to take the game-winning shot. He missed. Critics called LeBron pas-

sive. Kobe would've taken the shot, they said. Michael would've taken the shot.

"I go for the winning play," James brushed it off. "The winning play when two guys come at you and a teammate is open is to give it up. It's as simple as that."

By Game 5 the series had become a slugfest. James was carrying his team and logging a league-high 45 minutes per game. Halfway through the fourth quarter of another close game, James had 19 points. The book on James was that to beat him, you had to make him shoot. The Pistons backed off and LeBron made them pay.

He buried a 17-foot jumper. A few possessions later, he powered through the Pistons defense for a layup, and then he knocked down a 3-pointer to bring the Cavs within 1 point. He was entering the zone, that place players go where time freezes, opponents become pylons and the basket grows a foot wider. During a time-out, James told his teammates to concentrate on playing defense. He'd handle the offense.

Just as his jumper had earned Detroit's respect, James began to drive. With 30 seconds on the clock, James erupted for a ferocious baseline slam. Another monster jam at the close of the fourth quarter sent the game into overtime.

The Pistons switched every defender they had onto James, but he couldn't be stopped.

"I can honestly tell you we tried everything we had," Billups said after the game. "But with the great ones, it happens. I'd just never seen it happen like that."

In double overtime, James hit another 3-pointer to tie the game at 107. A Pistons miss put the ball in LeBron's hands with 11.4 seconds left. This time, he wasn't passing.

James tucked the ball under his arm and examined the floor like the T-1000 from the *Terminator* movies. His teammates got out of his way. With Pistons surrounding him, James lifted off the ground for a layup, brought the ball back down as he took a seat in midair and finished with a wild windmill lay-in. Final score: 109–107, Cleveland.

LeBron finished with 48 points in over 50 minutes of action. He scored the final 25 points for the Cavs, the only player on his team to make a field goal over the last 18 minutes.

James weaves between two Boston Celtics in the 2008 playoffs.

It was the signature moment the league and its fans were waiting for. No longer was LeBron the next big thing. He had ascended to the throne.

The Cavaliers blew Detroit off the court in Game 6 and made their first Finals appearance. There, they fell back to Earth with a 4-0 sweep at the hands of the San Antonio Spurs.

For James, it seemed like the first of many trips to the championship stage. And it was — in the coming years, he would appear in eight straight Finals. But few could have predicted that another three seasons would pass before LeBron made his Finals return. Or that it would be with another team altogether.

2007
THE REF GONE ROGUE

It was subtle. A non-call on a travel here, a quick whistle there, sending one team to the line and putting the other in foul trouble. It wasn't obvious at first, but the truth was clear: there was corruption in the ranks of the NBA's referees.

"NBA In a 'Fix'," read the headline in the *New York Post* on the morning of July 20, 2007. The story reported that a current NBA referee was under investigation by the FBI for betting on games. The investigation was part of a larger probe aimed at a mob-operated gambling ring in New York City. By the end of the day, it was revealed that the referee in question was Tim Donaghy.

In light of the report, Commissioner David Stern sent out a press release condemning Donaghy. "We would like to assure our fans that no amount of effort, time or personnel is being spared . . . to bring to justice an individual who has betrayed the most sacred trust in professional sports," he wrote.

Donaghy was the son of a referee. Born in a Philadelphia suburb, he attended the same Springfield, Pennsylvania, high school as three longtime NBA referees who came before him, and he quickly worked *his* way up the ranks. In 1994 he officiated his first game. By the close of the 2006–07 season, he had 772 NBA games under his belt.

While Donaghy climbed the ladder, so did a high school acquaintance named James Battista. Granted, Battista worked his way up in the world of gambling and organized crime. Looking for betting intel, Battista reached out to Donaghy, who began to relay information. Donaghy liked to gamble, and it wasn't long before he was betting on his own games.

In December 2016 they reached an arrangement whereby Donaghy would phone Battista or one of his associates. Speaking in code, he'd relay information on player injuries and other tips. Then he'd make his pick for the game he was refereeing that night. If his chosen team covered the spread, Donaghy got paid. It was a win-win. And he won a lot, hitting 88 percent of his picks. A court document later revealed that Donaghy had been placing bets as early as March 2003.

Unfortunately, basketball has a rich history of match-fixing. It was a recurring problem that had mostly played out at the collegiate level, where some of the game's biggest stars were implicated. There were two cases in NBA history — one involving a player named Jack Molinas, who was suspended, and the other a referee, Sol Levy, who was suspended and dropped by the league during the '53 season. Betting scandals peaked in the 50s and were few and far between in later years. One of the more recent events was a Boston College point-shaving scam in 1979 organized by Henry Hill, later the focus of the film *Goodfellas*.

The Donaghy case was the biggest scandal in years and painted the league in a harsh light. "How many games did he throw that I played in?" Shaquille O'Neal wondered, as the rest of the league likely did.

In August 2007 Donaghy turned himself in. He admitted to betting on his own games — two during the course of the 2006–07 season — and said he received $30,000 from bookies in exchange for information. But he denied that he conspired to intentionally fix matches. FBI and NBA investigations concluded the same. "Can't find it," Stern said of the evidence that Donaghy played a hand in altering the outcome of games.

There were suspicious games on Donaghy's record. A December 2006 matchup between the Detroit Pistons and New Jersey Nets raised eyebrows. Based on Donaghy's dealings with the bookies, the Pistons were to cover the spread, and they did.

In January 2003, on his way out of the arena following a game in Portland, Donaghy was reportedly threatened by Trail Blazers forward Rasheed Wallace, who was upset over a debatable technical foul call in the Blazers' game against Memphis earlier that night. Wallace was suspended seven games for his role in the encounter.

And then there was a Heat–Knicks game in which New York shot 31 more free throws than Miami. Both Heat coach Pat Riley and his assistant received technical fouls during

Referees Tim Donaghy (55) and Mike Callahan (24) hear it from Dennis Rodman during a game in 1996.

the game. The Knicks, favored by 4½ points. They won by 6.

"If this is widespread," said Bob Cousy, "it could do irreparable harm." It already had, bringing fans to question the authenticity of the game.

In June 2008 a statement delivered by Donaghy's attorney alleged that there were other referees "manipulating" games in the NBA. One game under fire was played during the 2002 Western Conference finals between the Sacramento Kings and Los Angeles Lakers. In a close game, the Lakers were awarded 27 free throws in the fourth quarter, compared to just nine for the Kings. LA won the game and the series. So egregious was the officiating that noted consumer advocate Ralph Nader called for a formal inquiry afterward.

The league denied the claims, and maintained that the corrupt referee was a "rogue." The head of the NBA's referees union, Lamell McMorris, said Donaghy "is a convicted felon who has not yet been sentenced for the criminal conduct he has already admitted to. He may be willing to say anything to help his cause. . . . Frankly, we're tired of Tim Donaghy's cat and mouse games."

On July 29, 2008, Donaghy was sentenced to 15 months in prison.

Until that point, no in-game official from any of the four major North American sports had ever been indicted for match fixing.

MOST CAREER FOULS

1.	Kareem Abdul-Jabbar	4,657
2.	Karl Malone	4,578
3.	Artis Gilmore	4,529
4.	Robert Parish	4,443
5.	Caldwell Jones	4,436
6.	Charles Oakley	4,421
7.	Hakeem Olajuwon	4,383
8.	Buck Williams	4,267
9.	Elvin Hayes	4,193
10.	Clifford Robinson	4,175

2008
SAVE OUR SONICS

On June 16, 2008, a group of 3,000 SuperSonics fans held a rally on Fifth Avenue in Seattle.

Their green and yellow jerseys, representing more than four decades of Sonics ball, gleamed against the reflective glass of the federal courthouse behind them. The fans held up signs and pointed out the irony of the Starbucks storefront across the street. (Starbucks founder Howard Schultz once owned the team.) They chanted "Save our Sonics" while former All-Stars Gary Payton and Xavier McDaniel spoke to the crowd.

Fourteen floors above them, a six-day trial was underway to determine the Sonics' future in the Emerald City.

When Seattle was awarded an NBA franchise in the winter of 1966, it brought the league's membership to 12 teams. In the early days, such stars Lenny Wilkens and Spencer Haywood played for the team, but it wasn't until 1975, after Bill Russell took over as head coach, that Seattle made its first playoff appearance.

Three years later, with Wilkens as coach, the SuperSonics were crowned NBA champs. In the 90s the team rose to popularity thanks to the dazzling duo of Payton and Shawn Kemp. Sonics jerseys were de rigueur for hipsters in that decade, and the team rose to prominence in the West.

In the 1993–94 season, the Sonics had the best record in the NBA but suffered a stunning loss to the Denver Nuggets in the opening round of the playoffs — one of the biggest collapses on record. "I sat in the hot tub drinking beer till about 2 o'clock in the morning," said head coach George Karl, "and it was an afternoon game." Their last game that season was also the franchise's final game at Seattle Coliseum. Major renovations to the arena began that summer, and it reopened in October 1995 as KeyArena.

With an exciting team on the floor and a city that rushed to support its first professional sports team from the very beginning, KeyArena became one of the most electric settings in the NBA. The most raucous home crowd in the league cheered on their team as the Sonics reached the Finals in '96.

But by the close of the Payton era in the early 2000s, Seattle's barn needed fixing again. It was outdated, and its 17,000-seat capacity was the smallest in the NBA.

In January 2001 the SuperSonics, along with the WNBA's Seattle Storm, were sold for $200 million to Schultz. As his first order of business, Schultz wanted to upgrade and remodel KeyArena to increase the capacity and create luxury boxes to attract wealthy fans. But there was a catch: he wanted local taxpayers to foot the $220 million bill, and threatened to relocate the team after its arena lease expired in 2010 if the city didn't pony up and cover the costs.

In 2006, five years after he purchased the team, Schultz sold it to an Oklahoma City–based group led by Clay Bennett, who had married into one of the wealthiest families in the Midwest and was briefly a minority owner of the San Antonio Spurs in the 90s. Bennett's group purchased the team under a "good faith" agreement that he would continue the fight for an improved arena in Seattle. Like Schultz, he wanted public money to fund the project.

In the wake of Schultz's threats to move the team, Sonics fans knew an arena deal

Lenny Wilkens at the 1979 NBA championship parade.

was central to keeping their team alive. A local group called Save Our Sonics began campaigning for the city to spend public money to renovate KeyArena. But a bigger group calling itself Citizens for More Important Things opposed what it deemed wasteful spending. In the November 2006 election, voters overwhelmingly said they did not want any more taxpayer dollars spent on sports teams.

Bennett then proposed a new $530 million facility in the sleepy suburb of Renton,

Washington. The arena plan was suspect from the start — if taxpayers wouldn't shell out for Schultz's $220 million renovations, why would they rush to pay more than double that amount for a new home outside the city? Conspiracy theories abounded regarding the Bennett group's true intentions.

In August 2007 alarm bells went off when one of the members of the ownership group, Aubrey McLendon, said that there was never a true effort to get the arena deal completed. "We didn't buy the team to keep it in Seat-

tle," he told an Oklahoma City newspaper.

Two years earlier, after the city of New Orleans was decimated by Hurricane Katrina, the Hornets temporarily moved to Oklahoma City, where they played for two seasons. OKC fans packed the local arena, and the city's NBA experiment was an all-around success. Most importantly, as Bennett noticed, it was profitable.

Following McLendon's comments, Bennett admitted he planned to move the SuperSonics to Oklahoma City as soon as the KeyArena lease expired in 2010. In September of '07, he tried to get out of the lease two years early and filed legal proceedings to get it done. Three days later the City of Seattle sued Bennett and his ownership group in an attempt to hold them to their lease agreement.

In the meantime, the Sonics were preparing for the 2007–08 season. Although the team's future in Seattle was up in the air, there was plenty of reason for excitement thanks to the team's second overall draft pick, Kevin Durant. Durant became the second-youngest player (behind LeBron) to average over 20 points per game, but the off-court drama distracted from the rookie campaign.

In November Bennett announced that he was officially in talks with the NBA to seek approval for the relocation. But he only wanted the SuperSonics. The WNBA's Storm, he said, could stay (in January 2008 the Storm were sold to a group of Seattle-area women).

Bennett became a villain in Seattle, and soon the NBA and commissioner David Stern would join him. In April 2008 the league's board of governors voted 28–2 in favor of relocation.

Court proceedings began in June, and the Save Our Sonics crowd gathered outside the courthouse. The two sides reached a settlement: Bennett and the Sonics ownership group would pay the city $45 million to break the KeyArena lease. If Seattle didn't get a new franchise within five years, the Sonics owners would cough up another $30 million.

The fight was over.

In the wake of the settlement, Howard Schultz tried to get the NBA to rescind his sale of the team seven years earlier, arguing that Bennett violated their "good faith" agreement. The league sided with Bennett, and Schultz dropped the suit.

The team was re-branded the Oklahoma City Thunder in time for the start of the 2008–09 season. In their last year in Seattle, Durant's rookie campaign, the SuperSonics won just 20 games. It was their worst record in franchise history.

In the years that passed, Seattle fans

mourned the loss of their team and watched in agony as Durant crafted a Hall of Fame career. But they were able to prove that Seattle's passion for pro hoops runs as hot as any NBA city's. The Seattle Storm established themselves as one of the WNBA's most successful franchises. In 2018 the team won its

Sue Bird celebrates winning the 2010 WNBA title.

third championship, and fans packed KeyArena to set a franchise record for sellouts.

The Sonics may be gone, but basketball is alive and well in Seattle.

ROUND 3
CELTICS VS. LAKERS

Kobe Bryant reacts as time runs out in Game 7.

After the Boston Celtics and Los Angeles Lakers met in the 1987 NBA Finals — their record 10th championship battle — the league's biggest rivalry lay dormant.

In the two decades that followed, the franchises took different paths. In LA, the Shaq-Kobe-Phil Lakers kept their winning ways alive, capturing three straight titles between 2000 and 2002. The Celtics, on the other hand, had only advanced beyond the first round twice between 1993 and 2007.

But in the 2007 off-season, the Celtics pulled off a pair of blockbuster trades that put them back into title contention. On draft night in June, Boston traded the fifth pick, Jeff Green, to Seattle as part of a deal for star shooting guard Ray Allen. One month later, Boston acquired 10-time All-Star Kevin Garnett from the Minnesota Timberwolves.

Allen, 32, was widely considered the best shooter in basketball — within three years he would break Reggie Miller's all-time record for 3-point field goals — and fresh off a career year in scoring. Garnett, 31, had been named league MVP in '04 and was the game's most ferocious two-way presence. But with their prime years winding down, the fact that neither had made their mark in the postseason hung over their legacies.

The same was true of Boston's existing star, 30-year-old Paul Pierce, who'd spent his 10-year career wearing Celtics green. Pierce had a well-earned reputation as one of the toughest players in the league. In September 2000, he was stabbed 11 times at a Boston nightclub, including in the face and neck. He suffered a collapsed lung, underwent emergency surgery and was out of the hospital in less than a week. He was back on the floor in time for the season opener on November 1 and played every game that season.

Pierce was also the Celtics' go-to scorer and had averaged 25 points per game over the past seven seasons. With Allen and Garnett in the fold, the Celtics instantly found themselves playing for a title.

Boston's Big Three carried the team to 66 wins — just one shy of the iconic '86 Celts.

Meanwhile, in Los Angeles, the Lakers had undergone a serious makeover themselves. After the team traded Shaquille O'Neal in 2004, Kobe Bryant's solo career wasn't going as planned. Between 2004 and 2007 the Lakers went 121-125 as Bryant carried a subpar roster, making the playoffs twice and losing in the first round both times.

In the 2007–08 season, Bryant was leading the league in points scored for the third straight year, and the Lakers were off to a 35–20 start. He'd go on to be named MVP for the first and only time in his career. On February 1, 2008, Los Angeles acquired former first overall pick and perennial All-Star Pau Gasol from the Memphis Grizzlies. Gasol was a well-rounded low-post force who, two years earlier, led Spain to the gold medal at the FIBA World Cup.

Gasol gave the Lakers the low-post star they'd been missing since they dealt Shaq. Along with emerging 20-year-old center Andrew Bynum, a 7-foot, 285-pound man-child (the last time the Celtics and Lakers met in the Finals, Bynum hadn't even been born) and Swiss Army knife forward Lamar Odom, the lone holdover from the O'Neal trade — the Lakers roster was as strong as it had been in years. The team closed the season on a 22-5 run and kept the momentum going all the way to the Finals.

The Celtics moved from the hallowed Boston Garden to a new, state-of-the-art arena just 30 feet from their old home — close enough that the old ghosts of the Garden could still haunt the Lakers.

Boston took a 2-0 series lead, and a 36-point performance from Bryant in Game 3 brought the Celtics' lead to 2-1. In Game 4, LA got out to a 24-point lead in the first half. Slowly, Boston chipped away at it.

With 3:48 remaining in the fourth quarter, the Celtics took their first lead of the game. Thanks to the hot shooting of Ray Allen, Boston was in the driver's seat down the stretch. A pass from Bryant that finished with a Gasol dunk cut the Celts' lead to 3, but a driving layup from Allen with 15.7 seconds remaining put Boston up for good, securing a commanding 3-1 series lead.

"We just wet the bed," said a dejected Bryant, who scored 17 points on 6-of-19 shooting and had been playing with a torn ligament in his shooting hand for the past three months.

Two games later, Boston finished the job with a 131–92 beatdown, capturing its first title in 22 years — an NBA-record 17th championship. "Anything is possible!" an emotionally drained Garnett screamed to the rafters between sobs during a postgame interview, nearly echoing the catchphrase from his popular Adidas ad campaign ("Impossible is nothing").

Pierce, who led Boston in scoring in the series, was named Finals MVP.

"Someplace, somewhere," said commissioner David Stern while awarding the team the Larry O'Brien trophy, "Red [Auerbach] is up there, lighting a cigar."

The next season, the Celtics fell to the Orlando Magic, who went on to lose the Finals in five games to the Lakers. Bryant earned his first Finals MVP award.

But 2010 saw a Celtics–Lakers rematch. Like the '87 Celtics before them, Boston's core was showing the effects of age. The group was still potent and got a boost from 23-year-old Rajon Rondo, who averaged 15.8 points and 9.3 assists during the playoffs.

Meanwhile, the Lakers had signed 30-year-old Ron Artest, both the NBA's top defensive stopper and its most volatile player, during the 2009 off-season. In Game 1 of the Finals, Artest proved his worth, helping to hold Pierce and Allen to 9-of-21 shooting, while the Celtics had no answer as Bryant and Gasol worked the inside-outside game.

In Game 2, Allen got back on track, setting a Finals record with eight 3-pointers en route to a Celtics victory.

The teams traded wins again over the next two games, tying the series at two. In Game 5,

Bryant scored 38, but no other Lakers managed more than 12. The Celtics won, only for Los Angeles to tie the series once again in Game 6, holding Boston to 67 points. For the fifth time in history, a Celtics–Lakers Finals would go to a deciding Game 7. Up to now, Boston had won each and every time.

The Lakers were in the driver's seat for much of the game, but the Celtics managed to bring the lead down to just three points with just over a minute remaining. With 1:03 on the clock, Bryant, who'd been maligned by teammates, coaches and media alike throughout his career for not trusting his teammates and giving up the ball, passed out of a double-team.

The ball sailed to Artest behind the 3-point line. He took a jab step and stepped back as Pierce scrambled to adjust on defense. Artest's 3-pointer hung in the air and swished through the basket as the Lakers home crowd lost their minds.

It was the death blow. The Lakers held on for an 83–79 win, capturing their second consecutive title and avenging their Finals loss to Boston two years earlier. Lakers coach Phil Jackson earned his 11th championship ring, giving him two more than Red Auerbach.

Artest finished Game 7 with 20 points. Bryant posted 24 points and 15 rebounds, earning his second Finals MVP award.

It was his fifth title. For a lifelong Laker like Kobe, who grew up in awe of Magic and the Showtime Lakers and was acutely aware of the Celtics' traditional domination of the Lakers, the 2010 championship stood out. Winning Game 7 against Boston was like exorcising those demons.

"This one is by far the sweetest," Bryant said, "because it's them."

MOST NBA TITLES

1.	Boston Celtics	17
2.	Los Angeles Lakers	16
3.	Golden State Warriors	6
	Chicago Bulls	6
5.	San Antonio Spurs	5

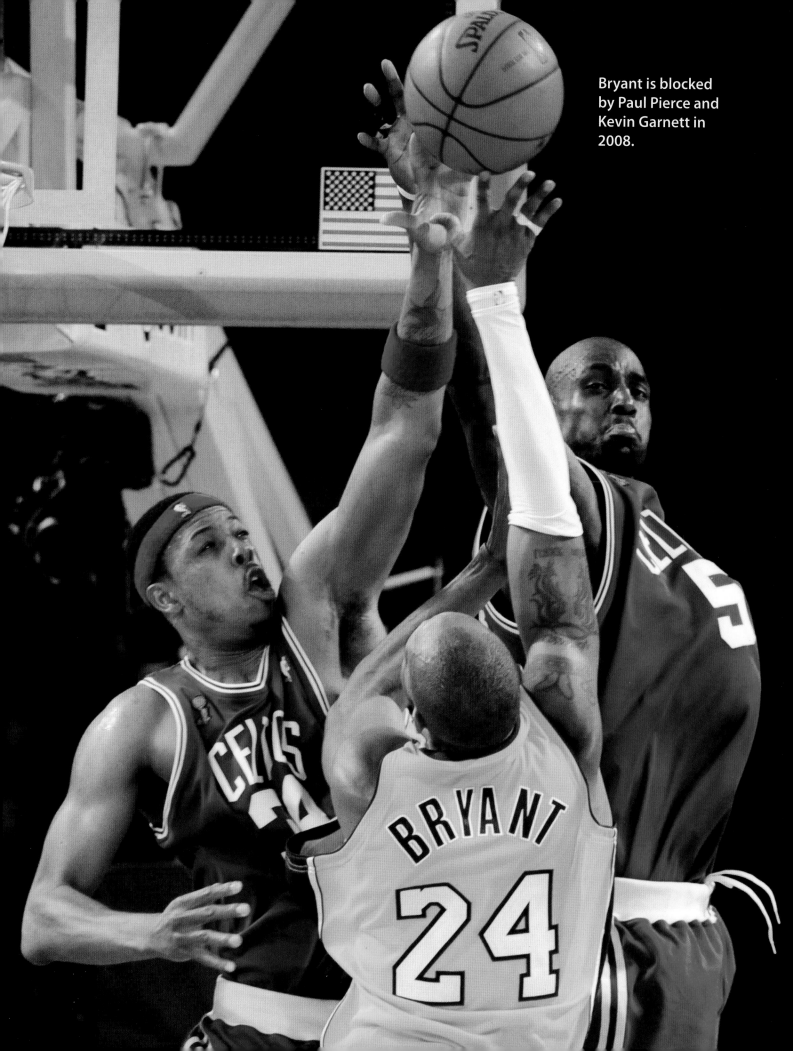

Bryant is blocked by Paul Pierce and Kevin Garnett in 2008.

2010
THE DECISION

Dwyane Wade finds LeBron James for the assist.

"This fall — man, this is very tough," LeBron James looked nervous. You'd think it was the fourth quarter of an elimination game.

It was the night of July 8, 2010. LeBron had traded in his wine-and-gold Cleveland Cavaliers uniform for a plaid shirt. He was set to make the biggest announcement of his career on live television.

The Decision, a 75-minute special broadcast, was the most anticipated NBA moment of the 21st century. At its peak, more than 13 million viewers — 10 million more than the FIFA World Cup match airing that night — tuned in to find out which jersey James would wear in the coming season.

At 25, James had already established himself as the greatest player on Earth. His time in Cleveland was a fairy tale: he was the prodigy from neighboring Akron who rescued the Cavaliers from the NBA's basement and took them to the Finals.

LeBron's Cavs were a one-man show. In the Eastern Conference finals in 2007, James scored Cleveland's last 25 points in a pivotal Game 5 win against the Detroit Pistons. In the Finals — their lone appearance to date — the Cavs were swept by the San Antonio Spurs. They looked like a high school team against the NBA's reigning dynasty.

In the summer of 2009 the Cavs tried to get LeBron some help. They traded for a 37-year-old Shaquille O'Neal and 33-year-old Antawn Jamison — two veterans whose All-Star days were well behind them.

The Cavs finished with the NBA's best record in 2009–10, and LeBron won his second consecutive MVP award. But his team blew a 2-1 lead to the Boston Celtics in round two. An ugly 3-for-14 shooting performance in a Game 5 loss added fuel to the notion that, unlike the all-time greats to whom he had drawn comparisons his entire career, James couldn't deliver when it mattered most.

Now, for the first time in his career, he was a free agent.

In Toronto, Chris Bosh had been suffering a similar fate to LeBron, only with far less to show for it. The fourth overall pick in the 2003 draft, Bosh was a low-post threat whose midrange shooting touch made him a nightmare to guard. He had been an All-Star every year since 2006, but his Toronto teams made the playoffs just twice in seven years and never won a series.

Bosh and James were part of a 2010 free-agent class that also included Dirk Nowitzki, Yao Ming, Amar'e Stoudemire and Dwyane Wade, who led the Miami Heat to a title in 2006 before the team around him was gutted.

The day before LeBron made up his mind, Bosh signed with Miami, where Wade had inked an extension.

Now all eyes were on LeBron.

Six teams were in the running to sign him: Cleveland, Chicago, New York, New Jersey, Miami and the Los Angeles Clippers.

James went on CNN and told Larry King that the Cavaliers had an advantage because of the familiarity he felt after a lifetime spent in Ohio.

Meanwhile, he met with each club as they pulled out all the stops to woo him. The Knicks, knowing James was a big fan of the show The Sopranos, even hired actors James Gandolfini and Edie Falco to film a scene in character as Tony and Carmela, explaining why LeBron should call Madison Square Garden home.

In the regular season, when the Cavs played the Heat, Miami GM Pat Riley arranged a sit-down between himself, LeBron and Michael Jordan. At their official recruitment meeting that summer, Riley poured his five championship rings on the table — four he had won with Magic Johnson and the Showtime Lakers, the fifth in Miami alongside James's close friend, Wade.

What more needed to be said?

On the set of The Decision, 30 long minutes passed before James finally made his announcement.

"In this fall, I'm going to take my talents to South Beach and join the Miami Heat."

"Never Has Being a Sports Fan Felt So Stupid," read the headline of a New York magazine feature. Another headline called it a "publicity disaster."

"Just as he did in Game 5 against Boston, LeBron James quit on the Cleveland Cavaliers," wrote one New York columnist. "And this guy thinks he can be another

James shoots during a 2012 game against the San Antonio Spurs.

in the Comic Sans font — calling LeBron's decision a "shocking act of disloyalty . . . a heartless and callous action."

James was shocked at the reaction. He hadn't planned for this. "I was 25 years old and wanted to be liked by everybody," he said years later.

A glorified "press conference" a few days after The Decision only stoked the flames. James, Wade and Bosh emerged onto a stage filled with smoke machines and strobe lights. "We came here to win championships," James told a delirious Miami crowd. "Not one, not two, not three, not four, not five, not six, not seven . . ."

Until then it had been easy to root for LeBron. He was the bright kid who overcame an impoverished childhood to carry his hometown team farther than it had any right to go. But now, with that one phrase — "taking my talents to South Beach" — he became an instant villain. In pro wrestling parlance, he "turned heel."

Whispers of a conspiracy that James, Bosh and Wade had made a pact to team up in the NBA after playing together for Team USA at the 2008 Olympics further soured fans.

They called Miami the "Heatles," a collection of super-talented individuals who combined to create a powerful force. The glaring difference being that the Beatles were beloved and the Heatles openly loathed.

Despite boasting the most talented roster in the league — in James and Wade, Miami had arguably the league's two best players — the Heat got off to a rocky start. James and Wade took turns playing the "alpha" role, while Bosh struggled to settle into an unfamiliar role as third banana. Fans reveled in Miami's pedestrian 11–8 start to the season.

On December 2, 2010, LeBron made his return to Cleveland for the first time since The Decision. It was hostile territory now, and the boos rained down on James like a typhoon.

"By far it was more intense, in terms of the crowd energy, than any playoff game, any Finals game I've been in," recalled Heat center Joel Anthony.

LeBron was the bad guy, and he took to

Michael Jordan? He's not even in the same league as Kobe Bryant."

The Decision was an unintentionally cruel act, as James publicly spurned his hometown and the fans who called him King. Looking back, James said he would have done it

differently if he could. But the damage had been done.

In Cleveland they burned James's jerseys and made bonfires out of LeBron memorabilia. Cavs owner Dan Gilbert published a letter in local newspapers — infamously

the role like Razor Ramon. The Heat decimated the Cavs that night. LeBron scored a season-high 38 points, playing up to the crowd, as a relentless Miami team whooped Cleveland, 118–90.

The game made it clear that, for the Heat to reach their potential, James would need to be their leader, with Wade playing the role of an overqualified sidekick.

Miami won its next nine games and didn't look back, cruising to the 2011 Finals and going 12-3 in the first three rounds of the playoffs, but was upset by Dirk Nowitzki and a veteran Dallas Mavericks squad. In a crucial Game 4, opposing fans delighted as LeBron turned in what was arguably his worst playoff performance, tallying just eight points. He turned the ball over 24 times in the series.

Chalk it up to growing pains. The following season, LeBron's Heat came back stronger and returned to the Finals. James had what was arguably his best season to date — and the most efficient NBA season since Jordan in 1987–88. He was named MVP for the third time.

Wade excelled in his new role as costar. But nobody sacrificed more than Bosh, who reinvented his game and became a 3-point shooter and rim protector, helping to solidify the blueprint for the modern-day big man.

After nine seasons, James won his first championship that year, easily ousting the Oklahoma City Thunder, 4-1. He was named Finals MVP. The next season, Miami repeated the feat, this time in a grueling seven-game series against the Spurs.

The series is best remembered for one of the greatest clutch shots in NBA history. In Game 6, with San Antonio one win away from being crowned champions, the Spurs were up three points with 18 seconds remaining. The Larry O'Brien trophy was waiting in the wings, and the arena staff had already put up ropes to separate the crowd from the court during the impending celebration.

After LeBron missed a 3-pointer, Bosh corralled the rebound and kicked the ball out to the right corner and into the hands of Ray Allen, the game's all-time leader in

The Miami Heat check into the game in the 2013 Finals.

3-point field goals. Allen backpedaled to behind the 3-point line and fired the ball with a hand in his face. Swish. Miami won the game in overtime.

Following a 37-point performance in Game 7, LeBron earned his second consecutive Finals MVP trophy, and the Heat were back-to-back NBA champs.

It became a lot more difficult to hate the Heat. James had, in essence, apologized for The Decision — not his actual choice, but the way he went about sharing the news. In the meantime, he shook the label as a gifted player who couldn't come through when it mattered most, and solidified his place among the game's all-time greats.

Wilt Chamberlain once said, "I'm a Goliath in a world of Davids. And nobody roots for Goliath."

After a roller-coaster ride in Miami, an exception was made for LeBron James.

2011

ROSE: THE ONE HIT WONDER

Derrick Rose is on a collision course with LeBron James.

He plants a vicious crossover on his defender and drives to the basket. James is waiting to take a charge. He gets his feet set and braces for impact.

It's late in the 2010–11 regular season, and Rose's Chicago Bulls and James's new-look Miami Heat are tied in the standings.

Rose sees James and erupts into the air upon approach, his sturdy 6-foot-3 frame soars as he contorts his body to squeeze between James and another Heat defender for an acrobatic layup, putting just the right amount of spin on the ball to send it high off the backboard and right through the net.

In just his third season, Rose has already cemented his status as one of the game's top point guards. On this night he's unstoppable, and the Bulls ride his coattails to a win.

This year, 2011, was supposed to be LeBron's year. Over the previous summer, he shocked the basketball world when he formed a superteam in South Beach. James promised that championships would immediately follow, and he was on track for his third straight MVP award.

But Rose is a disrupter. He disrupts opponents' game plans — no amount of Xs and Os can temper his talents. Growing up in Chicago's Englewood neighborhood, he disrupted pickup games against his older siblings, who let the kid they called Pooh

join in, even if it meant losing to him. In high school he disrupted the state championship game, burying a buzzer-beater to win the title. He disrupted college, too, taking University of Memphis to its first national championship game in 35 years.

The first overall pick of the 2008 draft, Rose was a silent killer — so quiet that teammates would complain they couldn't hear when he was calling plays. But he had a loud game.

A gifted playmaker, Rose's competitive advantage was an explosive athleticism rarely seen at the position. His first step was military grade. He took off like a F-15 Eagle fighter jet.

The Bulls hadn't found a true star since Michael Jordan retired — and it wasn't for a lack of trying. The team had drafted in the top 5 six times since 1998, but continually failed to land a franchise player. Then Rose fell into their laps. A Chicago kid starring for his hometown team, Rose led the Bulls to the playoffs in his first season.

In 2011, at the age of 22, Rose led the Bulls to 62 wins and a No. 1 playoff seed. He was named MVP, the youngest ever. He interrupted a streak that saw LeBron take home four MVP awards in five years between 2009 and 2013.

The following season he tore his left ACL during the first game of the 2012 playoffs and missed the entire 2012–13 season. Ten

games into his comeback season, he tore his meniscus — this time on the other knee. For a player who relied on his superhuman legs to propel him to greatness, the injuries proved too much to overcome. After making three straight All-Star appearances between 2010 and 2012, he was never an All-Star again. In just a few short years, Rose had taken the league by storm. His fall from grace was as swift as any.

The league began handing out the MVP award in 1956. In the 55 years between then and when Rose won, there had been just 16 one-time winners. All, save for Charles Barkley and Rose, won championships. And nearly all of them enjoyed long, successful careers.

You would never call them one-hit wonders.

Except, perhaps, for Rose.

In 2011 the groundwork had been laid for Rose to establish himself as a bona fide rival to LeBron for years to come. But he could never stay on the court in Chicago, and eventually the fans who appointed him their savior turned on him. "They were mad at me because they wanted to see me hoop," he said, "I understand that."

Rose missed 257 games in eight seasons with the Bulls. In the summer of 2016 he was traded to the New York Knicks. That season, he suffered another torn ACL and underwent his fourth knee surgery, a nearly

Derrick Rose goes for
a dunk in 2011.

Rose reacts to an injury in the 2012 playoffs.

unprecedented string of bad luck — or simply the result of a body that wasn't meant for longevity. As he entered his 30s, the one-time Dynamite Kid had lost his detonator. He continued to bounce around the league, accepting a role coming off the bench, his best years long behind him.

On Halloween night in 2019, he put on his cape one last time and reminded us all of how good he once was. Rose, the backup point guard for the Minnesota Timberwolves, erupted for 50 points, including two clutch shots in the final minute and a game-saving block at the buzzer. When the game ended, Rose burst into tears as his teammates engulfed him.

"That's why our game is so unbelievable," LeBron James said. "Even when a superhero's knocked down, he's still a superhero. . . . Derrick Rose showed why he's still a superhero."

The NBA named the performance its Moment of the Year.

Rose was supposed to go down in the history books. He was supposed to be Jordan's successor and LeBron's foe. He still might make history: he could be the first MVP not to be enshrined in the Hall of Fame.

The story of the NBA is told through its dynasties and the stars who ruled for years on end. But every now and then, a player comes along and disrupts all of that.

Rose was the most electric guard in the game, only for a flash.

ONE-TIME MVPS

Bob Cousy ('57), Oscar Robertson ('64), Wes Unseld ('69), Willis Reed ('70), Dave Cowens ('73), Bob McAdoo ('75), Bill Walton ('78), Charles Barkley ('93), Hakeem Olajuwon ('94), David Robison ('95), Shaquille O'Neal (2000), Allen Iverson ('01), Kevin Garnett ('04), Dirk Nowitzki ('07) and Kobe Bryant ('08).

2012

OKC: THE WOULD-BE CHAMPS

The Oklahoma City Thunder entered Game 6 of the 2012 Western Conference finals against the San Antonio Spurs with home-court advantage and a 3-2 lead.

It was the Thunder's breakout moment. Kevin Durant, Russell Westbrook and James Harden had combined to form the youngest contending team in the NBA. They were one win away from what was supposed to be their first of many trips to the Finals.

But the kids were suddenly trailing by 18 points. And it wasn't even halftime yet. This wasn't the plan.

The series was dripping with symbolism. It was a battle between the NBA's old guard (Spurs) and new wave (Thunder). The Immortals versus the Uprising.

The Spurs were the model for longevity, but the Thunder hit the scene like a flash flood. Durant and Westbrook were just 23, Harden only 22. Durant and Westbrook were already All-Stars (Durant had been named MVP of the All-Star Game just a few months earlier), and Harden would take home the Sixth Man of the Year Award that season. With their ultra-talented young nucleus in place the Thunder were pegged the NBA's team of the future. But they weren't waiting.

James Harden celebrates a 3-pointer in the 2012 Western Conference final.

Russell Westbrook drives passed Dwyane Wade in the 2012 Finals.

In the first round they swept the defending champion Dallas Mavericks, and they made quick work of Kobe Bryant and the LA Lakers in the second. But the Spurs were a different kind of challenge: How do you kill something that can't die?

San Antonio might have been a few years removed from its last championship, but the Spurs hadn't won fewer than 50 games since 1999. Their core was aging — Tim Duncan and Manu Ginobili were over 35, and Tony Parker wasn't far behind — yet it would be another five years before their streak was snapped. And in two years they would be crowned champions again, their fifth title in 15 years.

The Spurs' experience was showing in Game 6, and as the third quarter began their lead was 15. On the first play, Durant drove past Kawhi Leonard for a layup. A minute later, Westbrook threatened the defense with

his blazing speed and pulled up for a contested jumper that fell. The Spurs struggled to contain Serge Ibaka, the Thunder's 22-year-old Congolese center, while Harden was still feeling it after icing Game 5 with a last-second 3-pointer.

With 1:49 left in the third, the Thunder had cut the lead down to one. Durant grabs a rebound, brings the ball up court and steps into a 3-pointer at the top of the key. The crowd goes wild as it falls through the hoop. Oklahoma City 79, San Antonio 76.

The Thunder never trailed again. Durant put on a postseason show for the ages. He played all 48 minutes and posted 34 points and 14 rebounds. He, Westbrook and Harden combined for 75 points as Oklahoma City booked its ticket to the Finals.

The Thunder lost to the Miami Heat in five games, having been wholly outmatched by a more experienced squad led by LeBron

James, Dwyane Wade and Chris Bosh. But no matter; it was only their first crack at the title.

It would also be their last.

Oklahoma City and general manager Sam Presti had run a master class in building through the draft. In 2007 he selected Durant second overall (rendering first pick Greg Oden the Sam Bowie of *his* draft). In 2008 he drafted Westbrook fourth overall and Ibaka at No. 24. And in 2009 Harden was chosen with the third pick (rendering second overall pick Hasheem Thabeet the Greg Oden of his draft). All three would go on to be named MVP in the coming years, an unprecedented success rate.

Now the trio were emerging as superstars, and they expected to be paid accordingly. Durant and Westbrook had already signed long-term extensions totaling $166 million, and in the summer of 2012 the Thunder inked Ibaka to a four-year, $48 million deal.

But the team faced a crisis with Harden, who was entering the final year of his rookie deal and was next in line for a deserved raise.

Oklahoma City is a small market by NBA standards, and the franchise didn't have the bottomless pockets of wealthier organizations like the Knicks or Lakers. As its payroll mounted, the team was in jeopardy of going over the salary cap, meaning it would have to pay millions extra to the league in luxury tax penalties. Unlike richer teams, the Thunder saw the luxury tax as a legitimate deterrent to overspending.

Before the start of the 2012–13 season, the team offered Harden an extension for less than market value. He declined it. "I felt like I already made a sacrifice coming off the bench and doing whatever it takes to help the team," Harden said, "and they weren't willing to help me."

To avoid letting him walk in free agency for nothing in return, the Thunder traded Harden to the Houston Rockets one week before the season began. The team had cut off one of its limbs, but it still had Westbrook and Durant, who led the league in scoring each of the previous three seasons. The Thunder returned from their Finals loss against Miami better than ever. They won 60 games and entered the 2013 postseason as the favorites to emerge from the West.

While Durant was OKC's go-to star, Westbrook, the point guard, was emerging as the heart and soul of the team. He was a fiery competitor and explosive athlete who attacked defenders like a fighter jet.

In Game 2 of the Thunder's first-round series versus the LA Clippers, Westbrook tore the meniscus in his right knee after a collision with Patrick Beverly. The NBA's reigning iron man, Westbrook hadn't missed a game in his entire career — including high school and college — but required surgery and was sidelined indefinitely.

Without Westbrook, Oklahoma City was eliminated in the second round. Meanwhile, in Houston, Harden was becoming a bona fide star. His scoring average jumped nearly 10 points per game in his first season with

the Rockets, and kept climbing from there.

In 2013–14 Westbrook's knee ailments continued. He was limited to 46 games, and in February he underwent another knee surgery. But this time Durant picked up the slack. He led the league in scoring once more, averaging an even 32 points per game, and was named the NBA's 2014 MVP for carrying his team on his back.

He led the Thunder back to the Western Conference finals, where a rematch with the Spurs awaited. In another dramatic Game 6, Ginobili took over in the dying seconds as San Antonio got its revenge and OKC was sent packing.

That's when the Thunder's would-be dynasty began to unravel.

Before the start of the 2014–15 season, Durant fractured his foot and played only 27 games. With Westbrook battling injuries once more, the team missed the playoffs entirely. Looking for a scapegoat, the Thunder fired head coach Scott Brooks. "What did he do wrong?" Ibaka wondered to the media.

The following season, the Thunder got back on track and reached the Western Conference finals for the fourth time in six seasons. Facing a Golden State Warriors team that had just set a record with 73 wins in the regular season, Oklahoma City got out to a 3-1 lead, sounding the death knell for the Warriors. But Golden State came back to tie the series. In Game 6, Warriors guard Klay Thompson erupted for 11 three-pointers — the most ever in a single playoff game — to force a Game 7. Golden State advanced to the Finals and became just the 10th team in playoff history to erase a 3-1 series deficit.

Since their 2012 Finals appearance, the Thunder had experienced four straight years of heartbreak. For one reason or another — injuries, a mismanaged salary cap, an overreliance on their two stars— it seemed they had reached their apex.

In the summer of '16 the Thunder traded Ibaka for Victor Oladipo, a shooting guard tasked with filling the scoring void left by Harden years earlier.

It was too late. Durant was a free agent that summer. He had established himself as the NBA's preeminent scorer and the league's second-in-command behind LeBron James.

But the playoff failures were taking their toll. He was tired from having to hoist the Thunder on his back year after year with nothing to show for it. He just wanted to win, to be remembered as a champion.

On July 4, 2016, Durant phoned Thunder GM Sam Presti and told him the news that would shake the NBA's foundation: he was signing with the Golden State Warriors. If you can't beat 'em, join 'em.

The move officially put an end to the Thunder's status as contenders. What had once been the most promising roster in the league had been gutted.

With Durant in tow, the Warriors were unstoppable. In his first two seasons, they were crowned champions and Durant was named Finals MVP in both 2017 and 2018.

Westbrook, meanwhile, was the lone survivor in OKC. He did his best to keep the Thunder's winning ways alive and became a one-man show the like of which the NBA had never seen before. In 2017 Westbrook was named MVP and became the first player since Oscar Robertson in 1962 to average a triple-double for an entire season.

Robertson's record had always been lauded as Teflon, one of the most untouchable marks in all of sports. But Westbrook averaged a triple-double *three seasons straight*. Even so, the Thunder never made it past the first round.

In the meantime, Harden had lifted the Rockets to Western Conference finals appearances in 2015 and 2018. In 2019 he was named MVP after averaging a stunning 36 points per game — the most since Michael Jordan in 1987.

Like the Shaq-Penny Magic, or Olajuwon's Rockets of the 80s — teams that seemed poised to contend for years but saw their window shut ahead of schedule — the Thunder had all but burned out like a firecracker. They were the dynasty that could have been but never was.

In the summer of 2019, the Thunder traded Westbrook to the Houston Rockets, where he reunited with Harden.

In 2012 Durant, Harden and Westbrook were about to take over the NBA. Seven years later, they were gone. This wasn't the plan.

2014
KAWHI

His moves appear preprogrammed, and he operates with a machinelike efficiency. He rarely emotes and is often monosyllabic. He has an inhuman awareness of where the ball is at all times.

Kawhi Leonard is a robot. At least that's what we thought.

Kawhi was always quiet. He grew up in Moreno Valley, California, about an hour east of Los Angeles, where basketball was more than a game. It was where he could let his play do the talking.

He lived with his mother, Kim, while his father, Mark, lived in Compton. When Leonard was 16 years old, Mark was shot multiple times while closing up the car wash he operated. Leonard retreated to his bedroom when he heard the news to be in silence. "When we went to check on him," his uncle Dennis recalled, "he just said, 'I'm good.'"

Leonard played in a game the next day. It was difficult to get a read on Leonard at the best of times, but he was stone-faced as he led his team to a win against a rival. After the game, he collapsed in his mom's arms, hugged his teammates and cried.

"Basketball helps me take my mind off things, picking me up every day when I'm feeling down," he said. "I try to play as hard as I can each night. That's what my father wanted me to do."

After two standout seasons at San Diego State University, Leonard was selected 15th overall in the 2011 NBA draft. The San Antonio Spurs traded fan favorite George Hill for Leonard on draft night. On paper, Kawhi wasn't the ideal Spur. He couldn't

shoot, wasn't the greatest passer and didn't have an obvious feel for the game. But he was a hard worker who played defense and listened to his coach. That worked for Spurs bench boss Gregg Popovich, who put him in the starting lineup during the playoffs in his rookie season.

From day one his focus at such a young age was almost eerie. Leonard was immune to trash talk and went about his business so methodically, it was borderline worrisome. "There are times he does something well, and I have to tell him, 'That was super. That was fantastic. That was a helluva job,'" said Popovich. "'You can smile now.'"

Leonard quickly went from promising role player to unequivocal star. His breakout came in the 2014 Finals, when Pop sicced the 22-year-old on LeBron James of the Miami Heat. LeBron grimaced when Kawhi checked into the game; Leonard nearly matched James in size and made him work harder than ever.

On the other end of the floor, Kawhi was a stone-cold killer. Over the last three games of the series — all Spurs blowouts — he averaged 23.7 points, 9.3 rebounds, 2 steals and 2 blocks while shooting the lights out. San Antonio won the series, 4-1.

Despite sharing the court with Hall of Famers Tim Duncan, Manu Ginobili and Tony Parker, Leonard was an easy choice for Finals MVP.

But little was known about the Spurs' burgeoning star. Leonard preferred it that way. He avoided interviews and shunned social media. He dodged major endorsement deals

and widespread ad campaigns. "I don't like to make a scene," he said. In the look-at-me era he came up in, that stood out.

He drove the same '97 Chevy Tahoe he had saved up for as a teenager and sported Iverson-inspired cornrows long after they fell out of style. He became a spokesman for Wingstop because he was a regular and free coupons were a perk of the gig.

Kawhi is uncomplicated. Just like his game.

Leonard could do it all and took whatever the defense gave him. It was like opponents were playing a Choose Your Own Adventure game, only every option made things worse.

He had the strength of a football player, and his enormous hands allowed him to manipulate the ball in ways few players ever could — 40 years after Dr. J was bestowed with the nickname, Kawhi became known as the Klaw.

He was also a smart, intuitive player. In his career, he has more steals than fouls.

Each year, he added elements to his game until he had no weaknesses. Post moves, handles, turnaround jumpers. A 25 percent 3-point shooter in college, in his fifth NBA season he shot over 44 percent from deep.

The natural successor to Duncan, Leonard took the reins of the Spurs and in 2016 led them to a franchise-best 67 wins. In 2016 and '17, he finished second and third, respectively, in MVP voting.

Ahead of the 2017–18 season, Kawhi was diagnosed with a thigh injury that sidelined him until December. The Spurs doctors cleared him to play, but Leonard felt the injury hadn't healed and sought second opin-

Kawhi Leonard puts the clamps on Blake Griffin during the 2015 playoffs.

ions. He played just nine games that season. His teammates insinuated that he was healthy enough to play, and several in the organization reportedly questioned the injury.

Kawhi was incensed. With one year left on his contract, he demanded a trade. The unthinkable had happened: a Spur was breaking rank.

On July 18, 2018, Leonard was traded to the Toronto Raptors, who dealt the franchise's all-time scoring leader, DeMar DeRozan, for a one-year rental.

He was still a mystery when he arrived in Toronto, as was made clear by his answer to the first question lobbed his way at his introductory press conference: "What can you tell us about yourself?"

"I'm a fun guy," he said in monotone. His answer did little to change the narrative about his robotic persona.

The Raptors faithful learned about Kawhi in no time. They saw why he was a two-time

MOST FINALS MVPS

1.	Michael Jordan	6
2.	Magic Johnson	3
	Shaquille O'Neal	3
	Tim Duncan	3
	LeBron James	3

Leonard celebrates his 2019 NBA title.

Defensive Player of the Year. In one of his first games, Kawhi detected the ball as if he was built with sensors. With his back to the action, Leonard dove to intercept a pass and corralled the ball — the rare no-look steal.

They saw how he'd developed into a surgeon on offense, devouring defenders with a lethal throwback midrange game. He averaged a career-high 26.6 points per game and immediately transformed the team into title contenders.

In the playoffs, he shifted gears and began drawing comparisons to the all-time greats. He even had his own signature moment. In Game 7 of the second round, with the game tied, Leonard sunk a buzzer-beating baseline jumper that dramatically bounced on the rim four times before landing. The shot sent the Philadelphia 76ers packing and advanced the Raptors one step closer to a title.

Kawhi joined Michael Jordan as the only players to end a do-or-die playoff game with a walk-off at the buzzer. He also became the first player in 25 years to score at least 243 points in a playoff series — another Jordan-matching feat.

Leonard averaged 30.5 points in the playoffs. And, when the Raptors knocked off the dynastic Golden State Warriors in the Finals, he was named the Finals MVP once more, joining LeBron James and Kareem Abdul-Jabbar as the only players to win the award for two different teams.

And he was still in his prime. Leonard's impending free agency promised to alter the balance of the league, and it was covered like the royal wedding. In Toronto, news helicopters followed an SUV from the airport amid speculation Kawhi was in the car, en route to ink a new deal (he wasn't).

Leonard stayed mum while the Kawhi Watch became daily news, holding the NBA's off-season hostage as the biggest domino decided where to land. He opted to return home to Los Angeles and sign with the Clippers — but only after arranging for fellow LA native and All-Star Paul George to be traded to his new team. The Clippers headed into the season as title favorites as Leonard sought to carry yet another team to the Promised Land.

The NBA's "player empowerment" movement was in full swing, as players increasingly called the shots, and Kawhi was at the center of it all. Turns out we'd mistook quiet for unaware. Before turning 30, Leonard had crafted a legendary career unlike any other. He entered the 2019–20 season ahead of Magic Johnson for the highest career winning percentage in NBA history.

Sephen Curry after forcing a Cleveland Cavaliers' timeout in the 2015 Finals.

2015
CURRY AND THE WARRIORS

Curry nails a three against the Memphis Grizzlies in 2016.

MOST 3-POINT FG IN A SEASON

1.	Stephen Curry	402 (2015)
2.	James Harden	378 (2018)
3.	Stephen Curry	354 (2018)
4.	Stephen Curry	324 (2016)
5.	Paul George	292 (2018)
6.	Stephen Curry	286 (2014)
7.	Buddy Hield	278 (2018)
8.	Klay Thompson	276 (2015)
9.	Stephen Curry	272 (2012)
10.	James Harden	271 (2019)

MOST 3-POINT ATTEMPTS IN A SEASON

1.	James Harden	1,028 (2018)
2.	Stephen Curry	886 (2015)
3.	Stephen Curry	810 (2018)
4.	Stephen Curry	789 (2016)
5.	James Harden	769 (2019)

The Golden State Warriors trailed the Memphis Grizzlies, 2-1, entering Game 4 of the second round of the 2015 playoffs. The Warriors were in the midst of a breakout season, finishing with the top record in the NBA. Their star player, Stephen Curry, was on his way to earning his first of two MVP awards.

But whether or not the Warriors' high-octane offense could survive the grind of the playoffs was still up in the air. Against an oversized Grizzlies team built on hard-hitting defense, it wasn't looking good.

That's when Curry put his team on his back and exploded for 33 points, and the Warriors pulled off a convincing win. They won the remaining games in the series en route to the 2015 championship.

You'd have been hard pressed to know it at the time, but the Warriors were on the road to becoming a modern-day dynasty and one of the most dominant teams in NBA history.

Within five seasons they set — and broke — the NBA record for most wins over a five-year span. They won three titles and reached the Finals five seasons in a row. Yes, the Warriors *were* built for the playoffs.

You can spot the all-time greats — the players who lead their teams to multiple titles — long before they arrive in the NBA. They're top draft picks and highly touted prospects. Rarely do they come out of nowhere. Steph Curry is the exception.

Well, sort of. Curry was clearly a special talent from the start. The son of longtime Charlotte Hornets guard Dell Curry, one of the top 3-point marksmen of the 90s, Steph had the luxury of growing up around the pro game. By the time he was 11, he'd already hoisted thousands of shots on an NBA court.

Like Dell, Steph's strong suit was his shooting. When he was an eighth-grader, his family moved to Toronto after his dad signed with the Raptors. Around the same time, Steph nailed down his signature shooting motion — the dramatic, high-arcing bomb he flings from his hip, straight up and through the mesh. He led his middle-school team to an undefeated season, taking — and making — shots from *way* beyond the arc. He averaged 50 points per game that year.

Still, scouts at the college level saw a short, spindly, baby-faced kid with arms like broomsticks, and they collectively took a hard pass. He couldn't crack the top-150 player rankings coming out of high school, and only one major college program offered him a scholarship — on the condition he'd sit out a year to put on more muscle.

So, Curry attended North Carolina's Davidson College, which hadn't won an NCAA tournament game since 1969. By March of his freshman year, he shattered the NCAA freshman record by making 113 three-pointers. In his sophomore season, he made a name for himself scoring 30 second-half points in a comeback upset win over Gonzaga in front of a national television audience. Curry carried Davidson all the way to the Elite Eight, setting a single-season 3-point record in the process. After leading the entire NCAA in scoring his junior season, Curry declared for the draft.

His offensive skills were not questioned. But whether or not they'd translate to the bigger, stronger, faster NBA certainly was. One scouting report read, "Not a great finisher around the basket due to his size and physical attributes. Although he's playing point guard this year, he's not a natural point guard that an NBA team can rely on to run a team."

On draft night, four point guards were taken ahead of Curry — five if you include James Harden. He fell to the No. 7 spot, where the Warriors were happy to take the prodigious scorer.

He averaged over 17 points his rookie season, but it wasn't until his fourth season, 2012–13, that Curry's rise as the NBA's baby-faced assassin took hold. And it was thrilling to watch, as he broke the single-season 3-point record. He would the league in made threes five years running.

Curry became must-see TV. Every War-

riors game was a chance to watch the newest superstar let it fly. Because he was on the scrawny side, Curry had an everyman quality and an easily digestible style of play that brought in scores of new fans to the sport. By 2016 his jersey was the NBA's highest seller.

Curry became so popular among kids that youth coaches complained that more and more kids were trying to play like Curry, pulling up for maverick 3-pointers from impossible distances.

In Golden State, Curry had arrived in the perfect place. The Warriors were one of the NBA's worst, with just six playoff appearances in 30 years. They were a team with no real identity or direction. They could afford to put the ball in Curry's hands and see if he could recreate the magic that had made him a collegiate star.

He also arrived at the perfect time, when 3-pointers were valued more than ever and teams were looking to let it fly like never before. But it took a once-in-a-lifetime shooter like Curry to really put the new method to the test.

With each passing season, Curry pushed the envelope further until he established himself as the best shooter in the history of the sport. What made the Warriors so special was that the player who was arguably second best was standing next to him every night.

Golden State drafted Klay Thompson 11th overall in 2011. Like Curry, he was the son of an ex-NBAer: former first overall pick Mychal Thompson. And, like Curry, he was an unconscionable shooter, giving the Warriors an unprecedented one-two punch in the backcourt quickly dubbed the Splash Brothers. Away from the game, Thompson was calm and cool, a bit of a space cadet. But he was an absolute gamer on the court and one of the best two-way guards of his era.

Ahead of the 2014 season, the Warriors hired Steve Kerr as their head coach. As it was when Phil Jackson joined the Lakers in 2000, Kerr arrived at Golden State knowing perfectly well what it took to build and sustain a dynasty. As a player, he was part of two: Michael Jordan's Bulls and Tim Duncan's Spurs.

Kerr embraced his gunslinging backcourt and refined the offense, and the Warriors hit another gear. Between 2014 and 2018 they were the NBA's highest-scoring offense, and it wasn't close.

They put points on the board so quickly it put pressure on opponents to play their best — Curry's Warriors were always one run away from breaking the score out of reach. One defensive lapse and it was game over. Like the physical threat of the Bad Boys Pistons or the full-court destructiveness of the Showtime Lakers, Golden State had the mental game won before tip-off virtually every night.

Along with Steph and Klay, the Warriors' nucleus included Andre Iguodala, a former lottery pick who was traded to Golden State ahead of the 2013–14 season. A 30-year-old veteran, Iguodala became a powerful voice in the Warriors' locker room and the consummate glue guy on the court. A hyper-athletic wing, he picked his spots on offense and always guarded the other team's best player.

In the 2015 Finals he was assigned LeBron James, whom he held to under 40 percent shooting in the series, while averaging over 16 points himself. For his efforts, Iguodala was named Finals MVP.

But the Warriors' X factor was Draymond Green. A 6-foot-9 forward, Green could play multiple positions and was often cast as a small-ball center, where his versatile game opened up opportunities on both ends of the floor. He could bring the ball up the floor and distribute, protect the rim and shoot well enough from a distance.

What's more, Green gave them a swagger. He was hyper-confident and took pride in showing 29 teams that they made a mistake on draft night in 2012.

Green was a second-round pick out of Michigan State University who barely saw the floor his first few seasons. But injuries opened the door to playing time, and he took advantage, carving out an undisputed role in the starting lineup.

With the core in place, the Warriors' winning ways began. In 2014–15, they won 67 games, going from sixth in the West the season before to first. The season culminated in a title, and their first of four straight meetings with the Cleveland Cavaliers in the Finals. That year also marked the first of Curry's back-to-back MVP awards.

The Warriors began the 2015–16 schedule with 24 straight wins, topping 100 points in each of them. That set the stage for a season that saw Golden State win 73 regular-season games, breaking the record set by Jordan's 1995–96 Bulls, a team Kerr played on. But the Warriors ended the season on the wrong end of history, becoming the only team to blow a 3-1 series lead in the Finals.

That summer, the Warriors signed Kevin Durant and, in the words of Kerr, went from "a championship team to an all-time team." The team fell back to Earth, winning "just" 67 games again while claiming first place in the standings once more. This time, they finished the job and captured the title. They repeated the next year, with Durant claiming Finals MVP honors both times.

There was a specific play that Kerr looks back on as the perfect encapsulation of the Warriors at the peak of their powers. It was

in Game 6 of the 2018 playoffs against the Houston Rockets.

Curry and Green had been carving up Houston with the pick-and-roll throughout the game. In the fourth quarter, the Rockets finally adjusted, double-teaming Steph. But he managed to get the ball to Draymond, who then delivered a pass to Iguodala on the base-line, who instantly made the extra pass, kicking the ball back out to Thompson for a 3-pointer.

"The ball movement, the spacing, the beautiful vision and awareness of Andre and Draymond, and the lethal play of Steph and Klay . . . ," Kerr said. "It was special."

The entire Warriors experience was special. Three titles in five years. One of the deadliest five-man lineups the NBA has ever seen, and a generational icon keeping the wheels turning.

Each and every NBA campaign began with the same question: Can anybody stop the Warriors? For years, there was no answer. It turned out to be the Warriors themselves.

In the 2019 Finals against the Toronto Raptors, the team unraveled. They were decimated by injuries. In Game 5 in Toronto, Durant ruptured his Achilles tendon. In the next game, Thompson tore his ACL. Against a deep Raptors team, Curry and Green couldn't carry the Warriors alone.

That summer, Durant went in search of his next challenge and left the team for free agency. Thompson's injury ruled him out for all or most of the season. And then, four games into 2019–20, Curry broke his hand, sidelining him indefinitely. The Warriors plummeted to the bottom of the standings. In a matter of months, they became the worst team in basketball.

The Warriors set a standard for winning and left the rest of the league scrambling to compete. With each additional championship, more and more teams were reshaping their rosters for the sole purpose of trying to beat Golden State. No longer could teams afford to have players on the floor who couldn't score, and no longer did teams need a big, bruising center. The Warriors provided the model for capturing titles while relying on the 3-point shot.

Curry and the Warriors didn't just win. They changed the league.

2016
LEBRON
COMES BACK

When LeBron James left the Cavaliers in 2010 — a breakup aired on live TV — Cleveland fans burned his jerseys in the streets.

James's departure for South Beach sent the Cavaliers back to the Dark Ages. The team went from 61 wins in LeBron's last season pre-*Decision* to just 19 during his first year in Miami — literally from first to worst in the East. They won 64 games *combined* in their first three seasons without LeBron.

Losing has its perks, mind you. Cleveland landed three first overall picks in the span of four years. In 2011 the Cavs selected Kyrie Irving, a dribbling genius who quickly blossomed into one of the NBA's elite point guards. They also drafted a pair of Canadians with the top pick — Anthony Bennett in 2013, a surprising choice at the time who became a spectacular bust, and Andrew Wiggins the next year.

When James announced that he was coming back to Cleveland, there were no television cameras. "I'm Coming Home," read the headline of a self-penned *Sports Illustrated* essay announcing the news on July 11, 2014. In the piece, he expressed regret over the way he left Cleveland and mentioned how excited he was to play alongside Irving and others — but curiously made no mention of recent top pick Wiggins. A month later, Wiggins was traded to Minnesota in exchange for All-Star big man Kevin Love, a top-notch rebounder and 3-point shooter.

The King assembled his new court. Cleveland fans were quick to extinguish any smoldering resentment from LeBron's departure. It was as if *The Decision* never happened.

In LeBron's first season back, the Cavaliers made it all the way to the Finals. They ran into the Golden State Warriors — a rising power built around league MVP Steph Curry and Klay Thompson, the best-shooting backcourt the league had ever seen. LeBron was brilliant — he averaged 35.8 points, 13.3 rebounds and 8.8 assists, becoming the first player in NBA Finals history to lead *both* teams in points, assists and rebounds. But with Love and Irving both sidelined, he couldn't do it by himself. The Warriors dismissed Cleveland in six games.

Their rematch in 2016 established Cavs–Warriors as a bona fide rivalry and culminated in a dramatic Game 7, capping off the biggest comeback in Finals history.

It had been a long time since LeBron James was cast as the underdog. Early in his career, he'd carried those Cavs teams on his tattoo-covered back, but his tenure in Miami established him as the NBA's king of the court. But by the time the 2016 Finals rolled around, James and the Cavs were overshadowed by a burgeoning Warriors dynasty.

That season, Golden State set an NBA record with 73 wins in the regular season. The Warriors were a tornado that sucked in

LeBron James celebrates after winning Game 2 of the 2015 Finals in overtime.

anyone who got close, and even the King wasn't immune. James might have been game's most powerful figure, but Steph Curry was its most popular new icon. In 2015–16, following his second straight MVP season, Curry's jersey was the NBA's best seller, breaking LeBron's seven-year streak atop that list.

As the Finals got underway, Curry and the Warriors picked up from where they left off the previous year. They raced out to a 3–1 lead in the best-of-seven series, sounding the death knell for Cleveland, now one loss from

elimination. In the history of the NBA, 35 teams had fallen into a 3–1 hole in the Finals. No team had ever escaped it.

Tensions were high. At the close of Game 4, James and Golden State forward Draymond Green, a world-class agitator and the Warriors' defensive anchor, got into it. With two minutes left in the game and Golden State up by 10, LeBron was tied up with Green and knocked him to the ground. When James stepped over Green, the Warriors' firecracker took offense and threw a

punch at the King's jewels.

After the game, the league reviewed the incident and assessed Green a flagrant foul, ruling that he "made unnecessary contact with a retaliatory swipe of his hand to the groin." It was Green's fourth flagrant foul of the playoffs, resulting in an automatic suspension under NBA rules.

With Green out of the lineup for Game 5, the Cavs took control thanks to 41 points and 16 rebounds from a fired-up James. In Game 6 he scored 41 again as Cleveland

tied the series 3-3, setting up a do-or-die Game 7 in front of a Warriors home crowd in Oakland.

At its peak, over 41 million Americans tuned in to the final game to see if LeBron could finish the job — the most viewers for any game since Michael Jordan's last championship in 1998.

Like Mike had before him, James ruled his era. The self-proclaimed Chosen One was a four-time MVP and starred in each of the six championship series. And, like Mike, his signature sneaker was the NBA's best seller, with $348 million worth sold in the 2015–16 season — twice as much as anybody else's.

That year, LeBron joined Jordan in the 25,000-point club. At age 30, he was the youngest to ever reach the plateau — three years ahead of MJ.

James had evolved over his 13 years in the NBA. The svelte point guard who entered the league in 2003, weaving through defenses like an ambulance in rush-hour traffic, had given way to a hulking figure with the stature of a power forward. Instead of weaving, nowadays he drove straight through them like a tanker truck.

His physical style of play was giving the undersized Warriors fits, but toppling the league's most potent offense was a daunting task, as the year before had proved. For all the comparisons to Jordan that James was earning, he fell short where it mattered most. LeBron had been to six Finals by 2016, the same number as Jordan. The difference? Each time Jordan made it to the Finals, his team won a title. LeBron, meanwhile, was 2-4 with a championship on the line.

Game 7 in 2016 was a chance to rewrite the narrative.

For three quarters, the Cavaliers and Warriors went back and forth. But in crunch time, tied at 89 with 3:39 left on the clock, neither team could buy a bucket. They traded missed shots as the clock continued to wind down. And then it happened.

After a missed layup by Kyrie Irving with less than two minutes remaining, Andre Iguodala, the Warriors' 2015 Finals MVP, corralled the rebound and took off on a 2-on-1 fast break. Iguodala passed the ball to Curry, who returned the favor with a bounce pass leading Iguodala to the bucket. With James in hot pursuit, Iguodala collected the pass and went up for a layup, but James came out of nowhere to leap above the rim and pin the shot against the backboard with two hands.

With 55 seconds remaining and the score still deadlocked at 89, Kyrie Irving nailed a 3-pointer over Curry's outstretched hands to give the Cavaliers a 92–89 lead. After Curry missed a 3-point attempt at the buzzer, the

James gets the dunk in Game 6 of the 2016 Finals.

Cavs had pulled off the impossible: they were the first team to ever come back from trailing 3–1 and win it all.

"Cleveland, this is for you!" James said to begin his postgame interview. He finished Game 7 with 27 points, 11 rebounds and 11 assists, joining Jerry West and James Worthy as the only players to notch a triple-double in a Finals Game 7.

James turned the game into a symphony. "I felt like I watched Beethoven tonight," Irving said after the champagne had dried.

The Cavs and Warriors met in four straight Finals between 2015 and 2018. That 2016 title was the only time Cleveland beat Golden State. The next season, the Warriors added Kevin Durant, who was named Finals MVP in both 2017 and '18. In those series,

Golden State posted a 8-1 record against LeBron and Company.

Just as in 2010, it was clear that LeBron had taken the Cavs as far as he could. In 2016–17 and '17–18, his 14th and 15th seasons in the league, he led the NBA in minutes played. And each time, the Cavs fell short again.

In the summer of 2018 James said goodbye to Cleveland once more. This time he took his talents to Hollywood, signing with the Los Angeles Lakers and getting to work filming *Space Jam 2*.

This time, Cleveland fans sent him off like royalty. LeBron had brought the city its first championship in any major sport since 1964. The King had returned home and made history.

Kyrie Irving scores despite Draymond Green's defense in the 2016 Finals.

2017
THE RESTLESS SUPERSTAR

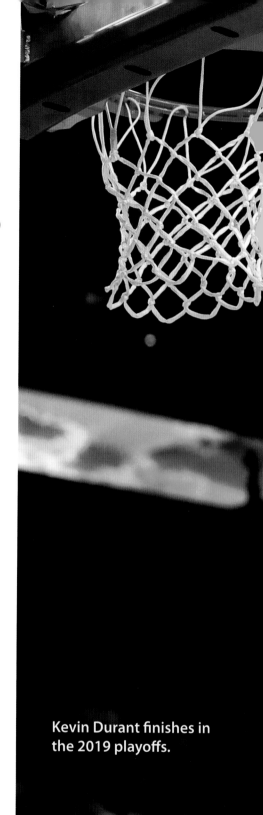

Kevin Durant finishes in the 2019 playoffs.

"I've been second my whole life," Kevin Durant said at the tail end of the 2012–13 season. "I'm tired of being second."

He wasn't talking about the scoring race, although he would finish in second that season after winning three years in a row.

Nobody doubted Durant's ability to put the ball in the hoop. At 24 years old and in his sixth NBA campaign, there was already chatter about Durant's ranking among the most gifted scorers of all time.

On every team he ever played on, Durant was the center of the universe. But outside of his own team, Durant was rarely No. 1.

In the D.C. area, where Durant grew up, his childhood friend and teammate Michael Beasley was long considered the better prospect. In high school, Durant ranked second behind center Greg Oden. And at the draft, Oden was taken first overall, despite Durant becoming the only freshman in college history to be named National Player of the Year at the University of Texas. In the NBA, his star ascended in a kingdom ruled by LeBron James; Durant finished second in MVP voting to him three times between 2010–11 and '11–13.

In his quest to become No. 1, Durant orchestrated one of the most shocking signings in the history of free agency — *twice*.

When the basketball gods set out to create the perfect player, we got Michael Jordan. When they got bored and revisited the mold,

we got Kevin Durant. Listed as a 6-foot-9 shooting guard in his rookie season of 2007–08, he quickly sprouted to nearly 7 feet and moved to forward, where his combination of size and skill was unmatched.

His smooth, effortless scoring touch reminded observers of George Gervin. His killer shooting instincts were reminiscent of Reggie Miller. And his ability to take over long stretches of games was Jordanesque.

Durant was a basketball puzzle that no defender could solve. How do you stop a player with no weaknesses? LeBron, especially in his early days, could be pushed to the 3-point line and dared to shoot. Shaquille O'Neal could be sent to the free-throw line. There was no answer for Durant.

In the 2009-10 season, he averaged 30.1 points and, at 21, became the NBA's youngest scoring champ. His Oklahoma City Thunder improved their record from 23 wins the year before to 50, earning a spot in the postseason.

That summer Durant signed a five-year extension with the Thunder. Management was building a perennial contender around him, with a talented young core of Russell Westbrook, James Harden and Serge Ibaka.

Soon the playoff runs ran deeper as Durant continued his ascent. His scoring numbers always rose in the playoffs.

In 2012 Durant dunked Dirk Nowitzki and the Dallas Mavericks out of the postsea-

son. Then he shot the lights out against Kobe Bryant and the Los Angeles Lakers, sending them home, too. OKC reached the Finals that year — an appearance that seemed like the first of many — but Durant fell short of capturing a ring when the Thunder lost in five games to LeBron and the Miami Heat.

They never made it back to the Finals.

He had established himself as a top-three player, had been named league MVP in 2014 and had taken home two All-Star Game MVPs for good measure. But after seven seasons of falling short in Oklahoma City, his eyes began to wander.

Playing for a thrifty, small-market team gave Durant the feeling he had taken the Thunder as far as he could. That staying put would be settling for second best.

And so his storybook career was rewritten on the fly. On the morning of July 4, 2016, Durant announced that he was signing with the Golden State Warriors, fresh off a gut-wrenching Game 7 loss to the Cleveland Cavaliers in the Finals.

In Golden State, Durant had an opportunity to play a more well-rounded style that better showcased his skills. Plus, he had a chance to win it all — a *very good* chance. The Warriors boasted the most dynamic offense in basketball. With Durant in the mix, the team now floored three of the deadliest shooters ever in KD, Steph Curry and

Klay Thompson. Throw in Green and 2015 Finals MVP Andre Iguodala, and the Warriors now rolled out what was arguably the most talented five-man unit of all time.

Instead of beating a rival, Durant joined one, and the decision rubbed people the wrong way.

"'I took the easy way out,'" Durant said, repeating the words of his critics. "'Easy.' That s★★t pisses me off, because I never had an easy way.'"

Growing up in Prince George's County, Maryland, Durant lived with his older brother, Tony, and his mother, Wanda Pratt, who worked multiple jobs to provide for her children and often went to bed hungry because there wasn't enough food to go around.

When he was eight years old, Durant walked into the nearby Seat Pleasant Activity Center during an open court run and was mesmerized by the sights and sounds. "It was love at first sight," he said of his relationship with basketball.

With his family constantly on the move from apartment to apartment, the court was a lone constant. He spent all his waking hours practicing. Through the game, life had purpose and the potential for prosperity, which seemed impossible to come by in his daily existence.

At a press conference when Durant was named NBA MVP in 2014, he told the story of moving into an unfurnished, unfinished apartment with Tony and his mom. Although the place was bare and the family had little means to furnish it, it was a place they could call their own. The three of them stood in the empty living room, hugged each other and didn't let go.

"We thought we'd made it," Durant recalled through tears. He turned to his mother, who was sitting in the audience. "A single parent with two boys by the time you were 21 years old. You the real MVP."

Durant's move to Golden State was not only controversial; it was almost without precedent for a superstar to sign with another team in his prime. "There's probably one guy in the history of the league who really understands," Durant said.

LeBron James was vilified for his infamous move to Miami, and upon his first visit to Oklahoma City as a member of the Warriors, Durant received the same treatment James had been given in Cleveland. He was greeted by a chorus of boos and an icy welcome from the Thunder staff.

"[There was] such a venomous, toxic feeling when I walked into that arena," he recalled. "Because I left a team and went to play with another team?"

Durant had given everything to OKC. He donated a million dollars to local tornado victims and entrenched himself in the community. When he left, he had to console his mother, Wanda, who was distraught when she saw the videos of fans shooting bullets into his Thunder jersey.

"I'll never be attached to that city again because of that," he said.

With Golden State, Durant got what he'd always wanted.

In his first season with the Warriors, the team reached the Finals in a rematch with LeBron and the Cavaliers. In Game 3, with his team up three points and less than a minute remaining, Durant brought the ball up the court, let the shot clock run down and pulled up for a dramatic 3-pointer that swished through, icing the game. Two games later, the Warriors were champs. Durant outplayed LeBron, and after averaging over 35 points, 8 rebounds, 5 assists and a steal and block per game, he was named Finals MVP.

The next year, the two teams met again. In Game 3 it was like déjà vu, only this time his team was down two points when Durant pulled up for a 3-pointer at the top of the arc at the close of the fourth quarter to win the game. "He's one of the best players I've ever played against [and] that this league has ever seen," LeBron said after the game.

This time the Warriors swept the Cavs. Durant was named Finals MVP for the second year in a row, joining Jordan, Hakeem Olajuwon, Shaq, Kobe and LeBron as the only back-to-back winners in history.

Durant wasn't in second place anymore. But he also wasn't satisfied.

"The same reason we got Kevin in the first place was the reason we lost him," said Warriors coach Steve Kerr. "He was restless."

In his third season with Golden State, with free agency just around the corner, Durant was eyeing another change. He might have been considered the league's best, but the hearts of Warriors fans belonged to Steph Curry. Once again, Durant was second.

During the 2018–19 season, Green got in Durant's face during a nationally televised game. The two argued on the sidelines as Green called him out for a lack of commitment, for having one foot out the door.

The writing was on the wall, but the Warriors were still poised for another run and they returned to the Finals, this time against the Toronto Raptors. Durant suffered an injury in the second round against Houston and made his return in Game 4 of the Finals with his team trailing 3-1. After just 11 minutes of action, Durant tore his Achilles tendon. The Warriors lost the series in six.

It was time for another change. After an entire season of rumors, Durant signed with the Brooklyn Nets. A new challenge. A new proving ground. A chance to reclaim his place atop the pyramid in the NBA's biggest market and add to his Hall of Fame legacy — although his Achilles injury meant he'd have to sit out a season before suiting up again.

For Durant, the stakes were much simpler. "It was another opportunity for me to play for another team," he said. "It wasn't that big of a deal. I could pick my game up and play anywhere. So I just did it."

NBA ALL-STAR GAME PPG

1. Giannis Antetokounmpo		27.3
2. Kevin Durant		25.0
3. LeBron James		24.1
4. Russell Westbrook		21.6
5. Paul George		20.7

Durant reacts to a dunk in the 2011 playoffs.

2018
ANALYTICS AND THE 3-POINT REVOLUTION

James Harden, the NBA's leading scorer, fires off a trey. *Clang* — front of the rim. Two plays later, Rockets teammate Eric Gordon pulls up in transition and hoists a three of his own. *Clang* — another miss. Shortly after, Harden draws a double-team and kicks the ball to a wide-open Trevor Ariza in the corner. *Clang.*

Throughout the 2018 season, the 3-pointer was undoubtedly the Rockets' greatest weapon. Houston attempted 3,470 of them, over 500 more than any other team.

But now, with their season on the line, they've gone cold.

It's Game 7 of the 2018 Western Conference finals between the Houston Rockets and defending champion Golden State Warriors, who deploy two of the most potent offenses the league has ever seen.

The two franchises have been perfecting the model for modern basketball; they are the poster teams of the 3-point revolution.

The Warriors have used the 3-pointer to sink opponents for years, creating a dynasty around the backcourt of Steph Curry and

Klay Thompson, two of the greatest shooters of all time. But the Rockets launched more long-range shots, and during the 2018 regular season Harden, who was named MVP, led the league with 10 three-point attempts per game. The team's general manager, Daryl Morey, a former statistician, built a roster around his data-driven vision of an offense that destroys opponents from beyond the arc and at the free-throw line.

But by half-time during Game 7, the Rockets have shot just 1-of-21 from deep and are on their way to missing 37 of their 44 3-point attempts. At one point, they bricked 27 three-pointers in a row. Years of number-crunching haven't accounted for a cold spell like this. The plan is backfiring.

In that 2017-18 season, 3-pointers were on the rise. The average NBA team attempted 2,378 of them (29 per game). Thirty years earlier, the average was 410 (5 per game). For context, in 2015–16 Steph Curry *made* 402 all on his own. So dramatic was the revolution that the league leader in 2000–01 (the Celtics, with 1,633) would have been dead last in '17–18.

MOST 3-POINT FG IN A GAME

1.	Klay Thomson	14 (2018)
2.	Zach LaVine	13 (2019)
	Stephen Curry	13 (2016)
3.	Stephen Curry	12 (2016)
	Donyell Marshall	12 (2005)
	Kobe Bryant	12 (2003)

James Harden reacts to a ref's whistle during the 2018 playoffs.

For all the advanced analytics that has invaded the game, simple math prevailed: three points are worth more than two. When Boston Celtics forward Antoine Walker led the league in 3-pointers by a hefty margin in 2000–01, he reasoned that he shot so many threes "because there ain't no fours."

It's a wonder it took teams so long to embrace the 3-pointer. In 1945 the 3-point shot was briefly tested out in college basketball, but it didn't become popular until the ABA instituted it in the late 1960s. The "home run shot," as it was marketed, gave ABA fans a glimpse into the future thanks to the likes of Louie Dampier, who hoisted over 7 threes per game.

It wasn't until the 1979–80 season that the NBA adopted the 3-point shot. The "gimmick" shot, as the *New York Times* called it at the time, was met with skepticism.

"It may change our game at the end of the quarters," said Phoenix Suns coach John MacLeod, "but I'm not going to set up plays for guys to bomb from 23 feet. I think that's very boring basketball." Celtics president Red Auerbach figured the 3-pointer was only added to boost poor TV ratings. In the first season with a 3-point line, the Atlanta Hawks averaged fewer than one attempt per game.

One of the first NBA players to routinely utilize the 3-pointer as a weapon was Celtics All-Star Larry Bird. He could shoot the ball from anywhere, and wasn't shy about it. Feeding off his popularity, the NBA staged its first 3-point-shooting contest in 1986. Before the event began, Bird entered the locker room and sized up his opponents. "Which one of y'all is gonna come in second?" he asked in his rural Indiana drawl. Bird proceeded to win the shoot-out, and never even bothered to take off his warm-ups.

In 1994–95 the NBA experimented with moving the 3-point line closer to the basket to encourage more shooting. Three-point rates rose and remained higher, even after the league moved the line back to its original position shortly afterward.

The 90s saw a wave of stellar shooters, including Reggie Miller, the brash Indiana Pacers star who ushered in a new era of 3-point specialists. None were more accomplished than Ray Allen, a cold-blooded shooter who retired in 2014 after 18 seasons with 2,973 3-pointers made — the NBA's all-time career leader.

But by the time Allen retired, teams still weren't building around the 3-point shot. It was the paint, but not the brush.

The winds of change came during the 2012–13 season — Steph Curry's breakout campaign. The son of accomplished shooter Dell Curry, Steph was a prodigious talent who had displayed a knack for shooting from the time he was four years old. With a funky, lightning-quick release and a range that comfortably extends to half-court, Curry was a savant. He made 272 three-pointers in 2013, breaking Ray Allen's single-season record. He would eclipse that mark four times over the next six seasons.

And Curry wasn't even the most effective shooter on his own team. That honor belonged to Klay Thompson. In addition to textbook shooting form, Thompson also mastered the art of the catch-and-shoot, minimizing any wasted time or movement.

In one game, he scored 42 points, including seven threes, and dribbled the ball just four times all game. On January 23, 2015, Thompson scored 37 points in one quarter thanks to a record nine 3-pointers. Warriors head coach Steve Kerr, who had played alongside Michael Jordan in his prime, was in awe after the game. "As many spectacular things as Michael did, which he did nightly," Kerr said, "I never saw him do that."

With the 3-pointer taking center stage, scoring records began to crumble. In 2017 Thompson became the fastest player to score 60 points — in under 30 minutes, thanks in part to his eight treys. The next year in October 2018 he set the mark with 14 3-pointers in one game.

The 3-point era was ushered in by generational talents like Steph and Klay. But its boom was largely the product of the rise of big data in basketball.

The reliance on data was changing the way players were being evaluated. Suddenly, how high a player could jump became less important than his shooting motion and how quickly he could release the ball.

Analytics rendered the traditional big man — who almost never ventured far outside the paint — extinct and put a new premium on perimeter play.

Coaching strategies changed. Instead of sending players to the rim on the break, coaches would have their players run to the corners, the shortest 3-point distance from the basket.

"Analytics are part and parcel of virtually everything we do now," NBA commissioner Adam Silver said in 2017.

In Houston, GM Daryl Morey was leading the analytics charge. He had studied at MIT, where he made a name for himself applying statistical analysis to basketball. After rising through the ranks of the Boston Celtics, he joined the Rockets in 2007.

Morey was building a team around the 3-point shot in general, and around James Harden in particular.

A lethal shooter and elite ballhandler, Harden could either create his own 3-point shot or attract defenders while driving to the basket, allowing him to pass the ball out of the paint to one of Houston's waiting shooters.

Morey even hired Mike D'Antoni, architect of the analytically advanced Seven Seconds or Less Suns of the early 2000s, to coach the team.

After acquiring Harden in 2012, the Rockets led the NBA in 3-point attempts in all but one season, when they finished second. In 2015 the Rockets set a record with 894 3-pointers made. Four years later, they made 1,323. Their 45.4 threes per game in 2018–19 were a record

That season, Harden shot over 13 threes per game, another record, and finished the season averaging 36 points per game. Only Wilt Chamberlain and Michael Jordan have averaged more in a single season.

The 3-point revolution produces exciting basketball and lofty scoring totals. It helped make the Rockets-Warriors series appointment viewing. But the statistical models that tell teams to fire at will from deep couldn't

Ray Allen holds his follow-through in 2008.

have anticipated that a roster of shooters like Houston's would miss 27 in a row. The data doesn't account for being human.

The Rockets fell short in their quest to build a championship team from the outside in, but the game had been changed for good. The long-distance shot evolved from spectacle, to rare weapon, to an absolute necessity for winning teams.

Time will tell how much farther the revolution will go.

MOST CAREER 3-POINT FG

1.	Ray Allen	2,973
2.	Reggie Miller	2,560
3.	Stephen Curry	2,495
4.	Kyle Korver	2,437
5.	James Harden	2,296

Klay Thompson unleashes his perfect jump shot in 2016.

2019
GIANNIS AND THE GLOBAL GAME

Giannis Antetokounmpo drives to the basket in 2019.

"I want to thank God for blessing me with this amazing talent."

The talent to cover the court in nine strides and to reach the rim from the free-throw line. The physique that landed Giannis Antetokounmpo the nickname Greek Freak.

"For putting me in this position I am today."

From impoverished kid from Greece to one of the NBA's megastars.

"I want to thank the front office for believing in me."

For not only rolling the dice on a lanky kid with next to no training but building a contender around him.

Giannis steps away from the mic and wipes away tears.

"This is just the beginning."

Antetokounmpo's earliest basketball memories are of outdoor courts in the Sepolia neighborhood of Athens, Greece. His parents emigrated from Lagos, Nigeria, to Greece before he was born. Greek immigration law prevented the couple from obtaining work permits, so the family grew up in poverty. Giannis shared a pair of sneakers with one of his four brothers, and when he wasn't on the court, he could be found selling knockoff handbags and watches on the streets of Athens.

When Giannis was 13, a local scout who'd been scouring immigrant communities in Greece saw a tall, lanky kid playing in the streets and arranged for him to play for a local youth team.

Giannis quickly took to the gymnasium in the suburb of Zografou. The team practiced twice a day, and Giannis would rise early to walk five miles. By the end of the day, he was so tired he'd often sleep in the gym, positioning a mat in the corner.

Antetokounmpo was a quick study and possessed obvious talent. In his mind, he was a point guard, and he would save up to go to a local internet café and pay a dollar per half hour to watch highlights of Allen Iverson. He couldn't have fathomed growing to 6-foot-10 by the time he was drafted. Or that, after he arrived in the NBA, he'd keep growing.

By the time Giannis's 18th birthday neared, word had spread about a gifted Greek kid with a raw game. NBA scouts began showing up to his games — it beat the grainy video footage they'd been sent back home. In 2012 he was signed to play the following season for a high-level Spanish club, but he never made it.

At the 2013 NBA draft, the Milwaukee Bucks selected the teenager from Greece with the 15th overall pick.

"The first time that I hear about the Bucks," he later said, "was at the draft."

Antetokounmpo might have been a mystery to most, but it wasn't altogether surprising that Milwaukee rolled the dice. For years, teams had been in search of the next Dirk Nowitzki — overseas gems gifted with freakish attributes and, hopefully, the foundation to become great players. There had been many attempts. Nikoloz Tskitishvili (fifth overall in 2001), Andrea Bargnani (first overall in '06) and Ricky Rubio (fifth overall

in '09) were among the many European projects NBA teams took a chance on. After Giannis began to rise, the trend continued, evidenced by first-round picks Bruno Caboclo, Clint Capela and Dragan Bender.

But just as the high school boom did for players like Kevin Garnett and Kobe Bryant, the rush to draft international players only served to highlight how rarely talents like Dirk or Giannis come around.

If Antetokounmpo was destined for greatness, it wasn't obvious from the start. He

was a wide-eyed rookie. He went on Twitter to profess his love for smoothies, amazed at the new world he'd entered. He was lighthearted and an instant favorite among the fans, despite their struggles to pronounce his name. They settled on nicknames: the Alphabet at first, and later the Greek Freak.

There have been very few players like Giannis. He is big enough to play center, yet slender and coordinated enough to run on the wing, with the ball skills and instincts of a point guard — plus a devastating impact at

the other end of the floor, to boot. His long arms erased the space between him and the basket. The possibilities were enormous.

Giannis was undeveloped, but the signs were there. He'd take a step from the foul line and dunk on anybody. He'd seem to teleport himself across the court to pin a shot against the backboard. He'd jump so high that he'd blocked the ball with his elbow.

The years spent running the point turned him into the NBA's tallest playmaker. Over his first few seasons, he added muscle to

become a ferocious rebounder and worked on his only real weakness: shooting.

It all clicked for Giannis during his third season. In the first game, he scored a loud 27 — poster dunks, bully moves, even a 3-pointer for good measure. After a few more games like it, he called his agent.

"I can do this *every night*," he said, excited by the revelation. He was 20 years old.

Growing up, Antetokounmpo just wanted to be in the NBA. Now he wanted more.

In 2017, at age 22, Antetokounmpo made his first All-Star team. Fans voted him into the starting lineup, even though he lacked the all-important 3-point shot. That same year, Giannis was named the NBA's Most Improved Player, becoming the first to finish in the top 20 in all five major stat categories (points, rebounds, assists, steals and blocks).

The rise continued. He was eager to get better. When he asked veterans for advice, first he grabbed a pen and paper. He soaked it all in and was a fixture at the Bucks' prac-

tice gym. As in Greece, sometimes he slept there instead of going home.

Year over year, Giannis's growth was staggering. He rebuilt his once-scrawny frame into one seemingly carved out of marble, now standing nearly 7 feet tall. His speed and control in the open court made it impossible to keep him out of the paint, and there was no way to stop him under the rim. What's more, he now seemed to go out of his way to out-muscle the competition, mean-mugging every bit of the way. The shy teen was long gone.

By the 2018–19 season he had become the single most destructive force in the game — the most unstoppable in the low post since Shaquille O'Neal. His 273 dunks were second in the NBA, and he was the only non-center in the top 10.

Giannis led the Bucks to an NBA-best 60 wins. And after the season, the 24-year-old estimated that he'd reached 60 percent of his potential as a player.

Giannis had risen to the top of the pack, but the amount of international talent

Giannis scores between two Celtics defenders.

around the NBA is staggering. The development of global scouting has made the bridge from abroad to the NBA shorter than ever. In Dallas, Luka Doncic is creating his own legacy. Unlike Giannis, no team rolled the dice when it came to Doncic, the third overall pick in 2018, who had been a EuroLeague MVP and champion by the age of 18. Others like Giannis and Denver Nuggets center Nikola Jokic continue to prove why teams will continue to mine the globe for talent.

In 2019 the NBA's yearly awards proved the extent to which the league's talent had gone global. Doncic (Slovenia) was named Rookie of the Year. Pascal Siakam (Cameroon) was Most Improved. Rudy Gobert (France) was the Defensive Player of the Year.

Eleven years after sleeping in the gym outside Athens, Giannis Antetokounmpo (Greece) was named MVP.

This is just the beginning.

2020
THE NBA HYPE MACHINE

All eyes were on Zion Williamson. The Duke forward and projected first overall pick in the 2019 NBA draft was putting on a historic show in his first and only college season. It had all contributed to the legend of the 18-year-old with unheard-of physical tools and a surprisingly skilled game.

At 6-foot-6 and 285 pounds, he recorded a Jordanesque 45-inch vertical leap. He threw cross-court bounce passes and practically blocked 3-pointers while leaping from the paint. His alley-oop finishes and dunks were like those of Charles Barkley and Shawn Kemp, but turned up to 11. By the time Zion entered the NBA, he would be its second-heaviest player — just five pounds lighter than 7-foot-3 giant Boban Marjanovic.

Williamson's highlight-reel moves led national sports programs and websites, often getting top billing over the biggest NBA plays of the day.

With the draft on the horizon, weaker teams around the league were in a race to the bottom in hopes of landing the No. 1 pick. It was no coincidence that the league changed the lottery rules so that the bottom three teams had an equal shot at the first overall pick, and therefore less incentive to tank. But it hardly stopped teams from trying.

LeBron James as a high school senior in 2003.

Zion Williamson in the 2020 Rising Stars game.

After all, landing Zion in the draft would be the biggest lottery win of them all. He could be the once-in-a-generation talent whose presence not only helped win games but got fans into the stands, buying jerseys and tuning in on TV.

One night late in February, a record audience of 4.3 million Americans tuned in to ESPN to watch Williamson square off against intrastate rival North Carolina. From the tip-off, Zion proved that even his mishaps were extraordinary. On the first play of the game, he swallowed up the ball and planted his left foot for a spin move, straining his knee. The force of the maneuver caused Zion's foot to explode through his Nike sneaker.

The following day, Nike's stock price dropped one percent.

The knee injury prompted pundits and players, including Scottie Pippen, to publicly plea with Zion to sit out the rest of his college season. With NBA superstardom months away, there was too much at risk. Undaunted, he returned for the playoffs and was named the ACC tournament MVP, shooting 77 percent and joining Kevin Durant as the only freshman to average 27 points and 10 rebounds in a conference tourney.

The injury had done nothing to derail the hype train. He was the most anticipated NBA prospect since LeBron James in 2003. Like King James, Williamson appeared to have it all. He had the game. He had the Madison Avenue–ready smile. And he had the name. Like Larry, Shaq and LeBron, he required no nickname or surname. Just call him Zion.

Zion had built a loyal following long before his games were televised. By the time he announced his choice of college, videos of his high school exploits had already received millions of views on YouTube and Instagram. The videos showed a man-child throwing down ferocious dunks on helpless kids.

His dunks were reminiscent of Vince Carter in his prime, with the difference being that Zion was built like a defensive lineman. In fact, growing up in gridiron-mad South Carolina, he would have been a football player — except his school didn't have a team. So Zion joined the basketball team.

By the time he graduated, he was a celeb. In 2018, public figures like rapper Drake and NFL star Odell Beckham Jr. had been spotted wearing his high school jersey and NBA luminaries like Kevin Durant praised his "once in a generation" athleticism.

Past icons like Julius Erving and Michael Jordan — even LeBron, to an extent — had been somewhat of a mystery when they first arrived in the NBA. You had to read the stories to buy into the myth. For Zion, all you had to do was look at your phone.

When he chose Duke, the nation's most publicized program, he called it "a business decision."

At Duke, Williamson's popularity only grew. He was overpowering and lauded as a good teammate. Even while starring for the most hated team in college sports, Zion was eminently likable. Brands noticed.

At the draft lottery, the New Orleans Pelicans jumped up six spots to land the No. 1 pick. With a trade in the works to send superstar big man Anthony Davis to the Los Angeles Lakers in the works, Zion would step in and assume the role of franchise player from day one.

Companies lined up to make Zion's confident smile the face of their product lines. The Jordan Brand inked him to a deal worth a reported $75 million, the largest for a rookie since LeBron 16 years earlier. "Kingdom Come," warned an ad campaign announcing the partnership. Gatorade, Mountain Dew and others added to the long list of sponsors.

Williamson's unofficial debut came at the NBA's annual Summer League in Las Vegas, where fans lined a sold out gym. Zion played like he'd been transported from another planet. He was a Monstar, dunking everything and literally tearing the ball out of opponents' hands. But another injury cut his Vegas appearance short. In the pre-season, he was back at full strength and appeared better than ever.

Zion's 23.3 points per game were the most by any rookie in their first preseason since 2006, when the league started keeping track. He was shooting a mind-numbing 71.4 percent from the field. In a matchup with 7-foot Utah Jazz center and reigning two-time Defensive Player of the Year Rudy Gobert, Williamson effortlessly outmuscled him at the rim.

It was Zionmania. His rookie cards were selling for $100,000 before he even played a real game. Which wouldn't be for a while.

On October 22, 2019, Williamson suffered a torn meniscus in his right knee. The injury sidelined him for the first three months of his rookie season. Meanwhile, the worst fears were being considered. Images of Barkley and LeBron were fading, being replaced with Bill Walton and Greg Oden.

The modern-day hype machine made a superstar out of Zion before draft night. For now, his legend is still being written. Williamson has promised just one thing: "I'm going to shock the world," he said in 2016, when the hype train was just gaining steam. When he signed with Nike's Jordan Brand three years later, Michael Jordan himself released a statement about the NBA's biggest prodigy.

"He told us he would 'shock the world,' and asked us to believe him," said Jordan. "We do."

Williamson finally made his NBA debut on January 22, 2020. He did not disappoint, putting on the rim-rattling show fans had patiently waited for. Within a month he became the first rookie since Jordan to score at least 25 in four games in a row while shooting better than 57 percent from the floor. In 19 games, he already amassed over 50 dunks. Zion was worth the wait.

ALL-TIME ROOKIE SCORING

1.	Wilt Chamberlain	37.6
2.	Walt Bellamy	31.6
3.	Oscar Robertson	30.5
4.	Kareem Abdul-Jabbar	28.8
5.	Elvin Hayes	28.4

2020
ROLE PLAYERS

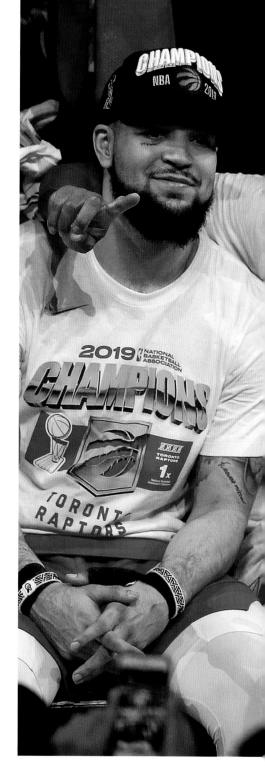

It's Game 6 of the 2019 NBA Finals, and Fred VanVleet is on fire. After hitting clutch shots and chasing Steph Curry around on defense, the Toronto Raptors' reserve point guard is a major reason why his team is minutes away from dethroning the Golden State Warriors in the last game ever to be played at Oracle Arena.

Down by three in the fourth quarter, he pulls up for a shot to tie the game with a defender in his face. Swish. Down 2 points just moments later, he drills another 3-pointer, this time with Curry draped all over him.

Three years earlier, VanVleet went undrafted after starring for Wichita State University. Scouts said he was too small and too slow. They couldn't envision him controlling the action on an NBA court and they overlooked the intangibles that had helped him lead a small school to the NCAA tournament three years in a row.

Signed after a preseason tryout, he spent most of his first season in the G League. When he reached the NBA, he carved out a role as a playmaker coming off the bench. Now, at 24 years old, he was swinging a Finals.

Tied at 101 with less than four minutes remaining, VanVleet crosses up the Warriors defense and steps back for another triple. The Raptors lead for the rest of the game. You'd think you were watching a game of *NBA Jam* — the only thing missing are the flames coming off his shoes.

VanVleet scored 12 points in the fourth quarter and 22 in the game as the Raptors captured the title. When it came time to tally up the Finals MVP votes, Kawhi Leonard got all but one. The other went to VanVleet.

The NBA's story is told through its stars and the teams they propel to greatness. From Elgin Baylor to LeBron James, there's a through line of legends who watch their jerseys lifted into the rafters. But underlying the success of every great team is the productivity of the lesser-heralded supporting players.

Role players come in all forms — a well-rounded sixth man, or a starter with a specialized set of skills — and it takes a particular mindset to accept a lesser role, embrace it and thrive.

Think about it: if you're in the NBA, odds are that when you were growing up, you were the best player not just on your team but in your city or area code. But once you reach the league, you enter a new basketball reality.

The names that appear on the marquee are the exception. In basketball, the role players are the rule.

Your role is reduced like never before. The ball is taken out of your hands, and you're asked to make your impact on the margins. Box out and set a hard pick, put the ball in your star players' hands, stretch the floor and be a marksman. In college, Duke's J.J. Redick was a flat-out superstar. He was a top-20 scorer in collegiate history, but in the NBA he was asked to be a complementary spot-up shooter. To prepare for the transition, coaches told him to attend Broadway plays and study the movements and timing of the background actors.

With a new perspective, he embraced his NBA destiny and managed to have a long career because of it.

Steve Kerr found success because he came into the league with a role player's mentality. He never questioned his place in the NBA pecking order. In college at Arizona, he was never his team's leading scorer. A second-round pick, by the time he signed with the Chicago Bulls in 1994 he had mastered the art of playing off of stars. He came off the bench and found his niche as a reliable shooter.

The Bulls dynasty under Phil Jackson and Michael Jordan knew how important role

Fred VanVleet poses with his teammates after Game 6 of the 2019 NBA Finals.

players could be. From Horace Grant to John Paxson to the most heralded role player of them all, Dennis Rodman, Chicago became unbeatable only when Jordan began turning to the players around him.

In Game 6 of the '93 Finals, while under pressure, Jordan passed to Paxson, who sank a 3-pointer with under four seconds left to hand Chicago its third title. Four years later, in Game 6 of the Finals against the Utah Jazz, Kerr found himself in the same position

and helped deliver the Bulls' fifth title of the Jordan era.

In 2003, as a 37-year-old veteran with another dynasty, the San Antonio Spurs, Kerr came through in the clutch once more. He had played sparingly during the playoffs, but in Game 6 of the Western Conference finals against Dallas, Kerr made all four of his 3-pointers to spark a comeback win that sent the Spurs to the Finals.

While superstars have the entire game and

the luxury of minutes and touches to work their way into a rhythm, the best role players are rustproof and have a knack for making an immediate impact.

And it's not just by shooting that the supporting cast can swing a game or series. It could be a timely block — as Tayshaun

Robert Horry sits at the end of the Laker's bench in 2000.

Prince did when he pinned Reggie Miller's shot against the backboard in the 2004 Eastern Conference finals. Or an offensive rebound, like the one Chris Bosh corralled to Ray Allen for a game-winning 3-pointer in the 2011 Finals.

The Spurs dynasty was lifted by the strength of contributions from the likes of Bruce Bowen, Rasho Nesterovic and Hall of Famer David Robinson, who accepted a backup role to Tim Duncan in the twilight of his career.

The greatest rivalry of all time, between the Lakers and Celtics, featured the biggest names ever to play the game. But it was the role players that helped cement their teams' legacies over the decades: John Havlicek, Frank Ramsey, Don Nelson, K.C. Jones, Gerald Henderson and countless others for Boston; Pat Riley, Michael Cooper, A.C. Green, Derek Fisher, Robert Horry and a playbill's worth of names for Los Angeles.

Perhaps no role player will ever carve out a career like Horry's. The 11th pick of the 1992 draft, Horry joined a Houston Rockets team gunning for a championship and quickly found his role as an energetic starting forward.

STOP THE BALL

Four teams had wrapped up their games on the evening of March 11, 2020, with two more games left in the NBA that night.

In Sacramento, the Kings and New Orleans Pelicans were nearing tip-off when a team doctor rushed the court with the news: Utah Jazz center Rudy Gobert, whose team was about to play a road game against the Oklahoma City Thunder, had tested positive for COVID-19.

The Kings game was canceled and fans were sent home. The Jazz-Thunder tilt was called off as well and, the two teams were sequestered at the arena into the wee hours of the morning as tests were administered to players and staff from both teams.

By then the NBA had announced that, for the first time in league history, the season would be suspended indefinitely.

The COVID-19 pandemic had already been on the league's radar. Ten days earlier the NBA sent a memo to all teams outlining precautionary measures that included keeping gatherings of media hordes out of locker rooms. Many teams pulled their scouts from the road, while business otherwise progressed as usual. In Los Angeles, LeBron James was continuing his resurgent season with the Lakers, leading the league in assists,

and giving front-runner Giannis Antetokounmpo a run for the MVP trophy. The Kawhi Leonard-led Los Angeles Clippers were finding their groove and setting up a Battle for L.A. in the playoffs, while Giannis and the Bucks had separated from the pack in the East.

But Gobert's diagnosis was the tipping point. Given the ease with which the virus transferred from person-to-person, the risk was too great to continue the season. Soon it was revealed that Gobert's teammate, Donnovan Mitchell, also caught the virus, as had several members of the Brooklyn Nets, including Kevin Durant.

The NBA's announcement of a suspended season was the first hammer to fall in the world of pro sports. Other leagues quickly followed suit, and soon enough to-play-or-not-to-play wasn't even a question. Two days after the NBA put the 2019–20 campaign on indefinite pause, the United States declared a national state of emergency. With the death toll rising, the sports world took a backseat.

Countless plans to salvage the season were tossed around league offices — including sequestering the league in a Las Vegas resort and constructing a mini-city of NBA courts — but as the spring turned into summer, the odds of the NBA witnessing its first lost season seemed just as high.

He hit clutch shots in the Western Conference finals and NBA Finals en route to Houston's first championship in 1994 and Big Shot Rob only added to his résumé from there.

He joined the Los Angeles Lakers in '97, and when the team acquired Shaq and Kobe the following summer, he accepted a role off the bench, where his size and shooting prowess let him have an instant impact whenever his number was called. He hit 3-point

daggers in 2001 and 2002 to help bring the Lakers closer to championships.

"If it wasn't for guys like [Brian] Shaw, Rick Fox and Big Shot Rob," said Shaquille O'Neal, "I'd probably only have one championship rather than four."

In the 2005 Finals with the Spurs, Horry's game winner in overtime gave San Antonio a 3-2 series lead. He barely played in the first half and hadn't scored until there were nine

seconds left in the third quarter, but he finished the game with 21 points. "That was the greatest performance I've ever been a part of," said Tim Duncan. The Spurs went on to claim the title.

Horry retired with seven championship rings — the fourth most of all time— matching the number of points he averaged during his 16-year career. He's the only non-Celtic in the top eight.

INDEX

PHOTO CREDITS